Diane Bair and Pamela Wright

FUN PLACES
to Go with
Children in

New England
3RD EDITION

CHRONICLE BOOKS
SAN FRANCISCO

Printed in the United States of America.

Library of Congress Cataloging-in-Publication Data:
Bair, Diane.
    Fun places to go with children in New England / by Diane Bair and
Pamela Wright. — 3rd ed.
        p. cm.
    Rev. ed. of: Places to go with children in New England. 2nd ed. c1994.
    Includes index.
    ISBN 0-8188-1865-9
    1. New England—Guidebooks. 2. Children—Travel—New England—
Guidebooks. 3. Family recreation—New England—Guidebooks. I. Wright,
Pamela, 1953– . II. Bair, Diane. Places to go with children in New England.
III. Title.
F2.3.B34   1998
917-404'34'083—dc21   97-34336
                                                     CIP

Cover design: Martine Trélaün
Book design and illustration: Karen Smidth
Composition: Words & Deeds
Maps: Ellen McElhinny
Cover photograph: Frozen Images, Inc.

Distributed in Canada by Raincoast Books
9050 Shaughnessy Street
Vancouver, B.C. V6P 6E5

10 9 8 7 6 5 4 3 2

Chronicle Books LLC
85 Second Street
San Francisco, CA 94105

www.chroniclebooks.com

Contents

For Charlotte, Connor, Sadie, and Jared

Introduction

WHEN WE WROTE the first edition of this book nearly a decade ago, we raised more than a few eyebrows when we trekked into museums and restaurants with young children and (gasp!) rambunctious toddlers in tow. Surely, we reasoned, there were great places to go, beyond the Chuck E. Cheese's of the world, where we could learn, play, and do, with our children. Well, we found 'em—and, ten years later, we're happy to report that New England is more family-friendly than ever. Even the most Boston-proper museums now have special tours for kids and family exploration days; sprawling family farms now offer horse-drawn hayrides for kids and livestock petting zoos. Even the fanciest lodgings—known for turning their noses up at kids—now offer family packages with milk and cookies, Disney videos, and the like to attract traveling families. After all, kids are tourists, too.

So, with an ever-expanding universe of fun places to go with kids, we've become a bit pickier. *Fun Places to Go with Children in New England* is full of places we think—and our "test kids" think—are really neat, places you're likely to remember long after you've returned home. We've focused on attractions that are uniquely New England, such as boat cruises where kids can play "lobsterman for a day," ancient cemeteries for making grave rubbings, a schooner cruise where you haul in and identify creatures of the deep, medieval castles to play "knight in shining armor," aerial train rides to mountain summits, and farms where you can not only pet the animals, but help milk cows and shear sheep. The emphasis is on interactive fun, places where kids can get involved in the action, not just watch. And, we looked for places where grown-ups will enjoy themselves. After all, it's your precious leisure time, too.

We admit a personal bias toward nature activities and outdoors pursuits. In this edition of *Fun Places,* we've expanded our coverage of New England outdoors, and how to enjoy it. You'll find lots of places to view wildlife, go hiking, paddle a canoe or kayak, tour on a bicycle. As mountain biking, kayaking, and snowboarding have become hot activities for kids, we've added lots of places where you can enjoy these activities. You'll also find our picks for best family beaches, "don't miss" attractions, and advice as varied as "Do you need a car on Block Island?" and what to pack for an incredible sunset picnic (including cheap transportation) on Nantucket Island.

We invite you to get into the spirit of it all and enjoy. Rediscover the fun-loving kid inside you, connect with your own children, and have a great time discovering an incredible place for everyone—New England.

Massachusetts

Boston

Boston loves kids. It's colorful, it's walkable, and it's chock-a-block with appealing attractions and museums, some with tours designed expressly for small fry. Venerable institutions, such as the Museum of Fine Arts (opened in 1870), offer activities tailor-made for families. But Boston's history isn't confined to museums—it's everywhere you look. The site of the Boston Massacre, for example, is marked by a plaque in the street, while famous patriots are buried in a downtown cemetery. Year-round, the heart of the city is abustle with families: the Public Garden is filled with kids ice skating on Frog Pond in winter and gliding along Lagoon Pond in a swan boat in summer. Boston hotels are more child-friendly than they once were, and most offer special packages for families, including "kids stay free" offers, milk and cookies at night, and more. Once comfortably ensconced in your hotel or bed-and-breakfast inn, get ready to discover why Boston is one of the most popular tourist destinations in the world.

You've heard the phrase, "Pahk your cah in Hahvahd yahd?" Forget about it. Boston's maze of narrow, one-way streets is best navigated by foot, trolley, or subway, not by car, since parking spaces are scarce. Don your most comfortable shoes (forget fashion; given Boston's climate and cobblestones, comfort and protection beat style every time), and start walking. When little feet get tired, board the "T." Boston's subway system is (relatively) clean and modern and will get you to all major points of interest in the city. Or, board a trolley (most will let you hop off and on as much as you like for one fare) and pick up a few factoids about the city as you cruise. (An example of trolley driver humor: "Paul Revere had 16 kids. Guess that's why they called him a minute man.")

Before you visit, consider sending for the "Kids Love Boston" kit ($4.95), a packet that includes a city map and family discount offers, as well as a run-down of hotel packages for visitors traveling en famille. Write to the Greater Boston Convention and Visitor Bureau, Two Copley Place, Suite 105, Boston, MA 02166-6501; 1-888-SEE-BOSTON.

DOWNTOWN

● Museum of Science

Science Park; (617) 723-2500. Tues.–Thurs., Sat. and Sun., 9–5; Fri., 9–9. Exhibit halls admission: adults, $8; 3–14, $6. Planetarium admission: adults, $7.50; 3–14, $5.50. Mugar Omni Theater admission: adults, $7.50; 3–14, $5.50. (Tues. night bargain shows, 7 P.M. and later.)
All ages.

You won't want to miss this world-renowned museum, with more than 400 participatory exhibits. Walk beside a three-story-high tyrannosaurus rex, see live animal and physical science demonstrations, or test your wits in the computer center. "Investigate!", a new permanent exhibit, challenges visitors to think like a scientist. Don't miss the lightning show in the Theater of Electricity. The Omnimax theater boasts the world's largest projection system and a four-story domed screen. It's the perfect venue for multi-image presentations such as "Whales" and "Special Effects." Even Hayden Planetarium is interactive; visitors don't just watch, but actually design a celestial adventure. Nighttime laser shows, set to the music of bands such as Smashing Pumpkins, are a great hit with the preteen and older set.

● Museum of Fine Arts

465 Huntington Ave.; (617) 267-9300. Tues. and Thurs.–Sun., 10–4:45; Wed., 10–9:45; Thurs. and Fri. (West Wing only) 5–9:45. Family Place: Oct.–June, first Sun. each month, 11–4. Children's Room: June–Aug., Tues.–Thurs., 3:30–4:45; Sept.–May, Wed.–Fri., 3:30–4:45. Adults, $10; 17 and under free. All fees Thurs. and Fri. after 5 P.M., $2 discount. Free to all (voluntary contributions accepted), Wed., 4–9:45. Family Place: free with museum admission. Children's Room: free. **Ages 6 and up.**

You'll probably be attracted to the Fine Arts for its terrific collections of Chinese, Japanese, Indian, Egyptian, Greek, Roman, European, and American art; happily, the kids can get a lot out of this wonderful museum as well. In the Children's Room, geared to ages 6 to 12, drop-in workshops highlight the museum's collections through dramatics, art projects, poetry, and music. (It's kids only here; you can tour the museum while they're busy with projects.) In the Family Place you can all get into the act by setting out on a museum scavenger hunt, for example. You'll meet at the Family Place, then explore the museum together. There's also a self-guided tour for families, pick up a booklet at the Information Desk.

Special Note: May is Museum-Goers' Month in Boston. More than 40 area museums participate, with special events and exhibits, free days, and more, a real bonus for museum hoppers.

● Faneuil Hall Marketplace

Merchants Row; (617) 242-5642. **All ages.**

Amazing to think that Quincy Market, the centerpiece of this shopping and dining complex, was built as a trading center for produce and livestock. These days, herds of people (more than 10 million tourists a year) amble through the cafes and clothing stores, and past pushcarts laden with all sorts of kid-tempting fare. Face it: If you visit Boston, you'll end up here at some point—it's practically the law. There are street performers galore, and they're good (they have to be—they audition for this plum position). Among their ranks: clowns and mimes, harpists, guitarists, and jugglers. This colorful, festive area has become a model for the restoration and conversion of older urban areas into shopping, dining, and entertainment centers. Little kids will want to check out the huge Disney Store; older ones will have a grand time picking out the coolest souvenir T-shirt from among hundreds of possibilities. And once they discover there's a whole hall filled with nothing but delectable edibles— look out.

Special Note: While at Faneuil Hall, stop by the Bostix Booth to see what's happening in the arts around town; buy half-price, day-of-performance tickets here.

● Boston Duck Tours

Tours leave from Prudential Center on Huntington Ave.; (617) 723-3825. Daily, early April–Nov. Tickets available 48 hours in advance, although they do save a block of tickets for same-day sales. Hotel concierges also have reservation privileges. Adults, $19; kids 12 and under, $10; 3 and under, $.25. **Ages 3–12.**

This is one tour of Boston that really makes a splash. The "ducks" in question are authentic WWII amphibious vehicles that take in most of the major tourist sites in town, then splash down into the Charles River for a brief cruise. The "conducktors" have no shame; they make goofy jokes, play kazoos, and honk at passersby. The coolest part (and a good photo op for families): Kids get to drive the half-boat, half-truck hybrid once it's in the water. This 80-minute tour doesn't take in all the must-sees, but it's great fun.

● Boston Common

Bounded by Beacon, Charles, Boylston, Tremont, and Park streets. **All ages.**

This is the oldest public park in the United States, occupying 48 acres in the city's busy downtown area. In colonial days the area was pastureland for animals and training ground for the militia. Today you're likely to find street musicians, art exhibits, political demonstrations, food vendors, even outdoor concerts. Pick up maps and information at the Visitor's Information Center located on the hilly east side. This is also the starting point for Boston's Freedom Trail. In winter, enjoy a Boston tradition: ice skating on Frog Pond. Bring your skates (or rent a pair for $3), and warm up with cocoa in the Pond Cottage.

● Freedom Trail

If you really want to see downtown Boston, put on some sensible shoes and follow the red-brick road. Boston's Freedom Trail is a self-guided, 2.5-mile walking tour of 16 historic sites. A bold red stripe on the sidewalk, beginning at the Boston Common Visitor's Information Center, leads visitors through the downtown financial and shopping district to Faneuil Hall, through the North End, and into Charlestown. Depending on how fast you walk, how many sites you see, and how long you stay at each site, the Trail can take anywhere from two hours to a full day to complete. Pick up maps at Visitor's Information Centers located throughout the city. Freedom Trail sites include: the State House, Park Street Church, Granary Burying Ground, King's Chapel, Ben Franklin's statue and the site of the first public school, the Old Corner Bookstore, Old South Meeting House, the Old State House, the site of the Boston Massacre, Faneuil Hall, the Paul Revere House, Old North Church, Copp's Hill Burial Ground, the USS *Constitution*, and Bunker Hill Monument. You might want to pick and choose sites along the tour that best match your family's interests.

● Boston-By-Little-Feet

Starts at the statue of Samuel Adams in front of Faneuil Hall (Congress St. side) on Sat. and Mon. at 10 A.M. and Sun. at 2 P.M. throughout the summer, rain or shine; (617) 367-2345. Per person, $6. Children must be accompanied by an adult. **Ages 6–12.**

This is a nifty idea, and we highly recommend it—it's an hour-long guided tour designed for children ages six through 12. It covers a major portion of the Freedom Trail and introduces kids to Boston history and architecture in a fun, participatory style. Kids get a special Explorer's Map with footprints leading to each location. This is a great way to introduce kids to the city of Boston.

● Public Garden

Bordered by Beacon, Charles, Arlington, and Boylston Streets. Swan boats: Mid-April–mid-Sept. Adults, $1.25; 12 and under, $.75. **All ages.**

An oasis of tranquility in the middle of a bustling city, the Public Garden is a wonderful place to relax and catch your breath before the next stop on your agenda. Sure to grab your attention, if you visit in season, are the swan boats, an enduring symbol of Boston. Do take a 12-minute ride and enjoy. This is the venue for Robert McCloskey's *Make Way for Ducklings*, the classic children's story of a mallard family looking for a home. (The kids can even pose for a picture with bronze replicas of the story's characters.)

● Wheelock Family Theater

180 The Riverway; (617) 734-5302 or (617) 734-4760. Late Oct.–May. Performances Fri., 7:30 P.M.; matinees Sat. and Sun., 3 P.M. Tickets, $9–$12. **Ages 3–12.**

This is a professional equity theater whose actors are members of the Boston theater community. Performances feature multicultural, intergenerational casts in such family-pleasing plays as *Stuart Little* and *The Secret Garden.*

● The Boston Children's Theatre

Performances at C. Walsh Theatre, Suffolk University, 55 Temple St.; (617) 424-6634. Performances Dec., Feb., April, and summer (outdoors). Matinees Sat., Sun., and Boston school vacations, 2 P.M. Tickets: $10–$12; summer performances free. **Ages 3–12.**

This is live theater, for children and by children. Local young actors star in three mainstage productions a year, all family favorites such as *Snow White, Narnia,* and *The Music Man.*

WATERFRONT

● Boston Tea Party Ship and Museum

Congress St. Bridge; (617) 338-1773. March–Dec., daily, 9–5. Adults, $7; 6–12, $3.50; 13 and up, $5.50. **Ages 3 and up.**

Relive one of the most colorful chapters in our country's history. Kids will love tossing a bundle of tea into the harbor below (and pulling it back up again, of course) as they act out the notorious rebellion aboard a full-size reproduction of one of the famous Tea Party ships. The adjacent museum houses colonial artifacts and exhibits.

● Children's Museum of Boston

Museum Wharf, 300 Congress St.; (617) 426-6500. Tues., Thurs., Sat., and Sun., 10–5; Fri., 10–9; closed Mon. except holidays. Adults, $7; 2–15, $6; 1-year-olds, $2; under 1, free. Fri., 5–9 P.M., $1 for everyone. **Ages 1–12.**

This multilevel space is fairly bursting with wonderful things to do; if the world were designed by kids, it would probably look a lot like the Children's Museum. Want to explore a Japanese house, appear on your own TV show, make giant bubbles, or put bones together to make a skeleton? It all happens here, and that's just a sampling. Traveling exhibits and special events are always part of the fun, too. Many events are tied in with holidays and celebrate cultural diversity. A special playspace is set aside for toddlers and preschoolers, where they can climb, play, and put together puzzles without the distraction of big kids.

Tip: The recycling center has lots of neat stuff (cheap) that's great for at-home craft projects.

● Computer Museum

Museum Wharf, 300 Congress St.; (617) 423-6758. Tues.–Sun., 10–5; Fri., 10–9; closed Mon. Adults, $7; 5–17, $5; 4 and under free. Sun., 3–5 P.M., admission half-price. **Ages 5 and up.**

Right next door to the Children's Museum, the Computer Museum is a user-friendly spot with enough activity to keep children happy and plenty of gee-whiz technology to impress techno-types. Much is interactive: Hold a conversation with a computer, change the look of your face, design a robot on the World Wide Web; you'll find the lastest in computer technology here, as well as a display of early computers. The changing exhibits are always intriguing, and have included "Robots! Robots! Robots!," "Design Your Own Racing Bike" (with computer graphics), and a walk-through computer.

● New England Aquarium

Central Wharf; (617) 973-5200. Mon.–Wed. and Fri., 9–5; Thurs., 9–8; Sat., Sun., and holidays, 9–6. Adults, $9; 3–11, $5; under 3, free. **All ages.**

Pardon their growing pains. The aquarium is in the midst of an expansion that will double its size by the year 2000. A new outdoor facility for seals and sea otters (temporarily located behind the aquarium) offers a free peak at these playful creatures. Inside, the world's largest circular, glass-enclosed tank—four stories high, 187,000 gallons—houses its own coral reef, bringing sharks, rays, turtles, and hundreds of underwater creatures within inches of your face. Kids adore hand-dunking for crabs, shells, and starfish at the Tidal Pool. In the harbor, see harbor seals cavort. Dolphin and sea lion shows are included in the price of admission; someone is always chosen from the audience to get a sloppy sea lion kiss.

● HarborWalk

15 State St.; (617) 242-5642. Daily. **All ages.**

Get in touch with Boston's shoreline on this two-mile, self-guided tour. Visit the National Park Service Visitor's Center at 15 State Street for a map and brochure that includes tidbits on Boston's maritime history. Sites along the way include New England Aquarium, the Children's Museum, and the Boston Tea Party Ship. Are you ready, Reeboks? Start walkin'. . . .

● Boston Harbor Islands

Tired of city sounds and sights? Consider a short ferry trip to one or more of the islands that make up the Boston Harbor island, recently designated a national park. There are more than 30 islands altogether, and most are included in the state park. Spend a day exploring an old fort, swimming in an ocean cove, hiking along wooded trails, and berry picking; each island has its own unique character.

Several cruise companies will take you by ferry boat from Boston's waterfront piers to Georges Island. (See Boat Cruises listing, below.) From there, take a free water taxi to the other islands.

BACK BAY

● John Hancock Observatory

200 Clarendon St.; (617) 572-6429. Mon.–Sat., 9–11; Sun., noon–11. Adults, $4; 2–10, $3. **Ages 3 and up.**

New England's tallest building offers sweeping views from its 60th floor. A multimedia presentation simulates a helicopter tour of the city.

● Skywalk

Prudential Center, 50th floor, 800 Boylston St.; (617) 236-3318. Mon.– Sat., 10–10; Sun., 12–10. Adults, $2.75; 5–15, $1.50. **Ages 3 and up.**

Get a 360-degree view of Boston and beyond from this 52-story building. Signs on the wall indicate points of interest.

● Where's Boston?

Copley Place, 100 Huntington Ave.; (617) 267-4949. Daily, shows on the hour. Free. **All ages.**

This multimedia show gives a quick, all-around introduction to the city's sights, sounds, and people. Stop in before you begin your visit to Boston.

● Mapparium

175 Huntington Ave.; (617) 450-2000. Tues.–Sat., 9:30–4. Free. **Ages 5 and up.**

Inside the headquarters of the First Church of Christ, Scientist, you'll find a walk-through glass globe, an intriguing sight for adults as well as kids.

BEACON HILL

● The State House

Beacon St.; Mon.–Fri., 10–4. Free. **Ages 6 and up.**

Samuel Adams laid the cornerstone for this gold-domed Boston landmark. Sitting atop Beacon Hill, the State House is now the seat of Massachusetts government. Two tours are offered; older children might enjoy the Legislative Process Tour that covers how laws are made; a historical/architectural tour features the Hall of Flags and House and Senate rooms. Be sure to pick up the special booklet for children at the tour desk.

● Granary Burying Ground

Tremont St., next to Park Street Church; Daily, 8–4. Free. **All ages.**

Step back into history and recall the lives and times of several American heroes. This is the final resting place of John Hancock, Samuel Adams, Robert Paine, and the parents of Ben Franklin and Paul Revere.

● Black Heritage Trail

This walking tour commemorates the history of Boston's 19th-century black community, which settled in this part of Beacon Hill. The trail begins at the African Meeting House (8 Smith Center), the oldest black church building still standing in the United States, and continues through Beacon Hill with stops at the Smith Court Residences, Abiel Smith School, the George Middleton House, Robert Gould Shaw and the 54th Regiment Memorial, the Phillips School, the home of John J. Smith, the Charles Street Meeting Houses, the Lewis and Harriet Hayden House, and Coburn's Gaming House.

Pick up maps and information at Visitor's Information Centers throughout the city.

NORTH END

● Paul Revere House

19 North Square; (617) 523-2338. Daily, 9:30–4:15; closed Mon., Jan.–March. Adults, $2; 5–17, $.75. **Ages 6 and up.**

Visit Boston without stopping by the Paul Revere House? Unthinkable. The famous patriot was living in this very house when he took his famous ride, shouting, "The British are coming!" This house is the oldest building in Boston (built around 1680) and contains many original furnishings.

● Haymarket Square

Haymarket St., adjacent to Quincy Market, behind the Bostonian Hotel. Fri. and Sat., dawn to dusk. **All ages.**

If you're near Boston's North End on Friday or Saturday, you won't be able to miss this open-air farmer's market. Push your way through the crowds and hear the staccato sales pitches of the vendors, amid the color and aroma of fresh produce, fish, and flowers. Bargains abound, especially at the end of the day. You might find fresh oysters on the half shell for a quarter a piece, or succulent peaches for a buck a bag. Yes, this can be a wild scene for kids, but it's pure Boston.

● Feasts and Festivals

North End (Hanover, Salem, and Prince streets), weekends throughout the summer. **All ages.**

The narrow streets of the North End, Boston's "Little Italy," come alive with celebration in honor of the saints. The statues are decorated, and the streets are blocked off to make way for pushcarts laden with pizza, sausages, pastries, Italian ices, and other treats. Add parades, music, and song and you have a colorful and lively outdoor festival. Walk over and join the fun. (See "Annual Events" section for more.)

● Scenic Strolls

Newbury Street and Beacon Hill. **All ages.**

Boston is a walker's paradise. You've probably visited several of the city's attractions on foot, or plan to; the following are suggestions for rambling along, with no particular itinerary in mind. After spending some time in Boston, you'll no doubt discover your own favorite spots to sit back and savor the city.

Newbury Street, from Arlington Avenue to Massachusetts Avenue, is lined with antique shops, boutiques, unique stores of every kind (some not so unique), and restaurants. Sit at an outdoor cafe, visit an art gallery, window shop, and people watch. If you have time, meander down Marlborough Street (our pick as the most beautiful street in Boston); stroll down Commonwealth Avenue, a tree-lined promenade of parks; or walk over to Copley Square, where you'll see the impressive Trinity Church and the Copley Square fountain.

There's no other place in the country quite like **Beacon Hill.**
The very first Bostonians resided here, and it's still regarded as a highly
desirable residential location. This is a neighborhood of charm and
antiquity, full of 18th- and 19th-century townhouses, cobblestone streets,
courtyard gardens, brick walkways, and gas-lit lanterns. The best way to
see it all is to wear comfortable shoes (most of the area is steep), start at
Charles and Beacon streets, and meander. You'll also find the Bull &
Finch Pub, model for the TV show *Cheers,* on Charles Street.

● Charles River Esplanade and Hatch Shell

Located off Storrow Drive, the Esplanade is a hub of activity
when good weather beckons Bostonians outdoors. Join them and you'll
see why this stretch along the river is perfect for walking or inline
skating, bicycling (along the Paul Dudley White Bike Trail), or simply
grabbing a picnic and a park bench and watching the sailboats and sculls
zigzag up the Charles. On summer evenings, the action centers at the
Hatch Shell, where there's often an outdoor concert, or (on Friday night) a
free movie screening under the stars. This is also the site of Boston's giant
July 4th fireworks gala, with dazzling pyrotechnics set to music by the
Boston Pops.

● Boat Cruises and Whale Watching

Discover a humpback whale playground, visit the Boston Harbor
Islands, or board a ship that will take you to the tip of Cape Cod and
back again.

A number of cruise companies offer several options for folks who
want a view of Boston from the water. All depart from points along
Boston's waterfront piers; call ahead for schedules and rates. A good
option for families: the 55-minute, narrated cruise of Boston's inner
harbor offered by **Bay State Cruise Co.** ($5 for adults, $3 for kids).
Departing from Long Wharf, it's just the right length for kids. Call (617)
723-7800. Other good trips are offered by **A.C. Cruise Line,** (617) 426-
8419; **Boston Harbor Cruises,** (617) 227-4321 (no charge for kids under
12 on some of their tours); **Boston Harbor Whale Watch,** (617) 345-
9866; and **New England Aquarium Whale Watch,** (617) 973-5281. If
this is your first whale watch trip, be prepared; it's colder out there than
you'd expect, so bring extra layers. The trip to Jeffrey's Ledge or
Stellwagen Bank (the whales' favorite local feeding grounds) can be rocky,
so seasickness is common. If you or yours are prone to this malady, take
precautions, because the boat won't turn around even if you turn green.

● Sailing

Community Boating, 21 Embankment Rd., Boston; (617) 523-1038. Mid-June through third week in Aug., weekdays, 1–sunset; weekends and holidays, 9–sunset. **Ages 10–17.**

If you're a sailing family, you've probably spotted the Tech dinghies and other craft dotting the Charles River. With Boston on one side and Cambridge on the other, sailors enjoy wonderful views from port and starboard. You can join 'em. Community Boating, off Storrow Drive on the Esplanade in Boston, offers two-day visitor's memberships for $50, allowing you the use of a 16-foot Mercury sailboat. Community Boating is a nonprofit organization dedicated to teaching local youngsters (age 10–17) to sail or row for just $1 per season. Students (with parental permission) get lessons and use of boats from 9 A.M. to 3 P.M., Monday through Friday. A 75-yard swim test is required.

● Boston Sports

While other cities have built mega-stadiums, Bostonians revere tiny, classic Fenway Park, home of the Red Sox, as an enduring symbol of the city. This intimate setting, with its in-your-face action, is perfect for kids. Would you rather see the Celts or the "Broons"? Perhaps the "Pats"? The Celtics and Bruins play in the new (yes, mega) Fleet Center, while the New England Patriots do their thing in Foxboro Stadium, about 24 miles south of Boston. Just pick your favorite spectator sport—Beantown is well known for its championship teams (not to mention enthusiastic fans). For tickets and information, call the following numbers: **Boston Red Sox,** (617) 267-1700; **Boston Celtics,** (617) 523-3030 (if the Celts are your dream team, good luck; tickets are hard to come by); **Boston Bruins,** (617) 523-3223; and **New England Patriots,** (508) 543-1776.

JUST OUTSIDE BOSTON

● Franklin Park Zoo

Franklin Park, off Blue Hill Ave., Dorchester; (617) 442-2002. Daily, 9–3:30 (grounds close at 4:30). Adults, $5.50; 4–11, $3; under 4, free.
All ages.

Just outside the city, this state-of-the-art zoo is something special. The centerpiece is a dazzling three-acre African Tropical Rainforest pavilion. The setting is so authentic that it has 60 to70 percent humidity and occasional rainstorms! Other features include an aviary, a children's zoo with New England farm animals, and a waterfowl pond. New residents include a pair of African warthogs named Elvis and Priscilla.

Special events include the annual Zoo Bash, when Sesame Street characters join the fun with songs, shows, and lots of photo opportunities. Ride the Zoo Mobile from Fanueil Hall Marketplace or Copley Square; call the zoo for details.

● Sports Museum of New England

100 First St., CambridgeSide Galleria, Cambridge; (617) 577-7678. Mon.–Sat., 10–9:30; Sun., 1–7. Adults, $6; 4–11, $4.50. **Ages 6 and up.**

Sports fanatics in your family might enjoy a visit to the Sports Museum, located in the CambridgeSide Galleria shopping mall. You'll relive some of the greatest moments in New England sports history here, and pose beside life-size statues of Bobby Orr, Larry Bird, and Carl Yastrzemski. Watch the magic of Bob Cousy's fast break and Ted Williams's perfect swing on film. See what it feels like to be a winning wheelchair athlete in the Boston Marathon.

● Harvard's Museum of Cultural and Natural History

26 Oxford St., Harvard University, Cambridge; (617) 495-3045. Mon.– Sat., 9–5; Sun., 1–5. Adults, $5; students, $4; 3–13, $3; free Sat., 9–12. **Ages 3 and up.**

If you're visiting Harvard, don't miss this four-museum complex. Most fun for kids: the four large rooms full of bones, skeletons, and trilobites. Junior rockhounds will be wowed by the massive specimens of gemstones and crystals (including diamonds in the rough) in the Mineralogical-Geological Museum.

● MIT Museum

Galleries at 77 and 265 Massachusetts Ave., Cambridge; (617) 253-4444. Tues.–Sun., 12–5. Closed major holidays. Adults, $3; under 12, $1. **Ages 6 and up.**

Never let it be said that nerds lack a sense of humor. This rather quirky museum, housed in two locations, features the "MIT Hall of Hacks," celebrating great Techie "hacks" (pranks), such as putting a police car atop the school's Great Dome. Elsewhere, current exhibits include a holographic rainforest installation, *Math in 3-D* geometric sculptures, rare ship models, and a collection of science and engineering photographs.

● Bunker Hill Monument

Monument Ave., Charlestown; (617) 242-5641. Daily, 9–5. Free. **Ages 6 and up.**

This towering obelisk marks the site of the first major battle of the American Revolution. Poised on the summit of Breed's Hill, this 220-foot monument was built to honor those who died on June 17, 1775. Older children will love climbing the 294 steps to the top; join them and you'll be rewarded with a great view of Boston, not to mention a good workout.

● USS *Constitution* and Museum

Charlestown Navy Yard, Charlestown; (617) 426-1812. Year-round, daily, 10–4. Adults, $4; 6–16, $2; under 6, free. Under 16 free on Sat. and Sun. when accompanied by an adult. **Ages 6 and up.**

A visit to Old Ironsides can be an intriguing experience for families. The ship, originally launched in Boston in 1797, is the oldest commissioned warship afloat in the world. Climb aboard for a tour, guided by one of the ship's active-duty sailors, and you'll learn all about life at sea. Kids love peeking into the nooks and crannies and climbing the ladderlike steps. Even better, at the Constitution Museum children can play sailor-for-a-day. Several interactive exhibits and even a computer simulator allow you to be ship's captain.

● Bunker Hill Pavilion

55 Constitution Rd., Charlestown; (617) 241-7575. Daily, April–May, 9:30–4; June–Aug., 9:30–5; Sept.–Oct., 9:30–4. Adults, $3; under 16, $1.50. Family rate (2 adults, up to 4 children age 16 and under), $8. **Ages 6 and up.**

During your visit to the USS *Constitution* stop by the Bunker Hill Pavilion. Catch "The Whites of Their Eyes," one of the liveliest half-hour history lessons you're likely to encounter. This multimedia presentation on the Battle of Bunker Hill is both entertaining and informative. You'll find yourself rooting for the badly outnumbered colonists who fought bravely until their ammunition was gone—an example of stubborn Yankee pride in action.

● Museum of Transportation and Larz Anderson Park

15 Newton St., Brookline; (617) 522-6547. Park: year-round, daily. Museum: Sat. and Sun., 10–5. Adults, $5; 12 and under, $3. **All ages.**

Larz Anderson Park, located about 15 minutes west of Boston, is a lovely urban oasis where you'll always find children somersaulting on the vast lawn or skipping rocks on the pond. In winter, the rolling hills are a favorite sledding spot for local kids, and you'll get a great view of the Boston skyline in the distance. Don't leave without a visit to the Transportation Museum, also on the grounds. Rare and unique automobiles are housed in an 1888 carriage house. Kids can climb on cars and motor-cycles, test their wits on the scavenger hunt auto quiz, or try out an antique bicycle. Special events might include a Model T Convention or Ferrari Fun Day; special exhibits feature subjects such as "Wild in the Streets," a celebration of "muscle" cars enhanced with Beach Boys music and surfing videos, and "Touring in America," chronicling Americans on the road from the horseless carriage to the luxury cars of the 1920s.

● Puppet Showplace Theater

32 Station St., Brookline; (617) 731-6400. Sept.–June, Sat. and Sun., 1 and 3 P.M.; July and Aug., performances also on Wed. and Thurs. at 1 P.M. Tickets, $6. **Ages 5 and up.**

Fairies, folk tales, fun, and fantasy all await you at Puppet Showplace Theater in Brookline (a short "T" ride from Boston).

● Blue Hills State Reservation and Trailside Museum

Rte. 138, 10 miles south of Boston, Milton; (617) 698-1802, (617) 333-0690. Museum: Wed.–Sun., 10–5. Adults, $3; children, $1.50; under 3, free. **Ages 3 and up.**

Just south of Boston, this unique area boasts a series of massive granite domes (monadnocks) rising more than 635 feet. The 7,000 acre reservation offers 150 miles of hiking, riding, and biking paths. A network of trails leads to a panoramic overlook on Great Blue Hill. Some of these trails are rugged; if your group includes young children or inexperienced hikers, stick to the lowlands of this vast area. Houghton's Pond is a popular swimming spot, while Ponkapoag Pond is best for fishing. A trailside museum operated by the Massachusetts Audubon Society features the natural history of the Blue Hills, including native animals, a Native American wigwam, a crawl-through log, and more. You can go cross-country skiing in winter.

● Motion Odyssey Movie (M.O.M.)

Jordan's Furniture, 100 Stockwell Dr., Avon; (508) 580-1335. Mon.–Fri., 10–9:30; Sat., 10–11; Sun., 12–6. Adults, $5; children, $4 (40-inch height requirement). **Ages 6 and up, if taller than 40 inches.**

Sounds odd, we admit. But this promotion-minded furniture store, south of Boston, is drawing crowds with this attraction, a motion-simulated movie "ride." First, you watch a five-minute laser show, then you head into M.O.M. Theater for two movies, *Dino Island* and *Red Rock Run.* Better strap in, this ride's as wild as the Southeast Expressway during rush hour! You pivot in eight directions. For the wimps in your tribe, there are stationary seats. There's even a snack bar. You can get a coffee, or a coffee table, for that matter. Net profits from M.O.M. go to charity.

● Stone Zoo
149 Pond St., exits 34N and 35S off I-93, Stoneham; (781) 442-2002. Daily, 10–4. Adults, $3; children, $1.50; under 3, free. **All ages.**

Located a short hop north of Boston on I-93, this zoo boasts a tropical rainforest exhibit with a huge aviary and a South American Grasslands exhibit featuring lovable llamas. Kids adore the polar bear exhibit, home of Major, the zoo's mascot, and the waterfowl at the wetlands exhibit. Plan your visit around one of the special events for children, such as the "Kids Run Wild" road race.

 RESTAURANTS

● Quincy Market
Faneuil Hall Marketplace, Merchants Row; (617) 242-5642. Mon.–Fri., 9–9; weekends 9 A.M.–10 P.M.

Between the numerous food stalls and pushcart vendors you can find every imaginable foodstuff here. Baked beans, brownies, bagels, big bowls of chowda, and that's just the 'b' category. Some of it's great, some of it is just okay, but it all makes great grazing. Stay away if you hate crowds. Grab a table in the center courtyard, or sit outside on benches. Now, if you're looking for a real sit-down restaurant at Faneuil Hall, consider . . .

● Durgin Park
Faneuil Hall Marketplace; (617) 227-2038. Daily, 11:30–10; Fri. and Sat., 11:30–10:30; Sun., 11:30–9.

Touristy as all hell? You bet. But this has been a Boston landmark since 1827. You'll get real Yankee cooking here—pot roast, succotash, Indian pudding—all served family style. Not for shy types; you'll be seated at long tables next to other diners, and the waitstaff will give you a hard time if you don't finish your vegetables. At one time, the servers were as crusty as the bread, which some patrons adored and others apparently didn't. These days, Durgin Park is trying a more friendly approach.

● Hard Rock Cafe
131 Clarendon St.; (617) 424-7625. Daily, 11–2 A.M.

Yeah, we know, it's not the only Hard Rock on the planet. But hey, the Boston venue of this chain is the only one billed as "Massachusetts

Institute of Rock" (not to be confused with the other Massachusetts Institute). And your kids will think you're totally cool if you bring 'em here. All the classic rock memorabilia you'd expect are here, along with good burgers and pie à la mode. If there's a preteen in your group, expect to spring for a T-shirt. (Hey—is that Steven Tyler from Aerosmith? Nah.)

● Imperial Tea House
70 Beach St.; (617) 426-8439. Daily, 9–2 A.M. Dim sum served 'til 3 P.M.

For children who love to eat with their fingers, we've got just the place. This airy restaurant in the heart of Chinatown is known for its dim sum, served at lunch. Choose whatever looks good, say, spicy shrimp or pork dumplings, then nibble happily till the next tempting cartful rolls by. You'll be charged per serving; most items are less than two dollars. Even the pickiest eaters should find something appealing.

● Pizzeria Regina
11½ Thatcher; (617) 227-0765. Daily, lunch and dinner; Sun., 2–11.

Not just a pizza place but a Boston landmark. Families have been coming here for more than 40 years to enjoy the thin-crust pizza and soft drinks by the pitcher. It's rustic as can be, so if someone knocks over an orange soda, no big deal. Another great place for pizza is Santarpio's, at 111 Chelsea St., near Logan Airport in East Boston. Not the easiest place to find, but the pizza is out of this world. Call (617) 567-9468 for directions.

Lexington and Concord Area

Prepare to soak up some 1775 spirit, and lots of history, when you retrace Paul Revere's famous ride. This is where the American Revolution began. As you stand on North Bridge, it seems you can still hear that first "shot heard 'round the world," and as you walk Battle Creek, you just might feel the presence of patriots long gone.

The historical landmarks are the big attractions in this area. But when children tire of history lessons, there are plenty of other things to do. Visit the top-notch Children's Discovery Museums in nearby Acton, hike to Thoreau's cabin on lovely Walden Pond, or surround yourself with gossamer-winged swallowtails at The Butterfly Place. A visit to this area is a popular day trip from Boston, but if you come from that direction try to avoid morning and evening rush hour traffic, which can be horrendous. In fact, locals joke that if Paul Revere were to make the ride today, he'd probably be delayed and opt to call John Hancock and Samuel Adams from his car phone. ("Sam? Hi, it's me, Paul. I'm stuck in traffic. The British are coming!") Or maybe he'd just e-mail.

● Minuteman Statue and Battle Green

Intersection of Massachusetts Ave., Harrington Rd., and Hancock and Bedford Streets, Lexington.

This is the spot where dramatic events began in the early morning of April 19, 1775. The mounting tension between the British occupiers and the independence-seeking rebels finally erupted at a place now known as Battle Green. Leading the Minutemen onto the green was Captain John Parker, immortalized by the Minuteman Statue. Captain Parker's rallying cry: "Stand your ground, don't fire unless fired upon; but if they mean to have a war, let it begin here!"

● Minuteman National Historical Park

Off Rte. 2A; (978) 369-6944. April–Dec., daily. Free. **Ages 6 and up.**

This 750-acre park spans three towns: Lexington, Lincoln, and Concord. Stop wherever you like, there are several visitor's centers in the park, each with maps and helpful staff to guide you. (A good place to start is Battle Road Visitor's Center, run by the National Park Service, with exhibits, films, and a diorama of what happened that fateful day in 1775.) Be sure to visit the reconstructed North Bridge, where the shot heard 'round the world was fired.

● The Wayside

455 Lexington Rd., Concord; (978) 369-6975. Daily, late June–early Sept. Tours: Tues., 1, 2:30, and 4 P.M.; Wed., Fri., and Sun., 1:15, 2:15, and 3:15. Fri.–Tues., 8:30–5. Adults, $1; 6 and under, free. **Ages 8 and up.**

Follow Battle Road (Route 2A) into Concord, and you'll see a number of historic houses. Young readers will enjoy visiting The Wayside, the 19th-century home of Nathaniel Hawthorne, the Alcotts, and Margaret Sidney, author of the *Five Little Peppers* series. In nearby Orchard House, Louisa May Alcott wrote *Little Women*.

● Sleepy Hollow Cemetery

Rte. 62, Bedford St., Concord. **Ages 6 and up.**

Visit the grave sites of famous people. Some heavy hitters are buried along Author's Ridge, including Thoreau, Emerson, Hawthorne, and the Alcotts.

● Walden Pond

Rte. 126, Concord. **All ages.**

Round out your trip to the Lexington and Concord area with a stop at Walden Pond, and you'll see why Henry David Thoreau (along with Don

Henley, the singer who has recently battled to save it) was so moved by its beauty. This freshwater kettle pond has been around a long time, dug out of the landscape by an Ice Age glacier. At the north end of the pond, you'll find a wooded walking path leading you to the site of Thoreau's cabin. This is where he lived and wrote from 1845 to 1847. Pack a lunch and bring your swimsuits—across the pond, in the 150-acre Walden Pond State Reservation, is a large picnic area and swimming beach.

● Drumlin Farm Wildlife Sanctuary

South Great Rd., off Rte. 117, Lincoln; (781) 259-9807. Grounds open Tues.–Sun., 9–5; closed Mon., except major holidays. Hayrides, weather permitting, Sun. 1–3, $1. Weekend demonstrations, 11 A.M. and 2 P.M. Adults, $6; children, $4. **All ages.**

Drumlin Farm, owned by the Massachusetts Audubon Society, is a great back-to-nature escape. The 180-acre property is made up of pastures, fields, ponds, and woodlands. The best part is that farm animals live here in several barns, as do wild animals native to the region. Hayrides are a special treat. Special events include Harvest Days, Bird Seed Day, and school vacation week activities. The Audubon Shop has lots of neat and also environmentally correct stuff, like binoculars, bird feeders, games, and books.

● Discovery Museums

177 Main St., Rte. 27, Acton; (978) 264-4200. During school year: Tues., Thurs., and Fri., 1–4:30; Sat. and Sun., 9–4:30. Children's Discovery Museum open Wed., 9–4:30, Science Discovery Museum open Wed., 1–6. Summer hours: Tues.–Sun., 9–4:30. Per person, $6; both museums, same day, $9; under 1, free. **Ages 1–8.**

What a find: two wonderful hands-on museums, right next door to each other in the town of Acton. This is no secret to local children, though. They love the cozy Children's Discovery Museum, housed in a 100-year-old Victorian. Best enjoyed by kids age one to eight, it has delightful things to explore everywhere, in rooms, hallways, even closets. Tots will like climbing aboard the Discovery Ship, constructing wondrous structures in the Lego room, setting off a roomful of chain reactions, and listening to the sounds of a humpback whale. There are 10 exhibit areas in all, an afternoon's worth of fun and learning.

Located behind the Children's Discovery Museum is the architecturally unique Science Discovery Museum for kids ages six and up. The spacious, colorful building is full of interactive science exhibits. Build dams and waterfalls in the Water Discovery Room, make patterns with sound waves, shout in the echo tube . . . there are hundreds of things to explore. Kids have so much fun they don't realize how much they're learning about science and technology.

● Lowell Heritage State Park and National Historical Park

Market Mills, Lowell; (978) 937-9300. Daily, 8:30–5. **Ages 8 and up.**

Travel a maze of canalways on river barges or hop an antique trolley to the 19th-century mill complexes as you learn about life during the American Industrial Revolution. As you tour the restored textile mills, you'll meet the mill girls and canal workers who first set the revolution in motion. The American Industrial Revolution began when Frances Cabot Lowell brought the power loom design to the United States from England. Situated on the Merrimack River at Pawtucket Falls, the town of Lowell had enough waterpower to create a cloth manufacturing industry. Walk the Esplanade along the river, stop by Market Mills with its changing displays and shops, or attend one of the special family programs held throughout the summer.

● The Butterfly Place

120 Tyngsboro Rd., Westford; (978) 392-0955. Mid-April–early Oct., daily, 10–5. Adults, $6; 3–12, $5. **All ages.**

Your kids will be awestruck by nature's beauty here, surrounded by hundreds of colorful butterflies. This 3,100-square-foot atrium is a living museum of North American species. Watch them in action here, where you'll see the most activity on sunny days, when butterflies are busiest.

 RESTAURANTS

● The Firehouse

130 Middlesex Rd., Westford; (978) 649-4118. Mon.–Wed., 11:30–9; Thurs.–Sat., 11:30–10.

Bring on the five-alarm chili! This firefighter-themed restaurant will tickle your funny bone as it fills your tummy. Decor includes a firepole, complete with life-sized dummy sliding down, a ceramic fire dog, a hostess desk that appears to be the front of a fire engine, and more. The menu runs to burgers, steaks, and seafood, while kid's choices are reliables like chicken fingers and fish 'n' chips. Resist the temptation to order them blackened.

● Willow Pond

745 Lexington Rd., Rte. 2A, Concord; (978) 369-6529. Mon.–Sat., 11–11; Sun., 12–11.

What's a rowdy roadhouse like this doing in an upscale town like Concord? Well, for starters, it's serving interesting food (fried frog's legs, anyone?) and amazingly inexpensive boiled lobster dinners. Kids get a kick out of the decor, which includes stuffed wildlife specimens and World War I relics, and the laid-back atmosphere of the place. And the frog's legs. Promise you won't tell a soul about this area's best-kept dining secret.

● Michael's
208 Fitchburg Tpke., Concord; (978) 371-1114. Daily, 11:30–10.

This small, busy Italian place serves lotsa pasta (try the chicken-broccoli ziti) along with steaks, chicken, and salads. It's friendly, reliable, and the portions are large enough for sharing.

North Shore

Beautiful beaches, picturesque seaside towns, a colorful history—these elements make the North Shore a popular destination for families. Of course, some people drive 30 miles from Boston just to sample the delectable Ipswich clams.

Many visitors are attracted by oh-so-bewitching Salem. If you're among them, you won't have to look hard to find traces of Salem's grim past. (Even its high school athletic teams are called the Salem Witches.) Salem has an official witch, Laurie Cabot, and museums that recount the events of the witch hysteria of 1692 in vivid detail.

Venture beyond Salem and you'll find nautical Marblehead, which calls itself the Yachting Capital of America and boasts a beautiful harbor; artistic Bearskin Neck in Rockport, home of the most-painted motif in America; two very different castles; and some of the best beaches in New England. You'll also find lots of magic.

● Le Grand David and His Own Spectacular Magic Company
286 Cabot St., Beverly; (978) 927-3677. Year-round, shows every Sun. at 3 P.M. (doors open at 2:15). Adults, $12; 11 and under, $8. **Ages 6 and up.**

Enter the beautifully restored Cabot Street Cinema Theater and leave reality behind. Le Grand David and his troupe will delight you with comedy, pageantry, and fast-paced fun. The 2½-hour show will be a bit long for the very young, but school-aged children will enjoy figuring out how to pluck rabbits from the air and how to make someone levitate (especially useful if one has siblings). Sit up front if you can. More nice surprises are a hand-painted puppet theater with performing puppets, magicians' props on display, and clowns bearing goodies.

● North Shore Music Theatre

Dunham Rd., Beverly; (978) 922-8500. Children's performances Mon.–Fri., 9:45 and 11:45 A.M. Ticket prices vary; usually around $6. **Ages 3–12.**

By night, Broadway revivals, pop singers, and comedians take center stage here. But by day, professional productions of children's plays and concerts are featured, such as *Peter and the Wolf, Snow White and the Seven Dwarfs,* and *Dinosaur Rock.* It's a theater in the round, so almost every seat is a good one.

● Lynch Park

55 Ober St., Beverly; (978) 922-0720. Memorial Day–Labor Day. Parking fee. **All ages.**

This waterfront park has it all: a small beach, two wooden playscapes (one for toddlers), picnic tables, a big grassy field for kite flying and Frisbee tossing, and a snack bar. (It features Dick & June's ice cream, the local favorite.) Family concerts are held here most summer weekends in front of the bandshell. Take a minute to meander, and admire the beautiful rose garden.

● Peabody Essex Museum

East India Sq., Salem; (978) 745-1876. Tues.–Thurs. and Sat., 10–8; Sun., 12–5. Adults, $7.50; 6–16, $4.50. Family rate: $18. **Ages 5 and up.**

World-renowned collections of maritime art and history and of Asian and Pacific art and artifacts are housed here, making the Peabody Museum an interesting place to visit. Children will most enjoy the special events and programs geared toward them. Past programs have included a maritime music festival, Morris dancing and sea shanty performances, sailor's knot-tying demonstrations, kite making, and a Doll's Day event, based on the annual Japanese holiday. Call for a schedule of events.

● Salem Witch Museum

Washington Sq., off Washington St., Salem; (978) 744-1692. Sept.–June, daily, 10–5; July and Aug., 10–7. Adults, $4; 6–14, $2.50. **Ages 8 and up.**

The tour buses parked out front will clue you in. This is the place. Probably one of the oddest "museums" you'll ever visit, this multisensory presentation recreates the witch hysteria of 1692 with 13 stage sets, eerie music, and voice-overs. It draws no conclusions about the chilling events but asks visitors to "be the judge." Outside the museum, you'll notice a large statue of a figure that looks like a witch. It's not, it's Roger Conant, one of the first settlers of Salem, garbed in a flowing cape. Nonetheless, mosts kids prefer to think of him as a witch and willingly pose for pictures beside him. How can you not like a place that implores you to "Stop in for a spell"?

● Witch Dungeon Museum

16 Lynde St., Salem; (978) 744-9812. May–Nov., daily, 10–5. Adults, $4.50; children, $3.50. **Ages 8 and up.**

Featured here is a live, pretty scary reenactment of a witch trial, based on actual transcripts, and a guided tour of a re-created dungeon (and you thought the Witch Museum sounded creepy).

● Salem Wax Museum of Witches and Seafarers

Derby St., Salem; (978) 740-2929. July–Oct., daily, 10–6; Nov., Dec., April, and June, 10–4:30; Jan.–March, Sat. and Sun., 10–4:30. Adults, $4; under 14, $2.50. **Ages 3 and up.**

In this era of virtual reality "this" and computer-generated "that," it's somehow comforting to know that kids still appreciate the humble wax musesum. This attraction explores the city's colorful past with 50 lifelike wax figures. Startlingly well-made, they're set in 13 tableaux, enhanced by music, sound, and lighting effects. There's also an interactive area where kids can learn how wax figures are made, make a gravestone rubbing from headstone replicas, try out a 17th-century jail cell, and learn to tie nautical knots.

● New England Pirate Museum

274 Derby St., Salem; (978) 741-2800. Daily, May–Oct.; weekends only in Nov. Adults, $4; children, $3.50. **All ages.**

Did you know that pirates lurked off the Massachusetts coast in 1692? Some (gasp!) are still here, cavorting among the exhibits of high seas plunder and shipwreck artifacts at the Pirate Museum. A highlight: an 80-foot-long pirate's cave, with a surprise at the end.

● Salem's Museum of Myths and Monsters

59 Wharf St., Pickering Wharf, Salem; (978) 745-7283. Open May–Dec., Mon.–Fri., 12–4; Sat. and Sun., 11–5. Adults, $5; children, $3.50. **Ages 8 and up.**

What does this attraction have to do with Salem's history? Absolutely nothing; it does not even pretend to be educational. But for kids who have graduated from Goosebumps to more bloodcurdling fare, these werewolves and vampires have squeal appeal. Walk through a "haunted maze," where detailed scenes feature animated monsters. It's creepy, but not truly scary—nothing reaches out and grabs you. In October, this place is transformed into a full-fledged haunted house.

● House of Seven Gables

54 Turner St., Salem; (978) 744-0991. Year-round, except first 10 days of Jan., Thanksgiving, Christmas, and New Year's Day. Daily except Thurs., 9:30–5; Thurs., 9:30–8. Adults, $6.50; 6–12, $3; 13–17, $4. Combination ticket with Pioneer Village: adults, $9.50; 6–12, $5; 13–17, $6.50. **Ages 8 and up.**

Of interest to older children and adults who have enjoyed Nathaniel Hawthorne's classic novel, this tour includes several houses: the Gables (1668); Hawthorne's birthplace (1750); Hathaway House (1682); Retire Beckett House (1655), and period gardens. A museum shop and coffee shop are also on the grounds. The site is not stroller accessible; bring a backpack for baby.

● Salem Willows

173 Fort Ave., Salem; (978) 745-0251. April–Sept., Mon.–Sat., 10–9; Sun., 11–9. Free. **All ages.**

It may be a little scruffy around the edges these days, but how can you not appreciate a place that claims to be the original home of saltwater taffy? This seaside park, shaded with willow trees, has a carnival-type charm all its own. Play skee-ball, have your fortune told by a mechanical gypsy in the old-fashioned arcade, or take a ferry ride around Salem Harbor. There are kiddie rides for small fry, including tiny tugboats and a 1920s carousel. And then there's the food. You could bring your own healthful picnic, but why miss an excuse to dig into fried clams, cotton candy, or—for the truly adventurous—a chop suey sandwich. Or stake out a picnic table and indulge in some classic New England cuisine: a lobster roll and onion rings, washed down with a raspberry-lime rickey.

● Pioneer Village

Forest River Park, West St., Salem; (978) 745-0525. Mon.–Sat., 10–5; Sun., 12–5. Adults, $4.50; 13–17, $3.50; 6–12, $2.50. Family rate, $12. Combination tickets available at House of Seven Gables. **Ages 6 and up.**

Living history museums are all the rage these days, and this is America's oldest. It's an authentic recreation of Salem in 1630 when

Salem was a Puritan fishing village, some 60 years before the witchcraft hysteria. Early buildings, gardens, and animals create the feel of life in the 17th century; you'll be guided by costumed interpreters and see demonstrations of crafts and day-to-day activities of the time. Special events are held throughout the summer. Combine your visit with some outdoor fun (swimming, picnicking) at Forest River Park, adjacent to Pioneer Village.

● Salem Trolley

Essex St. mall at National Park Service Visitor's Center; (978) 744-5469. April–Nov.1, hourly, 10–5; July–Oct., every half-hour, 10–5; weekends only, March and Nov. Adults, $8; 5–12, $4; under 5, free. Family rate (2 adults, 2 kids), $20. **All ages.**

Hop the trolley for a one-hour tour of the city's attractions. Salem Trolley stops at several, including museums, the House of Seven Gables, Salem Willows, and Pickering Wharf. Get on and off as often as you like.

● Endicott Park

Forest St., Danvers; (978) 774-6518, 777-0001. Year-round, 9 A.M.– dark. Parking fee on weekends.

This former estate property, now owned by the town of Danvers, is another great place to play. The 164-acre recreation area was the site of a working farm during the early 20th century. The original buildings are still there, but the attraction for kids is a large, inviting playscape. Wander over to the children's barnyard and meet horses, sheep, turkeys, and more. You'll also find walking trails and a pond, with a path leading to Glen Magna estate. Rest rooms are tucked away in the carriage house across from the barn.

● Myopia Polo

Rte. 1A, exit 20N off Rte. 128, Hamilton; (508) 356-7797. Late May– Oct., Sun., 3 P.M. (grounds open at 1 for picnickers). Adults, $5; 12 and under, free. **Ages 5 and up.**

Bring the kids to a polo match? Are we joking? Not at all. While polo's image is genteel, the sport itself is a rough-and-tumble competition in which bumping is allowed and players traverse the field atop 1,000-pound horses traveling at 30 miles an hour. There's plenty of action, and the horses (called ponies) are beautiful. To get into the spirit bring along a gourmet picnic (this isn't the place for fast-food cartons) and cheer the Myopia team from the grassy sidelines. At half-time, go out on the field and help tromp down the divots of turf kicked up by the horses (kids love to do this). A different, and pleasant, way to spend a Sunday afternoon.

● Wenham Museum

132 Main St., Rte. 1A, Wenham; (978) 468-2377. Daily, 10–4; Sat., 1–4; Sun., 2–5. Adults, $3; 6–14, $1. **All ages.**

This gem of a museum is now bigger and better than ever, thanks to a recent renovation. But the charm—and the historic Claflin-Richards House (c. 1660) portion of the museum—remains. Exhibits include a world-famous doll collection (more than 5,000 dolls!), incredibly intricate dollhouses, antique toys, and a room devoted to model trains. Special events and exhibits have included a teddy bear parade, a hands-on blocks exhibit, a kite exhibit, and a demonstration of how to turn "junk" into sculpture. Call ahead for current information. Have lunch or tea across the street at the Wenham Tea House and make it a really special day.

● Crane Beach and Castle Hill

Argilla Rd. off Rte. 1A, Ipswich; (978) 356-4354. Parking fee charged for nonresidents. **All ages.**

With more than 1,000 acres of white sand, Crane Beach is considered by many to be the North Shore's best. It is certainly the most picturesque, with swaying sea oats along the boardwalk, graceful dunes, and sailboats bobbing in the distance. Although the water never seems to get warm, children (and warm-blooded adults) don't seem to mind. But you will mind the dreaded greenhead, a pesky fly that often infests the area in—wouldn't you know it?—midsummer. The Crane Reservation Staff posts a greenhead warning at the gate if the flies are bad, so once you pay the nonrefundable (and stiff) parking fee, you take your chances. Bathhouses, a snack bar, and lifeguards are on the premises.

Up on the hill you'll see Castle Hill, a 59-room English Stuart–style mansion built for plumbing magnate Richard T. Crane in 1927. You can tour the castle or, even better, attend one of the children's events scheduled throughout the year. These include lawn concerts, an Independence Day celebration, a Halloween party, and Christmas programs. Call (978) 356-7774 for details.

● Goodale Orchards

Argilla Rd. off Rte. 1A, Ipswich; (978) 356-5366. Mid-May–Dec., daily, 9–6. Open Sat. and Sun. in April. Hayrides, $1 per person. **All ages.**

Cap off a trip to Crane Beach with a visit to Goodale's. Besides selling one of the world's best treats (a fresh cider donut with a cup of just-pressed cider), Goodale Orchards offers pick-your-own produce. Pick your own strawberries from mid-June through July. Raspberries are ready to be picked in July, and blueberries are ripe from mid-July through mid-

August. (Dates vary due to weather and crop conditions.) In the fall, pick a peck of apples and select a potential jack-o'-lantern from the piles of pumpkins. You can also watch cider being pressed or take a horse-drawn hayride through the orchard. Kids love meeting the farm's animals, including horses, goats, turkeys, and Vietnamese pot-bellied piglets. Check out the goodies in Goodale's barn store, featuring farm-grown produce, cider, preserves, cheese, and delicious fresh-baked pies.

● New England Alive

163 High St., Rtes. 1A and 133, Ipswich; (978) 356-7013. Daily, May–Oct., Mon.–Fri., 9:30–4; Sat. and Sun., 10–6. Open April–Nov., weather permitting. Adults, $5; 2–12, $3; under 2, free. **All ages.**

Stroke a scaly snake, nuzzle a baby chick, or feed a kid goat from the palm of your hand. This small petting farm is a favorite with North Shore children and a fun destination for a picnic. Meet such native New England wildlife as a bobcat, red fox, coyote, black bear, and two young mountain lions. There's also a collection of native and exotic snakes. Most of the animals here were found injured and were brought to owner Lyle Jensen to be nursed back to health. Jensen gives informational demonstrations, too, and will happily chat about any of the residents here.

● Ipswich River Wildlife Sanctuary

87 Perkins Row, Ipswich; (978) 887-9264. Donation requested for non-members; extra charge for special programs. **All ages.**

This site is Massachusetts Audubon's largest sanctuary, covering about 2,000 acres of meadow, swamp, islands, ponds, and part of the Ipswich River, along with an observation tower. The self-guided nature hikes are great for families; the "rockery" trail features huge boulder formations (no climbing, please), while the boardwalk takes you past a beaver dam. The sanctuary offers a great selection of family programs; a recent spring line-up included "Nature Detectives" for kids ages six to eight; "Sense of Wonder Walks" for tots and their families; a bat-house building workshop, and a maple-sugaring tour. All programs are held at the Ipswich River Sanctuary Barn. Preregistration is required; call for information and fees. (See Canoeing.)

● Canoeing

The Ipswich River's serpentine twists offer delightful canoeing, through wooded swampland and open marshland that's home to a variety of birds. The **Massachusetts Audubon Society's Ipswich River Wildlife Sanctuary** runs a number of guided family paddle trips, complete with story telling around a campfire. Call the sanctuary for a schedule of events. To paddle on your own: From May–Oct., the Sanctuary rents canoes to Mass. Audubon members on a first-come, first-served basis for $5 per hour. Canoes go out between 9 A.M. and 3 P.M., and must be in by 4:30. Call ahead to make sure canoes are available. Mass. Audubon members can also canoe-camp overnight on Perkins Island, a 40-acre, pine-covered river island owned by the Sanctuary. Call (978) 887-9264 for details. Canoe rentals are also available from **Foote Brothers,** 230 Topsfield Rd., Ipswich; (978) 356-9771.

● North American Wolf Foundation
Wolf Hollow, Rte. 133, Ipswich; (978) 356-0216. Sat. and Sun, 1–5; presentations at 1:30 and 3:30. Adults, $3.50; children, $2. **Ages 3 and up.**

Did the wolf get a bad rap in "Little Red Riding Hood"? Those who study them think wolves are generally misunderstood; here's a chance to learn about gray wolves and their habits in their natural environment.

● Willowdale State Forest
Linebrook Rd., Ipswich; (978) 887-5931. **All ages.**

This 2,400-acre forest has hiking trails, both marked and unmarked, and canoeing on the Ipswich River. Canoes can be rented from Foote Bros., 230 Topsfield Rd., Ipswich; (978) 356-9771.

● Bradley Palmer State Park
Rte. 1 to Ipswich Rd., Topsfield; (978) 887-5931. **All ages.**

Take a respite from the summer heat at this pleasant, relatively undeveloped state park. Hike along woodsy trails (the park has 20 miles of them marked) and enjoy a picnic among the pines. The trails double as bridle paths. Follow the path that loops around park headquarters and you'll see an old stone mansion. Mountain bikers test their quads on the roadway. In summer, a giant fountain pool provides a place for kids to splash and play. Adults watch the action from a grassy slope nearby. This is a popular and very beautiful site for cross-country skiing in winter. Separate trails are designated for snowmobiles.

● Wingaersheek Beach
Exit 13 off Rte. 128, Gloucester; (978) 283-1601. Memorial Day–Labor Day. **All ages.**

Looking for a perfect family beach? Wingaersheek has sand bars and warm, shallow inlets. Small children will be content to plop right down

in the warm water, while older ones will enjoy rock climbing and swim‐
ming in the calm waters. Arrive early (by nine on summer weekends) to
secure a parking space. Eats are available at the snack bar. Other beaches
to try in Gloucester: Good Harbor Beach and Stage Fort Park. The latter
has a beach that's small but offers a playground area.

● Hammond Castle Museum

*80 Hesperus Ave., off Rte. 127, Gloucester; (978) 283-2080. Memorial
Day–Labor Day, daily, 10–4; rest of year, weekends only, 10–4. (Call first;
special events may affect hours.) Adults, $6; 4–12, $4.* **Ages 3 and up.**

Like a fairy tale setting come to life, Hammond Castle has a moat
and drawbridge, parapets and turrets, even an indoor reflecting pool. This
re-created version was built in 1926 as the home of inventor John Hayes
Hammond Jr. and houses his unique collection of Roman, medieval, and
Renaissance art—not to mention a huge, working, 8,200-pipe organ.
Children especially enjoy the child-size suits of armor (man-size, in their
time) and the winding passageways. (The castle is not stroller accessible,
so bring a backpack for baby.) Visit on a rainy day for an added element
of spookiness, or during Halloween week when the castle becomes a truly
awesome haunted house.

● The Schooner *Adventure*

*Harbor Loop off Rte. 127N (next to Gloucester Marine Railways Corp.),
Gloucester; (978) 281-8079. Sun. morning breakfasts, shipboard, year-
round. Adults, $6; kids, $4.* **Ages 3 and up.**

Come aboard this 121-foot schooner and get a taste of shipboard
life without leaving the berth. Built in nearby Essex in 1926, the two-
masted *Adventure* is the real thing, complete with a large spoked wheel,
tiny bunks, and shipboard galley. Kids can play captain at the wheel,
poke around nooks and crannies, and perhaps watch the crew demonstrate
seaworthy skills such as knot tying and sail rigging while you're working
on that second cup of coffee. At this writing, the *Adventure* is undergoing
a major restoration. By the time you read this, she may be shipshape, and
taking passengers out to sea for cruises. Call first, to see what the ship's
status is.

● Whale Watching

Gloucester is a great place to get out on the water and learn about
the gentle giants. Typically, whale watch cruises go to Jeffrey's Ledge, a
favorite feeding ground (lots of krill) for humpbacks and minkes. Al‐
though the whales don't always cooperate, local cruise companies claim

sighting records of higher than 90 percent, and some guarantee you'll see whales—that's how confident they are. Onboard naturalists provide narration. Children—always the first to spot a whale's tail in the distance—squeal with delight as playful humpbacks leap into the air or pass near the boat. Bring a pair of binoculars, and bring warmer clothes than you think will be necessary (it's always cool out there) and rubber-soled shoes. The trip out to Jeffrey's can be rough, so consider taking precautions if seasickness is a problem for you or yours. Cruises leave daily from Gloucester's waterfront.

Companies to call: **Cape Ann Whale Watch,** Rose's Wharf, 415 Main St., (978) 283-5110; **Captain Bill's Whale Watch,** Captain Carlos Restaurant, 33 Harbor Loop, (978) 283-6995; **Seven Seas Whale Watch,** Seven Seas Wharf, Rte. 127, (978) 283-1776; and **Yankee Whale Watch,** 75 Essex Ave., 1-800-WHALING.

● The Paper House

52 Pigeon Hill St. (look for the sign on Rte. 127), Pigeon Cove in Rockport; (978) 546-2629. July and Aug., daily, 10–5 or by appointment. Admission by donation. **All ages.**

Kids are really into recycling these days, and this 1922 house is a recycler's dream home. The entire cottage—even the furniture—is made from old newspapers, rolled and varnished. A half-hour spent at this odd abode should inspire some interesting projects at home.

● Halibut State Park

Gott Ave. off Rte. 127, Rockport; (978) 546-2997. Daily, May–Oct., sunrise–sunset. **All ages.**

Pack a picnic basket, don your sneakers, and enjoy this beautiful spot overlooking Ipswich Bay. Once a granite quarry, this is now a prime spot for tide pooling and blueberry picking. Brochures will direct you on a self-guided walking tour.

● Maudslay State Park

Curzon's Mill Rd., Newburyport; (978) 465-7223. Year-round. **All ages.**

Once a private estate, this 450-acre park features 16 miles of hiking and nature trails. After a major snowfall, it's a mecca for cross-country skiers. In summer, the Children's Theater-in-Residence performs outdoors here. Watch for the summer arts festival, with plays, music, face painting, hayrides, and such regional big-name troupes as Vermont's Bread & Circus Puppets. Call (978) 465-2572 for a schedule of events.

● Parker River National Wildlife Refuge

Plum Island (take Water St. to Plum Island Tpke., then turn right to Sunset Blvd.), Newburyport; (978) 465-5753. Year-round, daily, one-half hour before sunrise to one-half hour after sunset. Parking fee, $5; $2 for visitors walking or biking. **All ages.**

Birdwatchers flock to this tranquil spot, where more than 300 species have been sighted. (Peak migration is from March to early June.) To help you identify what you see, you might want to visit one of the local shops catering to birdwatchers, such as Birdwatcher of Newburyport, 50 Water St. The refuge also offers miles of sandy beach that's great for strolling, though a bit rough for swimming, and nature trails. The two-mile Hellcat Swamp Trail is a standout; a boardwalk takes you past habitats of birds and other wildlife. Branch off from the trail to an observation tower where an easy climb will reward you with sweeping vistas of the marsh, and a nice vantage point to look for beavers near the beaver lodge.

Special Note: The beaches and dunes area here is sometimes closed, to allow piping plovers and least terns to nest in peace. The trails will still be open.

● Amesbury Sports Park

12 Hunt Rd., exit 54 off Rt. 495, Amesbury; (978) 388-5788. Open seasonally; snow-tubing and snowboarding in winter (when it's cold enough for snow-making), daily, 12–9:30; summer activities begin in May. Call first for current schedule. Snow-tubing: all-day pass, weekdays, $10; weekends and holidays, $20. 3-hr. pass: $15. Ages 4 and up; no toddlers. Helmets mandatory, ages 4–6. Snowboarding: $14 weekdays; $22, weekends/holidays. **Ages 4 and up.**

Totally tubular—that's the best way to describe New England's only snow-tubing facility. They even have snow-making coverage. Rope tows haul you up the hill; oversized rubber doughnuts carry you down a choice of slopes, some steep, some mogully. Tubes have attached loops, so you can all tie up together and make like a giant rubber roller coaster. Or, learn to snowboard at Jigger's Notch; if you decide to catch some phat air after you've bought your snow-tubing ticket, buy a beginner's package for $20. Summer activities include a driving range, miniature golf, bumper boats (outfitted with squirt guns), sand volleyball courts, and go-carts.

● Salisbury Beach

Rte. 1-A, exit 58 off I-95, Salisbury. Rides open Memorial Day–Labor Day, 12–10; arcades and shops open Memorial Day–Labor Day, 10 A.M.– midnight, and Labor Day–Dec. with reduced hours. **All ages.**

Since the 1800s, this little strip of beach has attracted fun seekers and, more recently, folks en route to Maine looking for a break from the car. One of the last of the seaside amusement parks, and suffering from a seedy reputation for a few years, Salisbury Beach is now a family-friendly destination, complete with a beach, kiddie rides, arcade games, and, thrilling for tots, a giant inflatable clown you can bounce on. (Find him at Pirate Fun Park, one of the family-run businesses that predominate here.) To go along with these pursuits, of course, the right treats are essential, like fried dough, homemade fudge, fried clams, and ice cream. Wednesday is Kiddie's Day, when children-only discounts are offered; Friday nights, there are fireworks, and Sundays, you're likely to see strolling musicians, a puppet show, or a petting zoo.

● Scenic Strolls—Marblehead Harbor and Bearskin Neck

Marblehead's scenic harbor is a sightseer's delight. Park your car in the waterfront lot on Front Street and explore the winding streets of quaint Old Town. Crocker Park, off Front Street, offers a great view of Marblehead Harbor. On weekends, watch sailing regattas from Castle Rock.

Rockport was a sleepy fishing village until artists discovered it after the Civil War. Today, Rockport's Bearskin Neck is a thriving arts center. Even if you've never visited Bearskin Neck before, chances are it will look familiar: the fisherman's shanty overlooking Rockport Harbor, called Motif #1, has been depicted by artists more often than any other building in the United States. Plan to eat in one of the casual-but-good seafood restaurants overlooking the harbor.

 RESTAURANTS

● The Rockmore Floating Restaurant

Salem Harbor, Salem; (978) 740-1001. Launch leaves from Pickering Wharf, Salem, and Village Street Pier, Marblehead. Late May–mid-Sept., Mon.–Fri., 11–9; Sat. and Sun., 11–10. (Last launch leaves prior to stated closing times.)

You've heard of waterfront dining. The Rockmore takes the concept one step further. To get to this restaurant (actually, a tricked out 110-foot barge, anchored in Salem Harbor), you scoot over by water in a bright red launch boat. For kids, the food is secondary to the motorboat trip. This is a fun way to go on a steamy summer night, so expect to wait a bit for the launch to pick you up. But once you get to the Rockmore, it's a festive scene. Eats consist of burgers, fish sandwiches, and seafood. Cute touch: Kid's meals are served in little boats. If the weather's not right for al fresco dining, try the Rockmore Drydock restaurant (at Pickering Wharf) where kids can watch Disney flicks in the living room while parents relax, post-meal. (Can you tell the owners are parents themselves?) The Rockmore Drydock is open daily, year-round, 11–10.

● Clam Shacks

Yeah, we know, "fat kills, yadda yadda yadda." Still, we can't imagine giving up one of the rites of summer, a trip to a clam shack for a mess of fried clams—plump, juicy, golden-crisp, bellies intact. Spend the rest of the week eating unadorned veggies, if you must, but don't miss a trip to one of the North Shore's best bets for fried clams. After much research, here are our picks. You can't miss **The Clam Box,** on Route 1-A at Mile Road in Ipswich; it's shaped like a box of clams. *Yankee Magazine* once named them "the world's best fried clam"—we agree. Kids won't eat clams, not even clam strips? Get 'em a box of chicken fingers, or a burger. Downside: it's a tiny place, so expect a wait. Upside: (besides the food) picnic tables outdoors. Open March–Nov., Sun.–Thurs., 11–8; Fri. and Sat., 11–8:30; (978) 356-9797. Another perennial favorite is **Woodman's,** 121 Main St., Rte. 133, Essex; (978) 768-6451. Just as much as Filene's Basement is famous for shopping, Woodman's is famous for clams. Billing itself as the birthplace of the fried clam, Woodman's also offers steamers, lobster-in-the-rough, chowder, and other (mostly fried) seafood. Noisy, rustic, and self-serve, this is the place to go for that quintessential taste of summer. Enjoy without guilt. Open daily, in season, 11–10.

● Prince Restaurant

517 Broadway, Rte. 1, Saugus; (617) 233-9950. Sun.–Thurs., 11–11; Sat., 11–midnight.

Located on Route 1 north of Boston, the Prince is hard to miss—its facade features a giant leaning tower. (Route 1 is not known for understatement, by the way.) Inside, the place is massive; so are the servings of pasta and made-to-order pizzas. You can tell they love kids: children's shows featuring Calvin the Clown are presented four times a week. Calvin also pops up frequently during school vacation weeks. Hours vary, so it's best to call first. Reservations are encouraged.

South Shore and South of Boston

Why make a stop when you're halfway to Cape Cod from Boston? For most families, the answer is Plymouth Rock. Sooner or later, nearly every child is carted to the spot where, in the autumn of 1620, the pilgrims first set foot in the New World.

Unfortunately, not much remains of this rock that looms giant-size in the minds of school children. Indeed, it once was giant—more than 3,000 pounds of Plymouth Rock have been chipped away by tourists. Today the rock is protected, and much of it remains underground.

Happily, there's more to Plymouth than a mostly buried rock. Plimoth Plantation is a favorite destination, and the *Mayflower II* awaits. Set aside time to visit some other South-of-Boston attractions, too, including a tiny town filled with a host of unique museums and 2,000 toy trains.

● Plimoth Plantation

Rte. 3A, Plymouth; (508) 746-1622. Pilgrim Village: April–Nov., daily, 9–5. Wampanoag Homesite: April–Nov., daily, 9–5. Admission (includes Plimoth Plantation, Wampanoag Homesite, Craft Center, and Mayflower *II): adults, $18.50; 5–12, $11; under 5, free.* **All ages.**

If you jumped into a time machine and set the dial to "Plymouth Colony, 17th Century," you'd be zapped to a place like this. Plimoth Plantation is no cutesy Pilgrim Theme Park—it's a living museum, peopled by folks posing as real Pilgrims to re-create life in the Plymouth Colony.

Portraying characters based on actual Pilgrims, each carefully researched by the Plantation, the Pilgrims here perform the chores of everyday life in 1627. As in real life, chores change with the seasons. Busy as they are, the Pilgrims take time to chat with visitors. They're really good at staying in character, too; if your child asks them about Nintendo or even Barbie dolls, they'll act totally clueless. Of course, kids love this.

Also on the grounds is the Wampanoag Homesite, where you'll see Indians (portrayed by Native Americans) perform their daily tasks in a re-created setting. Seeing these two very different cultures presented side by side provides a history lesson your children won't forget. The Craft Center features demonstrations of pottery making, furniture building, basket weaving, or cloth weaving. Don't miss the museum shop, with its good selection of children's books, craft kits, and Pilgrim-themed paraphernalia.

● *Mayflower II*

State Pier, Plymouth Harbor; (508) 746-1622. April–Nov., daily, 9–5; July and Aug., 9–7. Mayflower II *only: adults, $5.75; 5–12, $3.75.* **All ages.**

Berthed at the State Pier in Plymouth, the *Mayflower II* is Plimoth Plantation's full-scale reproduction of the ship that carried the Pilgrims in 1620. Climb aboard the gangway and you'll meet Mayflower passengers, realistically portrayed by Plimoth Plantation staffers. The stories they tell about the hardships of the voyage will capture your attention and make an impression on your kids that no textbook can match.

● Pilgrim Hall Museum

75 Court St., Plymouth; (508) 746-1620. Daily, 9:30–4:30. Closed Christmas Day and month of Jan. Adults, $5; 18 and under, $2.50; family rate (two adults, up to four children), $12. **Ages 3 and up.**

Did you know that the Pilgrims didn't really wear tall hats with buckles? (Yes, that means all those signs on the Mass. Pike are wrong.) Learn the facts about our famous forebears here, home of a premier collection of original Pilgrim artifacts. Take a look at a 10,000-year-old Native American arrowhead, Winslow's rapier, a suit of armor worn by a Pilgrim, a cannon, and much more. The museum also houses artifacts from subsequent generations. Activities geared toward kids, from tots to teens, include "treasure hunts" for intriguing artifacts, and "picture yourself as a Pilgrim" in a pre-drawn frame. Temporary exhibits cover topics such as "Popular Pilgrims," a look at how the Pilgrims have been depicted in the movies and other media.

● Plymouth National Wax Museum

16 Carver St., Plymouth (across the street from Plymouth Rock); (508) 746-6468. Mar.–Nov., daily, 9–5. Adults, $5; 5–12, $2. **Ages 3 and up.**

Wax museums tend to be a little creepy, maybe because of the deathly pallor of the characters' faces, and this one is no exception. But it is educational (sort of) depicting the Pilgrim story through 27 lifelike scenes. Special lighting, sound effects, and animation add to the experience; this is a good rainy-day activity.

● Cranberry World Visitor's Center

Water St., Plymouth; (508) 747-2350. May–Nov., daily, 9:30–5. Free. **Ages 3 and up.**

If your kids are world-class juice drinkers, they probably help keep this place in business. Sponsored by Ocean Spray Cranberries, Inc.,

Cranberry World is filled with exhibits tracing the history and development of the cranberry industry. (If you've driven around this area, you may have noticed some scarlet fields—those are cranberry bogs.) You'll see antique and modern harvesting tools and machinery and learn everything you ever wanted to know (and probably more) about this native American fruit. Children will enjoy sampling the numerous cranberry beverage combinations.

● Plymouth Beach

Rte. 3, Plymouth. **All ages.**

Right on the open ocean, this 3.5-mile sandy beach offers views of Saquish Neck to the northeast and Manomet Bluffs to the southeast. Plymouth Beach has lifeguards, concessions, and a bathhouse.

● Duxbury Beach

Rte. 3A to Rte. 139 N., Canal St., Duxbury. Memorial Day–Labor Day, 8–8. **All ages.**

Probably the nicest beach in the area, this five-mile stretch of sand is privately owned but leased to the town. It's clean, well maintained, and alcohol free. Lifeguards are posted; bathhouses, a concession stand, and a luncheonette are on the grounds.

● Duck Tours

Splashdown Amphibious Tours, Harbor Place, Plymouth; (800) 225-4000. Open May–Sept.; Adults, $12; under 12, $8; under 3, $.50. Another company: Water Wheels, (508) 746-7779. Village Landing, Plymouth. Adults, $15; 3–12, $10. **All ages.**

These amphibious land-and-sea tours, all the rage in Boston, are available in Plymouth, too. Splashdown Amphibious Tours offers one-hour cruises departing from Harbor Place (next to Isaac's Restaurant), from May through September. The tour takes in the town's historic waterfront district, then splashes down into Plymouth Harbor. Another company, Water Wheels, offers a 90-minute tour, departing from Village Landing. This waterfront tour features Plymouth Rock, *Mayflower II,* and the town's fishing fleet, by land and by sea. Kids take turns playing captain of the vessels when they're in the ocean.

● Colonial Lantern Tour

Meets at the Tin Lantern, 98 Water St., Plymouth. Call (508) 747-4161 for information. Nightly, 7:30 P.M., late March–late Nov. Adults, $8; children, $6. **Ages 6 and up.**

Now this is an appropriate way to explore an oh-so-historic town: on a candlelit walking tour. This 90-minute tour (too long for the very young or easily bored) covers sites including the waterfront, the Town Brook, the original Plimoth Plantation site, and other landmarks. A later tour, called Legends & Lore, begins at 9 P.M. Departing from the John Carver Inn at 25 Summer St., this one highlights the more macabre side of Plymouth's past. The sites are the same as the Colonial Lantern tour, but the narrative focuses on mysterious events in Plymouth's past. Special seasonal tours are offered for Halloween, Thanksgiving, and Christmas.

● Children's Museum of Plymouth

46–48 Main St., Plymouth; (508) 747-1234. Year-round, Mon.–Sat., 10–6; Sun., 12–6. $4 per person. **Ages 2–10.**

This interactive discovery museum caters to kids from two to ten. The 40-plus exhibits focus on the sciences and the humanities but, mostly, they're about fun. Want to go on a simulated whale watch, play on a fire engine, sink putts on a kid-sized golf course, climb a giant tree fort, or be mayor (or whatever role you choose) of Tiny Town, U.S.A.? You can here.

● Super Sport Family Fun Park

108 N. Main St., Rtes. 44 and 58, Carver; (508) 866-9655. Year-round, daily, 10–9; Memorial Day–Labor Day, 10–11. Price range: $4.50 and up, depending on activity. Combination passes available. **Ages 3 and up.**

Feel like riding a bobsled, skiing down double–black diamonds, or racing a motorcycle? You can do it all here, sort of. The Venturer motion simulator ride offers seven types of adrenalin rush. No chance of breaking a bone, unless you fall out of your seat. And that's just one of the fun options here. Others are a golf driving range, miniature golf, a bumper boat pool with waterfalls and geysers (you must be 38 inches tall to ride alone), batting cages, and a go-cart track (kids 58 inches tall can ride by themselves). A video arcade and restaurant are on the premises, too, in case you need to part with more cash.

● South Shore Music Circus

Sawyer St., Cohasset; (508) 775-9100. Children's performances, Thurs., 10:30 A.M. Tickets: $5.25. **Ages 3 and up.**

Kids love live theater, and what could be a better introduction to the stage than a performance of one of their favorite fairy tales? *Hansel and Gretel, Goldilocks and the Three Bears, Rumplestiltskin,* and other well-loved stories are presented in the children's series here. (This is the same line-up, different day, offered at Cape Cod Melody Tent. See listing.)

● A&D Toy-Train Village

49 Plymouth St., Middleborough; (508) 947-5303. Year-round, Fri.– Mon., 11–5; July, Aug., and Dec., daily, 11–5. Open during Massachusetts public school vacations and holidays, except Easter, July 4th, Thanksgiving, and Christmas Day. Christmas Festival from mid-Nov. through the first week in Jan. Adults, $5; 4–12, $3.50. **All ages.**

There's a certain magic about toy trains; they bring out the little kid in everyone. This charming, family-run museum celebrates the toy train with more than 2,000 on exhibit. Some are strictly for looking, including models made of candy, china, and lead crystal. And, there are 52 operating trains, in seven gauges. Children love pushing the buttons (a number of trains are visitor-activated) to set the toy trains in motion. Plan to spend an hour or so here, with a stop at the gift shop. Special children's days and theme weekends are scheduled, including a very nice Christmas display; call ahead for information. If you're bringing a toddler, ask if the "little tykes" ride-on train will be operating.

● Nantasket Beach

Nantasket Ave., Rte. 228 exit off Rte. 2, Hull; (781) 925-4905. Year- round. **All ages.**

This three-mile stretch of fine, hard-packed sand draws crowds from all over the Boston area and the South Shore. Swimmers, sun worshipers, surfers (there's often a pounding surf), joggers, shell seekers, and, of course, beach-loving families congregate here. Bathhouses and refreshments are available, and lifeguards are posted. At the mainland end of the beach is the Carousel Under the Clock.

● Carousel Under the Clock

George Washington Blvd., Nantasket Beach, Hull; (781) 925-0472. Weekends only, late May–late June, 12–6; daily, late June–Sept., 10–19. Per ride, $1.50. **All ages.**

Paragon Park, Hull's landmark amusement park, is long gone. But, happily, its 1928 carousel remains. Enjoy.

● Hull Lifesaving Museum

1117 Nantasket Ave., Hull; (781) 925-LIFE. Year-round, Sat., Sun., and Monday holidays, 12–5. July and Aug., Wed.–Sun. plus Monday holidays, 12–5. Adults, $3; 5–17, $1.50. **Ages 5 and up.**

Quick, put on a Coast Guard uniform and hop in the dinghy to rescue your friends. At this hands-on museum, kids learn what rescuers did when ships and boats were in trouble off the shores of Hull (at one time, the only entrance to Boston Harbor). At this genuine, 19th-century U.S. lifesaving station, children can climb to the loft and talk to each other using telegraph keys in the radio room, maneuver boats and blocks over a floor map of Boston Harbor, or make signal code flags out of construction paper. Throughout the year special demonstrations are held—children might be asked to go for a mock rescue ride or to pull the ropes in on a safety buoy.

● Myles Standish State Forest
Rtes. 3, 44, and 58, South Carver; (508) 866-2526. **All ages.**

This 15,000-acre preserve is a beautiful spot for communing with the great outdoors. Swimming (in College and Fearings ponds), fishing, canoeing, trails for hiking, bridle paths for riding, snowmobiling, cross-country skiing, camping—these options make this park a favorite with active families.

● Wompatuck State Reservation
Rte. 228, Hingham; (781) 749-7160. **All ages.**

This 3,000-acre state park offers hiking, fishing, and camping. Don't be surprised if you share the trails with horses—this is a popular place for trail riding.

● Hiking
In addition to the destinations mentioned above, this area offers some delightful places to hike. Family favorites are: **South Shore Natural Science Center,** Jacob's Lane, Norwell, offering nature trails (including a trail for the visually disabled), (781) 659-2559; and **World's End Reservation,** Martin's Lane, Hingham, designed by Frederick Law Olmsted, (781) 749-5780.

● Boat Cruises
Catch a codfish, spot a whale, or just relax aboard one of the excursion boats that cruise out of Plymouth Harbor. Or, cruise from Hull to Long Wharf in downtown Boston, or to Georges Island, Boston's most popular harbor island. For information, call these companies: **Captain John Boats** (deep-sea fishing, whale watching), departing from Town Wharf, Plymouth, (508) 746-2643 or (800) 242-2469; **Cape Cod Cruises** (Plymouth Harbor cruises, sunset cruises), departing from Mayflower State

Pier, (508) 747-2400; **Massachusetts Whale Watching** (whale and seabird watching, ecology activities), departing from Center Town Wharf, Plymouth, (508) 833-0181; or **Bay State Cruise Company** (Hull to Boston, Hull to Georges Island, and Harbor Islands, and whale watching), departing from Nantasket Pier and other sites in Hull, (781) 723-7800.

● Kendall Whaling Museum

27 Everett St., Sharon; (617) 784-5642. Tues.–Sat., 10–5. Closed major holidays. Adults, $2; children, $1; under 5, free. **Ages 5 and up.**

Inspired by your whale-watch trip? Here you'll find nine galleries of maritime artifacts and memorabilia, from paintings to navigational instruments. Most interesting for kids are the ship models, figureheads, and whaling gear.

● Wonder Museum

26 Chestnut St., Foxborough; (508) 543-1184. Tues.–Sat., 10–5; Sun., 1–5. Closed holidays. Admission, $3. **Ages 1–12.**

The wonders of science, art, math, and nature are presented here, in a lively, participatory style. A complex pendulum, a hot-air balloon, a walk-in kaleidoscope, an anatomy room, and a talking mynah bird (Max) are highlights. You'll also find a toddler room and special events and exhibits.

 RESTAURANTS

● Isaac's on the Waterfront

114 Water St., Plymouth; (508) 830-0001. Daily, 11:30–11.

No question about it, this is the place to go in Plymouth. The view can't be beat, with the *Mayflower II* on the right and Plymouth's fishing fleet on the left. Virtually every table at this contemporary, multilevel restaurant has a view. (In good weather, head for the outdoor deck.) Of course, fresh seafood is featured on the menu—it's good, and not pricey. Chicken, beef, and pasta dishes (try the Fettucine Neptune) round out the menu, and a children's menu is offered.

● The Clam Box

789 Quincy Shore Dr., Quincy; (617) 773-6677. Daily, March–Nov., 11–midnight.

This glorified clam shack is a local institution. It draws throngs of beach-goers from Wollaston Beach across the street, and regulars who've been coming here for a clam fix for more than 20 years. Forget the umbrellaed tables outside—too noisy—and head in to the atrium-style dining area to indulge in tasty fried clams, lobster rolls, shish kabobs, Greek salads, even fried oysters and (gasp!) fried lobster. Order ice cream and fried dough, too, if you really want to send that cholesterol count through the roof. (At least they use vegetable oil in the Fryolators.)

New Bedford and Fall River Area

About an hour south of Boston, this region has a colorful past. New Bedford was once the whaling capital of the world, and its revitalized waterfront offers plenty of evidence—from sea captains' homes to Seaman's Bethel, the mariner's chapel described in Herman Melville's *Moby Dick.* New Bedford's entire downtown and waterfront was recently designated as a National Historic Site. Melville described the city as home to "patrician-like" houses and "opulent" parks and gardens. "All these brave houses and flowery gardens came up from the Atlantic, Pacific, and Indian Oceans," he wrote. "One and all they were harpooned and dragged up hither from the bottom of the sea." Although the idea of killing whales is repugnant today, the whaling industry made New Bedford quite prosperous in the 19th century. Now, the city is a major commercial fishing port, but making one's fortune as a fisherman is a lot tougher. The Whaling Museum is the town's most popular attraction, and many visitors find that New Bedford's revitalized downtown is a nice place to knock around.

Fall River, on the Rhode Island border, was once a mill town, made famous by the Lizzie Borden ax-murder case. (The Victorian house where Abby and Andrew Borden were hacked to death is now a bed-and-breakfast inn, believe it or not.) Today, factory-outlet stores are the big draw—along with the World War II navy ships at Battleship Cove. Whatever you discover here, you'll most likely be surprised at how much this "untouristy" area offers to those who seek it out.

● Whaling Museum

18 Johnny Cake Hill, New Bedford; (508) 997-0046. Daily, 9–5; Sun., 1–5; July and Aug., daily, 9–5; Sun., 11–5. Adults, $3.50; 6–14, $2.50.
Ages 3 and up.

New Bedford's intriguing past is revealed at this museum. Children love climbing aboard the *Lagoda,* a half-scale replica of a square-rigged whaling ship. (At 89 feet long, it's the largest ship model in the world.) The museum also has an impressive collection of scrimshaw. You'll marvel at the intricate detail of these designs, engraved on the teeth of sperm whales or on pieces of whalebone. Whalemen usually whittled these as gifts for their mothers, wives, or sweethearts. The display *Down to the Sea for Fish* chronicles the tough life of men who fish for a living; *Windows on Centre Street* will point you toward other whaling-related sites along the waterfront area on a walking tour through historic New Bedford.

● New Bedford Fire Museum

Bedford St., New Bedford; (508) 992-2162. Memorial Day–Labor Day, Mon.–Fri., 9:30–3:30. Adults, $2; 6–16, $1; under 6, free. **Ages 3 and up.**

This fire museum is even more child-friendly than most. Downstairs, you'll find (surprisingly) a 1930s Barnum & Bailey circus miniature. Upstairs, there's a fire fighter's pole to slide down, and firemen's helmets, boots, and coats to try on, a bell to ring, and (with parental supervision) real fire trucks to climb aboard. Memorabilia dates back to the early 1900s.

● Zeiterion Theatre

684 Purchase St., New Bedford; (508) 994-2900. Year-round; performances Wed., 10:30 A.M. (mostly groups) and 2 P.M. (families). Sat. performances for kids, 2 P.M. Tickets: $5. **Ages 3 and up.**

Known locally as the "Z," this restored vaudeville theater offers wonderful family programming as part of its performing arts schedule. Recent performances have included *Doctor Dinosaur, Pinocchio,* and *Dr. I. Wonder's Science Circus.*

● Battleship *Massachusetts*

Exit 5 off I-95, Battleship Cove, Fall River; (508) 678-1100. Year-round, daily, 9–5; Sat. and Sun., 10–5. Adults, $8; children, $4. **Ages 6 and up.**

Admittedly, this attraction won't set everyone's hearts aflutter, but if this is your kind of thing, you'll love it. Climb aboard World War II warships and PT boats, and massive vessels from the Korean and Vietnam wars, including the destroyer the *Joseph P. Kennedy.* Check out the submarine USS *Lionfish.* There's a collection of World War II–related memorabilia, too, as well as a gift shop and snack bar.

● HMS *Bounty*

State Pier, Battleship Cove, Fall River; (508) 676-8226. July–mid-Oct., Sun.–Thurs., 10–6; Fri. and Sat., 10–8. Call to confirm closing times. Adults, $4; 4–11, $2; under 4, free. **Ages 3 and up.**

Just a short walk from the battleship *Massachusetts,* is the HMS *Bounty* replica. This 169-foot-long, three-masted Tall Ship was built for the 1962 movie *Mutiny on the Bounty,* starring Marlon Brando. It was donated to the Fall River Chamber Foundation by media mogul Ted Turner and TBS Properties. The ship is a replica of the British merchant vessel commanded in 1789 by Lieutenant Commander William Bligh. Visit this ship and recall the dramatic tale of the real *Bounty.*

● Fall River Carousel

Two Central St., Battleship Cove, Fall River; (508) 324-4300. Memorial Day–June, weekends, 12–4; June 30–Sept. 1, daily, 10–8; call for off-season hours. Per ride, $.75; book of 10 tickets, $6. **All ages.**

Pick your favorite steed and take a whirl on this restored 1920s carousel.

● Marine Museum

70 Water St., Battleship Cove, Fall River; (508) 674-3533. Wed.–Fri., 9–4; Sat., Sun., and holidays, 12–4. Adults, $3; children, $2. **Ages 3 and up.**

Young seafarers will get a kick out of this, as will anyone who's ever tried to put together a model ship (and how do they get those glass bottles around them, anyway?). More than 150 ship models are on display here; the centerpiece is the 28-foot-long *Titanic* replica. Exhibits include model steamships, yachts, sailboats, and the world's largest collection of HMS *Titanic* artifacts.

● Horseneck Beach State Reservation

Rte. 88 off I-195, Westport Point; (508) 636-8816. **All ages.**

Horseneck Beach is one of the state's most popular—and most stunning—beach destinations. Here you'll find more than 500 acres on the water's edge and enough activity to keep the most energetic bunch happy, including swimming, fishing, canoeing, boating, and picnicking.

● Children's Museum in Dartmouth

276 Gulf Rd., exit 12S off I-95, South Dartmouth; (508) 993-3361. Tues.–Sat., 10–5; Sun., 1–5. Open first Fri. of every month 'til 8. Closed Mon. except during school vacations, holidays, and early Sept. Admission, $3.75; under 1, free. Free, first Fri. every month, 5–8. **Ages 1–8.**

Housed in a former dairy barn, this museum is worth a visit if there's a toddler or young child in your bunch. Walk into a kaleidoscope, create a puppet show, or build the world's largest Lego creation. The animal petting area is also popular; animals are housed in cages, but museum staff members will bring them out to visit. During a recent visit, changing exhibits included a "Bubbles" area, a coral reef display, and a collection of teddy bears. Outside, you'll find a playground and nature trails to explore. The museum owns 60 acres of sanctuary land, made up of salt marsh, meadows, and forest.

● Capron Park & Zoo

Rte. 123, County St., Attleboro; (508) 222-3047. Year-round; April–Oct., 9:30–5; Nov.–March, 10–4. Adults, $2.50; 6–12, $1; 5 and under and handicapped, free. **All ages.**

Here's a find within a find: Inside this 63-acre park is a six-acre zoo housing everything from mice to sloth bears, llamas to snow leopards, about 90 specimens in all. Exhibits have a pro-conservation message. A picnic area, snack bar, gift shop, and playground are on the grounds, too.

 RESTAURANTS

● Freestone's City Grill

41 Williams St., New Bedford; (508) 993-7477. Daily, 11–11.

This is a rare find—a sophisticated little restaurant that welcomes kids. While the older kids and adults in your party are enjoying the contemporary artwork displayed, the little ones will be busy playing connect-the-dots on their menus; small fry receive a mug of crayons and a take-home kid's menu as soon as you're seated. The children's menu features the usual nonthreatening line-up, and a terrific option to soda pop: fresh-fruit smoothies.

● Big Top Kiddie Playland

35 Mariano Bishop Blvd., Fall River Shopping Plaza, Fall River; (508) 675-4800. Mon.–Thurs., 10:30–8:30; Fri., 10:30–9; Sat., 10–9; Sun., 10–8:30.

Animated animal shows, a ball crawl, video games, mechanical rides, pizza—sound familiar? It's not a Chuck E. Cheese (though it used to be), but it packs the same kid-pleasing punch. Besides pizza, the menu offers grinders, nachos, and the like. You buy tokens to operate the rides and games.

Tip: Go during the week to avoid the multitudes of pint-sized people and their parents.

Central Massachusetts

This region may lack ocean views and salt air, but visiting families don't seem to care. They're too busy enjoying the museums, parks, and attractions here. Take Springfield, for example: where else can you spend one day at a musket shoot and the next practicing your jump shot at the Basketball Hall of Fame? If there's a dinophile in your group, you'll want to put both the Springfield Science Museum and Dinosaur Land in South Hadley on your list of must-sees.

Worcester, the second-largest city in Massachusetts, boasts two destinations kids can't resist: Higgins Armory Museum and New England Science Center. And, if you're willing to roam a bit, there's plenty more to see and do, from state-of-the-art roller coasters to a centuries-old kid-sized cave. Beyond the big cities, you'll find rural towns dotted with farms and antique shops.

● Springfield Science Museum

State and Chestnut streets, Springfield; (413) 263-6800. Thurs.–Sun., 12–4. Planetarium shows: Wed.–Fri., 2:45; Sat. and Sun., 1:30 and 2:30 (2:30 feature is Magic Sky Show, *best for young children). Admission (includes all four museums in the complex: the Science Museum, the Connecticut Valley Historical Museum, George Walter Vincent Smith Art Museum, and the Springfield Museum of Fine Arts): adults, $4; 6–18, $1; under 6, free. Planetarium: $1 per person. Free on Fri. with Springfield library card.*
All ages.

Put this one in the "don't miss" category. Part of a quadrangle of museums, Springfield's lively Science Museum was designed with families in mind. At the hands-on Exploration Center, for example, kids can listen to Native American folk tales in a real wigwam and visit a turtle pond, where turtles "talk" to you (on audio tape) as you look through eye-level portholes and watch them swim. Other areas include Dinosaur Hall (where you'll see a full-size replica of a tyrannosaurus rex and can walk inside a giant dinosaur footprint), African Hall, with a huge African elephant, and a planetarium.

The Monsanto Eco-Center features an aquarium and live animals, with re-created examples of a mangrove swamp, a coral reef, the New England coast, and the Amazon rainforest.

Is there a fan of Springfield native Theodor Geisel (Dr. Suess) in your bunch? Stop by the Connecticut Valley Historical Museum and take a peek at the Suess exhibit.

● Naismith Basketball Hall of Fame

1150 W. Columbus Ave., adjacent to I-91, Springfield; (413) 781-6500. Daily, 9–6. Adults, $8; 7–14, $5; under 7, free. **Ages 5 and up.**

Don't expect hushed voices and "do not touch" signs at this Hall of Fame. When you enter the door, you join the great American game of basketball, which was invented in Springfield in 1891 by Dr. James Naismith. Try your skill at basket scoring in the Spaulding Shoot Out, the most popular spot here, where budding hoopsters shoot at baskets of varying heights and add points to the giant scoreboard. There's lots more, including video highlights of the great games, a special-effects motion picture that puts viewers in the middle of a game, and (great for nosy types) a peek at what some of today's famous NBA players keep in their lockers.

● Forest Park

Summer Ave., Springfield; (413) 787-6434 (park), (413) 733-2251 (zoo). Park: daily 'til dusk. Zoo: April–Oct., Mon.–Sat., 10–4; Sun. and holidays, 10–5; Nov.–March, Wed.–Sun., 10–3. Adults, $2.50; 5–12, $1.50; 4 and under, $.50. **All ages.**

This delightful city park boasts several fun features. You can rent paddle boats and pedal your way around Porter Lake, duckling style; then pay a visit to the Children's Zoo in the middle of the park to see wild and domestic animals from New England's woods and farmyards and such exotic species as a South American capabara, emus, and wallabies. There's also a petting area with goats and sheep. If you want more action take a trail ride on horseback ($10 per half-hour) or a pony ride ($1) from Forest Park Stable. Other options include swimmming, tennis, hiking, and picnicking.

● Holyoke Children's Museum

444 Dwight St., Holyoke; (413) 536-KIDS. Tues.–Sat., 10–4:30; Sun., 12–5. Admission $3; under 1, free. **Ages 1–12.**

This engaging museum houses three permanent exhibits that win rave reviews from small fry. At Paperworks, kids can create handmade paper out of recycled paper pulp (which is especially appropriate here, since Holyoke was once a leading paper producer). Cityscape is a child-size Main Street, with a half-dozen or so businesses to try out including a TV studio, health center, architect's office, and bodega (Latin market). Kids love The Scientific Company exhibit, offering exciting ways to explore scientific principles with bubbles, shadows, and objects in motion. If there's a toddler in your group, you'll appreciate the Tot Lot, where little ones can play without encountering rambunctious older kids. There's also a picnic area (and some indoor tables) in the complex, along with the 1920s Mountain Park Carousel.

● Robert Barrett Fishway

Holyoke Dam, Holyoke; (413) 536-9428. Mid-May–June, Wed.–Sun., 9–5. **All ages.**

Watch migrating salmon and shad on the fish elevator—that's what they call it, all right—at Holyoke Dam on the Connecticut River. Peep through the viewing windows or view from the observation platform overlooking the dam.

● Mount Tom State Reservation

I-91N to exit 17W, then Rte. 141 to W. Holyoke; (413) 527-4805. Reservation: year-round. Museum: Memorial Day–Labor Day; Sept.–Oct., Fri.–Sun. $5 per car. **All ages.**

Just minutes from downtown Holyoke, this area is worth exploring. You'll find more than 30 miles of hiking trails, many offering beautiful views of the Pioneer Valley. The Reservation Headquarters has trail maps. There's also a small nature museum, with collections of rocks, insects, butterflies, and birds, and a playground. You can cross-country ski and ice skate on Lake Bray in winter.

● Mount Tom Ski Area

Rte. 5, exit 17-A off I-91N, Holyoke; (413) 536-0416. Open Nov.–March, depending on snowfall. Lift tickets: adults, $26, weekdays and night skiing; $29, weekend days and holidays. Age 12 and under, $23/$26. Water attractions: mid-June–Labor Day. Adults, $15.95; 3–10, $12.95; under 3, free. Toddler ticket (wave and mushroom pools only), $5.95. Skiing: **Ages 4 and up;** *water attractions:* **Ages 1 and up.**

Many local kids get their "ski legs" here. With just 16 slopes and trails served by eight lifts, it's not a huge operation. But that suits many families just fine. Features include 100 percent snow-making and a family-friendly, discounted 3.5-hour "Right Time" lift ticket, usable any time of day. Junior ski school (for ages 4 to 14) is offered weekends and by the week during Christmas vacation and school vacation week in February.

In summer, Mount Tom turns wet and wild with a 9,000-square-foot wave pool, an Alpine Falls ride, a dual-tube waterslide, and a twisty Flash Flood waterslide. For tiny tots, there's a "mushroom" pool (the wave pool is also fine for small fry).

● Old Sturbridge Village

Rte. 20W, near exit 9 off Mass. Pike and exit 2 off Rte. 84, Sturbridge;
(508) 347-3362. Open Jan.–mid-Feb., weekends only plus President's Day,
10–4; mid-Feb.–March, Tues.–Sun., 10–4; April to Nov., daily, 10–5;
Nov.–Dec., Tues.–Sun., 10–4. Adults, $15; 6–15, $7.50; under 6, free.
(Tickets good for two consecutive days.) **All ages.**

What was it like to be a child growing up in rural New England
more than 150 years ago? Children will have a good time finding out at
Old Sturbridge Village, a living history museum that re-creates life in a
rural New England town, circa 1830s. The Village includes residences,
craft shops, meetinghouses, mills, a school, and a working farm. Everywhere you look, you'll see costumed interpreters busily engaged in early–
19th-century chores and pursuits. You'll see a printer, blacksmith,
tinsmith, and others plying their trades in authentically restored buildings (transported to the village from throughout New England). Visit
Freeman Farm, where you'll discover how much work, especially team-
work, was involved in raising crops and livestock, and in simply preparing
meals for the family. One of the newest features at OSV is a pontoon boat
ride on the Quinebaug River. The 15-minute interpretive cruise costs
$3 per person (under 3 ride free on an adult's lap). They've also launched
a kid's club for frequent visitors. In winter, horse-drawn sleigh rides are
offered.

Since this is a rural community, many of the daily activities will
change with the seasons. Spring brings sheep shearing, for example, and
autumn means a turkey shoot and an early–19th-century Thanksgiving
dinner. If you can, plan your visit to coincide with one of the special
participatory weekends scheduled throughout the year. Parades, musket
shoots, children's activities—these will make your trip to Old Sturbridge
Village more involving and more fun.

● Brimfield State Forest

Rte. 20, Brimfield; (413) 245-9966. **All ages.**

This hilly forest is a favorite destination among hikers, with lovely
views from several points along Mount Waddaquadduck. Cool off with a
dip in the pond or fish for trout in fast-flowing streams. You can go cross-
country skiing in winter.

● Dinosaur Land

Amherst Rd., off Rte. 116, South Hadley; (413) 467-9566. Year-round,
daily, weather permitting, 9–5. Adults, $3.50; 12 and under, $1.50. **Ages**
3 and up.

Dino-fanatics won't want to miss this—it's a quarry of dinosaur tracks made by prehistoric animals who once roamed these riverbanks and cliffs north of Springfield. More than 5,000 footprints have been quarried here. The oldest item is a 500-million-year-old trilobite fossil. An indoor museum features a collection of fossils, footprints, and related artifacts. Check out the gift shop for fossils, footprints, and dinosaur bones (all real) and dinosaur models.

● McCray's Country Creamery Petting Zoo

14 Alvord St., South Hadley; (413) 533-0775. Year-round, daily, 9–9. **All ages.**

This working farm is the home of two child-pleasing features: a petting zoo and an ice cream shop. Meet horses, goats, sheep, ducklings, rabbits, pigs, and peacocks. Take a 20-minute hayride around the grounds (adults, $2; kids, $1) to work up an appetite. Then sit at a picnic table and enjoy a homemade double-dip ice cream cone (there are inside tables, too). Ahh, simple pleasures.

● Red-wind Meadow Farm Trout Hatchery

500 Sunderland Rd., Amherst; (413) 549-4118. Memorial Day–Labor Day, Mon.–Fri., 9–4; Sat. and Sun., 9–5. Sept. and Oct., Sat. and Sun., 9–5, weather permitting. Please call for current rates. **Ages 3 and up.**

Few things are as thrilling to a young child as catching a fish. You can rent rods here, buy a bucket of worms, and fish all day for trout (rainbow, brook, and brown), large-mouth bass, sunfish, perch, and catfish. Staff members will provide pointers. Kids can learn a new sport— and maybe bring home the family dinner.

● Erving State Forest

Off Rte. 2, Erving; (508) 544-3939. **All ages.**

Swim in pretty Laurel Lake or fish for trout in the lake or streams. There's also a two-mile hiking trail and a half-mile nature walk, both marked. You can go cross-country skiing in winter.

● Riverside Park

Rte. 159, Main St., Agawam; (413) 786-9300. Mid-April–mid-Oct., Sun.–Thurs., 11–11; Fri.–Sat., 11–midnight. Admission, $18.99; under 54 inches tall, $10.99. **All ages.**

This rollicking amusement park has wild rides, corny family entertainment, costumed characters, and cotton candy, all sure to throw the kids into spasms of delight. Among the 120 rides and attractions are new rides including Mind Eraser, a suspended looping roller coaster, and Shipwreck Falls, Time Warp, and Chaos, all offering thrills aplenty. Gentler souls will appreciate the 150-foot Ferris wheel, the carousel, and antique cars. Don't miss the "Just for Kids" sing-along. NASCAR auto racing competitions are held on Saturday nights.

● Higgins Armory Museum

100 Barber Ave., Rte. 12N off I-90, exit 1, Worcester; (508) 853-6015. Year-round, Tues.–Sat., 10–4; Sun., 12–4. Closed Mon. and select holidays. Adults, $5.75; Seniors, $5; Ages 6–16, $4.75; age 5 and under, Free. www.higgins.org. **Ages 3 and up.**

This may be the only place in the country where your dream of being a knight in shining armor can come true. At this wonderfully unique museum, kids (adults, too!) can try on castle clothes and helmets in the Quest gallery. There's even armor for dogs.

Demonstrations of arms and armor are presented daily. Special kid's programs feature gargoyles, beastly dragons, and marionettes. The collections of medieval and Renaissance armor and related artifacts are fascinating.

● New England Science Center

222 Harrington Way, off Rte. 9, Worcester; (508) 791-9211. Year-round, Mon.–Sat., 10–5; Sun., 12–5. Adults, $6; 3–16, $4. Train rides, $1. **All ages.**

Exploration is the name of the game here. Set on 59 acres of woodlands, this three-story museum offers hands-on science exhibits, indoor and outdoor zoos, an observatory, a planetarium, a nature trail, a preschooler's area, even a working narrow-gauge train, the Explorer Express. Recent exhibits have featured Native American stories, earth activities, and comets, starring Hale-Bopp.

● Wachusett Mountain

Rte. 140, Mountain Rd., Princeton; 1-800-SKI-1234. Current lift ticket rates not available at press time (although this resort is always a bargain compared to North Country ski areas). Call for ticket prices and snow condition updates. **Ages 3 and up.**

Location, location, location. That's the best thing about Wachusett Mountain. Ski here, an hour or so from Boston, and you avoid the often-brutal traffic heading to points north. Obviously snow-making is important here, and they've got it, 100 percent from top to bottom. Features include night skiing (add $5 to the cost of your lift ticket and ski until

10 P.M.), NASTAR racing, a nursery, and the acclaimed SKIwee teaching program for kids ages 3 to 12. Children will have fun learning to navigate the Bamboo Bridge and Hoola Hoops in the Polar Playground; new-to-the-sport adults will feel comfortable in the beginner's area. These features make Wachusett Mountain—with 18 trails and 5 lifts—a great place to learn to ski.

● Farmland Petting Zoo

Redstone Hall Rd., off Rte. 62, Sterling; (508) 422-6666. Memorial Day–Oct., Thurs.–Sun., 10–5, weather permitting. Adults, $3; 12 and under, $2.
All ages.

Not your garden variety petting zoo, this one has pot-bellied pigs, llamas, Scotch Highland cattle, and more than 100 more animals to pet and feed. Go on a hayride (free) or a pony ride, and be sure to bring a picnic lunch; you can eat alongside the animals.

● Southwick's Wild Animal Farm

Off Rte. 16, Mendon; (508) 883-9182. May–mid-Oct., daily, 10–5. Circus shows at 12 and 4 daily. Adults, $7.50; 3–12, $5; under 3, free.
All ages.

Dedicated to the preservation of rare and endangered species, this farm houses the largest collection of wild animals in New England. Meet lions, tigers, and bears (oh, my), plus a baby giraffe, ostriches, and several varieties of birds. Catch the antics of clowns and trained elephants at the circus show. Make new friends—both furry and feathered types—at the petting area, ride a pony, and learn about them all through exhibits and demonstrations.

● Whalom Amusement Park

Rte. 13, Lunenburg; (508) 342-3707. Easter–Columbus Day, Fri. and Sat., 12–10; Thurs.–Sun., 12–9. Admission, $5; all-day ride pass, $13; all-day ride and waterslide pass, $17; Kiddie Land Pass, $9. Spring and fall, all-day ride pass $9. **All ages.**

Fifty acres of fun: rides, midway games, kiddie rides, waterslides, miniature golf, train rides, even a beach. We nominate as "most thrilling ride" the Comet roller coaster. The newest attraction here is Prism, an "experience in light and color," as it's billed—sort of a walk-through light show. We bet this is the only place in New England where you'll see Madonna, Simba the Lion King, and Michael Jackson (okay, so they're marionettes) sharing the same stage. Catch their performances and other, live shows throughout the day. Rent an aqua bike or paddle boat and get some exercise pedaling or paddling around Whalom Lake. Whalom Park offers lots of old-fashioned fun.

● Turner Falls Fish Viewing Facility

Fish Ave., Turner Falls; (413) 659-3714. Mid-May–June, Wed.–Sun., 9–5. **All ages.**

The name says it all—watch the annual migration of salmon and shad through underground viewing windows. The staff and informational exhibits will fill you in on all the facts.

● Maple Sugaring

Sweeten up your winter with a visit to a sugar house. Massachusetts has more than 100 (several in this area), open for demonstrations from February through early April. They give samples, too. Call the Massachusetts Maple Producers at (413) 628-3912 for a free directory. A recorded message gives updates daily in season.

● Hiking

If you guessed this region offers some great hiking, you're right, and it's especially rewarding during fall foliage season. Places to go include **Chesterfield Gorge,** off Rte. 153, in Chesterfield (a 30-foot gorge near the headwaters of Westfield River); **Laughing Brook Education Center and Wildlife Sanctuary,** 789 Main St., Hampden (nature and walking trails, and an animal exhibit); and **Northfield Mountain Recreation and Environmental Center,** Rte. 2A, Northfield (mile-long nature trail ringing Northfield Mountain).

● Boat Cruise—*Quinnetukut II* Riverboat

Rte. 63, Northfield; (413) 659-3714. Late May–mid-Oct., Wed.–Sun. Adults, $7; 14 and under, $3. Reservations recommended. **All ages.**

Cruise the Connecticut River, between the towns of Gill and Northfield, on this 1.5-hour interpretive tour. Narration covers local history, geology, and eco-facts, enhancing the leisurely trip.

● Purgatory Chasm State Park

Purgatory Rd., Sutton; (508) 234-3733. Daily, dawn–dusk, except during snow and ice conditions (usually, Jan.–Feb.). Guided tours Memorial Day–Columbus Day, Sat. at noon and 4 P.M., and Sun. at 4 P.M. **Ages 4 and up.**

This 900-acre state reservation is a boulder-strewn maze designed by Mother Nature. The chasm itself is an 80-foot-deep hole in the ground, with granite walls as high as 70 feet. This is a very cool place for a family adventure, but do keep in mind that the ledges of the chasm are wide open; nothing is closed off or roped off. We wouldn't recommend this for toddlers, as it takes surefootedness to climb the mossy boulders, but well-supervised kids will have a grand time crawling into "The Coffin" (a small cave), and shimmying their way through "Fat Man's Misery," a foot-wide, 10-foot-long space between two huge boulders. Even Moms and Dads can squeeze through "Devil's Corn Crib," although it may involve sucking in that tummy. Five trails have been carved through, and around, the chasm. So where did this family-friendly quirk of nature come from? There have been many theories over the years, but modern geologists believe that an enormous glacial lake melted nearby and Purgatory Chasm was carved by ice-fed torrents. Constant freezing and thawing results in natural sculpting, making the chasm a work in progress. On a hot summer day, this is a cool oasis. Bring some eats; there are picnic tables and (usually) an ice cream truck passes through the park.

● Breezy Picnic Grounds Waterslides

538 N.W. Main St., Douglas; (508) 476-2664. Weekends, Memorial Day–mid-June; daily, mid-June–Labor Day. Slides open 10–6:30; park open 9–7. Waterslide (unlimited rides): Adults, $11; 12 and under, $9.50. Picnic grounds and swimming only: weekdays, $4.50, kids $3.50; weekends and holidays, $5/$3.50. **All ages.**

Who doesn't love a waterslide? This waterside park and grassy picnic area, on Whitins Reservoir, boasts two 300-foot-long alpine waterslides, with lifeguard-attended lake swimming and a snack bar.

● Dunn Pond State Park

Route 101, Gardner; (978) 632-7897. Year-round, dawn to dusk. **All ages.**

This 119-acre park features walking trails, picnic tables, a playground area, and swimming on a 20-acre pond. Bring your own canoe or kayak, or rent a paddleboat from the vendor here. Naturalist-guided interpretive programs are offered throughout the summer; one popular program is an evening campfire with Native American story telling. Call for a schedule. Dunn Pond is a favorite venue for ice skating in winter.

RESTAURANTS

● Bub's Bar-B-Que

Rte. 116, Sunderland; (413) 259-1254. Mon.–Sat., 5–10 P.M.; Sun., 1–10 P.M.

This is a real down-and-dirty rib joint, very casual and often very busy. If you're not into red meat, that's okay—there's chicken, swordfish, salmon, catfish, shrimp, or whatever the current catch is, and even barbecued baked beans. Other tasty side dishes include dirty rice, collard greens, and dilled potato salad. The downside is that you can wait in line awhile, especially if you hit the place on Friday or Saturday night. The up side is that if the kids are rowdy no one is likely to notice.

● Gramp's

216 Lyman St., Holyoke; (413) 534-1996. Mon.–Fri., 7 A.M.–3 P.M.; Sat., 8–12:30.

This local favorite features great sandwiches and serves breakfast all day long. Try a roast beef melt or a Reuben, both with soup or salad. Most kids opt for a stack of Gramp's pancakes, regardless of time of day.

● Red Rose Pizzeria

1060 Main St., Springfield; (413) 739-8510. Tues.–Thurs., 11–11; Sun., 12–10.

Try the best pizza in Springfield, after you watch it being made right in front of you. Red Rose pizza makers toss dough into the air in an open kitchen. You can also get pasta, grinders, and eggplant dishes (the egglant Parmesan is superb). There's no children's menu, but the folks at Red Rose don't mind if you order, say, a plate of ziti and split it.

● Weintraub's Restaurant & Delicatessen

126 Water St., Worcester; (508) 756-7870. Mon., 10–4; Tues.–Sun., 9–8.

Voted best deli in New England by *Yankee Magazine*—need we say more? With so many possible choices and combinations, even the finicky will join the Clean Plate Club.

● Worcester Diners

True, diners are fairly small, and the sounds of one whiny child can really resonate, but if you're willing to take that chance and you love classic diners, Worcester's got 'em. Dining cars were once manufactured here, and there are still more than a dozen functioning as diners to choose from. We haven't tried them all, so we can't vouch for their quality, but would they have lasted so long if they didn't send out some mean Blue Plate Specials?

The Berkshires

The far western region of Massachusetts, called the Berkshires (short for Berkshire Hills), is an area as graceful as its name implies. Blessed with beautiful countryside and charming Main Streets, the area offers a wealth of cultural and recreational activity. Plan to take it slow and savor the pleasures of the Berkshires. Enjoy a picnic on the lawn of Tanglewood as the Boston Symphony Orchestra performs under a starlit sky. Visit a magnificent natural marble bridge with "graffiti" dating back to 1740. Or ride horseback through a forest of brilliant fall foliage. Even if you take a wrong turn along the way (and you probably will—it's easy to be distracted by the view), so what? You're bound to discover something special around the next curve in the road.

● Hancock Shaker Village
Rte. 20, Pittsfield; (413) 443-0188. May–Oct., daily, 9:30–5. Adults, $12.50; 6–17, $5. Family rate: $30 for two adults and all accompanying children under 18. **Ages 3 and up.**

Hancock was one of 18 communities founded by the Shaker sect in the 18th century. Although the last of the Hancock Shakers left the church family in 1960, this museum is a permanent memorial to the Shaker way of life. Twenty buildings have been restored on the site, including an unusual (but amazingly practical) round stone barn. You'll see farm animals, herb gardens, and craft demonstrations. In the Family Discovery Room, kids can try on bonnets and shoes, write with a quill pen, and get a taste of a child's life in an 18th-century Shaker community. You might be treated to a Shaker music program, where everyone joins in. Guided tours are scheduled daily; plan to spend about two hours here, depending on the ages and attention spans of your kids. Light meals and snacks are available.

● Berkshire Museum
Rte. 7, Pittsfield; (413) 443-7171. Sept.–June., Tues.–Sat., 10–5; Sun., 1–5. July and Aug., daily, 10–5; Sun., 1–5. Adults, $3; 12–18, $1; 12 and under, free. Free to all Wed. and Sat., 10–12. **Ages 3 and up.**

If Alexandra likes science museums but Christopher prefers art while Mom and Dad are history buffs, you've found the perfect museum. This one has something for everybody, and an aquarium to boot. Young children will be absorbed by the *Animals of the World in Miniature* exhibit and the Egyptian mummy. Special tours are offered for children.

● Pittsfield Mets Baseball

Wahconah Park, 105 Wahconah St., Pittsfield; (413) 499-6387 (499-METS). Late June–Labor Day. Starting times: Mon.–Sat., 7 P.M. (Labor Day, 1 P.M.); Sun., 6 P.M. Tickets, $1–$6.50. Call for a schedule of home games. **All ages.**

Hey, battuh, battuh! Catch the Pittsfield Mets, a Class A affiliate of the New York Mets, throwing the heat at historic Wahconah Park. You never know when you might discover the next headed-to-the-big-leagues superstar.

● Pittsfield State Forest

Cascade St., Pittsfield; (413) 442-8992. **All ages.**

This mountainous area offers plenty to see and explore, including caves, waterfalls, and cascades. Many species of mammals live here, and occasionally even a black bear or coyote is spotted. There are 30 miles of hiking trails, including several short ones. Drop a line in Berry Pond (which is stocked) or swim in the stream at Lulu Pond picnic area. Ten miles of cross-country ski trails are maintained in winter.

● Berkshire Scenic Railway Museum

Housatonic St. and Willow Creek Rd., Lenox; (413) 637-2210. Memorial Day–Oct. Train rides: weekends and holidays, on the half hour. **All ages.**

Don that conductor's cap and take a ride on a vintage railroad car. The little museum at restored Lenox Station offers interactive exhibits, model trains, a caboose, and lots of railroadiana.

● Berkshire Theatre Festival

Main St., Stockbridge; (413) 298-5576. July and Aug., Wed.–Sat., 12 noon. Tickets: $4. **Ages 8 and up.**

For nearly 70 years, this historic playhouse has showcased luminaries such as Joanne Woodward on its boards in plays written by the likes of Noel Coward and George Bernard Shaw.

Up-and-coming talents in grades four through six dazzle audiences in the Festival's Children's Theatre under the tent. These Berkshire County youngsters, part of the Young American Playwrights Program, work side by side with theater professionals to polish, cast, direct, and produce their plays. The one-act plays are performed—for appreciative audiences—in July and August.

● Sterling and Francine Clark Art Institute

225 South St., Williamstown; (413) 458-9545. Year-round, Tues.–Sun., 10–5; also Mondays, July–Aug. Free. **Ages 5 and up.**

This renowned museum offers a time-honored way to get youngsters involved in its galleries: a treasure hunt. Kids follow clues that direct them to specific paintings. If you can hold them back for a moment to savor the canvas before they sprint off to find the next one, so much the better! Collections feature important 19th-century paintings by Renoir, Degas, Monet, Toulouse-Lautrec, Homer, and many Old Masters, and sculptures by Degas and Remington, among others.

● Natural Bridge State Park

Rte. 8 (.5 miles from town center), North Adams; (413) 663-6392. May– Oct., daily, 10–8; Sat. and Sun., 10–6. **All ages.**

The highlight of this tiny state park is a natural marble bridge, the only one of its kind in the United States. The bridge extends across a gorge 60 feet above ground. It was formed when flowing water and ice gradually eroded the many layers of rock covering the marble, at the rate of one foot every 2,500 years. (Obviously, someone was keeping track.) Now, deep chasms are sculpted into the rock. Some of the walls of the chasms sport graffiti dating back to 1740. Picnic tables and rest rooms are available.

● Western Gateway Heritage State Park

B & M Freightyard, Rte. 8, North Adams; (413) 663-8059. Daily, 10– 4:30. Free; donations appreciated. **All ages.**

This collection of historical attractions, specialty shops, and restaurants is located in a restored railroad freightyard. Admittedly it's a pleasant place to stroll around in, but we're including it in this book for a more specific reason: The Tunnel Experience. This intriguing display, located inside a set of railroad boxcars, has lots of kid appeal. Through sight-and-sound effects, visitors learn what it was like to dig the Hoosac Tunnel during the mid-1800s. Explosions, dripping water, and the rapping of pickaxes against stone all re-create the drama of this undertaking. Nearly 200 workers died while digging the tunnel, which eventually linked the East, the Great Lakes, and the West. Tales of train wrecks and ghosts add to the experience. Junior conductors will enjoy taking a ride through the park on the Tot Train.

● Mount Greylock

Access road (Notch Rd.) off Rte. 2 between North Adams and Williamstown, North Adams; (413) 743-1591. Road to the summit is closed in winter (Dec.–early April). **All ages.**

The pinnacle of Massachusetts, Mount Greylock, can be reached by car. The nine-mile drive takes about a half-hour and rewards you with a five-state view. If you're visiting the Berkshires during fall foliage season, you won't want to miss it. At the top of the mountain, the Appalachian Mountain Club offers hikes, sunset walks, slide shows, exhibits, and evening campfires. You can spend the night at Bascom Lodge, run by the club. Meals and snacks are also available, from May–October.

● Tanglewood Music Festival

Rte. 183, West St., Lenox; (413) 637-1940, (617) 266-1492. June–Sept. Call in advance for ticket information. **Ages 5 and up.**

This 210-acre estate is world famous as the summer home of the Boston Symphony Orchestra. Bring a picnic and spread out on a blanket to enjoy classical music under a star-filled sky. Or, go earlier in the day and catch the BSO's rehearsal—a good option for families with young children, and the least costly way to go.

● Pleasant Valley Wildlife Sanctuary

472 West Mountain Rd., Lenox; (413) 637-0320. **All ages.**

Hike along the nature trail here and you'll see beaver ponds and lodges, with muskrats sometimes sharing the living quarters. Visit the Trailside Museum and encounter live and stuffed animals, as well as electronic nature games—a fun way for kids to learn about the environment. Fourteen miles of hiking trails cross the area; traverse them on cross-country skis in winter.

● Jiminy Peak Ski Area

Rte. 7, Hancock; (413) 738-5500. Web site: www.jiminypeak.com. Adult lift ticket, weekends/holidays, $38; junior (age 7–12), $27; toddlers (6 and under), $5. SKIwee/Explorers program, ages 4–12, weekends/holidays, $60, rentals additional. **Ages 6 mos. and up.**

This Berkshires-area resort is coming on strong as a family favorite, thanks to these appealing features: on-mountain lodgings; super snowmaking; a snowboard park with a quarter pipe; night skiing; kid's programs (including SKIwee) for youngsters from 4 through 17, offered seven days a week; and childcare for tots as young as six months. If your bunch isn't the first to make tracks in fresh powder (and what family manages to be up, ready, and on the slopes at 8 A.M.?) you can still get your money's worth at Jiminy Peak—day lift tickets are good 'til 6 P.M. Need a break from the slopes? Jiminy Peak offers free ice skating. If your kids are quickly leaving you in the dust, ski-wise, sharpen your skills with a Perfect Turn ski clinic. The stats: Jiminy Peak has a vertical descent of 1,140 feet, with 20 groomed trails and two glades, serviced by eight lifts.

For hotshots, it offers double–black diamond Jericho, and Whitetail, New England's steepest, longest night (lighted) run.

In summer and fall, you can ride up the chairlift for panoramic views of the Berkshires. Even better, the Alpine slide will zip you down again. An hour or so of this, and your children will be blissfully exhausted. Call for current schedule and rates.

● Norman Rockwell Museum

Rte. 183, Stockbridge; (413) 298-4100. May–Oct., daily, 10–5; Nov.– April, daily, 11–4. Adults, $9; 6–18, $2. **Ages 6 and up.**

If you're a fan of Rockwell's work, take a look at the originals on display here. During summer, you can also peek at the actual studio where he worked. On Family Days (once a month), special tours and activities are planned, and parents' admission is half-price. Call for information.

● Bartholomew's Cobble

Off Rte. 7A, Ashley Falls; (413) 229-8600. Mid-April–mid-Oct., daily, 9–5. Museum open Wed.–Sun., 9–5. **All ages.**

Let's keep this pretty spot a secret. Junior gardeners will be inspired by the rock garden, with 700 species of plants; the natural history museum has a neat collection of mounted birds, a bobcat, butterflies, arrowheads, and Mohegan Indian artifacts. Also head up to Hurlburt's Hill (the map at the entrance will direct you), a high pasture that's perfect for kite flying. (Fly before May, please, or you'll disturb nesting birds.) Round out your visit with an easy hike along Ledge's Trail or, beside the river, Bailey's Trail. Interpretive programs geared to kids, such as "Life in a Pond," are run several times a year. Call for a schedule.

● Beartown State Forest

Blue Hill Rd., 5 mi. east on Rte. 23, Monterey; (413) 528-0904. **All ages.**

Beartown Mountain is the major feature among a group of wooded peaks. Follow the signs to Laura Tower or the Alcott Trail lookout for scenic views. Hike along the Appalachian Trail, fish for bass, or swim in Benedict Pond. In winter, cross-country ski along 10 miles of marked trails.

¶¶ RESTAURANTS

● Miss Adams Diner

53 Park St., North Adams; (413) 743-5300. Tues.–Sat., 6:30–3; Sun., 7–1. Closed Mon.

This downtown landmark is a restored, 1949 Worcester Lunch Car. If you've always wanted to take your kids to a diner but figured they'd balk at the meatloaf special, this might be the ticket. There's meatloaf, all right, but there's also good homemade chili, pastrami sandwiches, and, at breakfast, really tasty muffins in 1990s combinations like pineapple-corn and cranberry-pecan. Other treats include malted milkshakes (much better than fast-food shakes) and the Mount Greylock Sundae, a triumph of coffee ice cream, hot fudge, peanut butter chips, blueberries, walnuts, and whipped cream. Wow.

● Hickory Bill's Bar-B-Que

403 Stockbridge Rd., Great Barrington; (413) 528-1444. Tues.–Sat., 11:30–9; Sun., 12–7.

Grab a pile o' napkins, roll up your sleeves, and dig into a big mess o' barbecue. It's hard to be neat when you're noshing on the likes of barbecued chicken, spare ribs, baby back ribs, boneless pork and (according to Bill) the world's best brisket. Tasty side dishes include collard greens and Mexican cornbread, a big hit with kids. Go ahead, pig out, you're eating in a barn (albeit a nice-ish barn), decked out in checkered oilskin tablecloths and planked wood floors. Eat indoors or grab a picnic table along the Housatonic River, and enjoy.

● Bev's Homemade Ice Cream

38 Housatonic St., Lenox; (413) 637-0371, and 5 Railroad St., Great Barrington; (413) 538-6645. Both locations: year-round, 9–10.

New Englanders eat more ice cream than anyone else in the country. In our opinion, places like Bev's are the reason why (it can't be the climate!). Try the locals' favorite flavor, Espresso Oreo, or—for the more adventurous palate—zabaglione gelato.

Cape Cod

More than four million people visit Cape Cod and the two tiny sister islands, Nantucket and Martha's Vineyard, each year. It is said that there are more people on this small elbow of sand on a summer day than there are in the entire city of Boston. Why do vacationers continue to flock to the Cape? Why do they endure the legendary Cape Cod bottleneck, waiting sometimes nearly three hours to cross the Sagamore Bridge? Despite the summertime crunch, Cape Cod has an allure that few can resist. Vacationers put up with the traffic and summer crowds because they know what awaits them: miles of sandy, white beaches, wide-open salt marshes and clam flats, scenic harbors, lighthouses, and picturesque, historic sea captains' homes and cedar-shaked beach cottages.

Families enjoy the casual seaside atmosphere, where lobster-in-the-rough and steamers fresh from local shellfish beds are daily fare. For fun, there's hiking, sailing, windsurfing, fishing, swimming, sightseeing, and any amusement your family desires. Think petting zoos, waterslides, video arcades, boat trips, train rides, aquariums, touch pools, museums, and more.

If your kids like lots of action, you won't be disappointed. The bustling resort towns of Hyannis and Provincetown sizzle with energy during the summer months. If you prefer more peaceful pleasures, they're here as well, tucked down the back roads of Falmouth, atop one of the striking cliffs in Truro, on a hike along spectacular beaches at Cape Cod National Seashore, or while digging for clams in Wellfleet. (Please check with local authorities before you dig, in case of "red tide" alert.) Nearly everywhere, despite the summer rush, it is possible to get away from the crush to enjoy the Cape's beauty. A local's best advice is to "get lost" (said with a bit of tongue in cheek!); meander the back roads and discover the lovely, hidden spots on the Cape. There, "Old Cape Cod" can still be found, far away from the shopping malls and fast-food eateries. But first you have to get there. Some words of advice:

1. Consider visiting Cape Cod off-season, if you can, during spring or fall. After Labor Day, the crowds diminish but the weather is still balmy—and most attractions stay open through September or October. Also, lodging prices drop dramatically after Labor Day. Personally, we think the Cape and islands are at their best in autumn. Springtime is a bit dicier, weather wise, and many attractions don't open until Memorial Day. Still, if you're looking for a real escape, and if you're not yet tied to school vacation schedules, think about an early visit.

2. Avoid the weekend rush hours; don't try to get to the Cape on Fridays between four and nine, or leave on Sundays between noon and nine (unless sitting in a virtual parking lot is your idea of a fine time).

3. If you find yourself trapped in the infamous Cape Cod congestion, don't despair. In just a few hours you'll be eating some of the best, freshest seafood in the world on some of the most spectacular beaches in the country. Pack car toys for the kids and an ocean-wave relaxation tape to achieve serenity of spirit, and try to make the best of it.

■ Upper Cape
(Includes Sandwich, Falmouth, Bourne)

● Heritage Plantation
Rte. 6A at Grove and Pine streets, Sandwich; (508) 888-3300. Mid-May–Oct., daily, 10–5. Adults, $8; 6–18, $4. **Ages 3 and up.**

A mixed bag of Americana spread throughout a beautifully land-scaped 76-acre site, Heritage Plantation has something for everyone. It's particularly enjoyable on a warm, sunny day when kids can skip along any of a dozen nature trails past flowerbeds, wood groves, and the shore of Upper Shawme Lake. But it's more than just a horticultural hotspot. A Shaker-designed round barn houses an impressive collection of antique cars, including one the kids can climb on. Other buildings house collections of Native American artifacts, antique military miniatures, firearms, early tools, and folk art. Don't miss the working antique wooden carousel.

● Thornton Burgess Museum
4 Water St., on edge of Shawme Pond, Sandwich; (508) 888-6870. April–Dec., daily, 10–4; Sun., 1–4. Winter hours vary. Story Hour, July and Aug., Tues., Thurs., and Sat., 10:30. Admission by donation. **All ages.**

The word "charming" springs to mind when you discover this place, a favorite of Cape Cod families. The museum is a memorial to author/naturalist Burgess, author of more than 15,000 children's stories, including *The Adventures of Peter Cottontail.* It was established in 1976 to inspire reverence in children for wildlife and the environment—long before such concerns were common. On sunny summer afternoons, join the parents and children who gather under a tree for Story Hour, often "illustrated" with live animals. The small museum houses Burgess memorabilia and an interactive exhibit tied to Cape Cod natural history themes. The Burgess Society sponsors several delightful children's events and activities during the summer. Call for a schedule.

● Green Briar Nature Center and Jam Kitchen
6 Discovery Hill Rd., off Rte. 6A, East Sandwich; (508) 888-6870. April–Dec., daily, 10–4; Sun., 1–4. Admission by donation. **All ages.**

Here's one of those things you'd only consider doing while on vacation: watching jams and jellies being made in an old-fashioned kitchen. This is no factory tour; they use turn-of-the-century cooking methods. Take home some beach-plum jelly. Visit the award-winning wildflower garden, and take the mile-long hike down historic Old Briar Patch trail. (Shorter walks are offered, too.) Before you leave be sure to check out the natural history exhibits, and say hello to Peter Rabbit, who resides here in his bunny hutch. The center is operated by the Thornton W. Burgess Society.

● Yesteryears Doll Museum

Old Main St., Sandwich; (508) 888-1711. Mid-May–Oct., Mon.–Sat., 10–4. Adults, $3; under 12, $2. **Ages 3 and up.**

Hello, dollies. If you like dolls, you'll adore this collection of antique dolls, many of them rare finds, along with dollhouses, each elaborately decked out. Got an injured doll around the house? Bring her/him along; this is the best doll hospital around. Between May and October about 200 dolls are treated here, for injuries ranging from broken limbs to torn neck sockets.

● Aptucxet Trading Post Museum

Aptucxet Rd., Bourne; (508) 759-9487. May–Columbus Day, Tues.–Sat., 10–5; Sun., 2–5. Open Mon., July and Aug., and Monday holidays. Adults, $2.50; children, grades 1–12, $1. **Ages 6 and up.**

Sure it's touristy, but this attraction has some redeeming historical value. Established as a trading post by Pilgrims in 1627, it's billed as the first-known commercial enterprise in English-speaking North America. Today, this replica of a Pilgrim-Dutch trading post is filled with Native American artifacts. The site includes a windmill, a Victorian railroad station (built for the exclusive use of President Grover Cleveland, who owned a summer home in Bourne), herb and wildflower gardens, and picnic areas on the Cape Cod Canal.

● National Marine Fisheries Aquarium

Corner of Water and Albatross streets, Woods Hole; (508) 548-7684. Mid-June–mid-Sept., daily, 10–4. Off season, Mon.–Fri., 9–4. Free. **All ages.**

This little gem—the oldest research aquarium in the United States—is a great place to get in touch with Cape sea life. Touch tanks house starfish, lobsters, horseshoe crabs, sea turtles, and snails. Watch the harbor seals' feedings at 11 A.M. and 3 P.M. during summer months.

● Cape Cod Children's Mini-Museum

Falmouth Mall, Falmouth; (508) 457-4667. Mon.–Sat., 10–5; Sun., 12–5. Admission: ages 1–4, $2; 5–59, $3; 60 and up, $2. **Ages 1–10.**

Outdoor plans rained out? Kids age one to ten won't balk at a trip to the Falmouth Mall; an in-mall children's museum offers lots of fun stuff to play with: a four-car wooden train, a dress-up area, puppets, a pirate's den, and lots of games and puzzles.

● Beaches

Upper Cape beaches include **Scusset Beach** (Scusset Beach Road, near the Sagamore Rotary in Sandwich), a nice state-run beach on Cape Cod Canal. **Town Neck Beach** (on the bay side, off Route 6A and Tupper Road, Sandwich) has pretty views and good swimming. It's a favorite spot of local photographers and artists. There's a nice hike along the boardwalk across Mill Creek. **Bourne Scenic Park** (Route 6, Buzzard's Bay on Cape Cod Canal, Sandwich) has 70 acres of hiking, fishing, swimming, and playgrounds. Take a dip in the unique sea-level pool—it changes with the tide.

Other fine beaches include **Surf Drive Beach** (on Vineyard Sound, off Surf Drive, Falmouth); **Old Silver Beach** (on Buzzard's Bay, off Bay Shore Drive, North Falmouth); and **Menauhant Beach** (on Vineyard Sound, off Menauhant Road, East Falmouth).

● Kettle Ponds

If you like gazing at the ocean but would rather dive into something, well, cozier, how about one of Cape Cod's little fishing holes, a kettle pond? Tucked behind the ocean beaches, these ponds were dug out of the landscape by Ice Age glaciers. They're round, deep (in the middle), clear, and warm. In short, they're perfect natural freshwater pools, great for swimming.

Locally, check out **Long Pond** in Harwich (covering more than 700 acres, it's a biggie) and **Wakeby** and **Mashpee** ponds, both in Mashpee. Pack a picnic and enjoy.

● Hiking

One of the best places to hike on the entire Cape is **Beebe Woods**, off Depot Road in Falmouth Center. The 400-acre property offers an abundance of trails for novices to experts. Intricate stone fences remind you that you're in New England.

● Bicycling

The **Shining Sea Bikeway** is a three-mile trail running from Falmouth Center to Woods Hole along the shoreline. Stop, take a break, and watch the activity at busy marinas along the way. Pick up the path on Locust Street in Falmouth; you'll end up at the Steamship Authority dock in Woods Hole.

● The Lobster Trap

290 Shore Rd., Bourne; (508) 759-7600. Daily, in season, 11:30–8:30. Spring and fall, Sat. and Sun. only.

So, you've just hit the Cape and can't wait another nanosecond for a taste of fresh seafood? This is the place. Located right off the Bourne Bridge (take an immediate right as you exit the bridge), it's ultracasual, and on the water (well, on the river). More important, the food is great and the prices are low. Try the Bourne scallops, lobster, fried clams, or, a good bet for kids, the expertly made lobster rolls, which are heavy on the lobster meat, light on the mayo. Already, the wretched ride is but a memory. . . .

● The Wharf

Grand Ave., Falmouth Heights; (508) 548-2772. April–Dec., daily, 11:30–10. Early bird special: 4–6 P.M., $6.95 (includes entrée, coffee, and dessert).

This is no family restaurant; it's more of a beachfront hangout. Part of a ramshackle structure that includes a dairy bar, T-shirt shop, and casino, The Wharf has lots to look at, making it the perfect place for kids. (We'd still avoid the peak dinner hour on Friday and Saturday night; it's just too smoky and noisy.) Inside, it's like a T.G.I. Friday's run amok—absolutely stuffed with junk like mooseheads, anchors, and buoys. Outside, there's the gorgeous sweep of Vineyard Sound and, in the distance, Martha's Vineyard. The best views, naturally, are from the deck. And the eats are great; blackboard specials usually feature fresh fish (often caught by the restaurant's owner) priced to move, German fare (the chef is from Germany), and steak, chicken, pasta, and prime rib.

● Hearth 'N Kettle

874 Main St., Falmouth; (508) 548-6111. (Other locations in Hyannis, South Yarmouth, Orleans, Centerville, and Plymouth.) Daily, 7 A.M.–9 P.M.; Fri. and Sat., 7 A.M.–10 P.M.; stays open an hour later from Memorial Day–Labor Day.

This local chain offers friendly family dining at great prices; nothing fancy, but reliably good. The Falmouth outpost was the first in the chain and has survived on the Cape for more than 25 years, as trendier places have come and gone. You can get anything from a hearty breakfast to grilled salmon fillet, served by chipper waitpeople. More reasons to give the H. 'n K. a try: lots of low-fat options, a good kid's menu (the cod nuggets 'n fries win rave reviews), and early-bird specials served 'til 6 P.M.

■ Mid-Cape
(Includes Hyannis, Barnstable, Yarmouth, and Dennis)

● Cape Cod and Hyannis Railroad
252 Main St., Hyannis; (508) 771-3788. June–Oct., Tues.–Sun., departures at 10, 12:30, and 3. Adults, $10.50; children, $6.50. **Ages 3 and up.**

Board a refurbished 1920s parlor car and take a scenic tour of undiscovered Cape Cod. You'll see Cape Cod Bay, historic villages, salt marsh, cranberry bogs, and more, with stops at Sandwich and the Cape Cod Canal. The trip takes one and three-quarter hours, departing from the station in downtown Hyannis. If you're planning a grown-up's night out, note the railroad also offers a three-hour dinner trip. Call for reservations.

● Cape Cod Potato Chip Tour
Breed's Hill in Independence Park (near Cape Cod Mall), Hyannis; (508) 775-7253. Mon.–Fri., 10–4. Free. **All ages.**

Looking for an unusual rainy day activity? Head to the potato chip factory, and watch them hand-cook these tasty chips in giant kettles. Tours are self-guided. Even if you've sworn off chips forever, you won't be able to resist a sample.

● Cape Cod Melody Tent
West Main St., Hyannis; (508) 775-9100. Children's performances, Wed., 11 A.M. Tickets, $5.25. **Ages 3 and up.**

Put a little culture into your Cape escape with a show at the Melody Tent. Productions feature all the kid's classics, like *Goldilocks and the Three Bears, Rumplestiltskin, Alice in Wonderland,* and *Hansel and Gretel.* (See South Shore Music Circus.)

● ZooQuarium
Rte. 28, West Yarmouth; (508) 775-8883. July and Aug., daily, 9:30–6:30; mid-Feb.–June and Sept.–late-Nov., daily, 9:30–5. Shows at 11, 1, 2:30, and 4. Adults, $7.50; under 10, $4.50. **All ages.**

Many a road-weary family, trapped in traffic along Route 28, has sought refuge here. Features include sea lion and dolphin shows, pony rides, and a petting zoo. You'll encounter monkeys, llamas, parrots, a shell exhibit—enough, in short, to chase away the worst case of kiddie car crabbiness.

● Crab Creek
Public dock, North Dennis Rd., Yarmouth. **Ages 3 and up.**

This is considered the best spot on the Cape for blue crabbing. No fancy equipment needed, just some leftover, cooked chicken (for bait) and some string. Crash-course in crabbing: stand on the dock, tie some string around a piece of chicken, lower string into the water, and wait for some action.

● Josiah Dennis Manse and Old West Schoolhouse
Nobscuset Rd. and Whig St., Dennis; (508) 385-2232. July and Aug., Tues. and Thurs., 2–4 P.M. Donations appreciated. **Ages 3 and up.**

This site features a 1770 schoolhouse with marine artifacts and a Children's Room. See spinning and weaving demonstrations in the attic workroom.

● Bicycling—Cape Cod Rail Trail
Trail begins in South Dennis off Rte. 134, across from Hall Oil Co. Bike rentals available. **All ages.**

Formerly the railroad right-of-way, this 19-mile tarred trail runs from Dennis to Locust Road in Eastham, where you connect with the National Seashore bike path. Take your swimsuits; you'll end up at Coast Guard Beach. You'll share the path with fellow cyclists, walkers, and horseback riders, through woods and bogs, around lakes and ocean shores. Parking areas are located in Nickerson State Park on Rte. 6A, in Brewster; Rte. 124 in Harwich, and at the Salt Pond Visitor Center off Rte. 6 in Eastham.

● Sea View Playland
Lower County Rd., Dennisport; (508) 398-9084. Late June–Labor Day, daily, 10–10. **All ages.**

This is pure honky-tonk fun. Skeeball, miniature golf, pitch and putt, and an old barn filled with nearly 100 different arcade games. Hey, you're on vacation—if not now, when? You'll find the newest and oldest coin-operated games. Ask anyone in the area for directions to the Barn of Fun; they'll be able to tell you.

● Boat Cruises
The mid-Cape area offers just about any kind of ocean adventure you could wish for: island excursions, harbor tours, Cape Cod Canal cruises, and whale-watching trips.

Local cruise operators include **Hy-Line Harbor Cruises,** Ocean St. Dock, Hyannis, (508) 778-2600; and **Hyannis Whale Watcher Cruises,** Barnstable Harbor, (508) 362-6088.

● Beaches

Sandy Neck Beach, on Sandy Neck Road (off Rte. 6A) in Barnstable, is considered one of the best public beaches on the Cape. It's easy to hang around here for an entire day, sunning, swimming, and exploring the surrounding dunes and marshlands. For a spectacular view of the unspoiled Cape, take one of the many trails along Sandy Neck. Walk quietly, and you're likely to spot rare birds and wildlife; you can also search for relics in the dunes along the way, and wade in the water along this magnificent stretch of beach. Be sure to return to the main entrance before dusk, where a wonderful surprise awaits: musicians, storytellers, and mimes performing around a campfire. **Sea Gull Beach,** off South Sea Avenue in Yarmouth, is another winner; on Nantucket Sound, it's calm, sandy, and considered the best beach for swimming in the Yarmouth area. It has a snack bar and picnic area. Teens or preteens in your group? They'll insist on making the scene at popular **Craigville Beach.** It boasts fine sand, gentle surf, and warm water. (An MTV beach party segment was shot here; enough said.)

RESTAURANTS

● Baxter's Fish 'N Chips

117 Pleasant St. Wharf, Hyannis; (508) 775-4490. April–Oct., Mon.– Sat., 11:30–10; Sun., 11:30–9; off season, Thurs.–Sun., 11:30–10.

Boat-less in Hyannis? Perish the thought! However, a meal at Baxter's is the next best thing. The outdoor deck of this classic fish house juts out into the harbor amid fishing boats and pleasure cruisers. Sometimes sea planes land alongside the restaurant, causing drinks to slosh. (Kids find this a hoot.) But don't get too distracted, or a seagull will make off with your entree. Lotsa luck getting it back. The menu features the usual fried seafood plates and fresh fish, grilled or broiled.

● Swan River Seafood Restaurant

5 Lower Country Rd., Dennisport; (508) 394-4466. Open late May–mid- Sept. Lunch, 12–3:30; dinner, 5–9.

Good, fresh seafood and breathtaking views of Nantucket Sound make this one hard to beat. Try the steamers, seafood pasta salad, or Cape-caught boiled lobsters. Not into fish? The menu includes paw as well as claw. There's a kid's menu, too.

● Barby Ann's

120 Airport Rd., Hyannis; (508) 775-9795. Daily, 11:30–11; Sun., 11–10.

Homestyle cooking is the draw at this popular family restaurant. Try their famous seafood stew or barbecued ribs, or one of the blackboard specials. The decor is casual but nice and the children's menu has an all-star line-up of chicken fingers, fish 'n' chips, hot dogs, and burgers.

● Four Seas Ice Cream

360 S. Main St., Centerville; (508) 775-1394. Late May–mid-Sept., daily, 9–10:30.

Still praline after all these years. When it comes to ice cream, Four Seas rules; they've won so many "Best of Cape" awards, they've lost count. A PBS special singled them out, among a scoopfull of other ice cream shops elsewhere, as one of the best in the U.S., no less. No need to gussy up this stuff with Reese's pieces. Try the penuche pecan or cantaloupe (all the fruit flavors are made with real fresh fruit.)

■ Outer Cape

(Includes Brewster, Chatham, Wellfleet, Truro, and Provincetown)

● New England Fire and History Museum

Rte. 6A, Brewster; (508) 896-5711. Memorial Day–Labor Day, Mon.–Fri., 10–4; Sat. and Sun., 12–4; Labor Day–mid-Oct., Sat. and Sun., 12–4. Adults, $5; 5–12, $2.50; 4 and under, free. **All ages.**

This museum contains a fascinating assortment of antique fire engines, one of the largest collections in the country. "They put out fires with buckets of water?" "They had to pull this by hand?" "How fast could the horses get them to the fire?" Children are full of questions as they view this interesting exhibit of 18th- to 20th-century fire engines and related memorabilia. Kids can climb aboard a fire truck, a fire engine, and a fire boat, complete with hoses.

● Bassett Wild Animal Farm

620 Tubman Rd., between Rtes. 124 and 137, Brewster; (508) 896-3224. Mid-May–mid-Sept., daily, 10–5. Adults, $5.75; 2–12, $4. **All ages.**

Meet mountain lions, zebu, alpaca, lemurs, Sumatran tigers, and other exotic creatures here. Of course, when you visit it's likely to be an entirely different lineup, as someone new is added every year to keep things interesting for repeat visitors. Kids love the monkeys and also the domestic animals in the petting zoo. There are pony rides and hay rides (each $.75), too.

● Cape Cod Museum of Natural History

Rte. 6A, Brewster; (508) 896-3867. Year-round, Mon.–Sat., 9:30–4:30; Sun., 12–4:30. Adults, $5; 5–12, $2; 4 and under, free. **Ages 3 and up.**

Play nature detective and discover mysterious species of sea life; put your hand in a secret box and try to figure out what lurks within; test your knowledge of underwater creatures when you take the hands-on discovery quiz. Watch live marine animals scuttle around in their tanks, and see bees at work (can you spot the queen?) in an indoor, working beehive. Stay awhile and hike one of the nature trails, or watch a movie. Small fry adore creating impromptu puppet shows with the family of animal puppets. The museum runs several creative and fun kids' programs and special events, like Bubble-Blowing Day, Make Your Own Kite Day, field walks, and museum sleep-overs.

● Salt Pond Visitor Center

Cape Cod National Seashore headquarters, Eastham; (508) 255-3421. Summer, open daily, 9–6; spring and fall, daily, 9–4:30; weekends only, Jan.–mid-Feb. Call to confirm tour schedule. Free. **All ages.**

Early birds: Take a guided, 8:30 A.M. Beach Walk and learn about the shoreline of Nauset Beach. Night owls: Plan to join an Evening Campfire Walk along the beach. Meet back at the campfire to tell stories and enjoy the aroma of woodsmoke and salt air. More than 40 tours are offered in summer, including beach and inland walks and fishing and shellfishing demonstrations. Children's Hours, held two to three times weekly in summer, feature fun projects like scavenger hunts for kids up to age six. Most activities are free, and they offer a great way to get acquainted with the Cape Cod National Seashore.

● Stony Brook Mill and Herring Run

Stony Brook Rd., Brewster. **All ages.**

If you're visiting in springtime (March through June) join local Cape Codders as they watch spawning herring run upstream. The herring swim against the current through a series of ladders that run from Cape Cod Bay to Upper Mill and Lower Mill ponds. A restored 19th-century grist mill shares the property; it grinds corn every Thursday through Saturday from 2 to 5 P.M., May and June (on Friday only July through August).

● Nickerson State Park

Off Rte. 6A, Brewster; (508) 896-3867. **All ages.**

This lovely, 1,750-acre park is perfect for hiking and biking (part of the Cape Cod Rail Trail passes through it). Swimming, camping, and fishing in one of four trout-stocked ponds are available for the sports-minded.

● Chatham Fish Pier

Shore Rd. and Bar Cliff Ave., Chatham. Daily, after 2. **All ages.**

Bring your camera and watch salty New England fishermen unload their daily catch. You'll stand atop a visitor's balcony and see nets full of haddock, flounder, halibut, cod, and more being pulled in and readied for shipping to local markets and restaurants.

● Kate Gould Park

Main St., Chatham Center. July and Aug., Fri. at dusk (around 8 P.M.). **All ages.**

If you're in Chatham and it's Friday night, catch the Chatham Band concert at Kate Gould Park. Bring a blanket and refreshments and join right in. It's a terrific, fun freebie.

● Chatham Railroad Museum

Depot Rd., Chatham. Mid-June–mid-Sept., Tues.–Sat., 10–4. Donations accepted. **Ages 3 and up.**

Attention, fans of Thomas the Tank Engine: This historic depot, once the Chatham Company Railroad Station, houses a restored 1910 caboose and numerous model trains. Lots of "railroadiana" (relics and photos) are displayed, much of it more than 100 years old.

● Clam Digging

This is the home of the world-famous Wellfleet oyster. For a true New England experience, roll up your pants cuffs, grab a bucket, and go clam digging. The shellfish beds here are abundant. Be sure to adhere to local laws regarding shellfish harvesting here and elsewhere on the Cape, especially if there's a red tide alert. This means it's unsafe to collect any shellfish. Check the local paper for times of low tide, when you can pick steamers, quahogs, mussels, oysters, cherrystones, and scallops from the shellfish beds along the shoreline. Shellfish licenses are available at the town shellfish offices near Mayo Beach and at Town Hall. You might ask local enthusiasts about recommendations for the best places to go, as these vary throughout the year.

● Highland Light and Highland House

Off Lighthouse Rd., North Truro. Early June–Sept., 10–5; (508) 487-3397. **All ages.**

Sometimes called Cape Cod Light, this is one of the most powerful beacons on the Atlantic Ocean. The lighthouse dates back to 1795 and is the first one seen by seafaring visitors traveling from Europe to Boston. It's a pretty drive to the lighthouse, which sits atop a bluff in a quiet, country setting. Nearby, the Highland House Museum houses a small collection of materials on shipwrecks and other local lore.

● Pilgrim Monument and Provincetown Museum

High-Pole Hill on Winslow St., off Bradford, Provincetown; (508) 487-1310. April–Nov., daily, 9–5; July and Aug., 9–7. (Door closes 45 min. before stated closing times.) Adults, $5; 4–12, $3. Admission includes monument and museum. **Ages 4 and up.**

This impressive monument—the tallest all-granite structure in the United States—was built to commemorate the landing of the Pilgrims here in 1620. Climb to the top of this 252-foot tower for a commanding view. (It's a stamina-testing 116 stairs and 60 ramps.) On a clear day, you'll see Boston skyscrapers as you look across the bay and, to the southeast, the Atlantic Ocean. Even if you choose not to climb the monument, you'll get a nice overview of Provincetown from this site.

Located at the base of the Pilgrim Monument, the Provincetown Museum houses some unique items of interest to adults and children. You'll see model ships (the *Mayflower* exhibit is especially good), marine and whaling artifacts, and a collection of toys and children's books from the 17th and 18th centuries. One of the newest exhibits is *Safe Harbor— Preserving Provincetown's Past;* ongoing special events include swing band concerts and lectures.

● Provincetown Heritage Museum

356 Commercial St., Provincetown; (508) 487-0666. Mid-June–Columbus Day, daily, 10–6. Adults, $2; under 12, free. **Ages 6 and up.**

Provincetown's past is celebrated at this little museum, offering a mix of art, Victorian memorabilia, commercial fishing artifacts, and—the centerpiece—a half-scale model of the fishing schooner *Rose Dorothea.*

● MacMillan Wharf

Commercial St., Provincetown. **All ages.**

This busy wharf on Provincetown Harbor is the perfect spot to park your car and watch the fishing boats and yachts come and go. (Leave your car here and explore the rest of the town on foot.) This is also the place you'll find charter fishing boats, harbor cruise excursion boats, and whale-watching tours. Cruise companies include **Portuguese Princess Whale**

Watch, (800) 442-3188 or (508) 487-2651; **Provincetown Whale Watch Inc.,** (800) 992-9333 or (508) 487-1582; and **Dolphin Fleet,** (800) 826-9300 or (508) 255-3857.

● Cape Cod National Seashore

The Cape Cod National Seashore is more than a beach; it's a unique national park (run by the National Park Service) that encompasses private residential and commercial land. Private businesses and residents are subject to strict building regulations and restrictions as part of an effort to protect the 400-mile coastline of the Cape's outer arm. The government owns about 27,000 of the 44,000 acres of land within the boundaries of the National Seashore. Six towns have boundaries within it: Chatham, Orleans, Eastham, Wellfleet, Truro, and Provincetown. Now for the fun part: the Seashore offers a wonderful variety of self-guided tours, bike trails, and ranger-guided activities, and they extend over six spectacular beaches.

● Province Lands and Salt Pond Visitor Centers

Salt Pond Road Visitor Center, off Rte. 6, Eastham; (508) 255-3421. Province Lands Visitor Center, Race Point Rd. off Rte. 6, Provincetown; (508) 487-1256. Summer, open daily, 9–6. Spring and fall, daily, 9–4:30. Salt Pond Visitor Center only, open weekends, Jan.–mid-Feb. **All ages.**

Visit either of these two National Seashore Visitor Centers and pick up information, maps, and a schedule of activities and programs. The centers offer exhibits and introductory audiovisual programs on the area. Nature films are shown on summer evenings in the amphitheaters.

● Beaches

Of the six National Seashore beaches, **Race Point Beach,** off Route 6 in Provincetown, is tops for families. It's a protected beach and is also a prime spot for watching the sun set. **Coast Guard Beach,** on Doane Road in Eastham, and nearby **Nauset Light Beach** (Cable Road, Eastham), are pretty, but the surf is rough. The former is good for boogie-boarding, the latter is known as the surfer's beach, having the highest waves of the National Seashore beaches. **Herring Cove Beach,** on Province Lands Road, in Provincetown, is another option; the left-hand side draws a gay and lesbian crowd, while the right attracts a mix of singles and families. Other National Seashore beaches are **Marconi Beach,** in Wellfleet, and **Head of the Meadow Beach** in Truro, which is not recommended because of seaweed. On Cape Cod Bay, in Truro, **Corn Hill Beach** is great for families, offering superb shelling.

● Beachcombing

Even when Cape beaches are deserted, they're teeming with life. When the tide is out, see for yourself. Look for horseshoe crabs, starfish, sea urchins, sand dollars, periwinkles, and shellfish (wearing a pair of reef shoes isn't a bad idea, since it's fun to dig in the sand with your toes). The best beaches for beachcombing are the ocean beaches from Chatham to Provincetown, although there's plenty to see along the beaches of Cape Cod Bay, Nantucket Sound, and Vineyard Sound.

● Bicycling

The following bike trails are within the Cape Cod National Seashore. Trail maps are available at the Visitor's Information Centers in Eastham and Provincetown. Bike rentals are available at **Arnold's,** 329 Commercial St., in Provincetown, (508) 487-0844, and **Holiday Cycles,** Grand Ave., Falmouth Heights, (508) 540-3549.

● Nauset Trail

Salt Pond Road Visitor's Center, off Rte. 6, Eastham. **All ages.**

This 1.6-mile paved bike trail offers views of the cedar banks, Nauset Marsh, old Nauset Coast Guard Station, and other points of interest. The trail ends at Coast Guard Beach.

● Head of the Meadow Trail

High Head Rd., Truro. **All ages.**

This two-mile marshland bike trail begins on High Head Road in Truro and heads toward Head of the Meadow Beach (you can also pick it up at the beach parking lot). Venture off the trail to the spring where the Pilgrims took their first drink of fresh water in America (follow signs to Pilgrim Lake and Pilgrim Spring Trail).

● Province Lands Trail

Herring Cove Beach, Provincetown. **All ages.**

This eight-mile paved bike trail crosses forests, ponds, bogs, and some of the most spectacular sand dunes along the Atlantic coast. Segments include a 5.25-mile loop trail; Herring Cove Beach spur (1 mile); Race Point Beach spur (.50 mile); Bennett Pond spur (.25 mile); and Race Point Road spur (.25 mile.)

● Hiking

Self-guided nature walks and ranger-guided tours and activities are offered throughout the year. You don't have to be an expert trail blazer—many are short but interesting nature walks suitable for beginners and children. Particularly enjoyable are some of the National Park Service hikes, such as the **Seashore Surprise** (parents and kids learn about the sea through scavenger hunts, stories, and games along the way); the **Sunset Beach Walk,** featuring stories around a campfire at sunset; and **Cape Cod Whales and Historic Beach Apparatus Drill** (divers demonstrate the methods once used to rescue shipwrecked mariners). Call the **Province Lands Visitor Center** for times and starting points; (508) 487-1256.

RESTAURANTS

● The Lobster Claw

Rte. 6A, Orleans; (508) 255-1800. April–mid-Nov., daily, 11:30–9.

This sprawling, rustic eatery is a real visit to Crustacean Land; the gift shop has more than 250 lobster-themed knickknacks, the menu is shaped like a lobster claw . . . you get the idea. It's extremely popular. We recommend it for families with a caveat: dine early, especially on weekend nights. You'll avoid long waits and get an incentive: free chowder, beverage, and ice cream with dinner between 4 and 5:30. That's a good deal, and the prices are pretty reasonable to begin with. Lobsters, mussels, and steamers are good buys, as are fish dinners, and the food isn't bad at all. There's a kid's menu, too. This is a good option when you want a step up from an eat-in-the-rough place.

● The Mayflower Cafe

300 Commercial St., Provincetown; (508) 487-0121. First Sun. in April–third Sun. in Oct., 11:30–9:30.

Need a break from seafood? This wonderful family-run place has served P-town natives and tourists for almost 70 years. The Italian and Portuguese specialties are delicious, and the waitresses fuss over you (well, over your adorable children) like doting aunties. Kale soup and pork chops *vinho dahlos* are house specialties, and for the kids, you can't go wrong with spaghetti and meatballs or pizza. (Children's portions are available.) Prices are remarkably low. Decor is plain-Jane, but what the Mayflower lacks in looks it makes up for in friendliness.

● Bayside Lobster Hutt

Commercial St., Wellfleet; (508) 349-6333. Memorial Day–Columbus Day, daily, 4:30–9.

Inside this old oyster shack you'll find some of the best seafood on the Cape. Eat in the rough and enjoy lobster, steamers, fried oysters, broiled flounder, or whatever else is fresh that day. Yes, there are cheeseburgers and hot dogs—sort of an unofficial kids' menu—but why not split up the generous Fisherman's Platter instead? Veggie lovers can opt for corn on the cob and a trip to the salad bar.

The Islands

Martha's Vineyard and Nantucket, accessible only by air or sea, are vacation playgrounds for thousands of travelers each year. Both islands offer miles of splendid beaches, tall, white sand dunes, nature trails, picturesque harbors, sleepy fishing villages, and bustling main streets lined with trendy boutiques and fine restaurants. And yet each island has a unique personality and charm of its own.

Martha's Vineyard, located just seven miles off Cape Cod, is the largest island in New England—20 miles long and 10 miles wide. The Vineyard, as it's commonly known, is full of surprises; its textures, rhythms, and amenities are as diverse as the people who visit it. Of course, one is never far from the sea, so the preferred pastimes are swimming, sunbathing, surfing, sailing, and exploring. Surrounding the sea are forests and salt marshes, meadows and cliffs, hills and plains. Much of the action—shopping, restaurants, attractions—centers in the towns of Edgartown and Vineyard Haven (also known as Tisbury). Oak Bluffs is famous for the Flying Horses antique carousel and charming gingerbread cottages in the center of town.

You'll find as much or as little to do as you want on this island, from bustling Edgartown to the rustic harbor village of Menemsha, where the current generation of fishermen still hauls in the daily catch.

Nantucket, meaning "far-away land," is 30 miles off the coast and offers a 100-year flashback in time. You'll step off the ferry to enter a perfectly preserved 19th-century village of cobblestone streets and red-brick mansions. Elegant sea captains' homes, reminiscent of a time when Nantucket was one of the great whaling centers of the world, now house fine restaurants, boutiques, and country inns. Pack up a picnic lunch and venture beyond the village to the shoreline, where cedar-shingled homes hug the coast. Swim in the surrounding island waters—the calm Nantucket Sound to the north, the mighty Atlantic to the south.

Travelers who plan ahead (book your accommodations as far in advance as possible) and avoid summer traffic congestion (consider leaving your car behind) can find the vacation they want in the islands. Most return revitalized, refreshed by the clear salt air that has the therapeutic power to wash away 20th-century stress.

Hy-Line Cruises, (508) 778-2600 or (800) 492-8082 (MA only), and the **Steamship Authority,** (508) 477-8600, provide regular ferry service to the islands from Hyannis and Woods Hole. Nantucket is 2 hours and 30 minutes from Hyannis and 3 hours from Woods Hole. If you're willing to pay a higher price to save time, a high-speed ferry run by Hy-Line Cruises will whisk you and yours from Hyannis to Nantucket in just one hour. Martha's Vineyard is 45 minutes from Woods Hole and 1 hour and 45 minutes from Hyannis. Call for schedules. You can bring your car on the Steamship Authority ferries, or rent a car on the islands, but you might want to consider bringing (or renting) bicycles, instead. Martha's Vineyard, in particular, is very bike-friendly, with paved bike paths covering much of the island (and more miles of pathway to come). (Also see bicycling section.)

MARTHA'S VINEYARD

● The Flying Horses
Circuit Ave., Oak Bluffs; (508) 693-9481. Easter Sun.–Columbus Day, daily, 10–10; weekends only before Memorial Day and after Labor Day. Per ride, $1; 10 rides, $8. **All ages.**

Doing the island thing with little ones? This may be the highlight of their visit. Grab the rings as you whirl around this antique carousel— nab the brass one and you win a free ride. The challenge is as exciting as the ride for most children. A short walk from the ferry dock in Oak Bluffs, the Flying Horses is said to be the oldest operating carousel in the country. This carousel has been designated a national landmark.

● Felix Neck Wildlife Sanctuary
Edgartown-Vineyard Haven Rd., Edgartown; (508) 627-4850. Grounds open year-round, daily, dawn–4; visitor's center, daily, 9–4. Adults, $3; children, $2. No charge for members of Mass. Audubon Society. **All ages.**

A wonderful place to commune with island wildlife, this 350-acre property offers six miles of self-guided nature trails and a small exhibit center. Natural features include a pond (home to native waterfowl), salt marshes, woods, and wildflower-studded meadows.

● Cedar Tree Neck Wildlife Sanctuary
Off Indian Hill Rd., West Tisbury; (508) 693-5207. **All ages.**

Walk off the effects of those ice cream cones from Mad Martha's with a day of hiking. This 300-acre preserve has 250 acres of North Shore headlands, with woods, ponds, brooks, and dunes, and several scenic trails.

● The Lobster Hatchery

Shirley Ave., Oak Bluffs; (508) 693-0060. June–Sept., Mon.–Fri., 9–12 and 1–3. Free. **All ages.**

A trip to New England wouldn't be complete without a real close look at one of these crustaceans. You'll see baby lobsters and large lobsters and learn all about the lobster life cycle. (Did you know it takes seven years for a lobster to grow to one-pound size in our waters?) And just wait 'til the next time you try to boil one...

● Gay Head Cliffs

Moshup Trail, Gay Head. **All ages.**

Formed by glaciers, this mile-long expanse of multicolored cliffs is a national landmark. They rise 150 feet above the shore, affording spectacular views. These russet-hued layers of clay, sand, and gravel tell the tale of the island's geologic past, as do the fossils revealed by the cliffs' erosion. Fossils of great sharks, ancient whales, camels, and wild horses have been found on the beach and in the cliffs. Many year-round residents of Gay Head are descendants of the Wampanoag Indians. The Wampanoag people have lived on the island for at least 600 years, mostly at Gay Head. There's a small parking lot at the top of the cliffs and a trail that leads to Gay Head Clay Cliffs Beach.

● Beaches

In general, the beaches on the Vineyard's south shore offer rougher surf but good body surfing than those on the north shore. (**Katama Beach,** or **South Beach,** is one example.) Beaches to the east and north offer gentler stretches of sand and shallow water. Good family beaches include **Bend-in-the-Road Beach** on Nantucket Sound, Edgartown; **Joseph A. Sylvia State Beach,** off Beach Road between Oak Bluffs and Edgartown (accessible by bike path); narrow **Menemsha Public Beach,** at the mouth of the harbor on Vineyard Sound (try to forget that the movie *Jaws* was filmed in Menemsha); and **Owen Park Beach** in Vineyard Haven, a calm public beach that's right next to a park and great for kids. Other nice beaches, requiring a bit more effort to get to, are **East Beach** (Cape Pogue Wildlife Refuge and Wasque Reservation) on Chappaquiddick Island, a wilderness barrier beach on the southeast tip of Martha's Vineyard. Much of this area is accessible by four-wheel-drive vehicle. **Lambert's Cove Beach,** on the north shore, is one of the island's best, but it is reserved for West Tisbury residents and guests only. To use it, obtain a permit from the West Tisbury town hall.

● Story Hours

What's not to like about an island that boasts seven libraries? Some offer story hours for little people, an especially nice outing on a rainy day. These include **Edgartown Public Library,** at 58 N. Water St., offering story hour on Wed. at 10:30 A.M.; **Oak Bluffs Public Library,** on Circuit Ave. (Wed. and Sat., 10–10:45); and **Vineyard Haven Public Library,** on Main St., hosting a preschool story hour on Tuesdays at 10 A.M.

● Fruit Picking

Fruit always tastes better when you pick it yourself. On Martha's Vineyard, **Thimble Farms,** in Vineyard Haven, is the place to pluck those plump strawberries and juicy raspberries that taste like summertime. Call (508) 693-6396 for hours and availability.

● Bicycling

Vineyard regulars agree: you haven't really *done* the Vineyard 'til you've biked it. Roads are mostly level, and paved bike paths run between Oak Bluffs and Edgartown, Vineyard Haven and Edgartown, and Edgartown to South Beach, with more on the way. Bikes can be rented in the three main towns, Edgartown, Oak Bluffs, and Vineyard Haven. For a look at the unspoiled heart of the island, head to Manuel F. Correllus State Forest. The forest encompasses 4,000 acres of scrub oak barrens and pine forest at the center of Martha's Vienyard. A paved bike trail follows the perimeter of the forest. Access it from parking lots, located in Oak Bluffs (on Airport Rd.); West Tisbury (Old County Rd.); and Edgartown (West Tisbury Rd.). As always, obey traffic laws. Keep to the right, single file, obey one-way street signs, and wear a helmet (they're required by law for kids 12 and under).

RESTAURANTS

● Giordano's Restaurant

107 Circuit Ave., Oak Bluffs; (508) 693-0184. June–Sept., daily, 11:30–10:30.

Bless this place—it's one of the few Vineyard restaurants where you can go in, plop down, and relax, kids in tow (although you might have to wait in line first). None of that Geez-I-hope-they-can-behave-themselves-in-this-place tension. Giordano's is cheerful and generally inexpensive, and the menu is a happy mix of pasta, pizza, fried seafood, and Italian specialties. Almost everything is made from scratch, including the sauces.

Try spaghetti with white littleneck clam sauce, or chicken parmesan (the most popular dish here), or shrimp cacciatore. A children's menu is offered, but prices are on the high side, so if yours are light eaters you might do well with a side of meatballs and some shared spaghetti.

● Black Dog Tavern

On the beach in Vineyard Haven; (508) 693-9223. Mid-June–Oct., daily, 11:30–10:30.

You've seen the T-shirts—everywhere—so you might as well try this local landmark (and monument to creative marketing) yourself. Sit on the open porch overlooking Vineyard Haven Harbor and feast on fresh seafood. Expect to pay around $20–$25 for a dinner entrée (perhaps grilled yellowfin tuna with spicy ginger sauce). Too much to pay for the privilege of saying "We've been there"? Show up for breakfast; the pancakes and muffins are a great hit with little people.

● The Aquinnah

Gay Head Cliffs; (508) 645-9654. Mid-June–Oct., Mon.–Thurs., 8–5; Fri.–Sun., 8–sunset.

More great views at this casual restaurant, high atop Gay Head Cliffs overlooking the Atlantic. It's open for breakfast, lunch, and dinner; naturally, you'll sit outside. Aquinnah means "land under the hill" in the Algonquin dialect of the Wampanoags.

NANTUCKET

● Whaling Museum

Broad St., head of Steamboat Wharf; (508) 228-1736. Mid-June–Labor Day, daily, 10–5; early April–May, weekends only, 11–3; mid-May–mid-June, daily, 11–3; Labor Day–Columbus Day, daily, 11–3; Columbus Day–Dec., weekends only, 11–3. Adults, $5; 5–14, $3. **Ages 3 and up.**

Learn what it was like during Nantucket's great whaling era as you study the museum's collections of maritime artifacts. Learn all about whales, every kid's favorite Giant Marine Mammal; see how they were caught and, well, processed. More fun are a whaleboat, scrimshaw, and the skeleton of a 43-foot finback whale. A lecture on the history of whaling is offered three times a day (few kids make it through this, in our experience!).

● Gail's Tours

(508) 257-6557. Van tours at 10, 1, and 3 daily, year-round. $10 per person in group tours, age 5 and under free; $130 for private tour. **All ages.**

If you really want to get to know the island, Gail Nickerson Johnson is the gal to see. She's been giving tours for ages, is a sixth-generation Nantucketer, and she'll give you a lively ride. Tours last about 1 hour and 30 minutes.

● Maria Mitchell Aquarium

28 Washington St.; (508) 228-5387 or 228-0898. Early June–Aug., Tues.–Sat., 10–4. Admission, $1. **All ages.**

This teeny-tiny aquarium and the Hinchman House (see listing) honor Nantucket astronomer Maria Mitchell, America's first female astronomer. See marine life collected from around the island here; during a recent visit, we viewed seven types of crabs, 15 kinds of fish, eels, and baby sharks. Some specimens can be taken out to touch; aquarium staffers will tell you all about them. You can even add to the collection here—join a marine life collecting trip (run twice a week), and you'll go out with nets and buckets to look for examples of local sea life. Your specimens may join the other inhabitants of the aquarium. The charge is $7 for adults, and $4 for kids age 6 to 14. Call for times.

● Nantucket Lifesaving Museum

Polpis Rd., Nantucket Center; (508) 228-1885. Mid-June–Sept., 9:30–4. Adults, $3; age 6 and up, $2. **Ages 3 and up.**

Step into this authentic recreation of Nantucket's Surfside Station, built in 1874, and see lifesaving boats and displays of rescue equipment. Check out the exhibit of treasures from the sunken ship *Andrea Dora,* which sank more than 40 years ago off Nantucket's southeast coast.

● Old Mill

At the intersection of Prospect, West York, and South Mill streets; (508) 228-1894. Mid-June–Labor Day, daily, 10–5; Memorial Day–June 15, daily, 11–3; Labor Day–Columbus Day, daily, 11–3, weather permitting. Adults, $2; 14 and under, $1. Kids program: $20; members of the Nantucket Historical Society, $15. **Ages 6 and up.**

Built in 1746, this is one of the last operating wind-powered mills in the country. It's preserved by the Nantucket Historical Association and is the sole survivor of four mills on the island. Watch the impressive-looking wooden gears turn the millstone, grinding the corn, and take home a freshly ground bag of cornmeal. In summer, join the children's living history program: kids run the old windmill and help the miller make cornmeal. Then the group heads to the island's oldest house to bake cornbread. The program runs on Wednesdays, July and August, twice daily, from 10 to 12, and again from 2 to 4 P.M. Reservations are required.

● Hinchman House

7 Milk St.; (508) 228-0898. Early-June–Aug., Tues.–Sat., 10–4. Adults, $3; children, $1. **Ages 3 and up.**

This building houses a unique natural history museum, featuring a collection of living reptiles and mounted birds and fauna from the island. There are also native wildflower and plant displays; exhibits focus on environmental issues of Nantucket. Tours are self-guided. Call for the schedule of bird and nature walks.

● Beaches

Children's Beach, on the North Shore (and an easy walk to town), is aptly named—it may well end up your family's favorite. On Nantucket Sound, the water is calm. Facilities include a playground, park, concessions, even tie-dying sessions, run Fridays at noon, mid-July–Aug. Other good choices include **Dionis Beach** (with sand dunes) and **Jetties Beach** (with sailboat rentals), both on the North Shore. Jetties Beach is an easy bike ride (or a long walk) from town and worth it—it's an inviting stretch of sand with a snack bar/ice cream takeout, sailboat and kayak rentals, and swimming lessons for kids ages 6 and up, mornings, from July 4 through Labor Day.

Looking for a beautiful beach for meandering? Take the shuttle bus from town to **Madaket Beach,** at the west end of Nantucket. The surf's heavy, but the views (and the sunsets) are splendid.

● Getting Around

Don't you dare bring a car to Nantucket! You haven't seen gridlock 'til you've seen Nantucket Town's narrow cobblestone streets in the height of tourist season. (They don't call it "Manhattan East" in August for nothing.) Who needs that on vacation? Better to stay someplace not far from the action, or near the beach, and vow to walk it, bike it, take taxis, or take advantage of the new, cheap way to get around the island, the NRTA shuttle. These buses make regular runs all over—around town, out to Madaket and Siasconset—for a small fee. Little kids ride free.

● Bicycling

Nantucket has several paved bike paths, leading to Surfside, Siasconset, Madaket, and (soon to come, at this writing) Polpis. Look for bike signs on sign posts, with destinations designated by color (i.e. Siasconset, red). Be sure to follow the rules of the road, stay off the soft sand and wildflowers along the path, and wear a helmet (required by law for kids 12 and under). For bike rentals, try **Young's Bicycle Shop** at

Steamboat Wharf, (508) 228-1151. They'll also provide a dandy map of bike trails.

● J.J. Clammps Great Atlantic Fun Co.
Nobadeer Farm and Sun Island Rd.; (508) 228-8977. Daily, in season, 9–11. **All ages.**

Even quaint Nantucket has a miniature golf course, nicely manicured, naturally. A free shuttle bus will get you there; call for service.

● Scenic Overlook
First Congregational Church & Old North Vestry, 62 Centre St.; (508) 228-0950. Church and tower open to visitors, mid-June–mid-Oct., Mon.–Sat., 10–4. Adults, $2; children, $.50. **Ages 4 and up.**

Get a bird's eye view of the island from the tower of the church. With sweeping views of the moors to Madaket, this is the loftiest view in town. It's 93 steps up, but you get a break halfway—there's an exhibit room at midpoint in the climb.

RESTAURANTS
First, a few words about Nantucket dining: to say that Nantucket has a bounty of wonderful dining establishments doesn't do it justice. Two of the finest restaurants in all of New England are on-island, The Chanticleer and Toppers at the Wauwinet. Of course, unless you brought the au pair along, you won't be setting foot in these bastions of gourmetdom. No matter—you'll still eat well. Nantucket has more than 50 eateries, offering everything from bean burritos to classic clambakes. In general, if your kids aren't always restaurant-civilized, stick with cafe-type places like the Atlantic Cafe and the Fog Island Cafe—these are fun, inexpensive, and casual. Here are a couple more perennials:

● The Hearth at the Harbor House
5 South Beach St.; (508) 228-1500. Summer, daily, 5–9.; after Columbus Day, Tues.–Sun.; after Jan. 1, Wed.–Sun. Sunset special: 5–6:30.

This appealing restaurant is in the 1860s Harbor House Inn, with high ceilings, exposed beams, and beautiful woodwork. They call it "civilized family dining," so if that describes your bunch, go for it. We like the Sunset Special. A special fixed-price menu is offered, with four entrée choices, appetizer, and dessert, along with a special menu for the under-12 set. Two children's dinners are free with each adult special. Has this concept caught on? You bet your lightship basket it has, so reservations are a must. Seafood, beef, and chicken are the bill of fare.

● The Downey Flake

At Children's Beach; (508) 228-4533. April–Oct., 6–2:30.

For melt-in-your-mouth pastries or a great breakfast, walk to this simple island eatery. Kids love the pancakes, stacked high and topped with fresh, locally made cranberry or blueberry syrup, and the homemade vanilla yogurt, topped with granola and served with a bowl of fresh fruit. Drop in at the counter for ready-to-go sandwiches and pastries on your way to the beach.

● Do-It-Yourself-Picnic

Local restaurateurs won't appreciate this insider's tip, but here goes: If you want to concoct your own fabulous picnic by the sea, stop by a local seafood market. They'll cook and crack lobster to go. Pick up some extras at the big A&P grocery store in Nantucket town (they even have ready-to-go items like chicken wings for kids who think lobster is yucky), then head to your favorite spot (say, Madaket Beach at sunset), relax, and enjoy.

New Hampshire

Portsmouth

There aren't many better places for a family to spend a day or two than in Portsmouth, New Hampshire. This gem of a city, New Hampshire's only seaport, is tucked away between the Maine and Massachusetts borders and often gets bypassed by hurried tourists.

In Portsmouth, being a visitor is just plain easier than in most other popular New England towns. In this pretty, historic seaport, you'll find more than 70 restaurants (some are rated the best on the seacoast), boutiques, art galleries and shops, and a list of activities to keep even the busiest of families happy. It also manages to maintain an unpretentious, relaxed atmosphere.

Don't rush through this town. Plan to spend at least a day visiting its unique museums (including a quaint hands-on museum just for kids), strolling lovely Prescott Park, cruising to the Isles of Shoals, or zipping down the wild Geronimo! water slide at Water Country. Be sure to stop by the town pier, where you'll see the massive tugboats, and, if your timing is right, the fish boats hauling in the daily catches.

● Strawbery Banke
Marcy St. (opposite Prescott Park and the Portsmouth waterfront); (603) 433-1100. May–Oct., daily, 10–5. (Annual Christmas Stroll held in December.) Adults, $10; 6–17, $7; under 6, free. **Ages 6 and up.**

This unique living history museum draws history buffs from around the country. When the first settlers landed in Portsmouth they found wild strawberries growing along the banks of the Piscataqua River and so named this seaport Strawbery Banke. During the next 150 years, the site became a thriving waterfront town, and later an immigrant neighborhood known as Puddle Dock.

Today, you'll see 30 of the 35 original buildings, all salvaged from demolition and in various stages of restoration. A number of archaeological and restoration exhibits illustrate how historians are able to piece together facts about the past. Part of the fun is seeing restoration projects still going on, in various stages of completion.

Some of the houses are furnished to reflect time periods ranging from the 17th to the 20th centuries; others contain exhibits and craft shops. You're likely to see gardeners at work on the grounds, as well as boat builders, barrel makers, archaeologists, carpenters, quilt makers, weavers, and more. Older children (six and older) can get firsthand knowledge of what it might have been like to live in an earlier time by signing up for daily workshops. During the 45-minute sessions, they might make a basket, spin yarn, or perform other 19th-century tasks.

● Port of Portsmouth Maritime Museum and Albacore Park

Market Street Extension; (603) 436-3680. Columbus Day–late-May, Thurs.–Mon., 9:30–4; late-May–Columbus Day, daily, 9:30–5:30. Adults, $4; 7–17, $3; under 7, free. **Ages 5 and up.**

Climb aboard on the USS *Albacore.* You get to go below to its tiny engine room, captain's quarters, radio room, and dining area. A short film describes the history of the 1,200-ton submarine, and a tour guide explains things as you go along. Where else can you sit at the controls of a real submarine?

● Children's Museum of Portsmouth

280 Marcy St.; (603) 436-3853. Sept.–mid-June, Tues.–Sat., 10–5; Sun., 1–5; mid-June–Aug., Mon.–Sat., 10–5, Sun., 1–5. Admission, $4; under 2, free. **Ages 10 and under.**

Watch as your children don rain slickers and fishing hats, jump aboard a lobster boat, and pull up a trap full of plastic flounders, lobsters, haddock, bass, and shrimp. Then, they can take their "catch" over to the fish market, where their playmates become make-believe customers. This cozy home-turned-museum is a child's paradise. When they're done fishing, children can head up to the rocket ship, taking turns at the controls, while a video screen helps them imagine their journey through space. A fun place for toddlers; older kids will enjoy the daily-scheduled arts and crafts projects.

Many children never make it past the big yellow submarine—the first thing they see when they walk in the door. This three-story play structure contains tunnels, platforms, peek holes, slides, and poles. Relax in the adjacent sitting area—your children are bound to come out sooner or later.

● Water Country

Rte. 1 (3 mi. south of downtown Portsmouth); (603) 436-3556. Memorial Day–mid-June, weekends, 10:30–6; mid-June–July, daily 10:30–6; July–late Aug., daily, 9:30–7:30; late-Aug.–Labor Day, daily, 10:30–6. Adults, $23.95; under 4 ft., $15.95. Admission does not include tube rental or lockers. **Ages 7 and up.**

What's summer vacation without at least one trip to a water park? In the seacoast area, this is the place to go. Tube down a quarter-mile river through waterfalls and caves; speed down the dips on the double dive-boggan slide; bank around the curbs on the triple giant slides; or swallow your stomach down Double Geronimo, the fastest waterslide in New England. Check out the two latest water adventures: Vortex and

High Five, a group tubing exprience. If that sounds too active, there are simple pools to soak in and lots of lawn chairs. (Take note: this place gets packed on hot days; come early, or during late afternoon to avoid crowds.) For kids under four feet tall, there are three large kiddie areas, including the Octopus Lagoon with miniwaterslides, wading pool, whirlpool, and playground equipment. But it's older kids and daredevil parents who get the most for the money here.

● Prescott Park

Marcy St. on Portsmouth waterfront; (603) 436-2848. **All ages.**

This lovely waterfront expanse is full of flower gardens and fountains and room to roam. Snack pushcarts are here if you need some quick replenishing, and often you'll see a variety of arts and crafts exhibits displayed throughout the park. Family art and music festivals are held during the summer; lots of folks turn out here on sultry summer nights to listen to concert music and watch the stars splash across the sky.

● Boat Cruises

There's no better place to view the coastline, harbors, and islands than from a boat. The **Isles of Shoals Steamboat Company,** (800) 441-4620, offers a variety of cruises, including fall foliage and naturalist tours, whale-watching expeditions, and a special lighthouse cruise that takes you to five lighthouses in the area. The Steamboat Company also offers a special excursion to Star Island (part of the Isle of Shoals) on which you'll be able to explore the island and learn its interesting history.

Portsmouth Harbor Cruises, 63 Ceres Street, (603) 436-8084, offers a 1-hour-and-30-minute cruise aboard the small (40 passengers) wooden M/V *Heritage.* Because of its size, the *Heritage* is able to travel to areas not accessible to a larger boat. You'll get an intimate look at the seacoast area, including its picturesque inland rivers and the Great Bay.

● Isles of Shoals

Discovered in 1614 by Captain John Smith, the nine shoal islands are natural havens for birds, wildflowers, and animals. You'll see several species of gulls on the islands; the most common is the herring gull. The largest is the black-backed gull, with a wing span of five feet. Harbor seals raise their young on one of the islands, and whales have been observed a few hundred yards offshore. Four of the islands are in New Hampshire and five belong to Maine. Sign up for one of the harbor boat cruises to reach them.

● Horse & Carriage Rides

Market Square; (603) 427-0044. May–Oct., daily; Nov.–April, weekends. 20-minute ride, $20; 30-minute ride, $25; 40-minute ride, $30. Prices are per carriage ride; carriages fit up to 4 adults or 2 adults and 3 children. **All ages.**

What kid doesn't like a horse-and-buggy ride? Mom and dad will enjoy it, too, in these quaint, historic horse-drawn open carriages that tour Portsmouth in style. The ride is particularly special during the winter holidays when the downtown area is decked out in its old-fashioned finery, and the sleigh bells add the perfect touch.

● Bow Street Theater

125 Bow St. **Ages 5 and up.**

Both the Portsmouth Academy of Performing Arts, (603) 433-7272, and the Seacoast Reperatory Company of PAPA, (603) 433-4472, perform at this intimate, comfortable theater. There's lots of quality, live theater going on year-round, including a top-notch Saturday and Sunday children's series. Call for a schedule.

● Urban Forestry Center

45 Elwyn Rd.; (603) 431-6774. Year-round, daily 'til dusk. Free. **All ages.**

This center is a peaceful nature escape just outside the city where you can walk Brook Trail alongside native wildflowers and herb and perennial gardens. Try your skill at identifying local trees—many are noted along the trail.

 RESTAURANTS

● The Stockpot

53 Bow St.; (603) 431-1851. Daily, 11–11:30.

The Stockpot began in 1982 as a soup-and-stew hangout for local artists. Today it draws a more diverse crowd that comes for its good, relatively cheap food and waterfront location. Housed in a remodeled 19th-century brewery, it offers nice views of Portsmouth Harbor and freshly made, simply prepared food, including lots of great homemade soups, salads, and sandwiches.

● Poco Diablo's

37 Bow St.; (603) 431-5510. Daily, 11–11.

This always-crowded eatery in Portsmouth is especially appealing on warm, pleasant evenings when you can snag a table on the outside deck, munch on a platterful of Nachos Grande, and watch the boats come in and out of the harbor. Inside, you'll miss the view, but the fare—tacos, enchiladas, burritos—is equally good.

New Hampshire Seacoast

This small, condensed region of New Hampshire encompasses only 18 miles of shoreline and centers on the busy resort area of Hampton Beach. Nearly 150,000 sunbathers crowd this long stretch of beach on sunny summer days. The hardy ones swim in the cold waters of the Atlantic (which average only 55 degrees in July); the rest soak up the sun's rays and the area's frolicking, carnival atmosphere. This is the Daytona Beach of the Northeast, full of noisy fun and enough activities to fill your days and nights.

If you're in need of a bit more solitude, don't despair. Visit the seaside town of Rye, where you can picnic at Odiorne Point State Park and take a quiet oceanside nature walk. Stroll the cobblestone streets of quaint downtown Exeter, or pick fruit at a nearby orchard. If you venture just a few miles from Hampton Beach in either direction, you're back in storybook New England.

● Hampton Beach
Ocean Blvd; (603) 926-8717. Year-round. Free. **All ages.**

Your kids will love this place. There are three miles of white, sandy beach surrounded by restaurants, games rooms, arcades, souvenir shops, waterslides, and hot dog, pizza, candy, fried dough, and ice cream stands. Don't try to drive around town; you'll spend too much time stuck in traffic. Hop the town trolley car (on which you'll hear about the day's list of area activities), or walk the boardwalk on Ocean Boulevard. Each night stars something different—talents shows, fireworks, concerts, and sing-alongs.

● Hampton Beach Casino
Ocean Blvd., Hampton Beach; (603) 926-4541. **All ages.**

This is where just about everything cool happens at Hampton Beach—at least according to kids. This seven-acre playground includes shops, food (like cotton candy, hot dogs, slushes, fried dough, clams, and sausages), minigolf, kiddie rides, arcades, waterslides, and a teen club. Always jam-packed and noisy.

● Odiorne Point State Park

Rte. 1A, Rye; (603) 436-8043. Year-round. **All ages.**

Located just a few minutes from Hampton Beach in Rye is this lovely, 230-acre oceanside park, the largest undeveloped stretch of shore on New Hampshire's coast. The area is expansive, offering great views and lots to do. Be sure to wear a pair of shoes that you don't mind getting wet. Odiorne is one of the best places around to go tidepooling. As you hop and peer into the pools, you'll likely find an abundant array of marine creatures, including sea urchins, snails, starfish, lobsters, shrimp, and more. (It's okay to pick them up, even to put them in a bucket for viewing—but everything needs to be put back before leaving.)

There are wading areas, picnic tables, grills, and a small playground. There are also a number of trails (lots of people bring their bikes) that take you along the rocky coastline or inland through salt marshes, ponds, and woodlands. The Science Center is a must-see, too.

● Seacoast Science Center

Odiorne Point State Park, Rte. 1, Rye; (603) 436-8043. Year-round, daily, 10–5. Admission, $1; under 5, free. **Ages 3 and up.**

Get your hands on a starfish, snails, sea urchins, and more at this pretty marine center that sits atop a bluff overlooking the ocean. The best strategy is to stop at the Science Center first to see and learn all about the creatures that inhabit the nearby ocean waters. Then go exploring the hundreds of tidepools outside for a look at some of the same critters.

The center houses a number of aquariums and marine exhibits that interpret the seven habitats found at the park, including a tidepool touch tank, a 1,000-gallon Gulf of Maine tank, and a "Look Under" tank. Local school kids act as volunteer guides during the summer and are eager to answer any questions.

● Rye Harbor Cruises and Whale Watches

New Hampshire Seacoast Cruises, Rye Harbor State Marina, Rte. 1A, Rye Harbor, (603) 964-5545, offers two-hour tours of the nine Isles of Shoals, and six-hour whale-watch excursions, led by research biologists.

The Atlantic Fishing Fleet, also at the Rye Harbor State Marina on Rte. 1A, (603) 964-5220, offers sunset cruises on its 80-foot M/V *Atlantic Queen II.* The evening whale watches offer a close-up view of these ocean giants. On the narrated trips, you're likely to spot dolphins, seals, and an array of seabirds.

● Wallis Sands

Rte. 1A, Rye; (603) 436-9404. Memorial Day–Labor Day. **All ages.**

This white, sandy beach is 800 feet long, 150 feet wide, and a popular summertime swimming spot. There are refreshments, rest rooms, and changing facilities. From the rocky bluff on the north end of Wallis Sands you can see Seal Rocks. During colder months, you might spot seals, who often sun themselves here. On the horizon, you'll be able to see the Isles of Shoals, nine tiny islands off the coast.

● Fort Constitution and Fort Stark

Fort Stark, Rte. 1B (take Wild Rose Ln. to the fort), Newcastle; (603) 436-6607. Memorial Day–Labor Day. Free. Fort Constitution, Rte. 1B (follow signs to Coast Guard Station), Newcastle. Memorial Day–Labor Day, weekends only. Free. **Ages 3 and up.**

These two sites in Newcastle provide a peek at early military installations and offer great views of the Atlantic coastline.

Fort Stark is a 10-acre former U.S. coastal harbor defense facility, where you'll get a historical look at the state's fortification system and a spectacular view of the Atlantic Ocean, Little Harbor, Odiorne Point State Park, and the Isles of Shoals. Be careful as you walk through the site: there are lots of rough ground and slippery rocks.

On December 13, 1744, Paul Revere rode from Boston with a message that the fort at Rhode Island had been dismantled and troops were coming to take over Fort Constitution (then named Fort William and Mary). The fort was damaged in the raid, which was an important link in the chain of events leading to the Revolution. Today, you can walk the site and enjoy the coastal views.

● Seacoast Science and Nature Center

Seabrook Station, just off Rte. 1, Seabrook; (800) 338-7482. Year-round, Mon.–Sat., 10–4. Free. **Ages 5 and up.**

Okay, this is a nuclear plant. That said, let's go on. The science center contains a number of informative, hands-on exhibits and sensitively presented educational programs about energy and the environment. There are more than 30 exhibits and displays. You'll take an imaginary journey nearly 260 feet below the sea level to Seabrook's cooling tunnels. Kids can test their "energy I.Q." with computer quizzes, and their "pedal power" at the bicycle-powered generator. There are also aquariums and a touch pool for a look at regional marine life, and a short nature trail through surrounding salt marshes and woodlands.

● Little Bay Buffalo Company

Langley Rd., Durham; (603) 868-2632. Daily, 9–sunset. **All ages.**

Home, home on the range . . . can this be right? Yes, native New Englanders don't have to head west to catch a glimpse of the mighty American bison. Come see the unexpected at this farm. There are tours and a small shop (anyone care for a bison burger?), but just a stop for a close-up look at these hefty beasts is enough.

● Emery Farm

Rte. 4, Durham; (603) 742-8495. Mid-May–Dec.; daily, 9–6. **All ages.**

There are more than 12 acres of pick-your-own fruit on this family farm, established in 1655 in Durham. A small animal petting farm and an old-fashioned country store are also on the grounds. During the summer, there are scheduled children's reading hours and activities, too.

● Kingston State Park

Off Rte. 125, Kingston; (603) 452-9621. **All ages.**

Swim in the fresh waters of Great Pond and have a picnic in this 44-acre state park; it's just outside Exeter.

🍴 RESTAURANTS

● Captain Newick's

431 Dover Point Rd. (exit 6W off Spaulding Tpke.), Dover; (603) 742-3205. Mon.–Thurs. and Sun., 11–8; Fri.–Sat., 11–9.

A great family place, especially if you have a taste for fresh fried seafood or lobster in the rough. This always-crowded, quick-service place serves hefty portions at fair prices. You'll sit at long picnic tables, probably eat most of your food with your fingers, and take home a doggie bag of leftovers.

● Loaf & Ladle

9 Water St., Exeter; (603) 778-8955. Mon.–Wed., 8–8; Thurs.–Sat., 8–9; Sun., 11–9.

Help yourself, cafeteria style, to an assortment of homemade breads, soups, chilies, and salads. Grab your plate and head outdoors to the deck overlooking the tumbling river. This is hearty, healthy fare, with great breads, vegetables, soups, and salads. At dinner, the chef prepares a couple of special entrees to choose from (like fresh veggie pasta dishes or lemon-baked herb chicken).

Merrimack Valley

More than half the population of New Hamsphire lives in the Merrimack Valley region, and most visitors see it only in passing on their way north to the more popular tourist destinations. Nashua, Salem, Manchester, and Concord offer an abundance of fun-filled family activities. You'll find a host of interesting museums, from the Children's Metamorphosis Museum in Londonderry to the larger Christa McAuliffe Planetarium in Concord. And, just outside the city centers, you'll find rolling, peaceful country-side, clear rivers and lakes, and some very scenic state parks.

Next time you're driving by get off the highway for more than a stop at a fast-food chain. Spend the afternoon at the Canobie Lake Amusement Park, take a refreshing swim at Silver Lake, try a canoe trip down the Merrimack River, or go mountain biking at Pawtuckaway State Park. You'll return to the car refreshed, and the kids will be tuckered out for the rest of the journey. Or you might just decide to stick around the area awhile to discover more of its hidden gems.

● Canobie Lake Park

Exit 2 off I-93, Salem; (603) 893-3506. Late-May–Labor Day, daily, noon–10; mid-April–late May, Sat., noon–10, Sun., noon–6. Adults, $17 (includes all rides and shows), under 48 inches, $10; under 2, free. **All ages.**

A kid's delight: all their favorite amusement rides, boats, games, haunted house, live puppet shows, music revues, and more are here. There's a large kiddie area with lots of rides, and a couple of great roller coasters for older children and teens. Bring your bathing suit; there's a swimming pool, and a wild log ride. You can also take a boat cruise around the lake, or a train ride around the park. The park features a wide variety of entertainment, including fireworks, live shows, and specialty acts. On your way home, head north a few miles for a look at America's Stonehenge.

● America's Stonehenge

Mystery Hill (off Rte. 111), North Salem; (603) 893-8300. March–Dec., daily, 10–5; summers, 9–7. Adults, $7; 13–18, $5; 6–12, $3; 5 and under, free. **Ages 5 and up.**

Some claim this series of unusual rock formations is the 4,000-year-old astronomical complex built by Celts who came here from the Iberian peninsula. It is most likely the oldest manmade construction in the United States. Formerly known as Mystery Hill, it has presented an intriguing puzzle to archaeologists and historians. It was, and still can be, used to determine specific lunar and solar events of the year. There are a few trails for the kids to run on while you ponder the site and take in the view.

● Busch Clydesdale Hamlet

Anheuser-Busch Brewery, Rte. 3, Merrimack; (603) 883-6131. May–Nov., daily, 9:30–3:30; Dec.–Apr., closed Mon. and Tues. Free. **All ages.**

Get a close-up and personal look at the famous Clydesdale horses on this free tour through the stables. Also on display are wagons, harnesses, and other riding equipment.

● Children's Metamorphosis Museum

217 Rockingham Park, Londonderry; (603) 425-2560. Tues.–Sat., 9:30– 5; Fri., 9:30–8; Sun., 1–5. Adults, $3.50; under 1, free. **Ages 1–12.**

Curiosity the Caterpillar, the museum's mascot, is always waiting to show children around. Best for kids ages two to eight, the Metamorphosis features a variety of hands-on, fun-filled activity rooms.

In the World Cultures Room, you're surrounded by giant maps and will learn about people from around the world. You can try on regional clothing, play traditional games, and listen to music. In the Emergency Room, kids take pulses, listen to heartbeats, give shots, and use a wheelchair and crutches. At the Construction Site, future achitects, builders, and engineers work a bulldozer, design with blocks, and use tools at the workbench. Other exhibits include the Sticky Room (full of Velcro boards and Legos), Five Senses Room (touch it first and then see if you can guess what's hiding in the box), Grocery Room, Nature and Science Area, Puppet Theater, and an arts and crafts activity area. A great place for kids.

● Amoskeag Fishways

Amoskeag Dam, Fletcher St. (exit 6 off I-293), Manchester; (603) 626- FISH. Year-round, Mon.–Sat., 9:30–5; during fish season (usually May– mid-June), daily, 9–6. Free. **All ages.**

Don't miss this site in the spring time when several species of ocean fish return to spawn in the Merrimack River. An underwater viewing window gives you a fish-eye's view of what's going on below. Dioramas and displays teach about fish migration.

● Science Discovery Center

324 Commercial St., Manchester; (603) 669-0400. Year-round, weekends, noon–5; late-June–Aug., Mon.–Fri., 10–3; Sat–Sun., noon–5. Admission, $3. **Ages 2–12.**

Every day is a new project at this family-focused Science Center. Throughout the summer the Science Enrichment Encounter organization offers daily workshops and activities for children. Stop by and learn how to build your own rocket. Or, how about spending a few hours making a bongo drum, or a paper tube kazoo? You might learn how to make pennies shiny, or construct a weather wheel or an air rocket. Call for a list of specific projects and the days they're offered.

● Christa McAuliffe Planetarium

3 Institution Dr. (off I-93), Concord; (603) 271-2842. Tues.–Sun., 10–5, Fri., 10–7. Adults, $6; 3–17, $3. **Ages 5 and up.**

Named after one of the *Challenger* teacher-astronauts (who was a Concord native), the museum is a pleasing mix of small hands-on exhibits and razzle-dazzle video presentations. Call ahead to get reservations for the shows; these sell out quickly and you're likely to be disappointed if you go without reservations. Once you enter the theater, you'll sit back for a self-guided tour of the universe and an up-close look at the moon, planets, stars, comets, and more. You press buttons and answer questions as you plot your journey through space. Everyone is likely to learn lots, and have fun doing it.

● State House Center

107 N. Main St., Concord; (603) 271-2154. Mon.–Fri., 8–4:30. Free. **Ages 5 and up.**

The hub of activities in downtown Concord is the State House Plaza; here, New Hampshire's most famous sons (Daniel Webster and Franklin Pierce) are immortalized in bronze. The gold-domed capitol building can be seen from around town, and its picturesque grounds are inviting. Inside, visit the Hall of Flags and view a variety of displays and interesting dioramas that depict New Hampshire historical events. You'll be greeted by a friendly staff of guides; come with questions—they love to answer them.

If the legislature is in session, you can catch a glimpse of state government in action.

● Little Nature Center

59 Boyce St., Weare; (603) 529-7180. By appointment only, usually several weeks in advance. Adults, $3; 5–12, $2. **Ages 3 and up.**

You won't find a single Do Not Touch sign at this place. This long-standing museum, housed in a private home, is open to the public and boasts an extensive collection of fossils, rocks, and minerals. This is all hands-on—and where else can you pick up and touch more than 50 to 60

fossils? Rockhounds, treasure hunters, and merely the curious will enjc
the visit here. Children will beam with wonder at flourescent minerals,
odd-shaped rocks, and shiny shells. A lovely nature hike is also on the
grounds. Call ahead to make arrangements.

● Audubon Society of New Hampshire Headquarters

*3 Silk Rd., Concord; (603) 224-9909. Mon.–Sat., 9–5; Sun., noon–5.
Free.* **Ages 5–15.**

What are those small black-and-white birds we see all the time?
What kind of woodpeckers peck in New Hampshire? How far do shore
birds go? What birds will we see in the mountains? Stop by the Audubon
Society headquarters to learn all about native feathered friends. You'll find
a number of exhibits, a nature store, and trails to explore. The society also
hosts a variety of programs throughout the year. Write or call for its
brochure.

● Society for the Preservation of New Hampshire Forests Conservation Center

54 Portsmouth St., Concord; (603) 224-9945. Mon.–Fri., 9–4:30. Free.
Ages 8 and up.

With conservation high on everyone's list, a visit to these headquarters is an interesting learning experience. A number of displays show you
how to conserve energy and natural resources. You'll enjoy a visit to the
passive solar energy building on the premises, and a walk on one of the
nearby nature trails.

● Silver Lake State Park

Rte. 122, Hollis; (603) 465-2342. **All ages.**

This is a popular family picnic area and beach in the Merrimack
Valley region. The sandy, 1,000-foot beach is great for toddlers. Older
swimmers will enjoy racing to the raft. The park has a bathhouse,
restrooms, and concession stand. Picnic tables and grills are nestled in
the pine groves surrounding the park.

● Bear Brook State Park

Rte. 28, Allentown; (603) 485-9874. **All ages.**

This 9,000-acre park offers a playground, picnic area, swimming
beach, and rental boats. You'll also find the Museum of Family Camping
located at the park. The museum houses exhibits, memorabilia, and
documents on family camping dating back to early days. But you won't
spend much time in the museum; this is a great spot to play outdoors,
and that's where you'll want to be.

● Pawtuckaway State Park

Off Rte. 156, Nottingham; (603) 895-3031. **All ages.**

This is a favorite among locals—the park boasts lots of room to roam and lots of things to do. There's a swimming beach, picnic areas, boats, and a number of trails to explore. Mountain bikers will love it; a number of backroad and off-road places to pedal are ideal for all levels of bikers. Strap your bikes to the rack, pack your swimsuits and a picnic basket, and you have the makings for a great outdoor adventure.

 RESTAURANTS

● Capital City Diner

25 Water St., Concord; (603) 228-3463. Sun.–Thurs., 6 A.M.–9 P.M.; Fri.–Sat., 6 A.M.–1 A.M.

Filled with 1950s memorabilia, neon lights, and a waitstaff with a sense of humor, this is a fun place for families. Good old standby diner fare is offered here, including meatloaf, burgers, macaroni and cheese, hot turkey sandwiches, grilled cheese, and more. There's also an offering of nondiner fare, such as grilled salmon, daily pasta dishes, and dinner salads. Everyone will love the soda fountain creations. Bring change for the jukebox.

● Shorty's Mexican Roadhouse

Rte. 3A, Litchfield; (603) 424-0010. Mon.–Thurs., 11:30–10; Fri.–Sat., 11:30–11; Sun., 1–9.

These Mexican restaurants have begun to pop up across New Hampshire; that doesn't make them any less appealing, however. Go easy on the basket of tortilla chips and salsa, because you'll want to save room for the chicken *pendaja* (marinated chicken breast in spicy tomato sauce, cilantro, and jalapeño peppers.) The kids will like the typical taco, burrito, and nachos fare. Lots of great choices, reasonable prices, and a casual, lively atmosphere.

● Green Ridge Turkey Farm

235 Daniel Webster Hwy., Nashua; (603) 888-7020.

Going to Green Ridge is like going to Grandma's house for Sunday dinner. This popular family restaurant is located off the major highway in Nashua. Smaller portions of turkey, mashed potatoes (real ones) and gravy, and all the trimmings are available for children.

Lakes Region

This region in central New Hampshire is dominated by Lake Winnipe-saukee, the state's largest lake, encompassing 72 square miles and more than 280 miles of shoreline. The picturesque lake is surrounded by three mountain ranges and speckled with 274 islands. Claiming to be home to the country's oldest summer resort (Wolfeboro), it also lays claim to having New Hampshire's "most popular vacation spot" (Weirs Beach), although the tourist folk in Hampton Beach and the White Mountain region might have something to say about that. But a look at the level of activity and number of visitors on any summer weekend makes the claim hard to dispute.

On the western side of the lake is busy Weirs Beach, often crowded but full of amusements. For a slower pace, visit nearby Lakes Waukewan and Winnisquam, or Lake Squam, the setting for the movie *On Golden Pond.*

Especially popular in the summer, this area by no means closes down the rest of the year. With the crowds gone, this is a great spot to spend a warm autumn day admiring the fall foliage, and winter brings cross-country and downhill skiing enthusiasts to the Gunstock ski area.

● Winnipesaukee Boat Tours and Rentals

The best way to appreciate this area is to get out on Lake Winnipe-saukee; merely driving around its borders is not enough. Several cruise ships operate from the Weirs Beach pier. The **M/S** *Mount Washington,* (603) 366-2628, offers daily summer cruises on the majestic 230-foot yacht, or aboard the classic *Sophie C.* The **Queen of Winnipesaukee,** (603) 366-5005, a 46-foot luxury sailboat, has one-and-a-half- and two-hour tours of the lake. Lake cruises are also offered on the **MV** *Judge Sewall,* (603) 569-3016, departing from the Wolfeboro town docks.

If you prefer to go it alone, you can rent a variety of boats, including jet boats, from **Thurston's Marina,** (603) 366-4811. It's located on Route 3 at the Bridge, Weirs Beach. Jet boats are also available for rent at **Sea Doo Watercraft Rentals,** (603) 293-7788, at the junction of routes 11 and 11A in West Alton.

Ready to get away from it all? Load a day pack with some goodies and a can of bug repellent, and catch the **Stoneham Island boat** from Weirs Beach. Now, relax. This is a 112-acre, unspoiled island in Lake Winnipesaukee, with two and a half miles of nature trails.

● Squam Lake Tours

The serene, picturesque setting of Squam Lake was the site of the classic movie *On Golden Pond*. The best way to see the lake's pristine beauty is on a boat tour. In fact, the lake is not easily seen from the roadside—you need to get on the lake to appreciate it.

The Original Golden Pond Tour departs from The Manor, Route 3 at Shepard Hill Road in Holderness, (603) 968-3348. Captain Pierre Havre takes folks to the movie's actual locations, and entertains with friendly narration. **Squam Lake Tours,** located on Route 3, just south of the center of Holderness, (603) 968-7577, takes passengers out on a 28-foot pontoon boat.

● Fishing Charters

Lake Winnipesaukee is known for its great fishing waters. But, you'll need to know how to get away from the crowds and find the hidden holes. Check out **Gadabout Golder Guide Service,** (603) 569-6426, at 79 Middleton Road in Wolfeboro, or **Landlocked Fishing Guide Service,** (603) 253-6119, at PO Box 1382, Centre Harbor.

● Kayaking

With 280 miles of shoreline and more than 250 islands, Lake Winnipesaukee is a kayaker's paradise. Never kayaked before? Not to worry; this sport is for everyone. A few short instructions and a couple of minutes on the water, and you'll get the knack. Even young children are able to conquer this sport. Try it first with a guide. **Lake Winnipesaukee Kayak Company,** (603) 544-3905, at PO Box 4, Melvin Village, offers lessons and excursions on the lake. You can also explore some of the lesser-known lakes in the region.

● Beaches

Despite its size, Lake Winnipesaukee has few public access points; most of the lodging places have their own private beaches for guests' use. Here are your choices:

Endicott Rock Beach, Route 3, Weirs Beach, (603) 524-5046, is a small, sandy beach located next to the Weirs Beach Water Slide.

Ellacoya State Park, Route 11, Gilford, (603) 293-7821, is a small beach on the southwest shore of Lake Winnipesaukee. There are rewarding views of the Ossipee and Sandwich mountains from the shoreline.

Wentworth State Beach, Route 109, Wolfeboro, (603) 569-3699, is a small park located on the shore of scenic Lake Wentworth.

● Molly the Trolley

*PO Box 119, Wolfboro; (800) 339-5257. July–Aug., daily, 10–5.
Adults, $3; 4–12, $1; under 4, free.* **All ages.**

Hop aboard a turn-of-the-century trolley car for a narrated tour of
Wolfeboro. The all-day pass is also good for getting from one side of the
town to the other and a quick history of the town.

● Weirs Beach Water Slide

*Rte. 3, Weirs Beach; (603) 366-5161. Memorial Day–mid-June,
weekends, 10–5; mid-June–Labor Day, daily, 10–5. 7-ride ticket, $6.99;
14-ride, $9.99; 2-hr. unlimited, $10.99; all-day, $11.99. Children under
4 ft., 10-ride toddler pass, $5.99.* **Ages 3 and up.**

There are waterslides for every level of bravery, from the 70-foot long
Tunnel Twister to the high-acceleration Sling Shot ("reserved for the
slider seeking the ultimate sliding experience"). Or, try Super Slide, billed
as the longest and highest water slide in New England. Daredevils will
love the Pipeline Express; it drops you down into a black hole and around
underground curves, then blasts you up into daylight and down the
flume. Whew! Let's do it again.

● Surf Coaster

*Rte. 11B, Weirs Beach; (603) 366-4991. Mid-June–Labor Day, daily,
10–8. Over 4 ft., $18.99; under 4 ft., $13.99.* **Ages 5 and up.**

If you're tired of sand in your shoes but still want to cool off in the
surf, a visit to Surf Coaster is in order. This attraction boasts a giant wave
pool (nearly a half-acre in size), four water slides, lagoons, lazy rivers, a
wave pool, and a Kiddie Play Park and minislides.

● Winnipesaukee Railroad

*Trains depart from Weirs Beach or Meredith; (603) 528-2330. Memorial
Day–Aug., daily. Sept.–Columbus Day, Weds. and Sat.–Sun. Trains depart
Meredith on the half-hour, 10:30–6:30. Trains depart Weirs Beach on the
hour, 11–6. Limited hours in the fall; special events held during the winter.
Call for schedules. Adults, $8.50; 4–11, $6.50; under 4, free. HOBO picnic,
$6.95.* **Ages 5 and up.**

The railroad's specialty is the kid-pleasing HOBO picnic. Lunch is
packed up in a bundle on a stick to be enjoyed along the way. The train
travels along the shores of Lake Winnipesaukee.

There are lots of special programs offered, including fall foliage tours
and Santa Claus rides.

● Science Center of New Hampshire

Rte. 113, Holderness; (603) 968-7194. May–Oct., daily, 9:30–4:30. Adults, $6; 5–15, $3, during May–June and Sept.–Oct. Adults, $8; 5–15, $4, during July–Aug. **Ages 3 and up.**

Live native bear, deer, raccoons, owls, eagles, reptiles, bobcats, and other animals roam the 200-acre sanctuary, contained by natural enclosures. Don't miss the newest exhibit: a native bird display, songbird aviary, and an outside birdfeeding station. Discover the wonders of nature, learning about plant and animal life through a number of unique indoor and outdoor displays and interactive exhibits. Children can push buttons, solve puzzles, and skip along a nature trail lined with exhibits. In the summer, attend the "Up Close Animals" program, a live demonstration held twice a day.

● New Hampshire Farm Museum

Rte. 125, Milton; (603) 652-7840. Mid-May–mid-Oct., daily, 10–4. Adults, $5; 3–12, $1.50; 2 and under, free. **All ages.**

Ever wonder what it was like in the old days, growing crops for your food, weaving your clothes on a loom, churning butter, pumping water from a well? You'll find out here.

Children get a chance to see and touch a large collection of old farm tools and equipment as they tour the museum. You'll see a blacksmith shop, cobbler shop, old house and tavern, herb garden, country store, and two large barns full of all sorts of harvesting, planting, and woodworking tools. Often children are invited to work the equipment—making butter in an old churn, working an antique loom, or cleaning clothes in the wash basin. Special family events are held each weekend throughout the summer.

● Castle Springs

Rte. 171, Moultonborough; (800) 729-2468. Mid-May–mid-June, weekends; mid-June–mid-Oct., daily, 9–5. Admission: adults, $4; 10 and under, free. Admission and castle tour: adults, $10; 10 and under, free. Horseback riding, $25/hr. **All ages.**

Thomas Plant, an eccentric millionaire, wanted to own a piece of land "from the mountains to the water." This 5,000-acre site in the middle of the Ossipee Mountain Range is testimonial to his desires. There are guided tours of Plant's spacious retirement home, but the real attraction is outside—this is a pretty spot. There are views everywhere you look, and lots of ways to enjoy them. Take the short path (off the driveway entrance road) to the Fall of Song or Bridal Veil waterfalls. Even if you opt to forego the house tour, be sure to walk the grounds surrounding the castle. It sits on the highest point of the site, and you'll have fabulous views of mountains, woods and lakes.

Guided trail rides on horseback are offered, covering some of the more than 80 miles of bridle paths on the property. The shorter half-hour or hour-long tours are best for younger children. If you have time, have a picnic at Shannon Pond. There are tables, grills, and paddle boats to rent. Castle Springs is especially beautiful in the fall, when the mountainside is ablaze with color.

● Polar Caves

Rte. 25, Plymouth; (603) 536-1888 or (800) 273-1886. Mid-May–late-Oct., daily, 9–5. Adults, $9; 6–12, $4.50; under 6, free. **Ages 6–14.**

Get your first taste of spelunking as you sink through the narrow passageways and climb rocky inclines. You'll explore an area where giant boulders were deposited by glaciers many years ago, forming a maze of caves. Kids who love a challenging climb and don't mind getting their knees dirty will enjoy finding hidden Smuggler's Cave, squirming through Lemon Squeeze, and screaming in dark Fat Man's Misery. You can back out along the way; there are detours to get you around some of the more challenging spots. A picnic area, museum shop, cafeteria, and ice cream bar are also on the grounds.

● Funspot Amusement Center

Rte. 3, Weirs Beach; (603) 366-4377. Year-round, 10–10; July–Labor Day, 24 hrs. a day. Admission free. **Ages 3 and up.**

A rainy day is the perfect excuse to visit Funspot, although kids need no excuse at all. This is home to more than 500 electronic games. You'll find all the latest machines, along with 20 lanes of bowling (ten pin and candlepin), minigolf, and a driving range. The preschoolers in your group will love the Aqua Blasta splash guns and kiddie bumper cars. You'll go through a lot of quarters.

● Mount Major

Rte. 11; Alton Bay. **Ages 5 and up.**

It's a steep climb to the summit but worth every grunt and groan along the way. The trail begins at a marked parking area on Route 11, about five miles north of Alton Bay, and climbs one and a half miles to the summit. It takes about two hours to reach the top. From here, you'll see commanding views over the mountain ranges and across Lake Winnipesaukee. You're likely to see groups of people along the way, including many small children. There are many alternate paths—choose any way; they all lead to the top.

● White's Miniature Horse Petting Farm

280 Dowboro Rd., Pittsfield; (603) 435-8258. May–Sept., daily, 10–5. Adults, $4; 2–12, $2. **Ages 2-12.**

This very low-key, small family farm features a hands-on, huggable visit with miniature horses. There's a handful of other friendly farm animals clamoring around for attention, too. Small tots get a kick (figuratively, of course) out of this place.

● Gunstock Ski Area

Rte. 11A, Gilford; (603) 293-4341. Lift tickets: adults, $39, night skiing, $19; 6–12, $24, night skiing, $15; five and under, free with an adult purchase. SKIwee (5–12), $49/day; Buckaroo (3 yrs.), $45/day; child care (6 mos. and up), $30/day. Rates listed are for weekends and holidays; special packages available. **All ages.**

This area offers more skiing than you might think at first glance. Tucked away in the Lakes Region, the area has trails for all levels of expertise, with 39 trails and seven lifts. It's a good, solid intermediate area, with a special user-friendly section for beginners, and a handful of black diamonds thrown in.

The staff shows a commitment to family and children's services. The Buckaroos Children's Center is located at the heart of Gunstock's base complex so parents can drop in frequently throughout the day, if they wish. The nursery and day-care programs include arts and crafts, outdoor play and social activities. Children 3 to 12 years can join the SKIwee program.

RESTAURANTS

● Hart's Turkey Farm and Restaurant

Rtes. 3 and 104, Meredith; (603) 279-6212. Daily, 11:15–8.

Every day is Thanksgiving at this turkey farm turned restaurant. On a busy day, Hart's serves more than a ton of turkey. It has all the trimmings, too, like mashed potatoes, cranberries, and squash pie. The children's menu includes the Tiny Tot Turkey Plate—a real feast.

● Yankee Smokehouse

Rtes. 16 and 25, West Ossipee; (603) 539-RIBS. Late-June–Labor Day, daily, 11:30–9; rest of the year, Thurs.–Sun., 11:30–9.

The Yankee Smokehouse proudly proclaims it will "serve no swine before its time," and it does not disappoint. This is real barbeque (not the kind you get out of a bottle). You eat at picnic-style tables among the

Smokehouse's vast collection of pig paraphernalia. All the meat is smoked slowly over hardwood coals in an open pit out back. The top seller is the Smokehouse Sampler for two—chicken, ribs, beef, and pork, served with fries, beans, cole slaw, corn on the cob, and garlic toast.

● Weirs Beach Lobster Pound

Rte. 3, Weirs Beach (across from the waterslide); (603) 366-5713. Mid-May–mid-June and Labor Day–Columbus Day, Thurs.–Fri., 4:30–8; Sat.–Sun., noon–8. Summers, daily, noon–9.

No need to dress up; just shake the beach sand out of your shoes and grab a table. This is perennial favorite, serving up chicken, ribs, and lobster in the rough. Popular with families.

Sunapee Area

The Sunapee area has been called the best-kept secret in New England. No boardwalks, no T-shirt and tacky souvenir shops, no fast-food stands. It's a relaxing, beautiful place to vacation, void of the typical tourist trappings.

Nestled high in the mountains of western New Hampshire, the Lake Sunapee area extends a quiet, slow welcome to its visitors. You'll find nothing pretentious or fancy. Despite natural beauty and bountiful opportunities for sports and activities, the Lake Sunapee area is fairly non-commercial, retaining much of its rural charm. Aware of its increasing appeal, its citizens have adopted the motto, "Preserve the Best of the Past." They're doing a good job. That's not to say you have to spend your entire time sitting under a giant white pine tree, skipping stones on Lake Sunapee (unless, of course, you want to). There are plenty of things to do: aerial rides, band concerts, boat cruises, hikes, waterskiing and snow skiing, apple picking, horseback riding, science and art museums, forts, and playhouses.

● Mount Sunapee State Park

Rte. 103, Newbury; (603) 763-2356. Beach open Memorial Day–mid-June, weekends, 9:30–8; mid-June–Labor Day, daily, 9:30–8. **All ages.**

Start your vacation in Sunapee with a visit to the state park. The entire family will enjoy the sandy park beach. Swimmers in the family will have fun racing to the raft; toddlers are safe along the calm, shallow banks. There are picnic areas in the park, a playground, and a small concession stand at the beach.

● Sunapee Harbor

Off Rte. 11. **All ages.**

Sit at the edge of the lake and watch the boats come and go, picnic on the lawn that stretches from the lake to the road. Nobody hurries here. During the day you can rent boats and waterskiing equipment from a nearby marina. (Sailboat, canoe, and motor boat rentals are also available a few miles north of the harbor.) Don't miss the free outdoor band concerts held every Wednesday evening during the summer. Bring a blanket—the kids can dance and play on the lawn while you listen to the music float across the lake.

● M/V Mount Sunapee

Sunapee Harbor (off Rte. 11); (603) 763-4030. Mid-May–mid-June, Sat.–Sun., 2:30; mid-June–Labor Day, daily, 10 and 2:30; Labor Day–mid-Oct., Sat.–Sun., 2:30. Adults, $10; 5–12, $6. **Ages 5 and up.**

"Who wants to take the wheel?" Captain Hargbol yells. By the end of the boat ride, nearly every child has taken the helm and played out the fantasy of "sea captain." This one-and-a-half-hour cruise, departing from Sunapee Harbor, takes you around the lake, past beaches, lighthouses, and summer homes. Captain Hargbol gives a lively narration on history, points of interest, and lore. It's a relaxing way to see this crystal clear mountain lake.

● Mount Sunapee Chairlift Ride

Rte. 3, Mt. Sunapee; (603) 763-2356. Late-June–mid-Sept., daily, 11–6. also open Memorial Day weekend and first two weekends in Sept. Adults, $5.50; 6–12, $2.50. **Ages 3 and up.**

A triple chairlift will whisk you to the summit of Mount Sunapee, where you'll be rewarded with panoramic views of the surrounding mountains and lakes. There are plenty of hiking trails and lots of perfect spots for a picnic.

● Ruggles Mine

On Isingglass Mountain (off Rte. 4), Grafton; (603) 448-6911. Mid-May–mid-June, weekends, 9–5; late-June–Aug., daily 9–6; Labor Day–mid-Oct., weekends, 9–5. Adults, $12; 4–11, $5. **Ages 2–14.**

Hammer and pound and chisel away as you look for precious stones. Prospecting in Ruggles Mine is a real adventure, no matter what your age. The mine is big, full of caves and tunnels, high ledges, and water pools. You're allowed to pick away at the walls and take whatever you extract.

The kids are sure to leave with a heavy load of "precious" souvenirs. In fact, more than 150 types of minerals have been found in the cave. You can rent hammers, chisels, picks, flashlights, and carrying sacks, or bring your own. Consider packing a lunch; the scenic view of mountains and valleys makes this a nice setting.

● Fort No. 4

Rte. 11, Charlestown; (603) 826-5700. Late-May–Columbus Day, daily (closed Tues.), 10–4. Adults, $6; 6–11, $4. **Ages 3–14.**

This living history museum is a reproduction of the original fortified settlement at No. 4, Charlestown, New Hampshire, during the French-Indian War era. The 20-acre site on the Connecticut River includes a stockade surrounding 14 buildings: a watch tower you can climb into, plus a blacksmith shop, cabins, and barns. As you walk through the village, you'll meet costumed guides demonstrating a variety of early crafts, such as musketball molding and candle dipping.

● Shaker Village

Shaker Rd., Canterbury; (603) 783-9511. May–Oct., daily, 10–5. Adults, $8.50; 6–15, $4. **Ages 5–15.**

Walking through this historic communal village, you'll get a glimpse of what life was like for the Canterbury Shakers. Watch artisans make a broom, spin yarn, or weave a rug in the self-sufficient tradition of Shaker life. Skilled craftspeople use other traditional Shaker skills to make baskets, tinware, herbal sachets, and ladderback chairs. There are six buildings on the spacious grounds, and walking tours are given, interpreting 200 years of Shaker history.

● Mount Kearsage Indian Museum

Exit 8N off I-89, Warner; (603) 456-2600. May–Oct., Mon.–Sat., 10–5; Sun., 12–5. Nov.–Dec., Sat., 10–5; Sun., 12–5. Adults, $6; 6–12, $4; 5 and under, free. **Ages 3 and up.**

Indian lore comes alive at this interesting New England museum. Walk along the paths in Medicine Woods, where you'll learn about medicinal plants and how they were used by the Indians. Imagine yourself living the life of an Eastern Woodlands Indian as you sit in the teepees. Or, put on one of the wolf robes, the kind the Indians used to wear on their buffalo hunts. The museum displays artifacts and exhibits covering the lives and lore of the Eastern Woodlands, Southwest, and Plains Indians. A great place for kids and adults alike.

● Barn Playhouse
Main St., New London; (603) 526-4631. July–Aug. **Ages 5–12.**

The summer stock theater in New London is a great way to introduce your family to the stage. The theater extends a warm welcome to children. Catch the magical Monday series throughout July and August. All programs are held in a refurbished barn. Call ahead for program information and schedule.

● Gould Hill Orchards
Gould Hill Rd. (off Rte. 103), Hopkinton Village; (603) 746-3811. Aug.–May, daily, 9–5. **All ages.**

If you're in the Sunapee area in the fall (and what a nice place to be), take a side trip to the Gould Hill Orchards for apple picking and fresh cider. The farm's scenic mountain setting is a good place to view fall foliage.

● Winslow State Park
Exit 10 off I-89, toward Wilmot; (603) 526-6168. **All ages.**

Take the auto road from the park entrance up to Mount Kearsage (2,937 feet), and you'll find a peaceful picnic area with a great mountain view. From here you can take a short hiking trail to the summit. This is an extra special spot at twilight, when the sunset is likely to be wonderful.

● Wadleigh State Park
Sutton; (603) 927-4727. **All ages.**

The 52-acre beach and picnic area on the south shore of Kezar Lake makes this park a special spot for families. It's rarely crowded.

● Pillsbury State Park
Rte. 31, Washington; (603) 863-2860. **All ages.**

This 5,000-acre hideaway is a great place for fishing, hiking, and camping. There are nine picturesque woodland ponds and several hiking trails in the park. Walk to Balance Rock, a large glacial erratic in such a teetering position that it's said one can actually move it by hand.

● Cross-Country Skiing
Young and old, big or little, novice or expert, if you're thinking of cross-country skiing, you'll find what you're looking for in the Sunapee area. Head for **Norsk Touring Center,** on Route 11 in New London, (603) 526-4685. It has 17 trails in a pretty location, and lots of amenities

on site: lodging, restaurant, and ski shop. **The Eastman Cross-Country Center** in Grantham, (603) 863-6772, offers plenty of novice terrain on 40 kilometers of trails.

● Mount Sunapee Ski Area

Rte. 103; Mt. Sunapee; (603) 763-5626. Lift tickets: adults, $28; 7–12, $19; 6 and under, free. SKIwee, 3–9, $55/day. Mountain Explorers, 9–11, $45 for two sessions, $35 for one session. Daycare, $25/day. Rates listed are for weekends and holidays; special rates and packages are available. **All ages.**

This small, friendly area has lots of relaxed, uncrowded skiing to offer, with 38 trails, serviced by seven lifts. If you're looking for a place away from the crowds, consider Mount Sunapee Ski Area. This is a great place to learn—or to perfect your skills. The majority of the trails are for intermediate skiers, with a special area for beginners and handful of black diamond runs. The pace is relaxed; the scenery inspiring.

● Pat's Peak

Rte. 114, Henniker; (603) 428-3245. Lift tickets: adults, $35, night skiing, $19; 14 and under, $26, night skiing, $15; 5 and under, free; child care (6–18 mos.), $30/day. **All ages.**

For 30 years families have been going to southern New Hampshire's Pat's Peak ski area. The modest area has 19 trails and seven lifts and is a local favorite with families and school groups. On selected evenings, Pat's offers night skiing; be prepared to share the trails with lots of hot-dogging teens.

This is a great place to get started. Most of the terrain is gentle and three isolated areas are just for beginners. It's also a great place to have fun, and keep costs down. Look for specials offered throughout the season. Pat's Peak hosts a number of family events, including an early-season free learn-to-ski week, family day, and a number of other themed celebrations.

 RESTAURANTS

● Peter Christian's Tavern

186 Main St., New London; (603) 526-4042. Daily, 11–10.

This 19th-century tavern-style eatery serves up hearty soups and stews and hefty sandwiches. Its relaxed, casual atmosphere is a favorite with families. There are lots of menu options, from full dinners to lighter soup-and-sandwich fare.

Lincoln and Franconia Area

This picturesque mountain area on the western flanks of the White Mountain National Forest is a pine-scented, four-season playground. Summer is the most popular season, when the valleys are full of flowers and the streams run with cool, clear mountain water. Each summer, thousands come to see the natural beauty of the White Mountains, to visit the Franconia Notch State Park gorges, flumes, and waterfalls, and to drive the scenic Kancamagus Highway, lined with mountain and valley vistas. Outdoor activities abound—take a hike to tumbling falls, swim in pristine mountain lakes and pools, canoe or kayak the Swift River, or take an aerial ride to the 4,200-foot summit of Cannon Mountain. The children can explore caves, zip down waterslides and roller coasters, visit haunted houses and petting zoos, and learn about nature, music, and history at a variety of local museums. In the winter months, there are sleigh rides, ski runs, and rinks and ponds perfect for skating.

● Lost River Reservation

Rte. 112, North Wooodstock; (603) 745-8031. Mid-May–Oct., weather permitting; May, June, Sept., Oct., 9–5; July–Aug., 9–6. Adults, $8; 6–12, $4.50. **Ages 2–14.**

Your children will be dirty, tired, and happy when you leave this place. You'll become explorers and navigators as you climb your way up and down ladders, belly-slide under rock ledges, and slither through caves. You can also take the easy way around—on the boardwalk—and simply enjoy the scenery. (But really, what fun is that?) The three-quarter-of-a-mile trip will take about an hour as you follow the river as it appears and disappears through giant glacier boulders. You'll learn about the geological and ecological history of the river along the way. Be sure to wear comfortable shoes and outdoor clothing. A snack bar and picnic area are on the grounds.

● Clark's Trading Post

Rte. 3, Lincoln; (603) 745-8913. Late-May–mid-June and Labor Day–mid-Oct., weekends, 10–6; late June–Labor Day, daily, 10–6. Admission, $7; 3–5, $2. **All ages.**

From an adult's point of view, Clark's Trading Post is a hodgepodge of amusements, including the performance of a family of trained black bears. But the kids will skip along in amused bliss, laughing at the slanted floors in Tuttle's Haunted House and the flying pianos in Merlin's Mystical Mansion. They will enjoy the antics of "Wolfman," who jeers at them as they ride aboard the White Mountain Central Railroad.

● The Whale's Tale Water Park

Rte. 3, Lincoln; (603) 745-8810. Early-June, weekends only, 11–5; mid-June–Labor Day, daily, 10–6. Admission, $16.50; under 36", $4.
Ages 5 and up.

Brave souls can zip down the Blue Lightning Speed Slide or the Serpentine Flume Slide. Or, try the 360-degree Beluga Boggin' Tube Ride. For a more relaxing pace, you can soak in the giant wave pool or unwind on the Lazy River. Young children have a special pool set aside for them. A fun place on a hot day.

● Hobo Railroad

Rte. 3, Lincoln; (603) 745-2135. Memorial Day–Halloween. Trains leave at 11, 1, 3, 5, and 7 in summer; as needed in spring and fall. Adults, $7.50; 6–11, $4.50. **Ages 2 and up.**

For outstanding mountain views (and a fun way to have lunch), consider taking the 14-mile trip along the Pemigewasset River aboard the Hobo Picnic Train. Your picnic lunch comes packed hobo-style— wrapped in a bandana and tied to the end of a stick. (If you can't make lunch, there are other rides throughout the day and evening.) Your children will probably not let you get away without a ride on Diamond Eddie's Ferris Wheel. This giant wheel takes you for a gentle 10-minute ride as you sit on benches in enclosed compartments.

● Loon Mountain Park and Skyride

Rte. 112 (Kancamagus Hwy.), Lincoln; (603) 745-8111. Memorial Day– mid-June, weekends; mid-June–foliage season (early Nov.), daily. Adults, $8; 6–16, $3. **Ages 2 and up.**

The beauty of the New Hampshire mountain ranges, forests, and lakes is spectacular from the mountain summits. In the Lincoln area, ride the Loon Mountain Gondola to the top of Loon Mountain, where you get a panoramic view of White Mountain peaks. The enclosed gondola ride takes about 10 minutes. On top, there's a four-story observation tower, cafeteria, and lots to explore: glacial caves, trails, and ongoing nature programs. At the base area, you'll find mountain bike and in-line skate rentals, horseback riding, archery, and a lodging and dining area.

● Franconia Notch State Park

Travel for eight miles through a spectacular mountain pass—the Franconia Notch Parkway—and through the 6,440-acre state park. The Notch Parkway is located between the high peaks of the Kinsman and Franconia mountain ranges. As you travel through the notch, from the Flume at the south end to Echo Lake at the north, you'll see wonderful vistas, waterfalls, mountain lakes, and natural attractions. Visit the Flume, then stop for a peek at the Basin. This beautiful waterfall has a granite pothole of 20 feet in diameter at its base. Below the Basin, look for the Old Man's Foot rock formation. Show the kids Boise Rock, where Thomas Boise, a teamster from Woodstock, New Hampshire, sought shelter during a blizzard in the early 1800s. Boise killed his horse, skinned it, and wrapped himself in the hide. Searchers cut away the frozen hide and found him alive.

Just north of Boise Rock, you'll see Profile Lake, headquarters of the Old Man's Washbowl. Look up; hovering above Profile Lake is the Old Man of the Mountains. This natural rock formation was formed nearly 200 million years ago. The Old Man is made of five separate granite ledges arranged to form a man's profile. At the northern side of the Notch Parkway, you'll find beautiful Echo Lake, the perfect spot to stop for a swim or picnic.

● Flume Gorge

Rte. 3, Franconia Notch; (603) 745-8391. Mid-May–Oct. (weather permitting), daily, 9–5. Adults, $6; 6–12, $3; under 6, free. **All ages.**

One of the most popular attractions in the area, this natural 800-foot chasm is a must-stop along the way. The rushing waters of the Pemigewasset River carved the wonder thousands of years ago, leaving walls that rise as high as 70 feet. If you don't mind sharing space with the inevitable summer crowds, you'll enjoy the cool, misty mountain air, and marvel at the surrounding natural beauty. Walk boardwalks and hiking trails across covered bridges to waterfalls, cascades, river basins, and pools.

● Cannon Aerial Tramway

Rte. 3, Franconia Notch; (603) 823-5563. Mid-May–July 4 and Labor Day–mid-Oct., daily, 9–4:30; July 4–Labor Day, daily, 9–7. Adults, $6; 6–12, $4; under 6, free. Summit cookouts, adults, $7; 12 and under, $5. **All ages.**

In Franconia Notch, the Cannon Aerial Tramway whisks you to the summit of 4,200-foot Cannon Mountain; on a clear day, you'll be able to see into Maine, Vermont, and Canada. The ride takes six minutes, but plan to spend some time at the top. Consider packing snacks or lunch (or buy something at the summit cafeteria) to enjoy along one of the summit trails. The Rim Trail is perfect for families. You'll be treated to some great mountain views, and you'll find plenty of picnic spots along the way. At the end of the trail is an observation deck for more viewing. It'll take about 20 minutes to walk, not counting time out for picnics and viewing. Summit cookouts are held July through Labor Day, Thursday through Sunday.

● New England Ski Museum

Base of Cannon Mtn., Franconia Notch; (603) 823-7177. Memorial Day–Columbus Day and Dec. 26–mid-Apr., daily (closed Wed.), noon–5. Free. **Ages 5 and up.**

Older children who have been bitten by the ski bug might enjoy a visit here. The exhibit that traces the evolution of ski equipment is particularly interesting. The museum also features changing ski-related exhibits and displays and archival film footage on video that outlines the history of New England skiing.

● Robert Frost Place

Ridge Rd., Franconia; (603) 823-5510. Memorial Day–Columbus Day, daily, 1–5 (closed Tues.). Adults, $3; 6–12, $1.50. **Ages 8 and up.**

The Frost farm homestead is an unpretentious, quiet tribute to the renowned poet. You'll find a small museum and an interpretive nature trail highlighting some of Frost's poems.

● Swimming

On hot days, head for **Echo Lake** (Route 3, Franconia Notch), a pristine, spring-fed lake at the base of Cannon Mountain. The white, sandy beach, cool mountain waters, and picturesque background make a hard-to-beat combination. There are changing and bathhouse facilities.

Travel the **Pemigewasset River** along Route 112 and you'll find a number of great swimming holes.

Other cooling-off spots include **Russell Pond,** in Woodstock, and **Franconia Notch State Park.**

● Horseback Riding

Horseback rides through meadows and forests, offering beautiful views of Mount Layfayette, Mount Moosilauke, and the Franconia Range, are available at the **Franconia Inn,** Route 116, Franconia, (603) 823-5542. You'll ride with a guide on trails through the 117-acre estate in the Easton Valley. Children must be at least 54 inches tall to reach the stirrups properly.

Trail riding is also available at **Loon Mountain Park,** Route 112, Lincoln, (603) 745-8111; and at **Waterville Valley Resort,** Route 49, Waterville, (603) 236-4666.

● Cross-Country Skiing

If you like to be on your own, skinny skiing through the countryside, check out the Echo Lake area. Cross-country skiing along Echo Lake is a visual treat. You'll see Cannon Mountain in the background and a glimpse of the Old Man of the Mountains. Or, there are lots of cross-country opportunities in Franconia Notch State Park, where you can follow the bike paths.

The Loon Mountain Cross Country Center, on Kancamagus Highway in Lincoln, (603) 745-8111, maintains more than 30 kilometers of groomed trails that run along the Pemigewasset River and traverse the mountains. There are lots of gentle trails for beginners and children. Information on trails, lessons, and rentals is available at the headquarters in the base lodge at Loon. There's also a skating rink and skate rentals available.

Waterville Valley, on Route 49, (603) 236-4666, selected as one of the top cross-country ski resorts in North America, offers a vast trail network laid out over 7,000 scenic acres. There's a variety of terrain; 70 kilometers of trails are groomed, 35 kilometers provide wilderness ski access. At the **Cross Country Ski Center** in Town Square, you'll find services and amenities, including refreshments, ski rentals, lessons, and special programs and activities.

Other cross-country ski opportunities can be found at the **Franconia Ski Touring Center,** (603) 823-5542, which offers 50 kilometers of groomed trails.

● Waterville Valley Ski Area

Rte. 49 (Waterville Valley Access Rd.); (603) 236-8311. Lift tickets: adults, $44; 13–18, $40; 12 and under, $30. SKIwee, $60/day. Rates listed are for weekends and holidays; discounts and special packages are available. **All ages.**

Waterville knows how to treat families. Come for the day and ski the 53 trails serviced by 13 lifts. But it won't be enough—to get the best out of Waterville you'll have to stay overnight to browse the Town Square, ice skate in the indoor arena, soak in a hot tub, or enjoy the twilight sleigh ride. Despite its amenities, this resort manages to retain a cozy, New England–village atmosphere.

Waterville Valley offers a professionally run nursery for infants six weeks and up, located at the ski area. If your children are old enough—that's three years and up at Waterville—enroll them in one of the children's learn-to-ski programs. "We believe in the all-smiles, no-tears approach to learning," says Joseph Jung, director of the Waterville Valley Ski School. Kids have their own small ski area and kinderlift.

In recent years, Waterville has gained a well-earned reputation as one of the best places for snowboarders in the East. On Mt. Tecumseh, the Boneyard Snowboard Park is for experienced riders featuring gaps, table tops, kickers, and railsides. (If you have to ask, don't go there.) Across the street is Snow's Mountain, a 2,050-foot peak for snowboarders only. Features include steep pitches and a half-pipe. Riders have their own base lodge at Snow's Mountain. If you have riders in your family, they're going to love it here.

Remember, this resort gets crowded on the weekends. Your best bet? Play hookey and head up midweek.

● Loon Mountain Ski Area

Kancamagus Hwy., Lincoln; (603) 745-8111. Lift tickets: adults, $45; 13–21, $40; 6–12, $28. P.K. Boo Bear (3–4), $60/day; Kinderbear (5–6), $65/day. Adventure Camp (7–12), $75/day; Teen Mountain Adventure (13–16), $89/day. Rates listed are for weekends and holidays; discounts and special packages are available. **All ages.**

Loon is a popular Northeast ski resort, offering 41 trails for skiers of every level. Loon's trails ski long. Even a beginner can ride to the top of the mountain and take a gradual, easy run down to the base. That's what makes it so appealing to intermediate and beginner skiers.

Don't plan on having the place to yourself—it gets crowded. Some tips to get more skiing for your dollars include getting your lift ticket the night before, getting to the mountain early, avoiding the gondola during peak usage (from 10:30 to 11:30 and from 1 to 2:30), and heading to the less-crowded West Basin double chairs.

● Cannon

Franconia Notch State Park, Franconia; (603) 823-5563. Lift tickets: adults, $37; 12 and under, $27. SKIwee, 4–9, $55/day; day care (min. age 1 yr.), $30/day; infant care, $5/hr. **All ages.**

Cannon has thousands of ardent followers and loyal return skiers. It's earned a reputation as a "skier's mountain," and you won't find a lot of frills and developments. Predominately known for its challenging ski runs and its ungroomed, off-trail skiing in heavy snow seasons, Cannon also offers some of the best views in the East.

Cannon has made several changes in recent years to lure families. The small, manageable area now has Peabody Slopes, offering a variety of intermediate and beginner trails. You'll find 31 trails in all, serviced by six lifts. If it's a windy, cold day, best to stay away. But, if the sun is shining in the White Mountains, head straight for Cannon, hop the chair to the 4,200-foot summit, and enjoy the view of surrounding mountains and forests, and the glistening Echo Lake, below. Then, cruise down.

RESTAURANTS

● Jigger Johnson's

On the Green, Plymouth; (603) 536-4FUN. Mon.–Sat., 11–10; Sun., 4–10.

Named after the New Hampshire folk hero and logger Jigger Johnson, this place works hard at not taking itself too seriously. Full of memorabilia and bad jokes, posters and souvenirs, it's casual, fun, and the food is suprisingly good. There's a big menu—pizza, burgers, nachos, sandwiches, salads, and a full section of dinner entrées. Kids have their own menu, and the chocolate milk comes with cherries.

● The Common Man

Main St., Ashland; (603) 968-7030. Lunch, Tues.–Sat., 11:30–2; dinner, daily, 5:30–9.

Rustic charm abounds in this restaurant. The old mixes with the new and you'll get a feast for your eyes as well as your palate. Neon clocks mix with lobster traps, Shaker baskets, and white tablecloths. Upstairs, you'll find a relaxing lounge with comfy chairs, books, board games, and puzzles. The place to go if there's a wait for a table. Or, elect to eat in the lounge, where young toddlers may feel more comfortable. The food is good old American fare—steaks, baked potatoes, salad. There's a handful of nicely prepared fish and poultry dishes, too.

Conway and Jackson Area

If your family has a love of the great outdoors, you'll revel in the natural beauty and abundance of activities at the pretty village of Jackson. This is the home of the Appalachian Mountain Club and center for hiking, mountain climbing, and cross-country skiing. The beauty of the area is best seen on a hike into the White Mountain National Forest, a picnic on the shores of a mountain lake, or a horse-drawn sleigh ride through a covered bridge and past a white-steeple church in the village center. There's fishing, swimming, hiking, canoeing, rafting, kayaking, golf, tennis . . . and more, more, more. Come winter, there's some of the best cross-country and downhill skiing in New England.

Drive a few miles south to North Conway, however, and you're in a different world of factory outlets, discount shopping, outdoor gear shops, boutiques, restaurants, minigolf, inns, hotels . . . and traffic. The end-of-day and Sunday afternoon bottlenecks are legendary.

Amid the surrounding natural beauty of the area, you'll find an abundance of commercial attractions to delight children. Your family can visit Cinderella at her castle, ride a gondola to the top of a mountain, and zip down it on a waterslide. It's a wonderfully diverse and popular area for family vacationing.

● Heritage New Hampshire

Rte. 16, Glen; (603) 383-9776. Mid-May–mid-June and Sept.–late-Oct., daily 9–5; mid-June–Labor Day, daily, 9–6. Adults, $10; 6–12, $4.50; under 6, free. **Ages 6–14.**

This museum puts you in the middle of history-in-the-making as you journey through time, from 1634 to the 20th century. You'll be carried across the ocean aboard the ship *Reliance*. From there you'll walk through history, as special effects and audiovisual techniques do a good job of putting you right in the middle of the action. Not quite Disney World, but you'll learn about early American history.

● Story Land

Rte. 16, Glen; (603) 383-4293. Early-June–Labor Day, daily, 9–6; Labor Day–Columbus Day, weekends only. Admission, $16; 3 and under, free. **Ages 1–10.**

Look, it's Cinderella and Little Bo Peep with her sheep. Youngsters will squeal with delight as they meet their favorite storybook characters. Take a ride on a pirate's ship, set sail on a swan boat, or travel around the track in a miniature Model T. You can also take a voyage to the moon or a rolling journey on the Polar Coaster. Cool off on Bamboo Chutes, a water flume ride. There are other amusement rides, a castle, live animals, and daily shows. A mixed bag of amusements, best enjoyed by little ones.

● Attitash Bear Peak and Fields of Attitash

Rte. 302, Bartlett; (603) 374-2368. Late-May–early June, weekends, 10–5; mid-June–Aug., daily, 10–6; Sept.–Columbus Day, weekends, 10–5. Single ride, $7; all-day, $17; under 4, free. **All ages.**

You can't beat this place for easy summer fun on the mountain; it has something for everyone. Take a scenic chairlift ride to the White

Mountain Observation Tower for a spectacular panaromic view of surrounding mountains and valleys. Too slow a pace for your family? No problem—zip down on a waterslide. Or, rent mountain bikes and follow the network of trails. At the Fields of Attitash, guided horseback rides along the scenic Saco River are offered. Special events are held throughout the summer.

● Conway Scenic Railroad

Valley train: mid-Apr.–mid-May and Nov.–mid-Dec., weekends; mid-May–late-Oct., daily. Notch train: late-June–early-Sept., Tues.–Sat.; mid-Sept.–mid-Oct., daily. Adults, from $8; 4–12, from $5.50; under 4, free. **Ages 5 and up.**

Hop aboard for a relaxing, nostalgic ride through the New Hampshire countryside. A variety of trips are offered. The Valley Train offers roundtrip rides to Conway and Bartlett, and the Notch Train travels through pretty Crawford Notch. On both, you'll see wonderful mountainside scenery. For a special treat, book the Pullman Parlor Car or a seat in the dining car "Chocorua," on the Valley Train. The Notch Train offers coach and first-class seating.

● Community Center Playground

Main St., North Conway. **Ages 1–10.**

This is where all the kids hang out. The outdoor playground is full of monkey bars, tunnels, slides, swings, and jungle gyms, and it's right next to the Conway Railroad Station in the center of North Conway Village. You can't miss it; just follow the sounds of children at play.

● Eastern Slope Playhouse

Main St., North Conway; (603) 356-5776. Tues.–Sat., 8. **Ages 10 and up.**

For a special evening, consider attending a performance of the Mount Washington Valley Theater Company, held throughout the summer at the Eastern Slope Playhouse. The renowned summer theater performs first-rate productions of Broadway musicals. A nice, upbeat, toe-tapping night out with older children. Call starting mid-June for schedule, reservations, and ticket prices.

● Arts Jubilee

Box 647, North Conway; (603) 356-9393. Performances held at Settler Green, intersection of Rtes. 16 and 302, North Conway. **All ages.**

You're likely to see anything under the Arts Jubilee tent in North Conway: magicians, dragons, and acrobats; folk dancing and ballet;

barbershop quartets, jazz reviews, classical orchestras, knee-slapping country music, and bagpipes. This ongoing arts festival is well known for its weekly summer family entertainment series (monthly events are held the rest of the year) and free evening concerts. Call for a schedule of events.

● Wildcat Mountain Gondola

Rte. 16, Jackson; (603) 466-3326. Mid-May–July 4, weekends, 10–4; July 4–Columbus Day, daily, 10–4. Adults, $8; 6–12, $4. **All ages.**

Enjoy the views atop the 4,100-foot summit at Wildcat Mountain without having to walk up or to ski down it. Take a 25-minute (roundtrip) sky ride to enjoy the fabulous views of the White Mountain National Forest and beyond. A great place for a picnic, if you have the time. Picnic areas, snacks, and nature trails are at the summit.

● Echo Lake State Park

Rte. 302 (just off Rte. 16), North Conway; (603) 356-2672. June–Labor Day. **All ages.**

This small park is the perfect spot to stop for a refreshing swim or a relaxing day outing. The clear, spring-fed lake has a good swimming area for children. There are trails to take you around the lake and to ledges above, depending on your time and inclination. There are picnic tables, grills, and boats for rent. This is a very popular summer spot.

● Swimming

There are plenty of places to pull off the road for a refreshing dip in the pristine mountain rivers and falls. On hot summer days, you'll see lots of people sunning on the rocks and swimming in the clear waters of the **Saco and Swift Rivers,** accessed from the Kancamagus Highway and Route 302. If you want to avoid the crowds, prowl around a bit. You'll find many good swimming holes a bit off the highway that are easily accessible. Tip: Ask a friendly local about his or her favorite spot.

● Canoeing

Rte. 302, Center Conway; (603) 447-2177. Also Main St., North Conway; (603) 447-3801. **Ages 5 and up.**

The Saco River is well known for its excellent canoeing. You don't need experience. Stop by the Saco Bound offices in North Conway, where you'll get all the equipment and instruction you need to go for a few hours or a day (or more) of it. The scenery is wonderful, the waters are calm (in spots) and shallow, and you'll find lots of great places along the way to stop for a picnic and swim. In the spring, when the waters are swifter, you might consider an exhilerating kayaking or white-water trip (for more experienced paddlers and older children).

Be sure to plan several weeks ahead for weekend rentals; the river gets crowded and rentals scarce. Write Saco Bound for a free brochure, at Box 119, Center Conway, NH 03813.

● Gold Panning

The locals swear there's gold in them thar rivers—the Saco and the Swift, that is. But, the rangers are quick to add that while many have found gold, no one's struck it rich yet. Pack a couple of shallow pans and try your luck. It's a fun way to spend a few hours on the river. And, who knows?

● Horse Logic Hay and Sleigh Rides

Rte. 116, Jackson; (603) 383-9876. **All ages.**

There's something special for kids and grown-ups alike about a sleigh ride through freshly fallen snow around a picturesque New England village. Relax in a wagon or sleigh pulled by horses as they prance around Jackson Village. Take the kids (of course, they'll love it), or get a baby-sitter and reserve it for a quiet, romantic night out.

● Hiking

Many who come to this area find they want to go farther into the woods and mountains. To really appreciate this part of New England, you have to get off the roads.

Your first stop should be a visit to the Pinkham Notch Camp at the base of Mount Washington. This is the hub of White Mountain hiking activity, and it serves as the northern New England headquarters for the Appalachian Mountain Club. Everyone is welcome to use its facilities and services. The AMC is a nonprofit organization offering a variety of recreation and conservation activities, including guided expeditions, research, backcountry management, trail and shelter construction and maintenance, mountain search and rescue, book publishing, and outdoor recreation.

At Pinkham Notch you'll see mountain climbers and backpackers, downhill and cross-country skiers—novices and experts—all gathering about, planning the day's activities. You'll want to talk to the people on staff for updated information on trail conditions and recommendations for families, and to pick up trail maps.

There are literally hundreds of hiking trails in the White Mountain area, and many are appropriate for the inexperienced hiking family. (Most, however, do not accommodate wheelchairs or strollers; put baby in a backpack.) Here's a selection of family-friendly hikes in the area:

Glen Ellis Falls. Off Route 16 (.8 mile south of the Pinkham Notch Camp), this trail is an easy walk to Glen Ellis Falls. The trail passes under the highway through a tunnel and reaches the falls in .3 miles. The main fall is 70 feet high, with many pools and smaller falls below.

Winneweta Falls. This trail leaves Route 16 three miles north of Jackson. You'll cross the Ellis River (watch out in the spring when the water is high) and follow the Miles Brook until you get to Winneweta Falls. A refreshingly wet, hot-day hike, this is about one mile long and takes about 40 minutes.

Mountain Pond Trail. This trail begins .6 mile up the road that leaves Maine Highway 113 at a spot .2 mile north of the Congregational Church in Chatham. You'll walk through a birch and fir forest to the pristine Mountain Pond. From here, take the northerly route around the pond and head back (stop first for a dip in the pond or a picnic along its shores). If you continue south past the AMC cabin, you'll be in for a much longer hike, about three hours. Otherwise, it's a short, easy hike to the pond and back.

Sawyer Pond Trail. This trail leaves the Kancamagus Highway two miles east of the Sabbaday Falls Picnic Area. You'll head north and cross the Swift River, pass between Coreens Cliff and Owls Cliff, and cross Sawyer Brook. The walk takes you through the woods (bring bug repellent!). Just about the time you've had enough of walking, Sawyer Pond will come into view. The pond is clear and inviting—a great place for a swim after your hike. You can continue on the trail and end up on Sawyer Pond Road (AMC runs a shuttle service; arrange for it before you start out.) A less complicated option is to head back the way you came. This will take about two-and-a-half hours on an easy 4- to 5-mile trail.

Sabbaday Falls Trail. This is a pleasant, easy walk to a picturesque series of cascades. The trail begins off the Kancamagus Highway (about 15 miles west of Route 16) and has a number of descriptive signs along the way pointing out wildlife and rock formations. It'll take about a half hour to go the .4 mile.

Black Cap Mountain. Drive to the top of Hurricane Mountain Road. There's an easy hike from here to Black Cap Mountain, where you'll be rewarded with great views of the national forest, mountain peaks, and

Maine to your east. Watch for migrating hawks often spotted here. The 1.2-mile trail will take about an hour.

● Ice Skating

There are three rinks open to the public in this area. Watch for signs in Conway Village, Jackson Village, and North Conway Village.

● Cross-Country Skiing

The Jackson, New Hampshire, area has been rated as one of the four best places in the world for cross-country skiing. The **Jackson Ski Touring Foundation,** (603) 383-9355, maintains more than 90 miles of trails throughout the area, beginning in the village of Jackson and running into the White Mountain National Forest. The trails are well maintained and marked for all abilities.

Many of the trails of the **Appalachian Mountain Club,** Pinkham Notch, (603) 466-2727, are open to cross-country skiers who love natural snow. Ask for trail descriptions and recommendations at the center.

The **Intervale Nordic Center,** North Conway, (603) 356-5541, offers lessons and ski rentals plus 40 kilometers of scenic trails. There's a pleasant dining area on the grounds.

You'll notice a number of cross-country skiers and snowshoers right in the middle of Jackson as they traverse the town golf course.

● Mount Cranmore Ski Resort

Off Rte. 16, North Conway; (603) 356-5544. Lift tickets: adults, $39; night skiing, $34; 14 and under, $22, night skiiing, $18; 5 and under, free. SKIwee, $60/day; nursery, $40/day. **All ages.**

Conveniently located in North Conway, Mount Cranmore has old-time appeal, nothing too flashy or fancy. In fact, this is where skiing began nearly 60 years ago. Today, Cranmore is a big hit with families, where they enjoy easygoing and gentle skiing on 36 trails, serviced by six lifts. Snowboarders like Bad Dog Snowpark, and everyone seems to love the night skiing.

● Attitash Bear Peak Ski Resort

Rte. 302, Bartlett; (603) 374-2368. Lift tickets: adults, $44; 12 and under, $27; Perfect Kids (4–6) $40/half-day; Adventure Kids (7–12), $40/half-day; child care (6mos.–5yrs.), $40/day. **All ages.**

This is a nice intermediate area offering 45 trails, serviced by 10 lifts. Recent improvements have expanded snowmaking on the mountain and added the more challenging Bear Peak area. It can get crowded on the weekends but the area tries to avoid congestion by limiting lift ticket sales. Skiers and riders have more than 200 acres to explore, most of them on intermediate runs.

● Wildcat Mountain

Rte. 16, Jackson; (603) 466-3326. Lift tickets: adults, $39/day; 6–12, $23/day; SKIwee (4–12), $59/day; child care, $39/day. **All ages.**

Wildcat's 2,100-foot drop and its 4,100-foot elevation make it an exciting ski area for the more experienced skier. The trails here run steep and narrow. There are concessions to beginners: a handful of easier trails, lessons, and nursery and learn-to-ski programs. And intermediate skiers will have a blast. You'll find all the amenities of a top-notch ski resort— base lodges, child care, services, and a number of special programs and events.

● Black Mountain

Rte. 16B, Jackson; (603) 383-4490. Lift tickets: adults, $32; 18 and under, $20; 5 and under, free. Kid's ski school (3–12), $45/day; child care (6mos.–5yrs.), $32/day. **All ages.**

Billed as the "Great American Family Ski Place," Black Mountain offers gentle, sheltered slopes and a slow, relaxed atmosphere that are welcoming for family skiers. There are 30 trails, serviced by four lifts, and a snowboard park to entice riders. This is a great place to learn.

Tired of skiing? Black Mountain also has a lift-serviced snow tubing park offering day and night tubing during the weekends and holiday periods. Sleigh rides and dog sled rides are also offered. Great fun.

RESTAURANTS

● Elvio's

Main St., North Conway Village; (603) 356-3307. Sun.–Thurs.. 11–9; Fri.–Sat., 11–11.

If you're in the mood for pizza (and when is your child not in the mood for pizza?), head to Elvio's. Locals argue that it's the best pizza in the world. You decide. Three different types are offered: the regular, round, thin-crust pizza baked in a stone deck oven; the rectangular, thick-crust, Sicilian pan-cooked pizza; and white pizza, a round-pie made with white cheeses, olive oil, garlic, and spices. Dine in or take out.

● Merlino's Steakhouse

Rte. 16, North Conway; (603) 356-6006. Daily, 11–9:30.

You can't miss the giant cow grazing atop the Merlino's Steak House sign on busy Route 16. This restaurant has been a mainstay on the North Conway dining scene for years. Pleasant atmosphere, serving the standard fare of steak, salad, and potatoes. Prime rib is their specialty. Children's portions are available.

Mount Washington Area

Majestic Mount Washington, the highest peak in the Northeast, looks down upon an area rich in natural beauty and abundant with family-friendly activities. The Presidential Range, a string of mountain peaks named after U.S. presidents, and the surrounding national forest offer miles of fine hiking trails, cascades, waterfalls, and mountain lakes. Chug along in a steam-powered railroad car, or take the slow, climbing auto road to the top of Mount Washington. The view, of mountain peaks and valleys below, is breathtaking.

Families who ski will enjoy the relaxing Bretton Woods ski area for cross-country and downhill skiing. Young children will enjoy a visit with Santa, and the entire family can get a taste of the Old West at Six Gun City in nearby Jefferson. Always, no matter what your day's agenda may be, you'll be surrounded by beautiful mountain scenery.

● Santa's Village
Rte. 2, Jefferson; (603) 586-4445. Mid-June–Labor Day, daily, 9:30–6:30; Labor Day–Columbus day, weekends, 9:30–5. Admission, $15; 3 and under, free. **Ages 1–8.**

Santa is never out of season with young children. If you can tolerate the "When is Christmas coming?" questions that will inevitably follow, stop in to see Santa and his elves. Besides a visit with the host of honor, children will enjoy splashing down the log flume, riding on the enchanted train, and circling on the old-fashioned carousel. There are music and bird shows, and Santa's Skyway Sleigh, a monorail ride that encompasses part of the park. Sure, it's a bit corny and touristy; but what else are you going to do with a two-year-old on a rainy day?

● Six Gun City
Rte. 2, Jefferson; (603) 586-4592. Late-May–early-June, weekends, 10–4:30; mid-June–Aug., daily, 9–6. Admission, $11.95; 3 and under, free. **Ages 1–10.**

This is a kid's fantasy come true—a visit to the Old West when cowboys ruled the land, sheriffs caught the bad guys, and horses were the mode of transportation. Children will love becoming deputies, helping the sheriff go after law-breaking outlaws, or taking a ride on a pony or burro. The live cowboy skits and Frontier Show are fun family-style entertainment. Throughout Six Gun City, you'll see more than 100 horse-drawn vehicles and many Old West antiques. And, there are plenty of rides, bumper boats, and a miniature golf course. Be sure to bring your bathing suit for a trip down the Tomohawk Run Waterslide.

● Mount Washington Auto Road

Rte. 16, Gorham; (603) 466-3988. Mid-May–late-Oct. (weather permitting), daily, 8–4:30. Car and driver, $15; each additional adult, $6; 5–12, $4. **All ages.**

This winding, steep, eight-mile toll road offers some of the most scenic views in the Northeast. The 45-minute trip to the summit—at 6,288 feet it's the highest in the Northeast—takes you through mountain forests until you reach the top, where on clear days views stretch across six states. Don't count on it being clear, though. It's usually not, and it's almost always windy and chilly. There's a weather station and observatory at the top, plus a cafeteria and small museum. If you prefer not to drive yourself, there are guided tour vans that will take you up, or you can catch a ride on the Cog Railway.

● Mount Washington Cog Railway

Rte. 302, Bartlett; (603) 278-5404. May–Oct. Adults, $39; 6–12, $26; five and under (on an adult's lap), free. **All ages.**

The mountain railway to the summit of Mount Washington is a lot like an old-fashioned wooden roller coaster ride. The steam-powered train, dating back to 1869, hits inclines that reach a 37 percent grade, making it the steepest railway in the world. It will chug, spit, and spew black smoke up the side of the mountain, threatening to give up each inch of the way. Get a window seat, and enjoy the mountain scenery. Be sure to dress warmly; the summit (where you'll find an observatory, cafeteria, displays, a small museum—and spectacular views!) is nearly always windy and cold.

● Hiking

Don't miss the chance to hike one of the many trails in the Mount Washington area; it's the best way to enjoy its natural beauty. Stop by one of the Appalachian Mountain Club camps or U.S. Ranger Stations for trails maps, recommendations, and up-to-date trail conditions. The following trails are short, easy hikes appropriate for families:

Jackson-Webster Trail. There are a few steep spots along the way, which makes this trail best for families with older children. The trail, marked in blue, leaves the east side of Route 302 just south of the Crawford Depot. (You'll see a side trail, Elephant's Head, veering to the right. Take this short side trip to the top of the ledge overlooking Crawford Notch for some fine views.) The main trail runs above Elephant Head Brook, crosses Little Mossy Brook, and rises, rather steeply, to Flume Cascade Brook. It's about 45 minutes and .9 mile to this point. Head back now, or continue on the Webster branch (to the right) to a beautiful cascade and pool. That'll be enough for most families.

Sylvan Way. This is a great trail for families, particularly in the fall when foliage is spectacular. Pick it up at the Link at Memorial Bridge on Route 2, .7 mile from the Appalachian parking area in Randolph. You'll pass falls and brooks on this easy 2.5-mile trip. It should take about an hour and a half.

● Jefferson Notch

A drive through Jefferson Notch is not recommended for the faint-hearted, but it's worth the effort. The narrow, steep road is one of the highest in New Hampshire, reaching almost 3,000 feet. From U.S. 2, three miles east of Jefferson Highlands, you'll turn south on the road heading from Labyan to the Mount Washington Cog Railway Station. You'll be rewarded with great mountain and valley panoramas, and a fine view of Jefferson Notch.

● Cross-Country Skiing

There are many natural, ungroomed trails in the **Appalachian Mountain Club** network open to cross-country skiers. Stop by the AMC headquarters in Pinkham Notch, (603) 356-5541, for information on conditions and for detailed trail maps.

Nordic skiers will also enjoy the well-maintained course at **Bretton Woods Ski Area,** Route 302, Bretton Woods, (603) 278-5000. The trails are generally old logging roads or rail beds that head through forests, over bridges, and down picturesque lanes. There are lots of nice views of Mount Washington, Crawford Notch, and the Ammonoosuc River along the way.

● Bretton Woods

Rte. 302, Bretton Woods; (603) 278-5000. Lift tickets: adults, $38; 6–15, $25; 5 and under, free. Kid's ski program, $45/day; child care (2 mos.–5yrs.), $30/day. **All ages.**

The slow and easy atmosphere and the wide-open beginning and intermediate terrain make Bretton Woods a favorite with families—or, for anyone looking for a relaxing ski getaway. You'll be skiing Mount Rosebrook, which has a 1,500-foot vertical drop mostly felt in long, cruising runs. There's not much of a challenge at this area for experienced skiers, but everyone will enjoy its views and happy-go-lucky ease. In recent years, Bretton has expanded its expert terrain (you'll find a couple of mogul-strewn, ungroomed trails), and added 25 wonderful acres of glade skiing.

The resort boasts lots of amenities: lessons, restaurants, nursery, special events and programs. Locals tell us the area gets twice as much snow as other resorts, a phenomenon they call the "Bretton Woods flurries."

RESTAURANTS

● Fabyans Station

Rte. 302 (next to the Cog Railway Road), Bretton Woods; (603) 846-2222. Daily, 11–9:30.

Housed in a restored railroad depot, this restaurant offers a selection of appetizers, salads, burgers, and sandwiches. Dinner entrées feature chicken, ribs, steak, pasta, and fish dishes. Ask for half-portions for children. Pleasant decor, reasonably priced, and tasty food.

● Darby's Restaurant

Rte. 302, Lodge at Bretton Woods; (603) 278-1500. Late-May–Columbus Day, daily, 7:30 A.M.–9 A.M. and 5:30 P.M.–9 P.M. Rest of the year, daily, 5–7 P.M.

This casual restaurant in the lodge at the Bretton Woods Resort offers great views of the Presidential Mountain Range. In winter, you'll be warmed by two fireplaces. The menu offers veal, chicken, steaks, and seafood. Make reservations for weekend dinners; it can get crowded.

Monadnock Region

White-steepled churches set in village centers, old-fashioned country stores, covered bridges, and rolling hills all set in quiet meandering valleys and farmlands welcome you to rural New Hampshire. You'll want to stroll the Main Street in the town of Peterborough, the model for Thornton Wilder's *Our Town*, or Main Street in Keene, the widest paved Main Street in the world. And if you like a parade, this is the place—the

Monadnock region may well hold the most parades per capita in the country. Stay more than a day or two in the summer, and you'll likely see one. This is small-town U.S.A.

The area surrounding Keene is classic New England countryside. You won't find neon lights, flashy hotels, or amusement parks. This is the place to come for lazy summer drives (be sure to drive Route 10 from Keene to West Swanzey, where you'll see six covered bridges along the way), hikes in the woods, swimming in the rivers, casting in lakes, and sleigh rides in the snow.

● Monadnock Children's Museum

147 Washington St., Keene; (603) 357-5161. Tues.–Fri., 10–5; Sat., 10–4; Sun., 1–4. June–mid-Aug. also open on Mon., 10–4. (Sometimes the museum closes for a couple of weeks in late Aug.; call for updates.) Admission, $3. **Ages 1–10.**

This hands-on children's museum is housed in a renovated 1850s colonial home that's chock-full of learning fun. There's a little bit of everything to please all interests and to help fulfill the insatiable curiosity of children. In the Crystal Room, budding scientists can perform tests to identify crystals. Children learn about other cultures in the World Room, and about sea life from the variety of fresh- and saltwater fish tanks. During the summer, there are special programs. Be sure to check out the treehouse filled with collections of objects that children have donated.

● Friendly Farm

Rte. 101, Dublin (a half-mile west of Dublin Lake); (603) 563-8444. May–Labor Day, daily, 10–5 (weather permitting); Labor Day–mid-Oct., weekends, 10–5. Adults, $4.75; 12 and under, $3.75. **Ages 1–10.**

Young children will enjoy a visit to this farm where they can pet and feed their favorite animals. At the hen house, you may see eggs hatching, and you can hold and cuddle baby chicks. Brilliantly plumed peacocks strut their stuff alongside a pen housing baby bunnies. Take a look at the observation beehive, too. You can bring a packed lunch to enjoy in the picnic area.

● New England Marionette Theatre

24-25 Main St., Peterborough; (603) 924-4022. **Ages 5 and up.**

If you can plan ahead, call about the wonderful marionette shows offered twice during the year for families (one during the Christmas holidays, another in late spring, March–April; call for details.) Billed as "an opera on a string," this unusual entertainment features two-foot-high puppets worked by a talented corps of puppeteers. The theater is located in a restored Baptist Church, with plush red velvet seats and fine acoustics. Throughout the year, the theater group puts on puppet shows to full-length operas, suitable only for adults.

● Mount Monadnock State Park
Rte. 124, Jaffrey; (603) 532-8623. **Ages 5 and up.**

Getting to the top of Mount Monadnock is a popular pursuit. First scaled by settlers in 1725, Grand Monadnock is the single most climbed mountain in North America! If you have the energy (sure you have!) for the two-mile trek up to the 3,165-foot summit, you'll be rewarded with lovely views of Boston to the east and Mount Washington to the north. It will take about three hours to complete the roundtrip hike (plus time for viewing and picnicking). If that sounds too ambitious for your group, there are more than 30 miles of other trails to choose from in the park. You'll also want to stop in the Ecocenter, where you'll find exhibits and programs on nature and ecology, as well as information on the various hikes.

● Ashuelot River Park
West St., Keene. **All ages.**

For a nice stroll along the river, you can't beat this pleasant town park. You can meander the trails, get in a good workout (look for the fitness markers along the way), sit in the gazebo, have a picnic, or simply admire the pretty plantings maintained by the Keene Garden Club.

● Sleigh Rides

Take a winter sleigh ride through snow-covered country lanes, rolling fields, and pine-scented forests. At **Silver Ranch,** Route 124E in Jaffrey, (603) 532-7363, you can ride in a covered carriage, or hop aboard a wagon for a fun-filled hayride. At **Stonewall Farm,** 243 Chesterfield Road, Keene, (603) 357-7278, you'll be pulled by Belgian draft horses through the fields of the 124-acre working farm.

● Greenfield State Park
Rte. 136, Greenfield; (603) 547-3497. **All ages.**

This is a nice family park of more than 350 acres along Otter Lake. The sandy beach is great for swimming, and children enjoy the small playground. If you'd like to do some rowing or fishing, you can rent small boats. The picnic area includes tables, grills, and a refreshment stand. There are also hiking trails in the park. Pack your trout-fishing gear and head for Hogback or Mud ponds; locals say the fishing is good.

● Cross-Country Skiing

Many of the trails in the **Greenfield State Park** (see entry above) and at **Pisgah State Park** (off Route 63 in Chesterfield or Route 119 in Hinsdale) are good for cross-country skiing. There are also a number of ski touring areas, including **B.U. Sargent Camp** and **Temple Mountain touring** in Peterborough, (603) 525-3311; **Tory Pines Resort** in Francestown, (603) 588-2000; **Inn at East Hill Farm** in Troy, (603) 242-6495; **Road's End Farm** in Chesterfield, (603) 363-4703; **Shattuck Inn Nordic Center** in Jaffrey, (603) 532-4300; **Windblown Ski Touring** in New Ipswich, (603) 878-2869; and **Woodbound Inn** in Jaffrey, (800) 688-7770.

RESTAURANTS

● Colony Mill Marketplace

222 West St., Keene; (603) 357-1240. Mon.–Sat., 10–9; Sun., 11–6.

Instead of opting for a fast-food lunch or dinner, consider stopping here, where your group can select anything from corn dogs to gourmet salads. Order from one of the take-out eateries, then find a table in the adjacent, sunny courtyard. Lots of great food. You'll also find the BrewPub and the Millyard Steakhouse, if you're in the mood for a sit-down feast.

● Nonie's Bakery and Luncheonette

Main St., Peterborough; (603) 924-3451. Mon.–Sat., 4 A.M.–2 P.M.

This is where the townies gather for a hearty breakfast or lunch, and all the local gossip. No one needs a menu—it's bacon and eggs, pancakes, and french toast; sandwiches and burgers for lunch. The blackboard announces daily specials, food like macaroni and cheese, or a long dog and slaw. Good prices, casual setting.

Maine

Southern Coast

If the word *Maine* conjures up visions of rocky shores, picturesque villages, and freshly caught lobsters, you won't be disappointed when you visit. Maine's southern coast is a favorite with vacationing families for those reasons and more. First, it's not difficult to get here. Many visitors to Boston are surprised to learn that Maine is only 55 miles away. Then there are the sandy beaches. That's right—sandy. Although there are 3,500 miles of shoreline in Maine, fewer than 100 miles are sandy beach. Southern Maine has a lot of them—long, silvery strands that stretch for miles. When it comes to swimming, some adults find the ice-cold North Atlantic waters a tad too brisk to be pleasurable. If you prefer being on the water to being in it, you'll find plenty of options, including a quintessentially Maine lobstering cruise on which you'll help pull up the traps.

Most families try to visit a museum or two while they're here, and rainy weather usually means a pilgrimage to family amusement centers and arcades along Route 1. A better remedy for less-than-sunny weather? Dress for it, then head outdoors so you won't miss the dramatic, foggy beauty that is Maine at its best.

● York's Wild Kingdom

Rte. 1, York Beach; (207) 363-4911. Zoo: Memorial Day–Columbus Day, daily, 10–5; adults, $9.75; 4–10, $9.50; 3 and under, $3.50. Amusement park: Memorial Day–Labor Day, daily, noon–6. Combination tickets (zoo and amusement park): adults, $12.75; 4–10, $9.50; 3 and under, $3.50.
All ages.

Kids have a terrific time at this combination zoo and amusement park, where they meet lions, tigers, monkeys, llamas, a zebra, and an elephant. There's also a petting area where children can feed the goats and deer. On the amusement side, there are 25 rides, including a Ferris wheel, a merry-go-round, bumper cars, the Octopus, and the Jaguar—the park's most popular ride.

● Old York Historical Tour

Lindsey Rd. (Off Rte. 1A), York; (207) 363-4974. Mid.-June–Sept., Tues.-Sat., 10–5. Admission for all buildings: adults, $6; 6–16, $2.50.
Ages 5 and up.

The Old York Historical Society offers guided tours of seven historic buildings, dating back to the days when York was a colonial village and seaport. You'll start at Jefferd's Tavern (1750), where you'll find period furnishings and a tap room. You're likely to see a demonstration of hearth cooking, basket weaving, or candlemaking during your visit.

Children enjoy touring the Old Gaol Museum, built in 1719 as the King's Prison for the Province of Maine and used as a prison until 1860. You can wander through the dungeons and cells that once housed criminals and debtors, and see the "gaoler's" living quarters. An exhibit room features the Museum of Colonial Relics, a turn-of-the-century display with old dolls, toys and unusual objects. Other sites on the tour include the Elizabeth Perkins House; the Emerson-Wilcox House; the George A. Marshall Store, a 19th-century general store; the John Hancock Warehouse; and the Old Schoolhouse, a one-room school built in 1745.

● Wiggly Bridge Footpath
Rte. 103, York Harbor. **All ages.**

For a lovely view of the York River that few tourists see, stroll the footpath that starts at Wiggly Bridge. Walk over the bridge, passing over an inlet to the York River, and follow the path along the river to Stedman Wood.

● Lobstering Cruise
Barnacle Bill's Dock, Perkins Cove, Ogunquit; (207) 646-5227. July– Labor Day, daily except Sun., every half-hour, 9–3:30. Call ahead for limited schedules in May–June and Sept.–Oct. Adults, $7.50; 4–11, $5.50. **Ages 3 and up.**

If you've ever wondered what it's like to trap lobsters for a living, this is your chance to find out. Take a 50-minute trip with Finestkind Cruises and learn how to bait lobster traps, read lobster buoy markings, and determine whether a lobster is a "chicken." Children are warmly welcomed.

● Sailing and Whalewatching Cruises

The best way to see the Maine coastline is to get out on the water. There are a number of cruises offered; most take off from Perkins Cove in Ogunquit. You're likely to spy humpback and finback whales, dolphins, seals, and porpoises on the half-day whalewatching cruises aboard the **Deborah Ann,** (207) 361-9501. Sail aboard the **Cricket** (207) 646-5227, a traditional wooden catboat for a 1¾-hour cruise of the Maine coast. Or, hop aboard the **Silver Lining** (207) 361-9800, a 42-foot Hinckley sloop, a classic wooden yacht.

● Marginal Way
Shore Rd., Ogunquit. **All ages.**

This 1¼-mile-long shoreline footpath is not to be missed. You'll see spectacular ocean views, tidal pools, wildflowers, rock formations, and, at high tide, waves crashing against the rocky shore. The benches that have been placed along the way are perfect when little feet need a rest. The footpath begins on Shore Road, near the center of Ogunquit, and continues to Perkins Cove.

● Bald Head Cliff
Shore Rd., Ogunquit. **All ages.**

Be sure to stop and take a look at this fascinating rock formation. Just south of Ogunquit, on Shore Road, you'll see the signs pointing out Bald Head Cliff. The cliff rises more than 100 feet from the edge of the Atlantic. Surrounded by stretches of sandy beach and rocky outcrops, the cliff is a striking spectacle.

● Sightseeing Tours

Lighthouses, ghost stories, shipwrecks . . . you'll hear lots of ghastly and goodly tales of land and sea on a number of special tours. Candlelit walking tours through historic York Village are given by a hooded tour guide. You'll hear the folklore of the 18th and 19th century as you stroll the historic streets. Call **Ghostly Tours,** Route 1A, York, (207) 363-000. **Seacoast Tours,** Perkins Cove, (207) 646-6326, conducts 2½-hour van tours that take you past witch's graves, forts, historic homes, and more. Lots of native gossip and lore.

● Wells Auto Museum
Rte. 1, Wells; (207) 646-9064. Mid-June–mid-Sept., daily, 10–5; open weekends only in May and Oct. (through Columbus Day), 10–5. Adults, $3.50; 6–12, $2. **All ages.**

More than 80 antique cars are on display here, some dating from the turn of the century, including gas, steam, and electric models. Kids will love taking a ride in a Model-T Ford. Arcade games and nickelodeons add to the fun.

● Wells National Estuarine Sanctuary
Off Rte. 1 (1.5 miles north of Well's Corner), Wells; (207) 646-1555. Daily, sunrise–sunset. **All ages.**

Budding birdwatchers can get their life list started. The sanctuary is also a good place to commune with nature while enjoying a picnic. This

1,600-acre site—mostly marshland—includes the Rachel Carson Wildlife Refuge and Laudholm Farm. The Sanctuary includes fields, woodlands, tidal rivers, salt marshes, dunes, and beaches, and offers a protected environment for wildlife. Marked nature trails lead through the woods and along the marsh.

● Cape Neddick Light
Off Rte. 1A. **All ages.**

Perhaps one of the most photographed lighthouses on the East Coast, the Nubble Light (as the locals call it) personifies the style of lighthouse for which Maine has become famous. Its white cast-iron tower, built in 1879, stands "atop the nubble," just off the shore, striking a beautiful pose against the rocky shoreline and blue waters of the Atlantic. Take Route 1A to Long Sands Beach; from the north end of the beach, a local road leads east to the tip of Cape Neddick and the lighthouse.

● Old Orchard Beach
Rte. 1, Old Orchard Beach. **All ages.**

Kids love the lively, carnival-like atmosphere of this seaside resort. One of the longest beaches on the Atlantic, Old Orchard Beach is lined with boardwalks full of fast food and fun. In fact, it's been called the Coney Island of Maine. The Atlantic waters here are shallow and warm, and the surrounding amusements are a hit with youngsters.

● Palace Playland
1 Old Orchard St., Old Orchard Beach; (207) 934-2001. Late-June–Labor Day, Mon.–Fri., noon–10; Sat.–Sun., 11–10. Memorial Day–late-June, weekends. **All ages.**

All a little heart desires for thrills are here: rides—big ones and little ones—and arcade games aplenty, an antique carousel, a waterslide, junk food, and more. Bet you can't pass by without going in.

● Seashore Trolley Museum
Log Cabin Rd. (off Rte. 1), Kennebunkport; (207) 967-2800. May–mid-Oct., daily, 10–5; mid-Oct.–mid-Nov., weekends, 10–5. Adults, $6; 6–16, $4. **Ages 3 and up.**

More than 200 antique trolley cars are housed here—the world's largest collection. You'll see a slide show and tour the cars on exhibit, but the real fun here is an old-fashioned trolley ride. You can hop aboard the authentically restored trolley cars from all over the world. All aboard!

● Ocean Drive

A ride along Ocean Drive to Cape Porpoise and Goose Rock Beach is a pleasant way to view Kennebunkport's coastline. Along the way, you'll see two unmarred natural wonders, too—Spouting Rock, a spectacular ocean fountain, and Blowing Cave, a rock formation where the waves roar in dramatically. Look closely so you don't miss them. When you reach Cape Porpoise, park the car and stroll around this quaint fishing village.

● Scarborough Marsh Nature Center

Rte. 9, Scarborough; (207) 883-5100. Mid-June–Labor Day, daily, 9:30–5:30. **All ages.**

Bring your bug spray and old sneakers—and a pair of binoculars. This 3,100-acre natural area contains a number of salt-marsh nature trails perfect for birdwatching and canoe routes through the inlets. The center offers guided nature walks, hands-on exhibits, and canoe tours. Canoe rental is available at the park. The park puts on lots of special naturalist programs for children throughout the summer.

● Smiling Hill Farm Barnyard

Rte. 22, Westbrook; (207) 775-4818 or (800) 743-7463. May–late-Sept., daily, 10–5. Adults, $5; 1–15, $3.50. **Ages 1–14.**

You might as well head directly to the ice cream barn upon arrival, and grab yourself a fresh, farm-made cup of ice cream. Now, everyone can relax and visit the rest of this working dairy farm. Meet the friendly barn animals in the petting area. More than 300 animals can be seen and touched at the farm, including some exotic farm animals from around the world. Plan to participate in a number of ongoing activities, like pony rides, horse-drawn hayrides, milk-a-cow, "Llead a Llama," or "Llunch with a Llama."

● Aquaboggin Water Park

Rte. 1, Saco; (207) 282-3112. Mid-June–Labor Day, daily, 10–7. Over 4 ft., $15.95; under 4 ft., $10.95. **Ages 5 and up.**

If your children love waterslides (and what kid doesn't?), this place is sure to please. Attractions include a wave pool, bumper boats, a swimming pool, and a go-cart race track. Gentler souls can tool around the pond on paddle boats.

● Funtown/Splashtown U.S.A.

Rte. 1, Saco; (207) 284-5139 or (800) 878-2900. May–Labor Day, daily, 10:30–10:30. (Call for limited hours in May and June.) Funtown:

adults, $18; 12 and under, $14 (height and weight restrictions on some rides). Splashtown: adults, $15; 10 and under, $12. **Ages 3 and up.**

Family fun is the name of the game here at Maine's largest theme amusement park. The Thunderfalls Log Flume is most popular, and is very tall and very wet. There's also a high-speed roller coaster, tilt-a-whirl, bumper cars, and kiddie rides galore. And what better to go with those tummy-twisting roller coasters than Mexican food, taffy, and cotton candy? Mellower folk will enjoy antique car rides. On a hot day, you'll enjoy Splashtown's waterslides, whirlpools, and tube run.

● Beaches

Maine's southern coast is dotted with several public beaches. Most are well marked; look for signs leading to beaches on the side roads off Route 1. Arrive early to snare a parking space. The best beaches for families with small children—offering gentler surf—are **Ferry Beach** in Saco, **Crescent Beach** in Cape Elizabeth, and **Long Sands Beach** in York Harbor. The surf can be lively at **Ogunquit** beaches, but toddlers can wade safely at a protected area near the mouth of the Ogunquit River.

¶ RESTAURANTS

● Mabel's Lobster Claw
Ocean Ave., Kennebunkport; (207) 967-2562. Daily, 11:30–9:30.

Known locally as Mabel's, this restaurant was featured in *Time* magazine for serving the best lobster rolls in the country. Adults can enjoy a glass of wine with their fresh seafood dinner, which might be the stuffed sole (a house specialty) or lobster prepared in one of several ways. Children can choose from the many sandwiches and fish items on the menu. Be sure to try the onion rings: "Fresh, not frozen," says Mabel. After dinner, the family can stroll next door to Mabel's ice cream shop for dessert.

● Bill Foster's Down East Lobster and Clambake
Rte. 1A, York Harbor; (207) 363-3255. Memorial Day–Labor Day, daily, noon–8. Reservations required.

Just what you'd expect: lobster, steamed clams, and all the trimmings. Steak and chicken are offered if you're not a crustacean fan (or if you've finally had your fill of 'em). Eat in the rough, then join in the old-fashioned sing-along. Little kids will love this; older children will, of course, be mortified, especially if you sing along.

Portland

Maine's largest city is an intriguing blend of old and new. Wander around the waterfront and you'll see fish-processing plants and warehouses just around the corner from specialty shops and fancy restaurants. Many stores and eateries are housed in renovated old warehouses, giving a quaint appeal to even the newest. This booming little city is rapidly becoming a cultural presence in New England, with museums, concerts, and festivals aplenty. After visiting Portland, you'll see why it keeps cropping up on those lists of "most livable" cities. The same factors make it a great place to visit.

● Children's Museum of Maine

142 Free St.; (207) 828-1234. Year-round, Wed.–Sat., 10–5; Sun., noon–5. Closed Mon.–Tues. Admission, $4. **Ages 1–10.**

"Please touch" is the operative slogan here. This terrific museum has so many things to do that your children will have the happy dilemma of deciding where to head first. Perhaps to the *Bubbles* exhibit, where kids can make a giant bubble screen? Or perhaps to the human skeleton, where kids can learn how "dem bones" really work? Children from one to 10 are certain to have a good time here, and you'll delight in watching them explore. Special activities and workshops are scheduled; contact the museum for details.

● Southworth Planetarium

96 Falmouth St., Science Bldg., University of Southern Maine; (207) 780-4249. Astronomy shows: Fri. and Sat., 7. Laser light concerts: Fri. and Sat., 8:30. Children's shows: Sat.–Sun. 3 P.M. Rates vary; call for schedule. **Ages 3 and up.**

Astronomy goes 20th-century tech at this planetarium. The sky dome theater is the perfect setting for high-tech light shows with full color motion and sound effects. Constellations and other objects currently visible in the sky are shown at the end of each show. There are also general astronomy shows—a good introduction to this dazzling science—and a special program for young children on Saturday afternoons. Call ahead for information and reservations.

● Maine Aquarium

Rte. 1 (Exit 5 off I-95), Portland; (207) 284-4512. Year-round, daily, 9–5. Adults, $6.50; 5–12, $4.50; 2–4, $2.50. **All ages.**

Giant octopuses, sharks, seals, and penguins all live here along with tidepool animals you can actually touch. The exhibits are fun as well as educational.

● Maine Rock Gym

127 Marginal Way; (207) 780-6370. June–Oct., Tues.–Fri., 2–10 P.M.;
Sat.–Sun., noon–6 P.M. Introductory package: adults, $20; 11 and under,
$10. **Ages 8 and up.**

Kids are natural climbers; why keep them on the ground? Let them
go at this first-rate climbing center. Holds are bolted on the climbing
wall, trained belayers and top-rope protection make it safe and easy to test
your skill and wits.

● Peak's Island

Don't miss the popular day excursion to this small island off the
coast from Portland. A 15-minute ferry boat ride will take you to the
720-acre island. When you hop off the ferry, head to the rental shops for
bikes—this is the best way to get around the island. The small community boasts only three restaurants, a gift shop, a market, and a library. But
you'll find a nice sandy beach near the ferry landing and lots of scenic
vistas and fresh salt air. Take a quick look in the Civil War Museum. It's
also possible to see where Longfellow's "Wreck of the Hesperus" was
inspired by the 1869 wreck of the *Helen Eliza* on the rocks off the island's
south shore. Peak's is the closest major island to Portland, and it can get
crowded in the summer.

● Two Lights State Park

Off Rte. 77, Cape Elizabeth; (207) 799-5871. **All ages.**

It's too cool for swimming but you want to stay outdoors? Head to
this state park to stroll the walkway, which offers great ocean views and
picnic sites along the way. It's located south of the city on the Cape
Elizabeth shore.

● Crescent Beach State Park

Rte. 77; (207) 767-3625. **All ages.**

A popular beach with Portland locals, Crescent has a 4,000-foot
sandy area. You'll find it south of Portland on the Cape Elizabeth shore.

● Portland Head Light

Just off Cape Elizabeth's Shore Road you'll find the Portland Head
Light, Maine's oldest lighthouse (built in 1791) and one of the most
frequently photographed. You'll enjoy the scenic coastal setting.

● Boat Cruises

The Atlantic Ocean beckons. Why not take a harbor tour, or cruise to
an island for a clambake? Or, if you want a real getaway, take the ferry to

Nova Scotia. A number of cruise companies offer a variety of options; you'll find them along Commercial Street in the Old Port section of Portland. Some possibilities: **Casco Bay Lines,** (207) 774-7871, and **Prince of Fundy Cruises, Ltd.,** (207) 775-5616.

 RESTAURANTS

● Village Cafe

110 Newbury; (207) 772-5320. Mon.–Thurs., 11–10; Fri.–Sat., 11–11; Sun., 11:30–8.

This local favorite is tucked away in a warehouse district just off the waterfront. It's worth looking for, especially if you're hankering after good, family-style Italian food. Children's portions are available.

● Cap'n Newick's Lobster House

740 Broadway; (207) 799-3090. Tues.–Thurs., 11:30–8; Fri.–Sun., 11:30–9.

This popular family restaurant offers delicious seafood at reasonable prices. The atmosphere is casual, so you don't have to worry if baby uses the drawn butter as a finger bowl or if junior discovers several unusual things to do with a used lobster leg.

● Ricetta's Pizzeria

29 Western Ave., So. Portland; (207) 775-7400. Mon.–Thurs., 11:30–10; Fri.–Sat., 11:30–11; Sun., noon–10.

Locals love the brick oven specialty pizzas served up here, voting it Maine's best in local magazines and surveys. Deciding what kind of pizza to order will be your biggest problem; there are lots of creative, delicious combinations, like "Melanzano Diavolo—the devil's eggplant, hot cherry peppers, pepperoni, and cheeses." Or, the "Futuro, wheat dough topped with tomato, spinach, roasted chicken, peppers, and cheeses." Or, create your own. There are also antipasti platters, salads, calzones, and a full menu of pasta entrées.

Mid-coast

You could spend a lifetime exploring the mid-coastal region of Maine and still you'd leave some hidden gem undiscovered. This area, running from Portland to Belfast, covers some of the prettiest spots in the country, characterized by quaint New England seaside villages, rocky coastlines juxtaposed against sandy beaches, idyllic peninsulas jutting out into the Atlantic, tidal rivers, classic Maine lighthouses, and more. And in each village you'll visit along the way, recreation and adventure abound.

You'll find outlet shopping in busy Freeport, home to the famous outdoor-goods company L.L. Bean, and also island hopping. Busy harbors have lots of choices for families who wish to try out their sea legs; just walk to any harbor and check out the offerings. You'll find charming, popular harbor villages, like Camden, Boothbay, and Rockport, with galleries, boutiques, and exquisite seaside dining, and others like Brunswick and Bath that are steeped in nautical history. There are numerous museums to visit, trails to hike, and trains to board, and lots of places to learn about the sea. There's even a scorching hot desert.

The downside of all this is the crowds. On a summer weekend, you'd better have a reservation for a bed and a meal waiting when you roll into town.

● Maine Audubon Society

Gilsland Farm (off Rte. 1), Falmouth; (207) 781-2330. Year-round, Mon.–Fri., 9–5; Sat., 9–5; Sun., 12–5. Donations accepted. **All ages.**

This is the home of the Maine Audubon Society and a great place to visit if you're in the area. You'll learn about solar energy through a variety of displays here and, of course, about native birds. Pack a picnic; there are lots of nature trails and places to stop along the way.

● Desert of Maine

Desert Rd. (off Rte. 1 and I-95), Freeport; (207) 865-6962. Early-May– mid-Oct., daily, 9–dusk. Adults, $6.50; 13–16, $4.50; 6–12, $3.50.
All ages.

The desert of Maine? Yep. Give your kids a real lesson in what happens when you don't respect Mother Earth. This spot was once the Tuttle Farm, located on a glacial sand deposit. After years of tree cutting and planting the topsoil eroded, exposing the sand beneath. Today this sand, covering more than 50 acres, forms dunes that tower over the trees and buildings.

But at Desert of Maine you'll also see rebirth. Surrounding the desert are lush forests. After a hot walk through the desert (this area sees temperatures that exceed 100 degrees), cool off with a walk on the forest trails, which are abundant with wildflowers. In fall, visitors can see 30 to 50 different kinds of mushrooms along the nature trail. Narrated tram tours give a good overview of the area. There's also a farm and sand museum, and a variety of sand design artists are at work.

● Maine Bear Factory

*Sparhawk Mill, 25 Bridge St., Yarmouth; (207) 846-1570. Mon.–
Sat., 10–5:30; Sun., noon–5. Free factory tours; bears extra.* **Ages 1–12.**

The Maine Bear Factory is one of the last makers of stuffed
animals in the United States. The kids will love a peek at how these
cuddly, furry friends are "born."

In the factory, you can pick your own unstuffed bear. The staff
will then help you stuff him or her. Next comes sewing and grooming,
and your new friend is ready to go home with you. At the store, you
can pick out a special outfit from a large selection of clothes and
accessories.

● Maine Sport Outdoor School

*PO Box 956, Rte. 1, Rockport; (800) 722-0826. Call for rates and
schedules.* **Ages 5 and up.**

There is no better way to explore the coast of Maine than by
sea kayak. Never done it? No problem. The folks at this premier paddling
school will show you how. Sign up for a four-hour, full-day, or multiday
kayak tour that will take you through Muscongus Bay, paddling the
coves and coastline. You're likely to see lots of shorebirds and marine
animals and great scenery. There are a number of special family tours
offered, too.

● Day Sails and Windjammer Cruises

Penobscot Bay is famous for its stunning coastline and sailing
waters. Short cruises out of Camden on motor vessels and traditional
sailboats are offered. Or, hop aboard a working lobster boat. Local ferries
also run daily in the summer to many of the islands in the bay.

Day sails are offered by **Appledore,** (207) 236-8353; **Olad,** (207)
236-2323; **Sail Shantih,** (207) 236-8605; **Schooner Surprise,** (207)
236-4687; **Windhorse,** (207) 236-7048; **Acadia Whale Watcher,** (207)
288-9776; and **Betselma,** (207) 236-4446.

● Winslow Park

*Staples Point Rd., South Freeport; (207) 865-4198. Memorial Day–Sept.,
8–9. Free.* **All ages.**

When you're tired of outlet shopping in Freeport, head to this park
for some cheap outdoor fun. Romp in the sand on the beach, rest at the
picnic area overlooking the bay, or take a short walk on the nature trail
that runs along the park perimeter.

● Boothbay Railway Village

Rte. 27, Boothbay; (207) 633-4727. Late-May–early-June, weekends only; mid-June–Columbus Day, daily, 9:30–5. Adults, $6; 12 and under, $3.
Ages 3 and up.

This turn-of-the-century village is sure to delight young visitors. The main attraction is a two-gauge railway with a working 1911 steam train that kids can ride. After purchasing a ticket at the railroad Station (relocated from Freeport), you'll board the Boothbay Central and chug your way on a 1½-mile, 15-minute ride. At the other end, there are old train cars, antique autos, and trucks to explore. Eat in the diner, or bring your own food and eat at the village's picnic area.

● Maine Aquarium

McKown Point, W. Boothbay Harbor; (207) 633-9500. Memorial Day– Columbus Day, daily, 10–5. Adults, $2.50; 5–18, $2. **All ages.**

Your child's first encounter with a lobster will probably be rather unpleasant for both parties, the lobster having been trapped and boiled, and the child thinking, "I'm supposed to eat this thing?" A visit to this small but interesting aquarium will provide a more complete picture of native sea life. A wonderful 20-foot touch tank is filled with sea urchins, starfish, periwinkles, and other inhabitants of the Gulf of Maine. Even more thrilling is a large, live shark tank with dogfish—some as long as two feet—and unusual lobsters that brave children can reach in and pat. Toddlers will love pressing their noses against the "baby tank" filled with tiny, squirming sea creatures. Be sure to pack a picnic; the Seaquarium has a pretty picnic area right on the water.

● Brunswick Fishway Viewing Area

CMD Dam, off Rte. 201, Brunswick; (207) 725-6623. May and June, Sat. and Sun., 10–2; Wed., 7–9 P.M. Free. **All ages.**

This is a fun place to visit when the fish runs are in progress, usually in early spring. There's a fish ladder, a counting room, and a viewing area.

● Peary-MacMillan Arctic Museum

Hubbard Hall, Bowdoin Campus, Brunswick; (207) 725-3416. Year- round, Tues.–Sat., 10–5; Sun., 2–5. Donations accepted. **Ages 5 and up.**

When the snow falls some things just come naturally to kids: snowball fights, snowman making, and building their own version of an igloo. Kids are naturally interested in igloos and Eskimos, and at this museum they can feed that curiosity and learn more about the Eskimo culture. Actually, the museum is a tribute to two Bowdoin alumni, Admiral Robert E. Peary and Admiral Donald B. MacMillan, and also contains equipment from and information about their arctic explorations.

● Maine Maritime Museum

243 Washington St., Bath; (207) 443-1316. Year-round, daily, 9:30–5. Adults, $7.75; 6–17, $5, under 5, free. **All ages.**

Here the imagination and fascination of Maine's maritime past are captured in a very child-friendly manner. Kids can get their hands on the capstan and into Morse Code and the World Trade Game, all equipment meant to be touched and played with. The museum hosts a number of changing exhibits celebrating the seafaring past, with lots of hands-on components for children. There are boat models and paintings on display as well. Be sure to stop by and talk to the apprentices in the boatbuilding school. During the summer there are also tours of the historic shipyard, visits to vessels, demonstrations of seafaring techniques, and a lobstering exhibit. Visitors to the area are invited along with locals to enjoy the weekly lobster bakes and special waterfront activities such as concerts, fairs, and parades.

● Thomas Point Beach

Cooks Corner, off Rte. 24, Brunswick; (207) 725-6009. Memorial Day– Labor Day, 9–sunset. **All ages.**

Ready to kick back and relax? Enough sightseeing for the day? Spend the afternoon at pretty Thomas Point Beach (it's also a campground) on a sandy ocean inlet. There's a calm beach area plus picnic spots, a playground, and lots of room to stretch out. Take in a deep breath of that fresh, salty ocean air while the kids run and play and splash in the surf.

● Popham Beach State Park

Rte. 209, Phippsburg; (207) 389-1335. **All ages.**

A favorite of visitors and locals alike, this pretty beach on the Phippsburg peninsula is the perfect spot for a sunny picnic and a refreshing dip in the ocean. The rocky coastline combines with a sandy beach area to make this a perfect place to spend a hot summer Maine day.

● Camden Hills State Park

Rte. 1, Camden; (207) 236-3109. **All ages.**

This park spreads across 5,000 acres at the foot of Mount Battie. Be sure to drive the road to Mount Battie's 900-foot summit. While not the tallest mountain in New England, from its summit you'll still get wonderful panoramic views of Penobscot Bay and the surrounding countryside.

● Owl's Head Transportation Museum

Rte. 73, Owl's Head; (207) 594-4418. April–Oct., daily, 10–5; Nov.–March, weekends, 10–4. Adults, $6; 6–12, $4, under 5, free. **All ages.**

Cars, trains, planes, boats . . . transportation vehicles make every kid's list of favorite things. Adults, too, will enjoy this collection of historic aircraft, automobiles, and engines—one of the world's top displays. Stop by the restoration workshop, where work on pre-1940s vehicles is in progress. Often you'll be able to hop aboard one of the antique autos for a ride. There are also energy exhibits, a small gallery, picnic areas, and nature trails.

● Fort Knox State Park

Rte. 174, off Rte. 1, Prospect; (207) 469-7719. Nov.–April, 9–5; May–Oct., 9–sunset. **All ages.**

Your kids can hide in the secret passageways, climb the underground stairways, pretend to shoot the giant cannons, and, along the way, learn about 19th-century armies, battles, and life. Fort Knox is a massive granite and brick fortification dating from 1844; it's now a state park. There's a guided tour each day at 1 P.M. Bring a picnic; there are tables and charcoal stoves. And bring a flashlight for exploring the underground passageways.

● Steve Powell Wildlife Management Area

Swan Island; (207) 547-4167. May–Labor Day, daily, 9–sunset.
All ages.

For a day in the wilderness, take the ferry from Richmond to Swan Island. This area, run by the Maine Department of Inland Fisheries and Wildlife, offers an opportunity for some successful wildlife viewing. Quiet, observant walkers are likely to see deer, eagles, and several types of native waterfowl. Bring binoculars and bug spray. There's camping on the island, too. Be sure to call ahead for reservations and ferry arrangements.

● Maine Coast Railroad

PO Box 614, Wiscasset; (207) 882-8000 or (800) 795-5404. Memorial Day–mid-June and Labor Day–Columbus Day, weekends; mid-June–Labor Day, daily. Trains depart at 11 and 1. Adults, $10; 5–12, $5. **Ages 5 and up.**

Hop aboard for a scenic excursion through the Maine countryside. On this 1½-hour roundtrip from Wiscasset to Bath, you'll see saltwater marshes, ponds, shorebirds, and a pretty look at mid-coastal Maine.

● Belfast Moosehead Lake Railroad

11 Water St., Belfast; (800) 392-5500. May–Oct. Call for up-to-date departure listings and rates. **Ages 5 and up.**

What a fun way to see the Maine countryside—chug-chugging along in a vintage 1924 Pullman Day Coach. You'll start at the water's edge and travel up the banks of the Passagassawakeag River. Pulling away from the river, you'll go farther inland, through the forests, across hills and fields. You'll be in the countryside once populated by Native American tribes and later farmed by the earliest settlers. Bring along some hands-on materials for young tots who may become antsy after the novelty of the train ride wears off and the thrill of scenic vistas wanes. The railroad features two excursions: one departing from Belfast, Maine, another from Unity, Maine. Or, try their unique Rail and Sail Excursion: a train ride through the countryside and a sail in beautiful Penobscot Bay.

RESTAURANTS

● Miss Brunswick Diner

Rte. 1, Brunswick; (207) 729-5848. Daily, 5 A.M.–9 P.M.

This roadside diner serves up quick, hearty food at wallet-pleasing prices. No need to keep the kids quiet—this is casual and friendly and full of small-town gossip and noise. There's a handful of daily blackboard specials. Fresh, fried seafood meals and Miss Brunswick Burritos are top sellers. And in true diner fashion, breakfast is served anytime.

● The Brown Bag

606 Main St., Rockland; (207) 596-6372. Mon.–Sat., 6:30–4, Sun., 7–2.

This is a bright, cheery little eatery with great tasting food. If you're around the area for breakfast, don't bother to go anywhere else. The small street facade belies the open, airy inside dining space with exposed brick, pine flooring, and country decor. You can feast on fresh Maine blueberry muffins, cinnamon swirl French toast, homemade sausages, three-cheese omelets, and smoked salmon, capers, and cream cheese bagels. The Brown Bag also serves great soups, salads, and sandwiches.

● Mama & Leenie's Cafe and Bakery

27 Elm St., Camden; (207) 236-6300. Mon.–Sat., 7 A.M.–8 P.M.; Sun., 8–4. Summer hours, Mon.–Sat., 7–11; Sun., 7–8.

Bet you can't pass this place up. You'll smell the homebaked cooking—fresh breads, simmering soups, and pastries. How about fresh blintzes filled with cheese, fruit, and sour cream or a slice of spinach and bacon quiche? Lunch brings a list of daily blackboard specials that include hearty soups and chowders, salads, and sandwiches. During evening hours, the blackboard announces the nightly specials, like fresh seafood and cheese pasta, marinated chicken breast with veggies, chili, or an assortment of pizzas.

● Shaw's Fish & Lobster Wharf

Shaw's Wharf, off Rte. 32, New Harbor; (207) 677-2200. May–mid-Oct., daily, 11–9.

This is a busy, busy place, and for good reason. You can sup on fresh steamed clams and corn on the cob overlooking picturesque New Harbor. You'll join people waiting to board boats for Monhegan Island, the lobstermen who haul in their catches, and tourists buying T-shirts and souvenirs.

Walk up to the counter and order your meal (lobster and other fish dishes), then enjoy the views and the people watching. Your dinner will be ready in no time.

Downeast, Including Acadia National Park

The Downeast region of Maine includes beautiful Acadia National Park and the prestigious resort community of Bar Harbor. You'll see striking stretches of coastline where ragged cliffs meet pounding surf. The combination of fresh salt air, fragrant pines, towering cliffs, and sparkling ocean is a sensory feast you're not likely to forget.

There's more to this area than spectacular scenery. Think of it as the ultimate place to play outside: You can hike, bike, camp, swim, paddle, cruise, or ski.

Even the museums are of the hands-on variety. At the Natural History Museum, for example, you can help assemble a 20-foot whale skeleton. And the local zoo has the largest petting area in the state of Maine.

The village of Bar Harbor, formerly a vacation mecca for wealthy East Coast families, is full of shops, restaurants, and galleries. While many of its mansions were destroyed in the Great Fire of 1947, some still exist and are now in use as inns. It's a fun place to stroll, with its streets at their liveliest during the Art Show and Musical Festival in late June and the Seafood Festival in early July. Enjoy.

● Acadia National Park

Park headquarters located on Rte. 233, near Eagle Lake; (207) 288-3338.

It's 22 square miles of wildlife, woodland, mountains, lakes, and valleys surrounded by the Atlantic Ocean. You'll call it paradise. The park is part of Mount Desert Island, a chunk of primitive beauty that owes its unique contours to the action of Ice Age glaciers. In 1919, President Woodrow Wilson set aside much of this lovely island as a national park. Acadia is eminently seeable, with more than 50 miles of car-free paths for hiking, bicycling, horseback riding, and, in winter, cross-country skiing. By car, a trip along scenic Ocean Drive follows the island's entire eastern perimeter.

Begin your visit at the Visitor's Center, Route 3, Hulls Cove. Open from May through October (although the park is open year-round), the Visitor's Center offers a free 15-minute film to introduce you to Acadia. Here you'll find information about Acadia's Naturalist Program, which has activities especially for children. The program offers several guided walks, ranging from easy to strenuous. You might want to join in a "Night Prowl" glimpse of the nocturnal animals who share the park. Others might include guided nature walks and photography workshops, all free of charge. Or sign up for "Nature's Way for Children," a program offered two to three times weekly.

Riding a bike is a wonderful way to see the park, with plenty of car-free paths to traverse. Bicycle rental shops are located in Bar Harbor.

While the ocean surrounds and beckons (especially on a hot summer's day), even the kids might find the waters here a bit too frigid for fun. Better to swim and play in Echo Lake, which has a nice sandy beach and warmer fresh water. Lifeguards are posted, too. Open mid-June through Labor Day, the lake is located along Route 102, Southwest Harbor.

There are lots of places to get on the water as well, from a variety of ocean-bound boat cruises to a pleasant paddle in a canoe. (Canoe rentals are available at the northern end of Long Pond, located within the park).

● Boat Cruises

Park naturalists conduct hourly or half-day cruises aboard privately owned boats out of Bass Harbor, Northeast Harbor, and Bar Harbor. Naturalists will describe geological history and area wildlife. (Bring binoculars so you won't miss anything.) You'll see seabirds and—to the delight of children—you may spot seals and porpoises. A variety of other sightseeing cruises are also available, including seal-watching, whale-watching, and lobstering trips. You may also choose a 12-hour round-trip cruise to Yarmouth, Nova Scotia.

For a more active excusion, consider a coastal kayak or canoe tour. **Acadia Bike and Canoe Company,** (207) 288-5483, and **Coastal Kayaking Tours,** (207) 288-9605, offer guided tours and island camping trips of varying lengths.

● Abbe Museum

Sieur de Monts Springs; (207) 288-3519. Mid-May–late-Oct., daily. Spring and fall, 10–4; July and Aug., 9–5. Adults, $2; 12 and under, $.50. **All ages.**

This tiny museum, located within Acadia National Park at Sieur de Monts Spring, contains decorative and practical items crafted by Maine Indians. Artifacts include unusual jewelry (fashioned from animal bones), pottery, baskets, and tools made of stone and bone. A museum shop offers Maine Indian crafts, books, and tapes.

● Cadillac Mountain

Ocean Drive follows the eastern perimeter of Mount Desert Island. Follow it from Sieur de Monts Spring, stopping along the way at scenic lookouts including Thunder Hole, until you reach Seal Harbor. There, a park road will take you north to the summit of Cadillac Mountain (1,530 feet), the highest point on the eastern seaboard. From this 360-degree vantage point, you'll see the surrounding ocean, distant mountains, and offshore islands. It's breathtaking. For a special treat, set the alarm clock for pre-dawn, pack a breakfast in a bag, and arrive at the top for sunrise. You may be the first in America to see the sun come up that day.

● Somes Sound

From Northeast Harbor, take Sargent Drive to the fjord at Somes Sound. The fjord was formed when Ice Age glaciers cut through existing mountains. Stunningly beautiful, Somes Sound is the only natural fjord on the East Coast.

● Mount Desert Oceanarium

Clark Point Rd., off Rte. 102, Southwest Harbor; (207) 244-7330. Mid-May–mid-Oct., Mon.–Sat., 9–5. Adults, $6; 4–12, $4.50. Combination tickets for the two Oceanariums and Lobster Hatchery (see below): adults, $11.95; 4–12, $8.75. **All ages.**

Why does the tide go out? Why is the sea salty? What do lobsters eat? If questions like these have come up during your trip to Maine, help is at hand. The Oceanarium's interactive displays offer a lively look at sea life, answering the kinds of questions kids might ask. And there's more.

In the lobster room, a lobsterer explains how a lobster eats, reproduces, and gets caught. The See and Touch room has sea urchins, starfish, and sea cucumbers that children can handle. In the Living Room, live specimens of local marine life are displayed in tanks.

● Mount Desert Oceanarium, Lobster Hatchery

1 Harbor Pl., Bar Harbor; (207) 288-5005. Oceanarium: May–mid-Oct., Mon.–Sat., 9–5. Adults, $6; 4–12, $4.50. Lobster Hatchery: Early-June– mid-Oct., Mon.–Sat., 9–5. Adults, $3.95; 4–12, $2.75. Combination tickets for two Oceanariums and Lobster Hatchery: adults, $11.95; 4–12, $8.75. **All ages.**

There's no better place than this Downeast waterfront location to learn about lobsters. The Lobster Hatchery was opened in 1990 to enhance Maine's lobster landing. At this facility, lobsters are hatched from eggs and raised for their first few tender weeks, then released in the local waters. You'll see thousands of tiny crustaceans in all stages of growth. You'll even get a microscopic view of very tiny lobsters. Friendly staff people are on hand to explain the whole process.

The Oceanarium, located on pretty Thomas Bay, is an expansion of the Southwest Harbor Oceanarium. You can visit both—this facility offers exhibits not available in the Southwest Harbor Oceanarium. The kids will enjoy the harbor seal program, where they get a chance to see the seals during feeding times, and the Maine Lobster Museum, where you'll learn everything there is to know about lobsters and lobster fishing.

● Acadia Zoological Park

Rte. 3, Trenton; (207) 667-3244. May–Oct., daily, 9:30–7. Adults, $6; 3–12, $5. **Ages 1–14.**

Heading north on Route 3, over the causeway from Mount Desert Island to the town of Trenton, you'll find this 100-acre nature preserve and petting farm. More than 150 native and exotic animals make their homes here, amid the woodlands, streams, and pastures. Children will delight in the petting area—the largest in Maine.

● Island Soaring Glider Rides

Hancock County–Bar Harbor Airport, Rte. 3; (207) 667-SOAR. May– Oct., daily 'til sunset. Rates vary. **Ages 5 and up.**

You can't miss this place on busy Route 3 heading into Acadia National Park. You'll see the glider planes, you'll be tempted . . . go ahead, stop in. What a thrill to soar in these one- to two-passenger aircraft!

● Craig Brook National Fish Hatchery

Hatchery Road, off Rte. 1, East Orland; (207) 469-2803. May–Sept.,
daily, 8–8. Free. **All ages.**

This is the oldest salmon hatchery in the country. You'll find exhibits
at the Visitor's Center, display pools, and an aquarium. It's also a nice
little park, with a beach area, boat launching facilities, and nature trails.
Stop by.

RESTAURANTS

● Jordan Pond House

Park Loop Rd., Acadia National Park; (207) 276-3316. Late May–Oct.,
11:30–8; July–Aug., until 9.

A trip to Acadia wouldn't be complete without a visit here. Enjoy
huge popovers and homemade ice cream on the lawn, with magnificent
views all around. Elegant dinners are served in the evenings with classical
music accompaniment.

● Beal's Lobster Pier

Clark Point Rd., Southwest Harbor; (207) 244-3202 or (800) 245-7178.
Year-round, daily, 9–sunset.

For more than 50 years, families have enjoyed seafood in the rough
here, on picnic tables along the pier. Fresh fish, lobsters, shrimp, clams,
and crab meat are available at reasonable prices. You'll soak up the
atmosphere of a busy fish pier, while feasting on the freshest fish around.

Bangor and Augusta

Just off the major interstate (I-95) in Maine, you'll find the two bustling
cities Augusta and Bangor, the state's commercial and cultural hubs.
While most vacationers closely hug the jagged coastline of Maine, much
of the state's business is done inland.

The mighty Kennebec River cuts through the center of capital city
Augusta. Here, you can get a close look at Maine's government in action.
The state capitol building dominates this lively city; its towering gold
dome can be seen from afar.

Traveling north, you'll discover Bangor, with its big-city style
shopping, restaurants, and lodging, and also Orono, where the University
of Maine makes its home. Visitors are welcome to tour the pretty 1,200-
acre campus and take advantage of its cultural and sports offerings.

Despite their modern day conveniences, both cities retain historic architecture and respect for their rural pasts. Venture just a short distance from these hubs and you'll find forests, lakes, and streams abundant with outdoor recreational opportunities.

● Maine State Museum

Capitol Complex, Rte. 201, Augusta; (207) 287-2301. Year-round, Mon.– Fri., 9–5; Sat., 10–4; Sun., 1–4. **Ages 5 and up.**

Located in the impressive Capitol Complex, this museum offers a thorough look at Maine, past and present. *Made in Maine,* the museum's central exhibit, includes a water-powered woodworking mill, a textile factory, and more than 1,000 Maine-made products. The *12,000 Years in Maine* exhibit features more than 2,000 artifacts and specimens dating from the last Ice Age to the 19th century. Kids will enjoy peeking at *This Land Called Maine,* including five nature scenes that show many of the plants and animals found in the state. Other exhibits show Maine's agriculture, fishing, granite quarrying, lumbering, and shipbuilding activities.

● State Capitol Tours

Capitol Complex, Rte. 201, Augusta; (207) 287-2301. Year-round, Mon.– Fri., 8–5. Free. **Ages 5 and up.**

The impressive Maine State Capitol Building can be seen rising above the mighty oak and elm trees that surround it from just about any point in Augusta. Constructed of native granite in 1829, the building's front facade, with its towering arcade, is a fine example of the work of noted American architect Charles Bulfinch. You'll enjoy a walk through the rotunda, where you'll see a large display of Maine battle flags. Also, for a first-hand look at government in action, visit the Legislative Chambers and the Office of the Governor.

● Fort Western Museum

City Center Plaza, Augusta; (207) 626-2385. Memorial Day–July 4, daily 1–4; July 5–Labor Day, Mon.–Fri., 10–4; Sat.–Sun., 1–4; Labor Day–Columbus Day, weekends, 1–4; Nov.–May, open first Sun. of every month, 1–3. Adults, $4.50; 6–16, $2.50. **All ages.**

What child doesn't like a fort? And there's no better way to learn about early American fortification and history than with a close-up look at the real thing. Fort Western, on the eastern bank of the Kennebunk River, was built in 1754 for protection from the Indians. The fort's original main house, once the barracks and the store, is still standing.

You'll also see reproduction blockhouses and watchboxes. In the adjacent City Hall, visit the Museum Services building with exhibits depicting military, settlement, trade, and family themes.

● Maynard Planetarium and Observatory

Wingate Hall, University of Maine Campus, off Rte. 2, Orono; (207) 581-1341. Public showings through the school year. Call for current shows and prices. **Ages 5 and up.**

The moon, the planets, the Milky Way, flashing comets, and falling stars . . . the nighttime sky has always held mystery and fascination for people of all ages. You can learn more about starry nights and space exploration at this small university planetarium. Shows on varied topics in astronomy, space exploration, and other sciences are offered year-round, but you'll need to call ahead for information on programs, schedule, and prices.

● Waterville-Winslow Two Cent Bridge

Front St., Waterville. Year-round. Free. **All ages.**

What will you give me to pass? This is one of the few remaining original toll footbridges in the United States. The toll-taker's house is on the Waterville side, but you'll be able to walk across free.

 RESTAURANTS

● Miller's Restaurant

427 Main St., Bangor; (207) 942-6361. Daily, 11–10.

Families love Miller's famous buffet. This all-you-can-eat feast includes more than 200 hot and cold items. Soups, salads, sandwiches, seafood . . . plus, you'll find an Italian section with spaghetti, lasagna, chicken, pizzas; a Mexican section with tacos, enchiladas, nachos; and classic American cuisine. Save room for the dessert table; you can make your own sundae or enjoy strawberry shortcake, cakes, pies, and more. Come hungry.

● The Greenhouse Restaurant

193 Broad St., Bangor; (207) 945-4040. Tues.–Fri., 11:30–9; Sat., 4–9.

This popular restaurant is on Bangor's waterfront, overlooking the Penobscot River. The kids will like the jungle-like feel to it; there are floor-to-ceiling plants—more than 200 in all. The kid's menu features familiar favorites like chicken fingers, sandwiches, burgers, and small orders of fried fish. Entrées run the span from seafood, chicken, lamb, and beef. Top sellers include the baked Riverside Chicken, a moist, cheesy, melt-in-your mouth chicken breast, and the charbroiled prime rib with horseradish dipping sauce.

Western Lakes and Mountains

As spectacular as Maine's rugged coastline is, there's more to the state, as those who've traveled its western lakes and mountain region can attest. This inland area encompasses the Sebago and Long lakes area, the beautiful Grafton and Evans notch regions of the White Mountain National Forest, and, farther north, the outdoor-recreation-rich Rangeley Lake and Carrabassett River Valley.

Sebago Lake, the second largest in Maine, covers 46 square miles and offers plenty of vacation facilities and recreational opportunities, including swimming, boating, fishing, floatplane rides, and more.

Traveling north, you'll find the classic New England town of Bethel (Hallmark once used the town for a Christmas card commercial). The town boasts a host of fine restaurants and country inns and also Sunday River, one of Maine's top ski resorts. Surrounded by the Mahoosuc Mountain Range and Grafton State Park, the region has also grown very popular with hikers and outdoor enthusiasts.

The Rangeley Lakes area has long been a mecca for vacationers, with a wide range of hotels, lodges, restaurants, and shops. Swim and picnic at lovely Rangeley State Park, attend the town cookouts in the square, play golf, or hike the numerous trails.

If you're a skiing family, no doubt you've heard of downhill giant Sugarloaf USA, near the Carrabassett River Valley. When your legs need a break from skiing, take an adventurous ride on a dog sled. Or come here in the summer for golf, tennis, mountain biking, trail riding, canoeing, hiking, and more.

● **Grafton Notch State Park**
Rte. 16, North of Newry; (207) 389-1335. **All ages.**

Located 14 miles north of Bethel, Grafton Notch is a great place to commune with nature and is one of Maine's best spots for picnicking, hiking, and swimming. Be sure to visit Screw Anger Falls; its rocky ledges are fun to climb, and the falls make a perfect backdrop for a picnic. Other points of interest: the Moose Cave nature walk and Mother Walker Falls.

● White Mountain National Forest

Rte. 2, Bethel; (207) 824-2134. **All ages.**

The Evans Notch Ranger District of the White Mountain National Forest is located here. Evans Notch is one of the five districts in the forest, which has lands in both Maine and New Hampshire. The U.S. Forest Service maintains a number of hiking trails that connect with the Appalachian Trail. Pick up trail maps at the Visitor's Center. Take a short loop hike or make a day of it, enjoying magnificent mountain scenery.

● Artist's Covered Bridge

Rte. 5, 2 miles beyond Sunday River Ski Resort Access Road, Newry.
All ages.

This frequently photographed 1872 bridge marks a great family swimming hole. Have a picnic on the rocky ledges beneath the bridge, downstream.

Special Note: This is private property, so please use discretion.

● Washburn-Norlands Living History Center

Norlands Rd., off Rte. 4, Livermore; (207) 897-2236. Year-round for overnight learning vacations. General tours: July–Labor Day, daily, 10–4. Labor Day–Columbus Day, weekends only, 10–4. Adults, $5.50; 5–18, $2.
Ages 5 and up.

This is the very best way to learn. When you check into this living history center, you are assigned an identity—and from then on you live it. You'll remain in costume. You'll probably be sleeping on corn-husk mattresses. No showers, no bathrooms (why, that's how they used to live!); in fact, Washburn-Norlands allows only two concessions to modern-day conveniences: window screens in the summer and toilet paper all year. You'll love every second and be amazed at how much everyone in the family learns. This place is repeatedly written about as the best of the best in family/learning vacations guides.

Of course, the ideal way to experience Washburn-Norlands is to stay for several days. But in July and August the center also conducts brief (two-hour) tours. You'll find an 1853 one-room school house and Maine's only living history farm. On 445 acres and complete with barns, horses, oxen, cows, sheep, pigs, and poultry, the farm operates year-round. The kids will enjoy lending a hand outdoors and you can also visit the library and Victorian home of the Washburn family, one of the country's greatest political dynasties. Bet you'll want to return for one of the vacation programs.

● Mountain Biking

If you want to skip the thigh-burning, uphill climbs and go directly to the cruise down, check out the two area ski resorts. Come summer, **Sugarloaf USA,** RR 1, Box 5000, Carrabassett, (800) THE-LOAF, and **Sunday River,** PO Box 450, Bethel, (800) 543-2SKI, turn into fat-tire paradises. Chairlifts whisk you up to the top; you pedal down.

At Sugarloaf USA, the 53-mile mountain bike park includes its nordic ski network and some of its alpine trails. Maps, tours, rentals, and shuttle drop-off and pick-up service are available from the Sugarloaf Bike Shop.

The Sunday River Mountain Bike Park has 35 miles of single track and wide-open dirt roads to cruise. With or without a guide, riders have access to a variety of terrain, with the western mountains of Maine as a backdrop.

● *Songo River Queen II*

Rte. 302, Naples; (207) 693-6861. July–Labor Day, daily; June and Sept., weekends. Songo River tour: adults, $10; 4–12, $6. Long Lake tour: adults, $7; 4–12, $4. **Ages 5 and up.**

Take a lazy one-hour riverboat ride on Long Lake or a 2½-hour cruise down the Songo River. Both are on a lovely 92-foot sternwheel riverboat. It's very relaxing and scenic. In the summer, several trips are made each day. In June and September one trip is offered each weekend day at 9:45 A.M.

● Willowbrook at Newfield

Off Rte. 11, Newfield; (207) 793-2784. Mid-May–Sept., daily, 10–5. Adults, $7; 6–18, $3.50. **All ages.**

History comes alive here, and the kids will enjoy looking at the toys, nurseries, schoolhouse, carriages, bicycles, and other artifacts of days gone by. The beautiful 1894 Armitage-Herschell Carousel is eye-catching for all—24 horses and four chariots fully restored and animated. You'll also see an early stagecoach, old-fashioned country store, and, in a nod to the present, restaurant, gift store, and ice cream parlor.

● Fish and Wildlife Visitor's Center

308 Shaker Rd., Gray; (207) 657-4977. April–Nov., daily, 9:30–4. Adults, $3.50; 4–12, $2. **All ages.**

Learn about native wildlife at this game farm. You are free to roam the farm and look at the displays of native animals, birds, and wildlife educational exhibits. There also are trout pools and picnic areas.

● Perham's

Rtes. 26 and 219, West Paris; (207) 674-2341. Year-round, daily, 9–5.
Ages 3 and up.

This area of Maine is noted for its wide variety of mineral and gem deposits, including tourmaline, mica, feldspar, and various types of quartz. At Perham's, you'll find out all about gem hunting. At its Mineral Museum, you'll have plenty of things to touch. Bring a bag and a shovel and pick—Perham's quarry is open to the public and you're free to take home what you find. Kids love this treasure hunt.

● T.A.D. Dog Sled Rides

Stratton; (207) 246-4461. Dec.–April, daily, 10–3. Adults, $40; 5–12, $25. **All ages.**

You won't want to miss this experience of a lifetime. Half-hour dog sled rides through the Maine snow-covered countryside are an experience you and your family won't soon forget. The team travels about one and a half miles. Call about summer cart rides.

● Mount Blue State Park

From Wilton or Dixfield, 15 miles off Rte. 2, in Weld; (207) 585-2261. Mid-May–mid-Oct. **All ages.**

This large scenic park nestled in the mountains of western Maine is popular with mountain climbers, hikers, and families looking for outdoor fun. Swim at Webb Lake and join in ranger-led activities that include gold-panning, nature walks, canoe trips, and mountain hikes. There's also a boat launch, and canoe rentals are available.

● Rangeley Lake State Park

Located on the south shore of Rangeley Lake, this 691-acre recreation area offers picnicking, swimming, fishing, camping, and boat launching facilities.

● Sunday River Ski Resort

Rte. 2, north of Bethel, (207) 824-3000. Lift tickets: adults, $46; 6–12, $29; under 6, free. Perfect Kids (4–12), $47/day; Mogul Mites (4–6) and Mogul Meisters (7–12) $76/day; child care, $43/day. Ticket prices listed are for weekends and holidays; special packages and discount rates are available.
All ages.

Sunday River is fast becoming one of the premier ski resorts in the East, if not in the country. Continually upgrading and improving, the resort now encompasses eight interconnected mountains, with 121 trails.

While skiing at Sunday River is geared toward the intermediate skier, it has recently expanded its expert terrain with the opening of Oz Mountain. Beginner's action is centered in the South Ridge Slope area, but novices can also ski from the top of the mountain and back to the South Ridge Base via Three Mile Trail. Are there new skiers in your group? Sunday River has a guaranteed Learn-to-Ski-in-One-Day and its well-known Perfect Turn learning programs.

Sunday River does a great job of welcoming families, offering a variety of programs for kids of all ages and abilities. A Children's Ski Center adjacent to the South Ridge Center serves as the base for the Mogul Meister and children's seasonal programs. Younger skiers in the SKIwee program are headquartered in the Merrill Brook II facility.

There are eight snow parks and playgrounds for riders. You won't find too many families who don't like skiing Sunday River. It's one of the best.

● Sugarloaf USA
Rte. 27, Kingfield; (207) 237-2000. Lift tickets: adults, $46; 13–18, $41; 6–12, $26. Mountain Magic (3–6), $54/day; Mountain Adventure (7–16), $40/day; child-care (6 wks.–6 yrs.), $42/day. **All ages.**

Skiing families who are tired of long waits in lift lines, crowded ski trails, and jammed parking lots should give serious thought to Sugarloaf. It's a bit off the beaten path, and that's why it's so relaxed. The closest major cities are Portland, two and a half hours away, and Montreal, four hours away, so you miss the big crowds that head to more southerly ski mountains. Located in Kingfield in the Carrabassett Valley, Sugarloaf is a destination resort. Drive up, park your car, and spend the rest of your time on skis, on foot, or riding the Sugarloaf Shuttle to the resort's shops and restaurants.

You'll find plenty to do. The resort has a well-equipped health club (including six indoor and outdoor jacuzzis), an Olympic-size ice skating arena, and a host of eateries and shops.

Now, about that mountain: It's big, challenging, and rough and tumble if you want it, slow, easy, and relaxed if you prefer. The vertical drop is 2,837 feet, with 107 trails, 11 glades, and lots of varied terrain. Black diamond skiers love it at Sugarloaf, where they find lots of big bumps, steeps, glades, chutes, and off-trail, out-of-bounds skiing.

Sugarloaf also works hard at pleasing families, and succeeds. Friendly staff and plenty of beginner terrain are hits with vacationing families.

RESTAURANTS

● Hugs

Rte. 27, Carrabassett Valley; (207) 237-2392. Summer, Thurs.–Sat., 5–10; winter, Tues.–Sat., 5–10. Closed mid-Oct.–Nov.

This is a great place to come with friends and family. The food is nothing less than fabulous, and the staff makes you feel right at home. This friendly place dishes up big baskets of just-baked pesto bread, bowls of fresh salad, and platters full of fine northern Italian cuisine. Select different entrées to pass at the table, mixing and matching to fit tastes and budgets. Dinners are served family style, and you can get all you want to eat. Save room for dessert.

● Red Top Truck Stop

Rte. 2, Bethel; (207) 824-2000. Daily, 5 A.M.–midnight.

When you ask the locals in Bethel about a good, cheap place to eat, the answer you almost always get is the Red Top. Actually there are two Red Tops in Bethel, both on Route 2. One stands alone, the other is a combination gas station, convenience store, and restaurant. That should give you some idea of the atmosphere. But, you'll get cheap, quick service of eggs, sausage, ham, or bacon, home fries, homemade toast, and home-made muffins and donuts. Free refills on the coffee. Lunch is $1.50 burgers, hot dogs, ham and cheese sandwiches, and the like.

Moosehead and Katahdin Region

If you have a love for the great outdoors and an appreciation for the beauty of unspoiled wilderness, this northern lakes region of Maine is for you.

This is considered one of the greatest hunting, fishing, and canoeing regions in the country. You'll see few commercial tourist attractions or concessions to modern-day extravagances. Rather, it's the wealth of natural resources that draws people to the shores of mighty Moosehead Lake or into the wilderness of Baxter State Park.

You'll stand in the shadows of Mount Katahdin, one of the highest peaks in the Northeast and the legendary home of the sacred spirits of the Abenaki Indians. Mount Katahdin, meaning "greatest mountain," rises nearly one mile above Baxter State Park. You'll get a good taste of northern Maine wilderness in this 201,018-acre park, where you can swim in secluded mountain ponds, hike through forests, and picnic along babbling brooks.

You'll get your thrills not from a waterslide or a roller coaster, but from a whitewater raft trip down the West Branch of the Penobscot River, or on a floatplane ride over the undeveloped shores of Moosehead Lake. It's easy here—and relatively inexpensive—to hire a seaplane for island exploring or to rent a canoe to get around the lakes and rivers. In the winter, you'll join snowmobilers, snowshoers, and ski tourers who traverse the surrounding forests on a network of trails and old logging roads. But whenever you come, be prepared to spend the time outdoors.

● Moosehead Lake

Moosehead Lake is Maine's largest lake, more than 40 miles long and up to 20 miles wide. There are several large islands, bays, and inlets in the lake, surrounded by rugged mountains and miles of dense forests. Much of the 420-mile shoreline remains undeveloped and accessible only by floatplanes, boats, or canoes. But don't despair; all these are easy to rent or hire. Stop in Greenville, on the southern tip of the lake, where you'll find lots of local seaplanes for lake sightseeing tours. There's nothing formal here; just walk up to the plane of your choice and talk to the owner. In Greenville you'll also find a number of places to rent canoes and rowboats. This is a great way to see the lake and explore its many islands.

Be sure to bring a pair of binoculars for moose watching. More than 10,000 moose reportedly live in the Moosehead Lake region. The best time to see them is early morning or twilight, when they come out to feed in the lake's swampy areas. If you feel adventurous, explore some of the old logging roads around the lake; they will take you to secluded bogs.

Special note: Though moose will seldom approach people, it's a good policy to watch from a distance.

● Mount Kineo

While you're exploring the lake, you'll notice Mount Kineo rising dramatically out of it for more than 700 feet. Located about a mile from the lakefront town of Rockwood, Mount Kineo is made entirely of green flint. Many years ago, the Abenaki Indians sought its flint to make arrowheads and tools. From here, you'll also get great views of the lake and surrounding mountains and forests.

● Lily Bay State Park

East side of Moosehead Lake, 8 miles north of Greenville; (207) 695-2700. Early May–mid-Oct. **All ages.**

This park, located on the shores of Moosehead Lake just north of Greenville, is a fine recreation center. Its 942 acres include a small beach for swimming, canoe rentals, and boat launching facilities. The kids will enjoy taking the short path to the playground or picnicking in the pines.

● S.S. *Katahdin* and Moosehead Marine Museum

Main St., Greenville; (207) 695-2716. Memorial Day–June, Sat. only cruise; 12:30 P.M.; July–Aug., Tues.–Sat., 12:30 P.M.; Sept.–Columbus Day, Sat.–Sun. 2:30 P.M. only. Three-hr. cruise: adults, $16; 5–15, $9; under 5, free. Six-hr. cruise: adults, $24; 5–15, $12; under 5, free. **All ages.**

Known locally as Kate, this restored 1914 steam vessel has been converted into the floating Moosehead Marine Museum. Besides taking a ride around Moosehead Lake—the cruise takes you up the southern tip of the lake—you'll be able to see displays and photographs of the logging industry and steamboat operations. The last Sunday in September there's an eight-hour, 80-mile Head of the Lake cruise.

● Baxter State Park

North of Millinocket; (207) 723-5140. April–Nov. **All ages.**

This premier, 201,018-acre park was given to the state by Maine Governor Percival Baxter in 1941, with one condition: "that it forever shall be held in its natural, wild state." The park is an unspoiled wilderness area dominated by Mount Katahdin, the highest mountain in the state. It includes 46 mountain peaks and ridges (18 of which exceed an elevation of 3,000 feet) and a network of about 150 miles of trails, all surrounded by natural wildlife, mountain streams, ponds, lakes, and dense forests. Visitors can wind their way through the park on a narrow road. The auto trip through the park takes about two and a half to three hours, but this doesn't include the stops you'll want to make for picnics, swimming, and hiking along the way.

There are trails for everyone in the park, and even families with small children can enjoy a number of hikes. Daicey Pond Nature Trail is perfect for small children. The trail is level and an easy trip around Daicey Pond. Be sure to pick up the free pamphlet on the trail that points out wildlife as you go. It's available from the ranger station at Daicey Pond Campground. Little Niagara and Big Niagara Falls Trail is part of the Appalachian Trail, and it's a great one to walk on a hot summer's day. (The Appalachian Trail, the only trail in Baxter blazed in white, terminates in the park at Mount Katahdin.) You'll pick up the trail at the Daicey Pond Campground and hike along the Nesowadnehunk Stream. There are lots of places to take a refreshing dip along the way. You'll pass a logger's dam before reaching Little Niagara Falls. Go a little farther down the side trail to Big Niagara Falls, a picturesque spot for a picnic.

From the campground to Big Niagara Falls is 1.2 miles. Families with older children will enjoy a 3.2-mile hike up Sentinel Mountain on the Kidney Pond Sentinel Mountain Trail. It's not too steep, and the summit view, overlooking a range of mountains, is beautiful. The trail leaves from the southwest corner of Kidney Pond.

There are lots of mountain pools and streams to swim in throughout the park. Families will also enjoy South Branch Pond; this is a busy camping and picnic area also open for day use. You'll find a nice swimming area and canoes for rent. Abol Pond is a popular spot for swimming and picnicking at the southern end of the park. Take Abol Pond Road three miles in from the park's southern gatehouse entrance. Togue Pond is open for general use. It's located just outside the entrance of the park.

Baxter State Park is a great place for animal watching. There are more than 170 bird species, and you're likely to see deer and moose in the ponds feeding on aquatic vegetation. (Look for them at Daicey and Elbow ponds.) There's also a large bear population in the park. People are warned not to feed the bears or leave waste around.

Parents should be warned that there is a serious bug population from May into August, and everyone will need the protection of insect repellent, nets, or both. Finally, there are no running water, electricity, lights, food, or supplies in the park.

● Lumberman's Museum

Rte. 159, Patten, at the northern entrance to Baxter State Park; (207) 528-2650. Memorial Day–Sept., Mon.–Sat., 9–4; Sun., 10–4. Oct.–Columbus Day, weekends; Sat., 9–4; Sun., 10–4. **Ages 5 and up.**

You'll learn about the active lumbering industry at this museum. The complex of nine buildings contains a working model of a sawmill, a blacksmith shop, old tractors, and 3,000 artifacts of the lumbering industry.

● Canoeing and Whitewater Rafting

This area boasts some of the most spectacular whitewater rivers in the East, including the West Branch of the Penobscot River, the Kennebec, and the Allagash Wilderness Waterway. Canoe trips can last for a day, a few days, a week, or longer and are designed for beginners as well as experts. A number of licensed outfitters can arrange canoe trips. The adventurous can try a thrilling ride down rushing waters in a rubber raft. Licensed outfitters arrange and guide the trips. Minimum age is usually 12 years. For a list of canoe trips, whitewater raft expeditions, and licensed outfitters, write the **Maine Department of Inland Fisheries and Wildlife,** 284 State Street, Augusta, Maine 04333; (207) 289-2043.

● Blacksmith Shop Museum

Park St., off Rte. 153, Dover-Foxcroft; (207) 564-8618. Memorial Day–Oct., daily, sunrise–sunset. Free. **Ages 5 and up.**

Do your children know what a blacksmith's shop is? Here's a good place to find out. This 1863 restored Civil War period blacksmith shop retains much of the original equipment, and kids will get a quick look into the past, when four-legged animals—not engines—were the mode of transportation.

● Gulf Hagas

Millinocket Rd., just north of Milo and Brownville. **Ages 10 and up.**

Gulf Hagas, accessible only by a four- to five-mile hike down a trail, has been called the "Grand Canyon of the East." This is where the west branch of the Pleasant River is deeply entrenched in a slate canyon, and waterfalls, sheer walls, and unusual rock formations form a spectacular site. Don't attempt this with young tots. But if you have older children and you've got the time, don't miss it.

RESTAURANTS

● Auntie Em's

Main St., Greenville; (207) 695-2238. Summers, daily, 5 A.M.–9 P.M.; winters, daily, 5 A.M.–7 P.M.

Yes, you read that right . . . this place opens at five in the morning in the winter, five in the morning come summer. Auntie Em wants to be sure all those day hikers, hunters, and fishing enthusiasts get a good, strong start on the day. Everyone knows Auntie Em's, where you'll get homemade donuts and muffins, large-size breakfast specials, and hearty lunches and dinners. You'll find unfussy, homestyle meals offering all the basics, like fried seafood platters, steaks, chicken, sandwiches, and burgers. Breakfast anytime.

● The Birches Resort and Restaurant

Birches Road, Rockwood; (207) 534-7305. Daily, summers, 7 A.M.–10 A.M. and 6 P.M.–9 P.M.; winters, 7 A.M.–10 A.M. and 5 P.M.–8 P.M.

Forget about dinner, just look at this room, a turn-of-the-century log building with a giant stone fireplace, and look at the view, a panorama of Moosehead Lake and surrounding mountain ranges. This is a great setting for a meal, and you'll likely share the dining room with fellow outdoor enthusiasts and vacationers. The food isn't bad, either. Dinners include appetizer, dessert, salad, vegetables, and potatoes. Standard menu items (steak, fish, chicken, and pasta) are offered, plus three or four daily specials.

Vermont

Manchester and the Mountains

Long before there were ski lifts and condominiums, Manchester was an elegant summer resort—Vermont's answer to Newport, Rhode Island, and Saratoga, New York. Instead of waiting in lift lines, guests queued up for a game of croquet. Then, as now, the combination of fresh mountain air and charming countryside proved too enticing to resist.

Happily some of that gentility remains today. Visiting families can tour Manchester Village in a horse-drawn carriage complete with a top-hatted driver. Guests can picnic on the manicured lawns of Hildene, the Robert Todd Lincoln estate, as past presidents once did. Or you can bundle up for a sleigh ride, stopping back at the mansion for hot mulled cider.

In Manchester Center, a more modern pastime predominates—shopping. You'll find a plethora of specialty stores, antique shops, craft studios, and designer outlets. In recent years, outlet shopping has also reared its (we won't say it) head.

But if you spend too much time poking around in the shops, you'll miss what this area has best to offer—ample opportunity to play outside. Southern Vermont is a great place for trout fishing, canoeing, camping, swimming, hiking, skiing, horseback riding—you name it.

There's also a prominent resident your children will want to meet: Santa. Where else would the Claus family choose for a summer home?

● Santa's Land

Rte. 5 (between Exits 4 and 5 off I-91), Putney; (802) 387-5550 or (800) 387-SANTA-99. Mid-June–Christmas, daily, 10–5; Memorial Day weekend–mid-June, weekends only. Adults, $8; 3-15, $6. **Ages 1–8.**

This very merry park has lots of child-pleasing features, including a petting zoo, a child's train ride, a carousel, and a playground. The highlight of your child's visit will likely be a chat with the Jolly Old Elf himself, who'll ask "Do you take care of your toys?" not, "What do you want for Christmas?" And, a close-up look at Rudolph and his animal friends. Marionette and puppet shows are featured on the weekends.

● Southern Vermont Natural History Museum

Rte. 9, Marlboro; (802) 464-0048. June–Oct., daily, 8–8; Nov.– Memorial Day, weekends, 8–4. Adults, $2; 12 and under, $1; suggested donation. **All ages.**

Don't miss this hidden gem tucked in behind the Vermont Country Market. This top-notch natural history museum has recently expanded and now includes nearly 600 different animals. Critters roam the forest, and birds fly the skies of New England in a collection of more than 80 dioramas. The native bird collection is astounding, featuring a very complete example of birds native to New England, including three extinct birds. Kids will love the big cases—one with four bald eagles, and another with at least 10 owls.

● Green Mountain Flyer

8 Depot St., Bellows Falls; (802) 463-3069. Late-June–Columbus Day; trains depart 11 and 2. Call about special winter and spring trips. Adults, $10; 3–12, $6. **Ages 3 and up.**

Climb aboard and journey through central Vermont's scenic countryside. The restored coaches, pulled by vintage diesels, travel 26 miles, from Bellows Falls to Chester. You'll view Brockways Mill Gorge, two covered bridges, and lots of rolling hills and valleys and pretty tumbling waterfalls.

● Hildene

Rte. 7A, Manchester; (802) 362-1788. Mid-May–Oct.; daily, 9:30–5:30 (last tour begins at 4). Adults, $7; 6–14, $3; under 6, free. **Ages 5 and up.**

This place is probably not number one on the "top fun things to do with children" list, but promise them an ice cream cone on the way home and they might go along. And, you'll get to see this gracious Georgian Revival mansion, built by Robert Todd Lincoln, the only one of Abraham Lincoln's four sons to live to maturity. Lincoln's descendants lived at Hildene until 1975. The kids will find the toy room, decorated with fairy-tale scenes, and the 1908 player pipe organ the most interesting. When they begin to get antsy, you can take them for a walk on one of the nature trails.

There are also picnic areas on the grounds, and open air concerts, performed by the Vermont Symphony Orchestra, are often scheduled in the summer.

● Village Carriage Company

Rte. 7A, Manchester. Departs daily, weather permitting, from the front of the Equinox Hotel or from the Equinox Golf Course. Ride of 20 minutes, $20; 30 minutes, $30. **All ages.**

Tour historic Manchester Village in the grand style of days gone by. Step into a fancy, horse-drawn carriage, complete with top-hatted driver, for this half-hour ride around town.

● Bennington Museum and Grandma Moses Gallery

Rte. 9, Old Bennington; (802) 447-1571. Daily, 9–5. Closed Thanks-giving, Christmas. Adults, $5; students and seniors, $4.50; under 12, free; family rate (two adults, two children), $12. **Ages 5 and up.**

You'll take a trip back to the 19th century when you view this collection of paintings, furniture, military artifacts, and toys. But most come for a look at the gallery devoted to Anna Mary Robertson, better known as Grandma Moses. This legendary woman began painting seriously at age 78 and continued to do so until her death at age 101.

● Bromley Alpine Slide

Rte. 11, Peru (6 miles east of Manchester); (802) 824-5522. Memorial Day–mid-June, weekends only, 9:30–6; Mid-June–Aug., daily, 9:30–6; Sept.–Oct., daily, 10–5. Adults and juniors (age 7 and up), $6; under 7, free, with an adult. **Ages 3 and up.**

The action at Bromley Mountain doesn't stop when the snow melts. Come spring, you can board the chairlift to the mountaintop, then careen down in a luge-style sled. You can take it as fast or slow as you like.

● Vermont Wax Museum

Rtes. 11 and 30, Manchester Center; (802) 362-0609. June–Oct., daily, 10–5; Nov.–Memorial Day, 11–5, closed Mon.–Tues. Adults, $6.95; 7–12, $3.95; under 7, free; family rate (four people or more), $19.95. **Ages 5 and up.**

What can we say? Where vacationers are, there's bound to be a wax museum sooner or later. This one is housed in three historic Victorian buildings. You'll meet John F. Kennedy and Jacqueline Kennedy, Mark Twain, and Marco Polo. You'll hear Churchill rally England and Andrew Carnegie give financial advice. There are 85 life-size figures, all set in multimedia displays.

● Swimming Holes and Picnic Spots

When it comes time to cool off and stretch out, you'll have plenty of choices:

Hapgood Pond Recreation Area, Rte. 11, Weston (2 miles north of Peru), is part of the Green Mountain National Forest, and a popular spot for swimming, hiking, fishing and picnicking.

Emerald Lake State Park, Rte. 7, North Dorset, is a 430-acre playground offering swimming, boating, and fishing. Picnic tables, snack bar, and boat rentals are available.

Stoughton Pond in Weathersfield is great for a quick dip. You'll find changing rooms here.

Jamaica State Park, Rte. 30, Jamaica, is on the banks of the West River, where you can fish, hike, canoe, kayak or swim. A nice nature trail leads to pretty Hamilton Falls. Boat rentals are available.

Lake Saint Catherine State Park, Rte. 30, Poultney, has swimming, fishing and boating. A marina on the west shore of the lake rents canoes and motorboats. You'll also find a nature trail, nature museum, playground, and picnic tables. Bring barbecue fixings; there are fireplaces, grills, and wood available.

Townshend Lake Recreation Area, Rte. 30, Townshend, has swimming, boating, picnicking, and hiking trails. There are boat rentals available.

● **Hiking**
Check in with the Manchester Ranger District, U.S. Forest Service, Rte. 11, Manchester; (802) 362-2307, for trailhead directions and information on local hiking opportunities. **All ages.**

You're likely to see a number of backpackers and hikers in this area. Two legendary trails merge here: **The Appalachian Trail** and the **Long Trail.** But you don't have to be an avid mountain climber to enjoy the trails.

There are plenty of opportunities for day hikes. Some easy treks in the area for families include:

Grout Pond Trails is a series of easy loop trails that pass Grout Pond and provide access to the north end of Somerset Reservoir. You'll find camping, picnicking, and swimming at Grout Pond. Catch the trailhead off Kelley Stand Rd., just east of Route 71.

Hapgood Pond Trail begins at the Hapgood Pond Recreation Area, forest Highway 3. The trail loops around the north edge of the pond to a dam. (Summer admission is charged at Hapgood.)

Griffith Lake Trail begins at the end of Forest Road 58, and heads north on an old road to Griffith Lake. It's just over two miles and well-marked.

● **Connecticut River Safari Canoe Touring Center**
451 Putney Rd., (Rte. 5), Brattleboro; (802) 257-5008. May–mid-Sept., daily, 8–6; mid-Sept.–mid-Oct., weekends by appointment. Rates are per canoe, 1–2 people: 2 hours, $10; half-day, $15; full-day, $20. Multiday rentals and pick-up service also available. **Ages 2 and up.**

Even small children will enjoy a paddle on the beautiful Connecticut River. This long, 412-mile stretch of water, flowing from the Canadian border to Long Island Sound, is wide and meandering. You'll paddle peaceful waters, sometimes around islands and under bridges. The overnight downriver trip from Bellows Falls to Brattleboro is the most popular water adventure. You'll camp on the river shores, or, if you prefer, stay overnight at the Putney Inn, a short walk from Putney Landing.

● Batten Kill River

The infamous Batten Kill, known for its great trout fishing, weaves through this southern Vermont region, inviting passersby to dip their toes or drop a line. Originating in Dorset and East Dorset, the Batten Kill flows into New York State and the Hudson River. Its waters are lively, clear, and perfect for canoeing and fishing. Your best bet is to stop in at the **Orvis Company** in town (Rte. 7A, Manchester) and pick up a detailed map of the river. Or just chat with the sales folk here. They'll tell you the best place to access the water, whether you want to sit on a rock and get your legs wet, or get serious about fishing. The store is a great place to browse, too, full of fishing gear and gadgets. You're likely to see a class outside by the Orvis Pond learning the finer points of fly casting.

Canoe rentals are available at the **Battenkill Canoe Company,** Rte. 7A, Arlington; (800) 421-5268. Shop staff will provide you with a map, go over your route, and point out interesting spots to watch for along the way. At the end of your trip, one of the shuttle vans will meet you and bring you back to your car. The rental shop is open daily from mid-April through Oct., and rental rates are $45 per canoe. Each rental includes paddles, life jackets, waterpoof bag, and shuttle pick-up.

● Scenic Chairlift Rides

Stratton Ski Resort, Stratton Mountain Rd., Bondville (off Rte. 30); (802) 297-2200. Late-June–mid-Oct., daily, 9:30–4. Adults, $10; under 6, free. Bromley Ski Resort, Rte. 11, Peru (6 miles east of Manchester); (802) 824-5522. Mid-May–July 4, weekends, 9:30–6; July 4–mid-Oct., daily, 9:30–6. Adults, $4.50; 7–12, $3.50. **Ages 3 and up.**

Grab a camera, pack a picnic, and don some sensible shoes for a trip to the top of the mountain. This is the easy way to get high-altitude panoramas: via a gondola or high-speed chairlift. See if you can name the five states you see standing on top of Bromley Mountain. Or, take the Starship gondola to the top of Stratton Mountain for equally fine views. On top, you can hike along the ski trails, and take the ride back down when you're ready.

● Mount Snow Mountain Biking

Rte. 100, Mount Snow; (800) 245-SNOW. Mid-June–Oct., Thurs.–Mon., 9–4. Trail access, $8/day; Lift access, $27/day. Bike rentals, adults, $30/

*day; 12 and under, $22/day (rental fees include a helmet, trail access fee
and trail map). Private and instructional group tours also available.* **Ages
5 and up.**

Whether you're a beginner or a fat-tire maniac, you're going to love
Mount Snow. And, if you haven't tried this fast-growing sport, this is the
place to do it. Mount Snow is famous for its world-class biking trails. The
Bike Center offers more than 140 miles of terrain on single-track, old
town roads, and ski trails. You'll find lots of variety, from meandering,
scenic back roads to rugged and steep up-and-down runs. The staff is
always available to help you choose which way to go, providing maps and
advice. Private and group instructional tours are also available.

If you'd rather peddle downhill than uphill, buy a chairlift pass and
ride it to Mount Snow's 3,600-foot summit. After a great four-state view,
point those fat tires down one of the many trails.

● Sun Bowl Ranch Horseback Riding

*Stratton Ski Resort (off Rte. 30); (802) 297-2200. Mid-June–Oct., daily,
9–5. One- or two-hour rides, $25–$50.* **Ages 8 and up.**

Take a guided horseback ride through the rolling Vermont countryside, past rippling streams, through forests, and to secluded spots. Parents
ride on gentle horses; children eight years and older hop on a donkey.

● Sleigh Rides and Snowmobiling

Dashing through the snow in a one-horse open sleigh—or, a speedy
snow machine . . . you decide. Sleigh rides are offered by the **Landgrove
Inn,** (802) 824-6673; **Horses for Hire,** featuring a two-horse team of
Belgians and an evening around the campfire (802) 824-3750; and **Taylor
Farm,** providing a scenic ride through the pastures of a working dairy
farm, (802) 824-5690.

Daily snowmobile tours through the Green Mountain National Forest
are offered by **North Country Sno-Tours** (800) 270-SLED.

● Cross Country Skiing

Southern Vermont is a nordic skier's paradise. There are numerous
ski touring centers nearby; these are great for families because you get
detailed maps, advice, rental equipment, groomed trails, and lessons. Here
are some possibilities:

Hildene, Rte. 7A, Manchester Village, (802) 362-1788, offering 15
kilometers of trails through the hardwoods on the historic Robert Todd
Lincoln estate; **Stratton Nordic Centers** at Stratton Mountain, Rte. 30,
Bondville, (802) 297-2200, with more than 30 kilometers of terrain at

two centers—the Sun Bowl for secluded forest trails and the Country Club for more gentle rolling terrain; **Viking Ski Touring Center,** Little Pond Rd., Londonderry, (801) 824-3933, with 40 kilometers of groomed trails through woods and open fields; and the **Wild Wings Ski Touring Center,** North Rd., Peru, (802) 824-6793, a family-friendly center with 25 kilometers of beginner through expert trails.

For those who want more natural terrain, head to **Merck Forest,** Rte. 315, Rupert Mountain, (802) 394-7836, for some fine backcountry skiing. Merck has 2,820 acres with 27 miles of ungroomed trails.

● Mount Snow/Haystack Ski Resort

Rte. 100, Mount Snow; (802) 464-3333 or (800) 245-SNOW. Lift tickets: adults (13 and up), $47; junior (6–12), $28. Mountain Camp and Mountain Riders (7–12), $57/day, including lessons and lunch, $77/day, with skis or snowboard rental; Snow Camp (4–6), $65/day, including lessons and lunch, $85/day with skis or snowboard rentals; Pre-Ski (3yrs.), $15/ day, including one-hour lesson and indoor/outdoor games; child care (6 wks.– 5 yrs.) $55/day. Rates are for weekends and holidays; discounted midweek rates and special packages are offered. **All ages.**

Recent expansions, improvements, and the takeover by the American Skiing Company has put a fresh face on this southern Vermont favorite. Families with beginner skiers and riders will find an expanded learning area and lots of beginner terrain. For those looking for a challenge, Mount Snow added 16 acres of tree skiing for a total of 137 acres and 12 specific acres devoted to expert skiers. In all, you'll find 130 trails and about 50 miles of slopes.

The resort is doing its best to welcome vacationing families. Special ski and stay packages and annual Teddy Bear Weeks are offered, and a host of kid's programs are available. Families will find lots of off-slope activities, including the Teen Extreme Program (coaching during the day for skiers and riders and social activities in the evening); the Planet 9 After Dark (a teen club for ages 15 to 20); and the Cave Club (ages 10 to 14). Both clubs feature DJ entertainment, adult supervision, and refreshments.

Riders will find a mix of beginner and expert trails. Un Blancho Gulch, one of the first snowboard parks in the East, runs about 2,700 feet long, with an average trail width of about 80 feet, and features more than 25 freestyle elements. The Gut is a new 400-foot competition-size halfpipe, featuring lights for night riding.

The resort can be a hoppin' place; very popular with the New York and Connecticut crowds.

● Bromley Mountain

Rte. 11, Peru (6 miles east of Manchester); (802) 824-5522. Lift tickets: adults, $39; teens, $32; juniors, $25; under 6, free. Mighty Moose (3–5) and Mountain Club (6–12), $55/day, including lessons and lunch. Kids Center (daycare for 6 wks.–6 yrs.), $35/day. Rates are for weekends and holidays; discounted midweek rates and special packages are offered.
All ages.

Tired of the crowds, the hassle, and the hustle-and-bustle of the big resorts? Then you're going to love this place. Bromley is low-key, friendly, and the perfect spot for beginners, or for those looking for a relaxing get-away. There's another great thing about Bromley: Its southern exposure, which makes the Alpine experience a tad warmer than at other New England ski resorts. It's also a bit kinder on the family budget; lift prices are about $8–$10 less a day than those at other, larger resorts.

There are 39 trails, mostly beginner and intermediate terrain, with a handful of expert runs. Riders will find two parks, including the Vew-Do Lounge, with lots of manmade obstacles, whales, and snow beasts.

On-mountain lodging is available, for ski-in, ski-out ease, and Manchester Center is just a few miles away if you're hankering for fine cuisine and apres-ski fun.

● Stratton Mountain

Stratton Mountain Rd., Bondville; (800) 843-6867. Lift tickets: adults, $48; 13–18, $40; 7–12, $30. Snowkids (3 yrs.), $57/day; Little Kids Kamp (4–6), $59/day; KidsKamp (7–12), $74/day; Kids Kare (6 wks.–3 yrs.), $57/day. Rates are for weekends and holidays; discounted midweek rates and packages are available. **All ages.**

Stratton believes in comfort—on and off the slopes. The mountain: the highest peak in southern Vermont, with a summit elevation of 3,875 feet; 92 trails; and 12 lifts including a 12-person gondola and a six-person, high-speed quad. The resort: a slopeside alpine village with dining and shopping options; and a mega sports center with swimming, racquetball, tennis, and more. Stratton draws crowds from the Big Apple.

RESTAURANTS

You won't go hungry in this region; there are plenty of dining options from fast-food chains, delis, family restaurants to upscale dining establishments. Head to Manchester Center or Brattleboro and take your pick. Here are a few notables:

● Laney's

Rtes. 11 and 30, Manchester; (802) 362-4465. Daily, 5–10.

This lively, popular restaurant features an open kitchen with a wood-fired brick oven. You'll be surrounded by lots of show-biz, sports-biz memorbilia, including signed movie posters and sports equipment. You can't go wrong with the barbecued ribs or chicken dishes, or one of their specialty pizzas. Noisy and fun.

● Mother Myrick's

Rte. 7A, Manchester Center; (802) 362-1560. Fri.–Sat., 10–10; Sun.– Thurs., 10–6.

This is goody heaven: an ice cream parlor, bakery, and chocolate shop all in one. Children will enjoy watching the candy makers prepare fudge and dip chocolates in the candy room. (Tell yourself this is an educational trip.) Can't decide what you want? Indulge in a scrumptious ice cream sundae now, and take some fudge home for later.

● Blue Benn

Rte. 7, North Bennington; (802) 442-5140. Mon.–Tues., 6 A.M.–5; Wed.– Fri., 6 A.M.–8; Sat., 6 A.M.–4; Sun., 7 A.M.–4.

This is a classic diner complete with barrelled ceiling, Formica counter tops, and lots of stainless steel and chrome. But this is not your typical greasy spoon. Blackboard specials might include cheddar cheese and asparagus or watercress and cream cheese omelets, whole wheat pancakes, veggie enchiladas, falafel and nut burgers. There's lots of traditional diner fare, too, like hot dogs, meatloaf and mashed potatoes, and Jell-O. Often crowded, but worth the wait.

Woodstock Area

If your family loves the outdoors, start packing. This gorgeous slice of Vermont mountains and valleys is a treasure trove of recreation.

Many visitors are attracted to this region for downhill skiing; most to mammoth Killington with its six mountains, and the nearby rollicking nightlife. Certainly, you could spend days on skis, while your kids are merrily making snowmen or perfecting their wedge turns. (Or, more often than not, waiting for you at the bottom of the hill.) Not a bad way to beat the winter doldrums.

Come summer, ski trails and the maze of old logging and carriage roads open to hikers, bikers, and strollers. And, summer visitors meander the quaint towns that existed before the ski resorts arrived, especially picturesque Woodstock; visit a world-class museum; or gaze down Quechee Gorge, a natural wonder that dates back to the Ice Age.

● Billings Farm and Museum

Rte. 12, Woodstock; (802) 457-2355. May–Oct., daily, 10–5; Nov.–Dec., weekends, 10–5. Adults, $7; 13–17, $5.50; 5–12, $3.50; 3–4, $1; under 3, free. **All ages.**

Watch cows being milked, churn cream into butter, nuzzle a sheep, pet newborn calves—these are some of the pleasures awaiting your family at Billings Farm. This working dairy farm has prize Jersey cattle, sheep, draft horses, oxen, and a petting nursery. You'll explore the busy life on this real working Vermont dairy farm, getting a good look at the rigors and traditions of farm life in the 1890s.

Be sure to visit the 1890 farm house, featuring an old-fashioned creamery. It's also the home of a farm museum, complete with an authentically restored farm home, workshop, and general store. There are demonstrations of how to hook a rug, spin wool, and do other country chores. Special events are scheduled each month, including an annual Children's Day.

● Vermont Institute of Natural Science

Church Hill Rd., Woodstock; (802) 457-2779. Daily, 10–4; Nov.–Apr., closed Sun. Adults, $5; 5–15, $2. **All ages.**

This unique living museum, a favorite among adults and children alike, houses 26 species of birds of prey native to northern New England. This is your chance to get up close and personal with an owl, hawk, or eagle. All the raptors at the center are permanently injured and unable to survive in the wild. You'll also see injured birds in the infirmary. The institute treats hundreds of injured birds of prey each year; most are released back to the wild.

Leave time for a walk on one of the many self-guided nature trails (there are 77 acres of nature preserve), and for a look at the visitor's center. Housed in a remodeled dairy barn, it usually has a small display of nature exhibits.

● Montshire Museum of Science

Rte. 10A, Norwich; (802) 649-2200. Daily, 10–5. Adults, $5; 3–17, $4; under 3, free. **All ages.**

This peaceful setting has been called "one of the finest museum sites in New England" by the American Association of Museums. The natural world is the focus at Montshire, featuring a wide range of hands-on exhibits and programs, and outside exhibits on the museum's 100-plus acres of forest along the Connecticut River.

Inside, the two-story museum offers dozens of exhibits on astronomy, natural history, and general science. One exhibit is a self-contained colony of more than 250,000 leaf-cutter ants. Other live animals include boa constrictors, a see-through bee hive, and an aquarium with freshwater fish found in northern New England.

The museum continues outside. A footbridge connects the building with the trail system, which has exhibits on cloud formations, ultraviolet light, and other weather-related phenomena. Other trails offer opportunity to see native wildlife, or to learn about geology, trees, insect life, and more. The short walks are perfect for families with even young children, and offer lots of scenic overlooks of the Connecticut River.

● Wilson Castle

West Proctor Rd. (near Rutland, off Rte. 4), Proctor; (802) 773-3284. Late-May–late-Oct., daily, 9–6 (last tour, 5:30). Adults, $6.50; 6–12, $2. **Ages 5 and up.**

If you've ever imagined living in a fairy tale castle, you might have envisioned a place like this. Built by a local physician and his monied British wife, Wilson Castle boasts turrets, arches, parapets, and balconies, the whole thing made of imported materials, including the bricks. On the grounds are cattle barns, stables, and, to the delight of children, an aviary with Indian peacocks.

The Wilson Castle fairy tale, alas, has an unhappy ending. Soon after the castle was built, the lady of the house fled, taking all her money with her.

● The New England Maple Museum

Rte. 7, Pittsfield; (802) 483-9414. Late-May–Oct., daily, 8:30–5:30; Nov.–Dec. 23 and mid-March–late-May, daily, 10–4. Closed Jan.–Feb. Adults, $2.50; 6–12, $.75; under 6, free. **Ages 2 and up.**

Vermonter's call it "nature's gold." And you won't want to miss a sample of the state's sweetest product. Visitors learn how the Native Americans first taught Vermonters to tap the trees and turn sap into syrup. Go during maple sugaring time, from about the end of February until early April, when you'll get a hands-on lesson.

● Pico Alpine Slide

Rte. 4, Pico Mountain Resort, Sherburne; (800) 898-7426. Late-May–mid-Oct., daily, 11–5. Single ride: adults, $5; 6–12, $3.50. Five-rides: adults,

$20; 6–12, $15. All-day pass (includes slide, minigolf, and driving range): adults, $35; 6–12, $25. **Ages 6 and up.**

Every kid loves a wild ride on a slide, and face it, most grown-up kids do, too. In summer, ride the chairlift up the side of Pico Peak, enjoying the beautiful mountain views, then whoosh down the giant alpine slide. There are two tracks, for all ages. If you opt for a one-ride ticket, the kids will be begging for more.

Also at the base lodge, you'll find minigolf and a driving range. And, ever considered bungee jumping? Here's a way to get your feet wet: try Pico's latest Bungee Thing.

● Killington Gondola and Chairlift

Rte. 4, Killington Ski Resort, Sherburne; (802) 422-3333. Gondola: mid-Sept.–mid-Oct., daily. Adults, $16; 6–12, $9. Chairlift: mid-June–mid-Oct., Mon.–Fri., 10–4; Sat.–Sun., 9–4. adults, $5 (one-way), $10 (round-trip); 6–12, $5 (for both one-way and roundtrip tickets). **Ages 2 and up.**

Summer, winter, or fall, you can ride to the summit of Killington Mountain without ever putting on a pair of skis. During the foliage season, the enclosed gondola, or, in the summer, the chairlift will take you three-and-a-half miles up. At the peak you'll find a lounge, cafeteria, and an observation deck. From the deck, you'll see the Green Mountains, the White Mountains (see if you can spot majestic Mount Washington in the distance), the Berkshires, and the Adirondacks. The views, especially during foliage season, are spectacular.

● Killington Playhouse

Killington Rd., Sherburne; (802) 422-9795. July–Labor Day. **Ages 2–12.**

Treat your kids to an afternoon of musical theater at a just-for-kids Wednesday matinee. The Green Mountain Guild performs Broadway favorites at Killington Ski Resort's Snowshed Base Lodge during the summer season. Call ahead for details.

● Vermont Marble Company

62 Main St., Proctor; (802) 459-2300. Daily, 9–5:30. Call for winter hours. Adults, $5; 12 and under, free. **Ages 5 and up.**

You'll learn about marble formation, quarrying, and finishing at the world's largest marble museum. An informative film, exhibits, and interpretive displays show the history of the marble industry in Vermont. The kids will enjoy seeing the sculptor at work. There's also an interesting outdoor display and gallery, including carved marble busts of several U.S. presidents.

● Quechee Gorge

Rte. 4, Quechee; (802) 295-7600. **All ages.**

One of Vermont's most intriguing natural wonders, Quechee Gorge is a mile-long, 165-foot-deep channel that dates back to the last Ice Age. From the bridge spanning the gorge on Route 4, you can stare down into the seemingly bottomless chasm. If your group includes older children, try the shaded mile-long trail to the bottom. It's a fairly easy hike along the fenced-in edge of the precipice. Or, take the short stroll to the falls at the top of the gorge and indulge in a picnic.

● Mountain Biking at Killington Peak

Rte. 4, Sherburne; (802) 422-3333. Mid-June–mid-Oct., daily, 9–6. All-day lift and trail access, $25; one-time ride and trail access, $15; trail access only, $5. Bike rentals: $32–$52/day. **Ages 8 and up.**

There are lots of pretty places for off-road biking in this region of Vermont, but if you like the adrenaline rush of going downhill (and not the huff-and-puff work of uphill pedaling), head to the Killington Ski Resort. Come summer, the Killington Peak chairlift transports bikes and riders to the top of the second highest peak in Vermont. From there, let 'er rip, as you cruise 25 miles of marked trails. Guided tours, helmets, and rental bikes are available at the base.

● Great Outdoor Adventure Tours

Cortina Inn, Rte. 4, Killington; (800) 451-6108. Bike rentals and maps: adults, $25/day; 6–12, $19/day. Drop off and pick up shuttle service, $10 per person. Multiday rates and guided adventure trips are also offered. **Ages 6 and up.**

Some of Vermont's prettiest country—waterfalls and swimming holes, forests and wildflower meadows—lies in its backcountry interior, hidden from the main routes and highways. Hop on a fat-tire bike and it's all yours to discover. Your best bet is to stop by the Cortina Inn (or sign up for one of its weekend adventure getaways). The inn is smack dab in the middle of a network of trails, old logging roads, and backcountry lanes. At its doorstep lie more than 100 miles of mountain biking. The Inn offers bike rentals, maps, guided trips, and shuttle and pick-up service. You can pick from a variety of bike routes, from quiet, easy cruises on backcountry roads to more challenging climbs.

● Horseback Riding

From horse-drawn wagon rides to ponyrides and trail riding, there's something for all ages and experience levels. You can ride for hours through pastoral valleys, pine-scented forests, and along lakes and streams. At **Kedron Valley Inn & Stables,** Route 106, Woodstock, (802) 457-1473, guided trail rides and hourly and daily rentals are offered. Other places to check out if you're hankering to get in the saddle include: **Pond Hill Stables,** Route 4A, Castleton, (802) 468-5166; **Hay/ Sleigh Rides,** 78 Hartland-Quechee Rd., White River Junction, (802) 295-2910; and **Mountain Top Stables,** Mountain Top Inn, Mountain Top Rd., Chittenden, (802) 483-2311.

● White River

Be sure to throw your bathing suit or an extra change of clothes in the trunk when you're traveling this area. The beautiful White River snakes its way through central Vermont, around bends and over rocks. There are lots of places along its banks to stop for a dip, to jump across its width on rocks and fallen logs, or to picnic next to a picturesque waterfall. A favorite summertime sport among locals and visitors alike is tubing down The White on a hot summer's day. There are several places in the area to rent tubes (watch for the hand-scrawled signs and piles of rubber).

● Hiking

Hiking opportunities abound, from easy strolls to rigorous mountain climbs. The trail around Quechee Gorge, for example, offers easy hiking with great views into the gorge.

At Mount Tom in Woodstock, there's a graded footpath with benches along the way. Start at Faulkner Park and follow the switchback trail to the top of Mount Tom. Or, for an easier way up, start at the Woodstock Inn on the Green. The walk follows paved paths, leading gently to the summit with a rewarding 360-degree view. For more hiking and walking trails, contact the local Chamber of Commerce. Several old carriage roads, constructed by the Rockefeller family, crisscross the Woodstock area and make beautiful backcountry strolls.

● Cross-Country Skiing

Nordic skiers will find abundant trails, varied terrain, and plenty of extras at the **Woodstock Ski-Touring Center,** Route 106, Woodstock, (802) 457-2114; **Mountain Meadows,** Thundering Brook Road (off Route 4), Sherburne, (802) 775-7077; **Fox Run,** Ludlow, (802) 228-8871; **Trail Head,** Stockbridge, (802) 746-8038; and **Wilderness Trails,** Quechee, (802) 295-7620. **Killington and Okemo ski resorts** also have cross-country ski centers.

● Killington Ski Resort

Killington Rd. (off Rte. 4), Sherburne; (800) 621-MTNS. Lift tickets: adults, $49/day; 12 and under, $29/day. Superstars (6–12), $83/day, including ski or snowboard instruction and lunch; Ministars (4–5), $96/day, including ski or snowboard instruction and lunch; First Tracks (2–3), $65/day, including on-snow instruction and indoor games. Childcare Center (6 wks.–6 yrs.), $48/day. Rates listed are weekend and holiday rates; midweek discounts and special packages are available.
All ages.

Killington is undeniably a popular place with skiers, and for good reason: it's huge. With six mountain peaks and 170 trails, it's the largest resort in the East. Even those who are new to the sport will find plenty of territory to cover from top to bottom. Killington Peak, the highest mountain of the six, has a vertical rise of 3,000 feet. Since it gets crowded here, plan to hit the slopes early. Also, you may want to head over to the less-populous Sunrise Mountain or Bear Mountain areas, where you'll get more runs in. Some complain that you spend too much time just trying to get from one trail to another. Killington has made it easier for families with the addition of its new Rams Head Family Mountain. The self-contained area has a family center, child care, food emporium, and other services, and the Snow Play Park has beginner and intermediate terrain. An underpass from Rams Head to Snowshed makes it easy for families to access the rest of the mountains.

Beginner riders will like the eight-foot minipipe, offering an easy, less intimidating route to drop in and learn the sport. More advanced riders can twirl, flip, and soar in the 12-foot halfpipe on Snowdon Mountain. Freestylers will also like the 1,300-foot snowboard park at Bear Mountain (for riders only). Jimburritos, a food and music hut, is located at the base of the halfpipe. Lots of rock-and-rollin'.

● Okemo Mountain Resort

Mountain Rd., Ludlow; (802) 228-4041. Lift tickets: adults, $48/day; 13–18, $40/day; 7–12, $30/day. SKIwee (4–8) and MINIriders (5–8), $40; Mountain Explorers and Young Riders (7–12), $65/day; Get Attitude Package (13–18), $25/half-day (morning sessions only); TEENriders (13–18), $65/day; child care, $45/day. Rates listed are weekend and holiday rates; midweek discounts and special packages are available. **All ages.**

If you're thinking of a family ski vacation at Okemo, you better book early. This popular ski resort draws crowds from New York, New Jersey, and southern New England. It's the biggest area in southern Vermont—

88 trails and 13 lifts. It's a wonderful place for families, offering a variety of terrain. Beginners will find lots to ski, including a 4½-mile trail from the summit and one of the longest and widest novice slopes in the country. The upper mountain glades are challenging (and the views are great), and more experienced skiers will be challenged on the mogul-strewn black diamond runs like Sel's Choice, Punch Line, and The Plunge.

Okemo is becoming a hot spot for snowboarding, too. Boarders can catch the waves on The Pipe, a 420-foot halfpipe; The Park, a giant snowboard park; and The Pull, a new riders-only surface lift.

 RESTAURANTS

● The Grist Mill

Summit Pond on Killington Road, Killington; (802) 422-3970. Mon.–Fri., 11:30–10; Sat.–Sun., 7:30–10.

The food is classic New England—hearty steaks, seafood and chicken dishes. But, the view is wonderful. The dining room is surrounded by windows on three sides overlooking Sunnit Pond, with Killington Peak in the distance. If it's a nice day, grab a chair on the deck, and order from the lounge menu.

● Mother Shapiro's

RFD 1, Box 3175, Killington; (802) 422-9933. Winter: Mon.–Fri., 7 A.M.–2 A.M.; Sat.–Sun., 6:30 A.M.–2 A.M. Summers: Mon.–Fri., 8 A.M.–2 A.M.; Sat.–Sun., 7 A.M.–2 A.M.

Both early risers and serious night owls haunt this place. This is the spot to go for breakfast, especially if you're a hash lover. Shapiro's made-from-scratch hash is its best-selling item. Other traditional break-fast items are also available. Sandwiches, soups, and burgers sell at lunch, and dinner entrées include the popular prime rib plate, and chicken and seafood dishes. There's also an extensive kosher menu offered. Children's portions are available.

● Ludlow Cooking Company

29 Main St., Ludlow; (802) 228-3080. Daily, 11:30–9.

Homemade soups, sandwiches, stews, salads, and more are the specialities at this deluxe deli. You can order in, or have them pack it to go for your own classic New England roadside picnic. Don't forget dessert—lots of scrumptious baked goods.

Lake Champlain Valley

Burlington, the largest city in Vermont, reigns over the Lake Champlain Valley region, blessed with spectacular views of mountain peaks on both sides and a large, glistening lake in the middle. The most urban of Vermont's cities sits on the eastern slope of Lake Champlain and is home to nearly a quarter of the state's population. But "urban" to most of us does not mean what it does to Vermonters. You'll find a thriving, vibrant city but one that has not lost its small-town charm and rural influences.

The rejuvenated waterfront area, once one of the country's busiest seaports, is a nice place to stroll; at dusk you'll be rewarded with breathtaking sunsets across the lake. Nineteenth-century buildings have been restored and now house cafes, specialty shops, and pedestrian marketplaces. There are five public parks from which to enjoy water views and lake activities.

If you have time, be sure to visit Champlain's Grand Islands, only a short half-hour drive from downtown Burlington. You'll discover the rural town of South Hero, the countryside of Grand Isle, the tiny village of North Hero, and the beautiful seashore of Isle La Motte. The islands are connected by bridges, surrounded by mountains, and laced with lovely state parks and lakeside beaches.

Everywhere there are opportunities to enjoy the sparkling, 110-mile-long Lake Champlain. Beaches are plentiful; there are powerboats, sailboats, kayaks, and windsurfing equipment to rent; ferries and schooners to carry you across; and scenic vistas everywhere you look. Be on the lookout for Lake Champlain's legendary sea monster—Champ. In 1609, Samuel de Champlain noted in his diary the sighting of a strange creature in the lake. Since, other sightings have been made, prompting the Vermont House of Representatives to pass a resolution in 1982 protecting Champ from "injury or harrassment." The Lake Champlain Chamber of Commerce annually hopes for a banner year of sightings.

Waterlogged and happy, you can travel inland to visit horse and dairy farms, a 1783 log cabin, and the popular Shelburne Museum and Farm.

● Champlain Ferries

Lake Champlain Transportation Co., King Street Dock, Burlington; (802) 864-9804. **All ages.**

An easy way for the family to see Lake Champlain is to hop on one of the ferries that cross the lake to New York. Along the way you'll be treated to beautiful vistas of the New York Adirondacks on one side and the Green Mountains of Vermont on the other.

There are three crossings on Lake Champlain. Catch the ferry in Charlotte just south of Burlington for the 20-minute ride to Essex, New York. You'll enjoy the stopover in Essex; it's a charming lakeside village. The drive from Burlington to Charlotte is worthwhile, too, and you might want to visit a few sites (Wildflower Farm, Mount Philo State Park) in Charlotte, before or after the ferry ride. The ferry leaving Charlotte is open April through early January.

A 12-minute ferry between Grand Isle and Plattsburgh, New York, is open all year. This is a good side trek to remember on your visit to Grand Isle.

A longer, one-hour ferry between Burlington and Port Kent operates mid-May through Columbus Day and provides great views of Lake Champlain.

The boat charter company also offers daily, historic cruises in the summer. You'll trace the path of Samuel de Champlain and hear tales of battles, shipwrecks, and heroes. Cruises depart 11:30, 2, and 4 from the King Street Dock. Rates: adults, $7; 6–12, $3.50; under 6, free.

● Spirit of Ethan Allen

Departs from the Burlington Boathouse, Burlington; (802) 862-8300. Late-May–mid-Oct. Adults, $7.95; 3–11, $3.95; under 3, free. **Ages 3 and up.**

This is a lively, 1½-hour narrated lake excursion aboard a replica of a vintage sternwheeler. With small children, you might want to opt for the shorter day cruise, or, perhaps, a sunset ride. On either one, you'll see fine scenery. Keep your eyes and ears open for the elusive Lake Champlain sea monster, Champ, whom only a few have seen. The sea serpent is said to be about 20 feet long with a horselike head.

● M/V Carrillon

Departs from Teachout's Lakehouse Store & Wharf, Larabee's Point (end of Rte. 74); (802) 897-5331. Father's Day–Labor Day. Two-hour cruises depart 10:30, 12:30, and 2:30; adults, $8; 3–12, $4.50. One-hour cruises depart 11, noon, 1, 2, and 3; adults, $5; 3–12, $3. **Ages 3 and up.**

While other Champlain boat charters opt for the wide-open waters and expansive lake views, this special excursion boat takes a different route. The *Carrillon*, a 1920s lakeboat, moves up and down the narrowest stretch of Lake Champlain. In a vivid history lesson along the way, the boat makes stops at Fort Ticonderoga on the New York side and at several Revolutionary War battlefields in Vermont.

● Shelburne Museum and Heritage Park

Rte. 7, Shelburne; (802) 985-3344. Late-May–late-Oct., daily, 10–5. Adults, $17.50; 6–14, $7 (second consecutive day is free). **All ages.**

The Shelburne, one of the world's great museums of American folk art, artifacts, and architecture, is often referred to as New England's Smithsonian. This is a museum for people of all ages. The children will enjoy its parklike setting, covering 45 acres and filled with an interesting collection of buildings and memorabilia. You'll be able to board the 220-foot steamboat Ticonderoga, cross a covered bridge, peek in a typical New England one-room schoolhouse, shop in an 1840s general store, circle the round barn, and climb the lighthouse.

There are 37 exhibit buildings, seven furnished historic houses, more than 200 horse-drawn vehicles, and 80,000 pieces of Americana in all. The museum grounds leave lots of room to roam, and are perfect for strolling. Lilac gardens, some of the finest in New England, and perennial and herb gardens grace the grounds. A fun peek at the past, and a great family outing.

● Shelburne Farms

Bay and Harbor Rds. (off Rte. 7), Shelburne; (802) 985-8442. Visitor Center and Farm Store open year-round, daily, 9–5. Children's Farmyard: early spring and late fall, weekends only, 10–4; mid-June–Labor Day, daily, 10–4. Adults, $4; 2–14, $3. Tours: late-May–mid-Oct., daily. Adults, $6.50; 2–14, $3.50. Inn rooms and restaurant open late-May–mid-Oct.
All ages.

This is a true gentleman's farm, with 1,000 acres of rolling hills, gracious gardens, and lake views. Always on the kids-favorite list, the open-air wagon tour stops at the dairy barns where you can try your hand at milking; at the Coach Barn Education Center; and at the beautiful Shelburne House gardens. You'll see cheese-making and dairy operations and majestic 19th-century buildings and landscapes along the way. Save time for the walking tour; it begins at the Visitor's Center and winds through fields and woodlands about a mile, past the Farm Barn to the top of Lone Tree Hill for a magnificent view of Lake Champlain and the Adirondacks. Small children will like the up close and personal look at the farm animals in the Farm Barn.

Stop by the gatekeeper's cottage on your way out to pick up some cheese courtesy of the herd of Brown Swiss on the farm.

● Birds of Vermont Museum

900 Sherman Hollow Rd., Huntington; (802) 434-2167. May–Oct., daily, 10–4. Adults, $4.50; under 12, $2. **Ages 5 and up.**

Bring your binoculars and hiking boots and try your luck at spotting some of Vermont's most common birds on the museum trails. Inside you'll find a lovely display of wood-carved Vermont birds and lots of information on these native friends.

● The Vermont Teddy Bear Company

2236 Shelburne Rd., Shelburne; (802) 985-3001 or (800) 829-BEAR. Year-round, daily, 10–4. Adults, $1; under 18, free. **All ages.**

The factory that makes the popular handcrafted Vermont teddy bears has opened its doors, allowing a look inside the magical business of teddy bear making. The colorful complex had its inspiration from the movie Willie Wonka and the Chocolate Factory, and kids of all ages enjoy the entertaining factory tour. The tour guides, or Bear Ambassadors as they are called, throw in lots of teddy bear history and lore, as you watch the Toymakers cut, sew, and stuff the bears. You'll wave as the bears "head off to their new home" inside a pretty box, complete with air hole. Kids can create their own bear in the Make a Friend for Life section of the factory (for $24.95). First, they'll select a "hungry" bear (unstuffed) and then fill him or her with love, dreams, wishes, and giggles on the stuffing machine. The bear, carrying case, and birth certificate is theirs to take home. After the tour, you'll have a chance to browse the Bear Shop, with more than 100 teddy bears for sale.

● The Discovery Museum

51 Park St., Essex Junction; (802) 878-8687. June–Sept., Tues.–Sat., 10–5; Sun., 1–5. Call for winter hours. Adults, $3.50; 2–12, $2.50. **Ages 1–10.**

This wonderful hands-on museum includes a natural science area with live animals; a physical science area where kids can make giant bubbles or work at WFUN-TV station; and an art hall, with changing art exhibits and programs. In July and August, the outdoor animal wildlife center is open, where you can meet native Vermont critters like the great horned owl, fox, and raccoon.

● UVM Morgan Horse Farm

Rte. 23, Middlebury; (802) 388-2011. May–Oct., daily, 9–4. Adults, $3.50; 13–18, $2; 12 and under, free. **All ages.**

This farm, once owned by Joseph Battell, an eccentric landowner, was one of the first centers for the development of the purebred Morgan Horse. Now operated by the University of Vermont, the stables are open for guided tours to see the Morgan descendants. From the short audiovisual presentation shown on the tour you'll learn that the Morgan was the first breed of horse developed in America.

● Robert Frost Trail

Rte. 25, west of Middlebury Gap. **All ages.**

"[A]nd I—I took the one less traveled by . . . ." Whatever road
you travel, don't miss the short (three-quarters of a mile) walk on this
commemorative trail. You'll wind through woods and across a beaver
pond, coming upon seven mounted Robert Frost poems along the way.
Why here? Poet Frost spent 39 summers in a log cabin just down the road
and surely must have walked the same path years ago. While you're here,
visit nearby Texas Falls.

● Texas Falls

Rte. 125, east of Middlebury Gap. **All ages.**

These falls must have been an inspiration to long-ago resident
poet Robert Frost. You'll see a sign marking the falls on Route 125 and
a designated parking area; walk across the bridges to view the series of
falls. There are picnic tables along the way.

● Dakin Farm

*Rte. 7, Ferrisburg and the Champlain Mill, Winooski; (802) 425-3971
or (800) 993-2546. Year-round, daily, 9–5:30. Free.* **All ages.**

Vermont is known worldwide for its farm products. At this
family-owned farm, you'll gain a greater understanding of the processing
of food between the farm field and the grocery store shelves. Farm
products include corncob-smoked ham, bacon, poultry, syrup, and
cheeses. Kids can watch the production of food products and taste free
samples.

● Lake Champlain Maritime Museum

*Basin Harbor, (802) 475-2022. May–mid-Oct., daily, 10–5. Adults, $7;
6–15, $3.* **Ages 2 and up.**

Lake Champlain's colorful nautical past comes to life at this museum
dedicated to preserving the lake's heritage. Top on kids' lists are the
working shops, where they can watch craftspeople carry on the traditional
skills of boatbuilding and blacksmithing. You can view a large collection
of original small watercraft, built over the last 150 years; learn about
shipwrecks in the Nautical Archaeology Center; talk to conservators and
archaeologists on current research being conducted in the lake; climb
aboard a replica of Benedict Arnold's Revolutionary War gunboat, the
Philadelphia; and take a look at marine technology. The museum has a
pretty lakeside location, too.

● Ethan Allen Homestead

Off Rte. 127, Burlington; (802) 865-4556. Mid-May–late-June, daily, 1–5; late-June–late-Oct., Mon.–Sat., 10–5; Sun., 1–5. Adults, $3.50; 5–17, $2; under 5, free. **Ages 5 and up.**

You'll learn all about Ethan Allen, Vermont's founder and hero of the American Revolution, as you tour his restored 1787 farmhouse. The struggles of 18th-century Vermont farm families come alive as you reconstruct their daily lives. (Maybe the kids will stop complaining about picking up their toys and making their beds after a visit here. Sure.) Through exhibits and shows, visitors also learn about the Indians, French colonists, and English settlers in the Champlain region. There are authentic working gardens on the property and in-progress archaeology projects. Bring a picnic basket of goodies to complete the outing; besides plenty of walking trails with river access, there's a picnic area.

● Swimming and Picnicking

There are five public beaches in Burlington where you can enjoy the clear, cool waters of Lake Champlain. **North Beach** is the largest and most popular of the town's beaches. It has a sandy area for sunbathers and swimmers. You'll also get a view of the Adirondacks in the distance. **Oakledge Park** is a more rugged, scenic beach. It has a picnic area and rocky ledges to toss your towel on. **Red Rocks,** a small, sandy beach in South Burlington, is good for kids. Lifeguards are always on duty. **Leddy Park** has a playground and a small beach area.

Mount Philo State Park, off Route 7 in Charlotte, (802) 425-2390, is a great place for a picnic. Be sure to take a drive to Mount Philo's 980-foot summit. Sure, it's small, but you'll have some of the best views in the area. An access road in the park (there's a nominal fee) leads you to the summit.

Burton Island State Park is perfect for those who like a bit more solitude. There are no cars on the island; you reach it by boat or a launch service from Kill Kare State Park, off Route 36 in Saint Albans. There are hiking trails, and a small nature center on the island.

● Catamount Family Center

Governor Caittenden Rd. Williston; (802) 879-6001. May–mid-Oct., Mon.–Fri., noon–8; Sat.–Sun., 9–6. Summer rates: adults, $5; 13–17, $4; 6–12, $3; 5 and under, free. Winter: Mon.–Fri., 10–8; Sat.–Sun. 10–5. Adults, $12/day (trail fee); 13–18, $7/day; 7–12, $5/day; 6 and under, free. **All ages.**

At his 500-acre recreation center, you can run, mountain bike, hike, cross-country ski, ice skate, golf, and more. There is an extensive network of trails for all levels of experience. Ambiance is friendly and casual, with a very helpful staff. Cross-country ski and mountain bike rentals are available. Also check out the wide array of sports programs offered. Refreshments and services are offered in the summer kitchen of the Catamount family's 1796 historic farmhouse.

● Lake Champlain Aquarium

1 King St., Burlington; (802) 862-7777. Mid-May–mid-Oct. Adults, $2; 5–10, $1. **All ages.**

This museum is just getting going but already has more than 80 known Lake Champlain fish species on display. Eleven tanks house giant channel catfish, prehistoric gar, eel, crayfish, turtles, lake sturgeon, and more. It's worth a quick peek, especially if you're pedaling the Burlington Bike Path (the aquarium's right on the path at the waterfront).

● Burlington Bike Path

This 10-mile recreation path follows the lake from the mouth of the Winooski River. You'll share the route with strollers, joggers, and bikers. Pick up the path at Perkins Pier, Leddy Park, Oakledge Park, or North Beach.

● Champlain's Grand Islands

If you have time, take a drive through these peaceful lakeside gems. Traveling north from Burlington, you'll cross the lake to the islands of South Hero, Grand Isle, North Hero, and Isle La Motte. The island villages, connected by bridges, are 30 miles long and eight miles wide. Surrounded by water, with views of the Adirondacks to the west and Mount Mansfield to the east, they offer some of the best in solitude and scenery. Parks and beaches on the islands include:

Grand Isle State Park, with great views, a small beach cove, and rowboats to rent, U.S. 2, Grand Isle, (802) 372-4300; **Knight Point State Park,** a good family beach with a large, sandy swimming cove, picnic area, nature trails, concession stand, and boat rentals, U.S. 2, North Hero, (802) 372-8389; and **North Hero State Park,** where the beach is only open to campers, but noncampers can fish, bike, hike, and rent boats, U.S. 2, North Hero, (802) 372-8380.

● Ice Skating

There are lots of places to ice skate along the shores and inlets of Lake Champlain. Also, you'll find skating at **Leddy Arena** in Leddy Park,

Burlington, (802) 864-0123; **Essex Junction Education Center,** Essex Junction, (802) 878-1394; **Fenton Chester Ice Arena,** Lyndon, (802) 626-9361; and at the **Collins-Perley Sports Center,** Saint Albans, (802) 527-1202.

RESTAURANTS

Stroll through Burlington's downtown Church Street Marketplace and you'll find all kinds of things to eat at lots of delis, take-out stalls, candy shops, sidewalk cafes, and indoor and outdoor restaurants. Two family favorites are featured below.

● Carbur's

115 Saint Paul St., Burlington; (802) 862-4106. Mon–Sat., 11–10; Sun., noon–10.

Like no other, this zany restaurant is perfect for families. From the moment you glance at the menu (a 16-page newspaper with more than 100 "granwich" combinations) 'til the moment you wipe your face with the fluffy hand towels, you'll enjoy your meal here. There are close to 200 items on the menu. (The staff recommends you glance at the table of contents, decide what you're in the mood for, and turn to the pages for descriptions.) The favorite items on the kid's menu are the peanut butter, jelly, honey, and sliced banana sandwich or the peanut butter and fluff sandwich (fluff of marshmallow). If these offend your good taste, there's the kid's bowl of tricolored pasta and sauce, minipizza, fish and chips, and more.

● Henry's Diner

Bank St., Burlington; (802) 862-9010. Daily, 11–10.

A real diner, with real diner food and pocket-pleasing prices. Try the pig-in-a-poke—a hot dog wrapped in bacon and cheese on a grilled roll. The kids will love swinging around on the stools at the counter.

Montpelier Area

As you gaze up at Montpelier's elegant, gold-domed capitol building, you'll get a sense that time has passed you by. The nation's smallest state capital is nestled in the valley of the Winooski River and surrounded by rolling green hills. There's a simple elegance and beauty about Montpelier. But it's not at all pretentious; it's a friendly place to be. Your family will feel comfortable running about the town streets or tumbling on the front lawn of the capitol. Best of all, from here you have all of Vermont to explore. You won't need to go far for recreation. The area mountains, forests, lakes, and streams offer great skiing, hiking, biking, swimming, fishing, and sightseeing.

Meander the back roads for a view of rural Vermont's rolling farmlands and tiny villages. Follow the winding mountain road through dramatic Smuggler's Notch or the twisting side road that follows the Lamoille River through scenic covered bridges. If you're looking for something more lively, visit the cosmopolitan, four-season resort town of Stowe.

This is also a great place to learn about how things are made. Visit the Cabot's Visitor's Center to see cheese being made. At the Maple Grove Museum, you'll see a maple-sugaring operation. In nearby Barre, you can visit the world's largest granite quarries. Take the tour of the capitol and learn how laws are enacted. And everyone's favorite is a tour of Ben & Jerry's Ice Cream Factory.

● Vermont State House Tour

State St., Montpelier; (802) 828-2228. July–Oct., Mon.–Sat., 10:30–4. Free. **Ages 5 and up.**

On this friendly, 20-minute tour of the State Capitol, visitors get an introduction to how state government works. You'll see old Civil War flags in the governor's ceremonial office and take a look at Representatives' Hall. If you are here when the Legislature is in session (January through April), you can watch the proceedings, although tours are not given at this time.

Directly behind the Capitol, there's pretty Hubbard Park. This 121-acre network of trails is a favorite place to go for short hikes. Pack a picnic to enjoy en route; there are scenic places along the way to stop.

● Morse Farm Sugar Shack and Woodshed Theater

County Rd. (3 miles from the State Capitol), Montpelier; (802) 223-2740. Year-round, daily, 9–5; summers, 8–8. Free. **All ages.**

The Morse family members have been maple sugar makers for eight generations and they love to tell the story of maple sugar. The best time to visit this rustic sugar house is in March or April, when the sap is gathered and transformed into syrup. But you can tour the farm and learn about the process of maple sugaring at all times. You'll watch a short slide show in the unique Woodshed Theater, and get a chance to taste samples of the syrup. Few visitors leave without purchasing Sugar on Ice ($2), the traditional Vermont treat.

● Rock of Ages

Exit 6 off I-89, Barre; (802) 476-3121. May–mid-Sept. (closed July 4), Mon.–Sat., 8:30; Sun., noon–5; mid-Sept.–mid-Oct., Mon.–Sun., 8:30–5. Adults, $4; 6–12, $1.50. **Ages 3 and up.**

You can stand atop an observation platform and look over the world's largest granite quarry. From a 350-foot pinnacle at the 20-acre quarry, you'll watch skilled granite miners carve out huge blocks with machines, then lift up to 150 tons with giant granite derricks towering 150 feet above the quarry's edge. Kids will enjoy the tour to the giant ice wall, created for the lair of Dr. Freeze, one of Batman's rivals. Warner Bros. shot one of its Batman movies at the quarry.

Rock of Ages has been operating since the Civil War, producing granite for buildings and monuments around the world. On the guided walking tour, you'll see and hear (this is a nosiy place!) the work being done. You can also take an open-air rail car to the work areas farther uphill. Visit the Craftsman Center on your way out to see how granite is used in final products. Just the sheer size of things here will amaze you.

● Stowe Gondola and Alpine Slide

Mountain Rd., Stowe; (802) 253-7311. Gondola: late-June–late-Oct., daily, 10–5. Adults, $9; 12 and under, $4. Slide: late-June–Aug., daily, 10–5, weekends only Sept.–Oct. Adults, $7.50 (1 ride), $25 (5 rides); 12 and under, $6 (1 ride), $22 (5 rides). **Ages 2 and up.**

Take a scenic ride to the summit of 4,393-foot Mount Mansfield aboard the enclosed, four-person gondola. Too tame? Hop a ride down on the alpine slide that zips down the face of Spruce Peak. You control your own speed through woods and fields, and around the curves.

● Mount Mansfield Auto Road

This 4½-mile gravel road twists and turns its way to the top of Mount Mansfield. At the top—put on your coats, it's likely to be cold—the 33,881-acre Mount Mansfield State Forest stretches before you. Because of the cold climate, you'll see alpine plants found only in arctic temperatures. (Stay on the marked trails to avoid damaging these fragile plants.)

● Stowe Aviation

Rte. 100 (7 miles north of Stowe); (802) 888-7845. May–mid-Nov., daily, 8–sunset. Rates vary. **Ages 3 and up.**

For a bird's-eye view of Mount Mansfield, and an experience you won't soon forget, stop by Stowe Aviation and inquire about its airplane, sailplane, and hot-air balloon rides. If you've always wanted to soar above the mountaintops or float sliently across the treetops, this is your chance. Even small children are welcome.

● Stowe Recreation Path

Hiking or biking the Stowe Recreation Path is, perhaps, the best way to get a look at this mountain city. The 5.3-mile, handicapped-accessible path meanders back and forth across the West Branch River and over 11 gracefully arched bridges. It connects and links a number of attractions in Stowe. In winter, it's a popular cross-country tour. The path begins behind the white-steepled Community Church on Main Street.

● Ben & Jerry's Ice Cream Factory

Rte. 100 (exit 10 off I-89), Waterbury; (802) 244-5641. Year-round, daily, 10–5. Adults, $1.50; 12 and under, free. Note: There is no ice cream production on Sun. **All ages.**

It's not quite Willy Wonka's Chocolate Factory—but close enough. For ice cream lovers, it's next to heaven. The fun-filled tour takes you through the factory where all that famous Ben & Jerry's ice cream is made. You'll learn the steps it takes to produce the ice cream, and just when you think you can wait no longer, you'll reach the Scoop Shop. (The tour does include free samples of ice cream, but just enough to make you want more.) Enjoy your Chunky Monkey cone (or any of your other favorite flavors) at a picnic table overlooking a pasture of cows with a backdrop of Vermont's rolling Green Mountains. In the summer, Ben & Jerry's offers free outdoor family movies once a week at dusk. Call ahead for a schedule. If you're here in June, inquire about the timing of the Ben & Jerry's annual ice cream festival—lots of fun.

● Cold Hollow Cider Mill

Rte. 100, Waterbury; (802) 244-8771. Daily, 8–6; June–Oct., 8–7. Free. **All ages.**

Cold Hollow is Vermont's largest producer of fresh apple cider. Come to watch the cider being made and to partake of a barnful of homemade Vermont goodies, including fresh pies, donuts, jams and jellies, cheeses, hams, syrup, and more.

● Lamoille Valley Railroad

Rte. 100, Railroad Depot, Morrisville; (802) 888-4255. Mid-July–mid-Oct., daily, 10–1. Rates vary. **Ages 5 and up.**

Take a scenic mountain trip aboard 1920 rail cars. The 60-mile excursion takes about two hours and is very popular during foliage season. Call ahead for reservations.

● Cabot Visitors' Center

Main St., Cabot; (802) 563-2231. June–Oct., daily, 9–5; winter, Mon.– Sat., 9–4; closed Jan. Adults, $1; under 12, free. **All ages.**

If your family has not yet tired of factory visits, go to the Cabot Creamery, where you'll see all kinds of dairy products being made. The cooperative is the largest in the region, owned by 1,800 farm families. From this small, quiet Vermont village come award-winning, world-renowned cheddar cheeses. The countryside setting is pleasant, the staff always friendly, and the video presentation interesting. Of course, you won't want to leave without sampling the creamery's excellent products. An annex store is also located in Waterbury, between Ben & Jerry's Ice Cream Factory and Cold Hollow Cider Mill.

● Groton State

Rte. 232, Groton; (802) 584-3822. **All ages.**

This is one of the best places in the area for outdoor family recreation. The 28,000-acre area is the state's largest recreational center, covering six towns. There are several lakes in the forest for swimming and boating (you can rent boats and canoes in the park), and more than 40 miles of hiking trails. The summer nature programs are fun for the entire family.

● Lake Elmore State Park

Rte. 12, Lake Elmore; (802) 888-2982. **All ages.**

A pleasant park about 25 miles from Stowe, you can swim, rent boats, hike, and walk up a lookout tower for a view of the Green Mountains here.

● Smuggler's Notch

If you can endure the hairpin turns and narrow curves on this steep, winding scenic drive, you'll be rewarded with a dramatic view of Smuggler's Notch. Travel Route 108 just beyond Spruce Peak, where you'll begin your climb to the top of the notch. It's said to have been used as a hideout and, during the War of 1812, as a passageway between Canada and the United States. At the top, there's a small rest area from which to view the gnarled chasm created by glacial waters. You'll be at an elevation of 2,162 feet, where the air begins to cool. On the way down the back side, you'll pass a waterfall before reaching the Smuggler's Notch Resort. The road is closed from late fall until May.

● Smuggler's Notch Resort

Rte. 108, Smuggler's Notch; (802) 644-8851 or (800) 451-8752. The resort specializes in multiday family packages, offering a variety of options. Write or call for free brochures, listing packages, and rates. **All ages.**

Smuggler's has accumulated just about every "best family resort" award given out. It's always rated at the top of the list for quality and fun. It has everything children want—lots of activities, lots of freedom, and lots of other kids. Drive your car to the resort (the drive itself is beautiful) and park. You'll need to go no farther to find dining, swimming pools, games, sledding, ice skating, movies, arcades, saunas, hot tubs, tennis, parties, bonfires, parades, and top-notch resort lodging. The really nice part? While the kids are off having fun (everything is within walking distance), the parents are free to do the same. Smuggler's takes care of your kids, and all the details, so you can relax and have fun, too.

In the winter, there's plenty of skiing on 60 trails across three inter-connected mountains. Most of the terrain is beginner to intermediate, but black diamond skiers will find a handful of runs to get the adrenaline going, including the first triple black diamond run in the East. In a good snow season, Snuffy's Trail opens, connecting Smuggler's with the Stowe ski area. (Interchangeable tickets are available.) Kids have their own Learning and Fun Park. Kids are Smuggler's specialty. The smallest children do their first skiing indoors on the carpeted ski ramp. They get the feel of sliding on skis before they head outdoors for their first 20- to 30-minute lesson. Children, ages 3 to 5, learn to ski in Discovery Dynamos; six- to 12-year-olds ski or snowboard in Adventure Rangers; and teens, 13 to 17, have their own program, Mountain Explorers. Everyone graduates with the appropriate degree—bachelor of skiing or snowboarding for novices; master's for intermediates; and a Ph.D. for those who've conquered the black diamonds.

In summer, a variety of nature, hiking, and exploration programs and activities are offered.

● Sugarbush Resort

RR 1, Warren; (802) 583-2381 or (800) 53-SUGAR. Lift tickets: adults, $47; 7–13, $25; 6 and under, free. Microbears (2¹/₂–3), $53/day; Minibears (4–6), $58/day; Sugarbears (7–12), $68; Catamounts (13–16), $75/day. Daycare (6 wks.–3yrs.), $48/day. Programs include instruction, lift tickets, lunch, and ski rental equipment (snowboard rental is additional). Rates are for weekend and holidays; special discount packages are available. **All ages.**

With the recent infusion of $28 million in improvements, Sugarbush has become one of the premier ski resorts in the East. The world's longest, fastest quad chair now travels from the Mount Ellen area in the north to Lincoln Peak area in the south. Skiers and riders have six mountains to explore, including 111 trails. Experts will find some of the best runs in the region, including the legendary Castlerock runs—bumpy, gnarly, steep, narrow, unpredictable. But there's plenty for intermediate and beginner skiers, too: lots of blue-square cruisers, plenty of pretty glades, and a separate learning area for beginners. Small children will enjoy the Sugarbush Forest, a special kid's area with a covered bridge, obstacles, and artificial bumps and rolls. (Adults must be accompanied by a child to enter.) Riders encounter rolls, waves, hits, and pipes on several trails. At the Mount Ellen area, the Wizard Bus blasts out tunes all day on Sunday. At Lincoln Peak, riders can get their thrills on Nancy, a half-mile pipe.

The best part about the Sugarbush expansion is that it managed to maintain most of its character. Off the slope, vacationing families will find the quintessential Vermont countryside and quaint villages. Lots of pretty country inns, rustic taverns, and traditional charm surround the resort.

● Stowe Mountain Resort

Mountain Rd., Stowe; (802) 253-3000 or (800) 253-4SKI. Lift tickets: adults, $48; 6–12, $28; 5 and under, free. Children's ski programs (3–12), $65/day; child care, $50/day. **All ages.**

You'll get real spoiled skiing at Stowe. It makes skiing as easy, convenient, and comfortable as possible. You'll find some of the finest on-mountain services (like homemade pizzas, fresh-baked pastries and designer-style sandwiches and salads at the boutique-style Midway Cafe), an enclosed (no need to brave the sometimes-brutal New England weather), and the deluxe mountaintop Cliff House restaurant (where the views and the fare are equally superb). And you'll find some great skiing—big-time skiing. Experts can tackle a 2,360-foot vertical drop, offered in a variety of terrain. The intermediate runs at Stowe ski long and hard all the way down, and beginners have an entire mountain area to explore. Stowe has often been cited as one of the best vacation ski areas in the country, and its reputation draws plenty of trendy, lively crowds. In recent years, Stowe has actively targeted the family business, offering special family packages and top-notch daycare and children's ski programs.

● Bolton Ski Area

Bolton Valley Access Rd. (off Rte. 2), Bolton; (802) 434-2131. Lift tickets: adults, $35/day; 6–14, $25. **All ages.**

The friendly atmosphere of Bolton Valley is especially apppealing to families. Tucked away high in the mountains of northern Vermont, Bolton offers two mountains to ski with 46 trails. This is a relaxing, effortless skiing experience, with gentle cruising runs and an emphasis on the slow and easy. Bolton loves families and goes that extra mile to welcome them. It was one of the first ski resorts in America to offer a full-service daycare and instruction program for kids. Bolton is an all-inclusive, self-contained resort, offering dining, recreational facilities, and nightlife (making it even more pleasant for vacationing families). An added plus: night skiing, too.

RESTAURANTS

Stowe, Mad River Valley, and Montpelier are all well known for a variety of eateries, from elegant to casual. In addition, the major ski resorts offer a wide selection of family-friendly restaurants. Here are a few of the most popular.

● The Shed
Mountain Access Rd., Stowe; (802) 253-4364. Daily, 11:30–midnight.

More families probably eat here than at any other restaurant in Stowe. It serves breakfast, lunch, and dinner—fast, friendly, and predictable. This place goes through a lot of barbequed baby back ribs and mighty Shed burgers (the best in town).

● China Moon
Sugarbush Village, Warren; (802) 583-6666. Nov.–mid-Apr., daily 5:30–10:30; winter, weekend lunch also served 12–3. Spring/fall, closed Tues.; summer, daily, 5:30–9:30.

You can't beat this place for great Chinese food—casual atmosphere, reasonable prices, and a menu that goes on forever. All the traditional fare: noodles and rice dishes, pork, beef, fish, and seafood prepared in a variety of ways, bean cakes, and much more. Take out is also available if you decide to stay in the condo. Reservations are usually necessary.

● About Thyme Cafe
40 State St., Montpelier; (802) 223-0427. Mon.–Fri., 7–7:30; Sat., 9–3. Closed Sun.

This gourmet take-out/deli is the perfect antidote for a hungry crew. The sandwiches come on thick-sliced homebaked breads; the salads—an impressive array is always offered—are fresh, creative, and great tasting. Breakfast is homemade muffins, waffles, fresh fruit, and more. At dinner, there's a selection of daily entrées, reflecting the cafe's international flavor.

Northern Vermont

Some call it the Northeast Kingdom. Some call it the quiet corner. Some call it the last vestige left of "real" Vermont. Whatever you call it, you won't argue about its scenic, unspoiled beauty. The Vermont territory closest to the Canadian frontier offers the most variety of terrain and range of topography, from rolling hills to high mountaintops to wide, flat rural regions. There are places where you'll be able to see for miles, unbroken by the marks of civilization, and others where you'll find surprising pockets of lively culture, interesting museums, and frolicking activity. Your options for travel are just as diverse, from a hot-air balloon or gondola, a car, train, or mountain bike to canoe or afoot. Poking about the vast rural lands, you'll discover some unexpected pleasures, such as an extraordinary natural history museum, a challenging ski resort, and a hidden mountain lake to enjoy.

● Fairbanks Museum and Planetetarium

Main St., St. Johnsbury; (802) 748-2372. Museum: year-round, daily, Mon.–Sat., 10–4; Sun., 1–5. Adults, $4; 5–17, $2.50. Planetarium: summer, daily; weekends, year-round; 1:30 show. Adults, $1. **All ages.**

This must-see museum was founded in 1891 by Colonel Franklin Fairbanks, a naturalist and born collector of wildlife. The building itself, a red sandstone Victorian with a 30-foot barrel-vaulted oak ceiling, is something to see. But you'll be more dazzled by the exhibits inside.

You'll be nose to nose with stuffed polar bears, wild boars, alligators, penguins, bison, foxes, moose, opossums, an armadillo, and more. You'll be surrounded by an unbelievable collection of mounted birds and mammals peeking out through holes, from under limbs, and from behind glass in environmental displays. The eclectic collection also includes Indian artifacts, dolls, photomicrographs of tiny snowflakes, dinosaur bones, Fairbanks scales, and lots of folklore, from doll furniture made by Mark Twain to colorful mosaic tapestries depicting the Revolutionary War—made out of bugs!

Be sure to visit the lower level, where you'll see one of the country's oldest continuously operated weather stations and get a glimpse of regional weather broadcasts being prepared. If you have time, travel to the stars at one of the ongoing planetarium shows, offered daily in July and August and on weekends the rest of the year.

● Maple Grove Maple Factory

Rte. 2, St. Johnsbury; (802) 748-5141. Museum: May–Oct., daily 9–5. Factory tours: year-round, Mon.–Fri., 9–5. Adults, $1; under 12, free. **All ages.**

Vermont is maple syrup country, and you can't leave the area without at least one visit to where it is being made. Maple Grove is one of the world's largest. You'll learn how the sap is gathered—a tap is driven into the tree and a tin bucket hung from it. When the bucket is full, it's emptied into a vat, transported to a shack, and boiled down. The Maple Grove Museum re-creates this process. Housed in an original sugar shack, the museum includes the displays of both antique and modern sugar-making equipment. You'll also see how maple syrup is converted into candy (and get a free sample) on the tour.

● Bread & Puppet Museum

Rte. 22 (off Rte. 16), Glover; (802) 525-3031. June–Oct., daily, 10–5. Donations accepted. **All ages.**

Show us a kid that doesn't like a puppet or can resist the lure of full-size masks, and we'll show you a kid that hasn't seen them. As you travel the Northeast Kingdom and find yourself near the tiny town of Glover (just off I-91), stop by this small museum. You'll enjoy looking at the nice collection of puppets and masks in all sizes.

● Lake Willoughby

Near Westmore. **All ages.**

Okay, you've been traveling through the northern region of Vermont, gazing at the gorgeous scenery, rolling hills, and rural pastures. Nice, but now it's time to get out of the car for fresh air, a little exercise, maybe even a swim. This is the place. Although a bit off the major highways, Lake Willoughby is worth the extra time it takes to get there. This is a 600-foot deep lake carved by ancient glaciers, tucked between two mountain ranges. Secluded and relatively undiscovered, it has great views and hiking trails, too.

● Jay Peak Ski Resort

Rte. 242, Jay; (802) 988-2611. Various package rates available. **All ages.**

Ready to get away from it all? Want to escape the southern crowds? Longing for some skiing on real, natural snow? Consider a trip up to Jay Peak. This area is famous for receiving the greatest natural snowfall of any Eastern resort. This is a relatively small resort, unpretentious, and relaxed. You'll find 2,153 vertical feet of skiing, 40 diverse trails and glades, and numerous slopeside accommodations and amentities. Jay Peak welcomes families and offers SKIwee programs for all ages and abilities. Family specials are offered, including "children stay free" programs and complimentary day and evening child care.

¶¶ RESTAURANTS

● Miss Newport Diner

E. Main St., Newport; (802) 334-7742. Mon.–Fri., 5:30 A.M.–1 P.M.;
Sat., 6–noon; Sun., 7–noon.

This authentic 1947 dining car has been a favorite watering hole for
many a year offering homemade, old-fashioned food at yesteryear prices.
It's a great place for families. Hot turkey sandwiches, real mashed potatoes
and gravy, fresh-baked breads, burgers and fries—even Jell-O.

● Miss Vermont Diner

Memorial Dr., St. Johnsbury; (802) 748-9751. Mon.–Thurs., 6 A.M –
8 P.M.; Fri.–Sat., 6 A.M.–9 P.M.; Sun., 7 A.M.–8 P.M.

This is the quintessential cheap-eats restaurant—and the kids will
love the swivel seats. Clean, bright, and cheery, Miss Vermont serves up
huge portions of homemade food at old-fashioned prices. You'll get jumbo
eggs, thick slices of toast, and chunks of ham, or for lunch, a fresh, flaky
haddock sandwich or thick, marinated chicken breast with roasted
potatoes and cole slaw. At dinner, you're likely to find roast turkey,
homemade soups and chowders, and fresh pies for dessert.

Connecticut

Mystic and the Shoreline

The Mystic area is tremendously popular with families, and for good reason: it boasts two world-class attractions, Mystic Seaport and Mystic Marinelife Aquarium. Downtown Mystic—sliced down the middle by the Mystic River—has a seafaring charm all its own. Here you can participate in the town's most popular spectator sport, watching boats go by. You may not have a choice regarding this activity: the bridge goes up in the middle of downtown approximately every hour and a quarter in summer.

Neighboring towns, including Stonington, Norwich, Groton, and New London, offer appealing attractions, too, such as the Science Center of Eastern Connecticut, the Nautilus Submarine Museum, and Ocean Beach Park.

Where there's lots of fun and activity, you can bet there'll be crowds. This is especially true of Mystic Seaport. So arrive early, and be prepared to spend some time waiting in lines if you visit in summertime. Or plan your trip to Mystic in the less-hectic spring or fall. Another possibility: consider Christmastime. Mystic makes the most of it. Mystic Seaport holds Children's Victorian Christmas Tours, and downtown Mystic re-creates the spirit of a 19th-century Christmas, complete with carolers and yuletide refreshments.

● Mystic Seaport

Exit 90 off I-95, Mystic; (860) 572-0711. Year-round, daily, except Christmas Day. Open April–mid-June, 9–5; mid-June–Sept., 9–6; Sept. and Oct., 9–5; Nov.–March, 9–4. Adults, $16; 6–15, $8. Horse-and-carriage ride: adults, $2 (15-min. ride) or $1 (10-min. ride); children, free. Steamboat Sabino river cruise: adults, $3; 6–15, $2; under 6, free. **All ages.**

This is the attraction that put Mystic on the map. Mystic Seaport is America's largest maritime museum, a 17-acre site boasting tall ships and a re-created 19th-century seaport village. If you're visiting Mystic Seaport in summer, stop at the gate for your copy of Kids Today, a chronological guide to all the fun stuff scheduled for kids. This might include a session on tying sailors' knots or helping set sails, and special planetarium shows. Small fry will adore the quaint Children's Museum (despite the long wait to enter it in high season). A treasure trove of 19th-century toys and games awaits inside; outside, on the green, children can try rolling a hoop or walking on stilts.

Your family could spend a whole day at Mystic Seaport and not be bored. For starters, you'll want to explore the seaport's historic homes and village, where role-players demonstrate such 19th-century skills as boatbuilding and wood carving. Climb aboard the 1841 whaleship, *Charles W. Morgan,* and you'll see the magnificent result of one of the lenghthiest resoration projects in the seaport's history. The *Morgan* is the last of the wooden whaleships. You won't want to miss a river cruise on the *Sabino,* the last coal-fired steamboat in America. The *Sabino* departs hourly for 30-minute cruises from mid-May to mid-October.

A great way to end your day at Mystic Seaport: give your legs a rest and take a ride on a horse-drawn carriage at Chubb's wharf. Children will enjoy clip-clopping around the seaport village, and you'll get one last look at this special place before heading back to the 20th century.

● Mystic Marinelife Aquarium

Exit 90 off I-95, Mystic; (860) 572-5955. July 1–Labor Day, 9–6; rest of year, daily, 9–5. Closed Thanksgiving, Christmas, New Year's Day, and last full week in Jan. Adults, $10.50; 3–12, $7. **All ages.**

More than 3,500 marine animals live here, and the best part about this aquarium is that you can get really close to most of them. The aquarium houses 40 exhibits, with every kind of fish and sea creature you can imagine, including a blue lobster and an octopus.

Most kids are fascinated by sharks, and they'll love exchanging menacing stares with three kinds of them in the Open Sea exhibit. There's even a special step up, alongside the tanks, so that toddlers won't miss anything. Of course, you'll want to see as many of the marine mammal shows as possible. Dolphins, sea lions, and whales perform here; children are especially delighted when the dolphins walk on their tails and the Beluga whale kisses its trainer. Outside, Seal Island features five species of seals and sea lions in natural settings, and the Penguin Pavilion houses a colony of African black-footed penguins. Plan to spend a couple of hours here to see it all.

● Denison Pequotsepos Nature Center

Pequotsepos Rd., Mystic; (860) 536-1216. Open May–Sept., Mon.–Sat., 9–5, Sun., 1–5. Oct.–April, Tues.–Sat., 9–5; closed Sun. and Mon. Adults, $4; children under 12, $2; under 5, free. **Ages 3 and up.**

If you're worn out from fighting the crowds at Mystic Seaport and Mystic Marinelife Aquarium, the peaceful nature center could provide the perfect respite. You'll find more than 125 acres of wildlife sanctuary and four miles of hiking trails, with ponds, fields, lowland and upland woods to explore. The Nature Center maintains a year-round trailside museum, where you'll learn about birds, insects, reptiles, and pond and marine life. The nonprofit center is dedicated to environmental awareness. Special programs are offered on weekends throughout the year; call ahead. Nearby, the Denison Homestead (1717) showcases heirlooms from several generations of the Denisons, one of Connecticut's first families.

● The New England Carousel Museum/Mystic Carousel & Fun Center

193 Greenmanville Ave., Mystic; (860) 536-7862 (museum), (860) 572-9949 (Mystic Carousel & Fun Center). Mon.–Sat., 10–5; Sun., 12–5. Adults, $4; ages 4–14, $2.50; under 4, free. **All ages.**

An offshoot of the Carousel Museum in Bristol, Connecticut, this site offers more than 70 pieces of wonderful, whimsical carousel art, reflecting the styles of turn-of-the-century carvers. The museum's goal is to foster appreciation for the classic wooden carousel; certainly, kids' eyes light up when they see these magical creations. At the same site, the Mystic Carousel & Fun Center—one of the largest indoor fun spots in the state—offers a working carousel, pizza, rides, and games for little ones.

● Scenic Stroll: Downtown Mystic's Bascule Bridge

You really can't miss this famous bridge; it runs right through the center of town, rising so that sailboats can navigate the **Mystic River** without snapping their masts off. Watch the boat traffic, wander into a shop or two, perhaps stopping for a meal at a riverfront eatery. Or, try **Mystic Pizza,** the setting for the movie of the same name, where Julia Roberts got her start.

● Old Lighthouse Museum

Water St., Stonington Village; (860) 535-1440. May–Oct., Tues.–Sun., 11–4:30. Adults, $2; 6–12, $1. **Ages 3 and up.**

Drive out to the Lighthouse Museum on Stonington Point (a short trip from downtown Mystic on Route 1) and you can see three states at the same time: Fisher's Island, New York, to the south; Watch Hill, Rhode Island, to the east; and Connecticut, under your feet. Stonington Lighthouse was operated as a lighthouse until 1889; now it's a museum, housing 19th-century portraits, a collection of whaling and fishing artifacts, swords and firearms, and, in the children's room, toys and a dollhouse. To most kids, the best part is just being inside a lighthouse.

● Rocky Neck State Park

Rte. 156, exit 72 off I-95, Niantic; (860) 739-5471. **All ages.**

The best feature of this park is a mile-long crescent beach. Enjoy hiking, fishing, picnicking, a boardwalk, and concessions.

● Children's Museum of Southeastern Connecticut

409 Main St. (Rte. 156), Niantic; (860) 691-1255. Tues.–Sat., 9:30–4:30; Sun., 12–4. Open Mon. in summer and on CT school holidays. $3 per person; under 2, free. **Ages 1–12.**

"We all vis-it a yellow submarine". . . Kids from one to 12 will find plenty to engage, delight, and challenge them here, including a pipe organ to play, an Amtrak train exhibit, Kidsville, a kid-size town, and a real, 21-foot yellow submarine. Theme areas include The Sciences, The Arts, Safety and Health, and Culture and History. Live performances are often featured, including folksingers, storytellers, jugglers, magicians, and dancers.

● Millstone Information and Science Center

278 Main St., exit 74 off I-95, Niantic; (860) 444-4234. Year-round, Mon.–Fri., 9–4; special evening and weekend hours in summer (call for times). Free. **Ages 3 and up.**

The Millstone Nuclear Power Station offers exhibits on nuclear energy and other energy sources, computer games, multimedia shows, and the Millstone Nature Trail, a one-mile walking path through woodlands and lagoons with views of native wildlife.

● Putts Up Dock Mini Golf

One Chelsea Harbor Dr., Norwich; (860) 886-PUTT. June–Sept., daily, 10–10; weekends only, spring and fall. Open weather permitting. **Ages 3 and up.**

While there are several miniature golf courses in Southeastern Connecticut, this one claims to be New England's most challenging course. Features include an actual spouting volcano, a misty cave under a waterfall, and a play-through boathouse. Bumper boats, too.

● Norwich Navigators Minor League Baseball

Sen. Thomas W. Dodd Memorial Stadium, 15 Stott Ave., Norwich; (860) 887-7962 or 800-64-GATOR. Call for a schedule of home games and ticket prices. **All ages.**

Catch all the action (and a fly ball, if you're lucky) of the New York Yankee's AA minor league affiliate team at their spiffy new stadium.

● Maple Breeze Park

Rte. 2, exit 92 off I-95, Pawcatuck (near Stonington); (860) 599-1232. May and June, weekends; July–Labor Day, daily, 10–10. **Ages 3 and up.**

Here's just the place for the kids to expend some pent-up energy after a too-long road trip or museum session. This amusement park offers a waterslide, go-cart tracks, bumper boats, and mini-golf. All this, and an ice cream shop, too.

● Seal Watching and Whale Watching

Wildlife watchers will want to check out these intriguing adventures, offered by **Captain John's Sport Fishing Center.** In March and April, take a three-hour cruise to visit harbor seals, departing from Waterford. From May through Labor Day, excursion boats head to the waters of Montauk Point for all-day whale watching, departing from Captain John's dock near the Niantic River bridge, Route 156. Call (860) 443-7259 for information. Rates for bald eagle and sealwatching cruises are $25, adults, and $15 for children under 12; free for kids under 4. Rates for whalewatch trips in July and August: adults, $35; under 12, $20; under 4, free.

● Historic Ship *Nautilus* and Submarine Force Museum

Exit 86 off I-95, Groton; (800) 343-0079 (recorded information), (860) 449-3174. Open Wed.–Mon., 9–4; closed Tues.; also closed the first full week of May, first full week of June, and second full week of Dec. Closed Thanksgiving, Christmas, and New Year's Day. Free. **Ages 3 and up.**

Many a child has fashioned a periscope out of a cardboard tube and played submarine. At the Nautilus Museum—part of the U.S. Naval Submarine Base—kids can peer through real periscopes and tour a real submarine, the USS *Nautilus.* The world's first nuclear-powered vessel, the *Nautilus* was commissioned into the U.S. Navy in 1954. Once on board (you might have to wait in line, as only 60 people are allowed aboard at one time), you'll carry an electronic wand that activates narration about each area of the submarine. You'll see the navigation center, the radar room, the attack center, and watch films about submarines past and present. Elsewhere in the museum, there are working periscopes, an authentic submarine control room, and several midget submarines.

● Project Oceanology Marine Studies Cruise

Cruises depart from Avery Point off Eastern Point Rd., Groton; (800) 364-8472. Late June–Labor Day, daily, 10 and 1. Adults, $17; under 12, $12. Reservations recommended. **Ages 5 and up.**

Climb aboard a 50-foot Enviro-Lab research vessel for a cruise you won't forget. Marine scientists and instructors will teach you how to use oceanographic instruments, help pull a trawl net, test seawater, identify lobsters, crabs, and fish, and measure lobsters. You'll also help take core samples of mud and sand (wonderfully messy work) from the bottom of the ocean and examine them. Best for kids age five and up, the trips last two and a half hours. Project Oceanology is operated by a nonprofit association of public and private schools and colleges in Connecticut, Massachusetts, Rhode Island, and New York.

● Fort Griswold State Park

Monument St., exit 85 off I-95, Groton; (860) 445-1729. Park open year-round. Museum and monument: Memorial Day–Labor Day, daily, 9–5; Labor Day–Columbus Day, weekends only, 9–5. Free. **All ages.**

This 17-acre park was the scene of a massacre in 1781. Benedict Arnold led an attack by the British forces, taking the fort and burning Groton and New London. On the hilltop near Fort Griswold, a 135-foot monument dedicated to the victims of the massacre bears their names. Today you'll find the spot a considerably more pleasant place, with beautiful views of the Thames River and Fisher's Island from the memorial tower. Bring a picnic.

● Bluff Point State Park

Depot Rd., off Rte. 1, Groton; (860) 566-2304. **All ages.**

Located between Mystic and Groton on Long Island Sound, this unspoiled stretch of shoreline is a great place to take a hike or nature walk, have a picnic, or fish from the shore. Take to the trails on cross-country skis in winter.

● Lyman Allyn Art Museum

625 Williams St., New London; (860) 443-2545. Open July–Labor Day, Tues.–Sat., 10–5; Sun., 1–5; open Labor Day–June, Tues.–Sun., 1–5. Adults, $3; under 12, free. **Ages 5 and up.**

This small museum, a memorial to whaling captain Lyman Allyn, houses period furniture, a glass collection, and displays of Oriental, Greek, Egyptian, and Roman art. We recommend it for families because of the terrific collection of dollhouses and toys including an exhibit of rare 19th- and 20th-century dolls. At Christmas, a special exhibit, *The Victorian Toy Shop,* is featured.

● Connecticut Arboretum/Science Center of Eastern Connecticut

Gallows Lane off Williams St., exit 83 off I-95, New London; (860) 442-0391. Open Tues.–Sat., 10–4; closed Sun. Adults, $6; 3–12, $4; under 3, free. **Ages 3 and up.**

Two sites on the Connecticut College campus are worth a visit. The 415-acre arboretum offers several hiking trails, including one that leads to Balles Wood, a hemlock forest. At the Science Center, enter cyberspace via the internet and explore a jungle of microbes as a "microscope master." Also among the fun, interactive exhibits here: a pipe organ, just waiting to be played by tiny hands.

● U.S. Coast Guard Academy

Mohegan Ave. and Rte. 32, exit 83 off I-95, New London; (860) 444-8270. Visitor's Pavilion: May–Oct., daily, 10–5. Free. **Ages 3 and up.**

There are two advantages to visiting the academy in spring and fall: you might see the cadet corps on dress parade (usually on Friday afternoons) and you can board the 295-foot training barque, *Eagle,* Fridays through Sundays from 1 to 4 P.M. when it's in port. (Call first to avoid disappointment.) The Visitor's Pavilion features a multimedia show depicting cadet life, while the museum at Waersbe Hall displays historical nautical items.

● Ocean Beach Park

Ocean Ave., exits 75N and 83S off I-95, New London; (860) 447-3031; (800) 962-0284 (CT only). Memorial Day–Labor Day, 9 A.M.–10 P.M. Adults, $2; 3–14, $1. Parking, $2 per hour/$6 maximum, Mon.–Thurs.; Fri.–Sun., $10 maximum. **All ages.**

You can have family fun galore at Ocean Beach Park, one of the most popular recreation areas on Long Island Sound. In addition to a wide white-sand beach, you'll find a boardwalk, eateries, a pool, a triple waterslide, minigolf, a playground, and an arcade (open year-round). The kids won't leave willingly.

● Harkness Memorial State Park

Rte. 213, 4 mi. south of New London, Waterford; (860) 443-5725. Year-round. **All ages.**

Once a private summer estate, this grand Italian-style villa is set on 116 acres on Long Island Sound. Grown-ups will enjoy poking around the 42-room mansion and formal gardens; kids will like beachcombing, picnicking, and fishing.

● Garde Arts Center

329 State St., New London; box office (860) 444-7373. **Ages 5 and up.**

The historic Garde Theatre, the region's last remaining vaudeville/cinema house, offers a family theater series among its program of performances. Call for a schedule and showtimes.

● Mohegan Park

Judd Rd., Rtes. 2 and 32, Norwich; (860) 886-2381, ext. 259. Year-round. Free. **All ages.**

The best feature of this 385-acre park, overlooking the city, is a children's petting zoo. Residents include tropical birds, monkeys, and an American eagle. In season, don your suits for swimming in Mohegan Park Lake. A beautiful rose garden, honoring World War II dead, is in full bloom from late June to early July. Other features include hiking trails, picnic areas, and a playground.

● Slater Memorial Museum

108 Crescent St., Norwich; (860) 887-2506. Sept.–June, Tues.–Fri., 9–4; Sat. and Sun., 1–4. July and Aug., Tues.–Sun., 1–4. Closed holidays. Adults, $2; under 12, free. **Ages 5 and up.**

Visit the Norwich Free Academy with your kids for a look at the Slater Museum complex's Joseph P. Gualtieri Children's Gallery. Appointed with work that appeals to children, the gallery features authentic African masks, a parade of circus figures carved in wood, sculpture and painting, and porcelain dolls. The Romanesque Slater Memorial Museum houses sculpture; Egyptian, Greek, Roman, and Native American artifacts; American primitives; and African and Oriental art. Kids will be inspired to get out the Play-doh and modeling clay once they get home.

● Tantaquidgeon Indian Museum

Rte. 32, Montville; (860) 848-9145. May–Oct., Tues.–Sun., 10–4. Donation requested. **Ages 3 and up.**

This unique museum offers a personal look at the Mohegan Indians. Begun in 1931 by direct descendants of Uncas, chief of the Mohegan Nation, the museum houses numerous artifacts. Among the unusual and beautiful objects here are headdresses made of deer hair and tiny, intricate straw baskets. Objects made by Plains and West Coast Indians are also displayed, including a wolf kachina doll. Behind the museum are replicas of Indian dwellings.

● Boat Cruises

Windjammer cruises and sightseeing ferry trips are popular ways to explore the Connecticut coastline and Long Island Sound. Several companies offer trips; here's a sampling of those most suited for families. **Mystic Whaler Cruises** offers 2-, 3-, and 5-day cruises (including a 3-day pirate cruise) on a refurbished 83-foot schooner. Kids ages 10 and up are welcome on the longer cruises, while kids 5 to 10 are appropriate on daysails and evening cruises. Call (860) 536-4218 or (800) 697-8420 for details. The Mystic Whaler departs from Whaler's Wharf in Mystic.

Thames River Cruises offers narrated trips on the Thames River (you can see the subs by riverboat); and excursions on Long Island Sound for kids and adults of every age. Trips run daily from June through September, departing from New London's City Pier. Call (860) 444-SUBS for details. And don't forget the steamboat **Sabino** at Mystic Seaport, (860) 572-5315.

● Clyde's Cider Mill

129 N. Stonington Rd., Mystic; (860) 536-3354. Late Sept.–Thanksgiving, 9–5. **All ages.**

Looking for a way to mark the arrival of autumn? Visit the last steam-powered cider mill in New England and see the cider pressing operation in action. Of course, you'll want to take home a jug of cider and a fresh apple pie.

● Sugarhouses

Show your kids that some things are still done the old-fashioned way; maple sugaring, for instance. There are several places in southeastern Connecticut where you can watch sap being collected and boiled to make maple syrup and candy. The season typically runs from early February to late March. Call ahead for a boiling schedule. Places to visit include: **Maple Dawn Sugar House,** Wintechog Hill Rd., N. Stonington; (860) 535-1915; and **Applewood Farm,** 137 Mile Creek Rd., Old Lyme; (860) 434-9883.

RESTAURANTS

● Salem Valley Farms

Rtes. 11 and 82, Salem; (860) 859-2980. Daily, March–Dec., 11–9.

Could ice cream be any fresher? The milk used for the dairy products here come from the herd of 50 resident Guernseys and Holsteins. Besides ice cream, the farms offer frozen yogurt, sherbet, and sorbet made of fresh, natural ingredients. Another good bet for ice cream—of the sinfully indulgent variety—is Michael's Dairy, 629 Montauk Ave., in New London; (860) 443-2464. Open year-round, Michael's offers sweet treats made on the premises using 16 percent butterfat.

● Abbott's Lobster in the Rough

117 Pearl St., Noank (10 minutes from Mystic off Rte. 215); (860) 536-7719. May–Labor Day, daily, 12–9; Labor Day–Columbus Day, Fri. and Sat. only, 12–7.

This waterfront, eat-in-the-rough restaurant has won fans far and wide, including the folks at *Gourmet* magazine. Eat at a picnic table outdoors, where you might see lobster boats bringing in their catch, or grab a table indoors if the weather is foul. The bill of fare includes boiled lobster, hot lobster rolls (excellent), shrimp, clams, mussels—and hot dogs. Ice cream, too.

● Avanti's

Rte. 1, Mystic; (860) 536-2639. Daily, 11–10; Fri. and Sat., 11–11.

Most children love Italian food, and this small family restaurant is a local favorite. There's nothing fancy, but all your favorite pasta dishes are on the menu, as well as Avanti's popular pizza.

Hartford and Central Connecticut

Hartford calls itself "The Insurance Capital of the World," not "vacation wonderland." However, the city of Hartford—Connecticut's second largest—offers several attractions that will delight visiting families. Museums are the main event, with a wonderful hands-on science museum, the Mark Twain house, a fire museum, and an art museum with a super program for kids. Hartford also serves as a good base for exploring other sites in central Connecticut. They're varied and loaded with kid appeal, ranging from a state park with real dinosaur tracks to an aviation museum.

Looking for a cheap, easy way to get around Hartford? Here's a tip. Try a Scooter. Brightly painted Scooter buses zip around downtown Hartford to East Hartford from early morning to early evening, Monday through Friday. The cost? Just a buck a ride. Call (860) 247-5329 for more information.

● State Capitol and Legislative Office Building

210 Capitol Ave., exit 48 off I-84 or exit 29A off I-91, Hartford; (203) 240-0222. Free one-hour tours Mon.–Fri., (except holidays), 9:15–1:15; July and Aug., Mon.–Fri., 9:15–2:15. Open Sat., April–Oct., 10:15–2:15.
Ages 5 and up.

Visiting a state capitol building makes history lessons come alive. Connecticut's state executive offices and legislative chambers are housed in an impressive gold-domed structure built in 1897. See bullet-riddled battle flags and more on a guided hour-long tour.

● Mark Twain House

351 Farmington Ave., exit 46 off I-84, Hartford; (860) 493-6411. Year-round. Hour-long guided tours Mon. and Wed.–Sat., 9:30–4; and Sun., 12–4. Daily, Memorial Day–Columbus Day and month of Dec., Mon.–Sat., 9:30–4; Sun., 12–4. Closed Tues., rest of year. Open Mon. holidays. Closed New Year's Day, Easter, Labor Day, Thanksgiving, and Dec. 24 and 25. Adults, $7.50; 6–12, $3.50. **Ages 6 and up.**

Twain's bright red Victorian-Gothic house reflects the eccentricity of its owner. For example, Twain slept with his head at the foot of his bed so he could admire the ornate Venetian headboard, and he kept his telephone in the closet because it drove him crazy. You'll see the study where Twain wrote about Tom Sawyer and Huckleberry Finn—and took billiards breaks at the full-sized pool table. Visitors soon realize that the author enjoyed drinking, smoking, and billiards at least as much as he liked writing. The Twain House is part of Nook Farm, an intellectual community formed in the mid–19th century by Twain and cultural luminaries Isabella Beecher Hooker, who was a women's rights activist, William Gillette, a playwright, author Harriet Beecher Stowe, and others.

● Harriet Beecher Stowe House

Nook Farm, 77 Forest St., Hartford; (860) 525-9317. Year-round. Daily, June–Columbus Day and Dec., Mon.–Sat., 9:30–4; Sun, 12–4. Closed Tues., rest of year. Adults, $6.50; under 16, $2.75. (Includes Katherine S. Day House.) **Ages 6 and up.**

Adjacent to the Mark Twain House is the restored Victorian cottage of *Uncle Tom's Cabin* author Harriet Beecher Stowe. Most of Stowe's original furniture is here, including the small desk where she wrote 33 books.

● Science Center of Connecticut

950 Trout Brook Dr., exit 43 off I-84, West Hartford; (860) 231-2824. Tues.–Fri., 10–4; Sat., 10–5; Sun., 12–5. Open Mon., 10–4, during summer and Mon. school holidays; closed Thanksgiving and Christmas. Adults, $5; 3–15, $4; under 3, free. Gengras Planetarium: star shows, $1 per seat; laser shows, $2 per seat. **All ages.**

From kinkajoos to computers, this science center offers lots to see and do. Explore the mysteries of the solar system and the planetarium, shake hands with a starfish in the touch tank (part of a 25-tank aquarium), and learn by doing in the Discovery Room, where there's an echo tunnel and a giant 30-foot walk-in kaleidoscope. The center also has a computer laboratory, and a small indoor/outdoor zoo with 50 species of animals. Many kids take a shine to Teddy, the kinkajoo; other zoo inhabitants include a mountain lion, a raccoon, an eagle, ferrets, owls, and snakes.

● Hartford Whalers Hockey

Hartford Civic Center, 242 Trumbull St., Hartford; (860) 728-6637 or (800) WHALERS. Season: Oct.–May; games start at 7 P.M. Ticket prices range from $19–$42. **All ages.**

We New Englanders do love our hockey. Watch Connecticut's home team face off against NHL opponents at the Hartford Civic Center, downtown. Call for a schedule of home games.

● Connecticut Sports Museum and Hall of Fame

Civic Center Mall, Hartford; (860) 724-4918. Mon.–Fri., 10–2. Free. **Ages 3 and up.**

Changing exhibits offer a look into the lives of Connecticut's best athletes, featuring the accomplishments of men, women, and children in the world of sports.

● Hartford Police Museum

101 Pearl St., Hartford; (860) 722-6152. Mon.–Fri., 9–4:30. **All ages.**

Calling all cars! Take a peek behind the scenes at the police department of Hartford. Pictures, artifacts, and exhibits trace the history of Hartford's men and women in blue. Kids get a sense of a day in the life of a police officer, and can get behind the wheel of a police car—even listen to actual police dispatches on the radio.

● Travelers Tower

700 Main St., 1 Tower Sq., Hartford; (860) 277-2431. Free. **Ages 3 and up.**

At 527 feet, this building—home of Travelers Insurance Company—is one of the tallest in New England. Climb up 72 steps to the observation deck for a panoramic view of the city.

● Bushnell Park and Carousel

Jewel St., Capitol Area exit off I-84, Hartford Park: (860) 522-6400; carousel: (860) 246-7739. Mid-May–Aug., Tues.–Sun., 11–5. Mid-April–mid-May and month of Sept., Sat. and Sun., 11–5. Carousel rides, $.50. **All ages.**

What child doesn't adore a carousel? And the one at Bushnell Park, built in 1914, is something special, with 48 hand-carved horses and ornate lovers' chariots. It operates daily in summer and weekends in spring and fall. Also on the grounds are two Farragut cannons. Located in the center of the city, within steps of the capitol, this 37-acre municipal park is a great place to people watch or just relax under a tree. Grab a hot dog and a juice from a pushcart vendor.

● Elizabeth Park

915 Prospect Ave. at Asylum Ave., exit 44 off I-84, Hartford; (860) 722-6514. **All ages.**

Another urban oasis, this park features gorgeous rose gardens (more than 14,000 plants of 90 varieties), in full bloom late June through early July. Lots of space to play; lawn bowling, perhaps? You can go ice skating in winter.

● Wadsworth Atheneum

600 Main St., Hartford; (860) 278-2670. Tues.–Sun., 11–5. Adults, $5; under 13, free. Free to individuals all day Thurs. and before noon on Sat. Tours on Thurs., 1 P.M.; and Sat. and Sun., 2 P.M. **Ages 3 and up.**

America's first public art museum (more than 150 years old), the Atheneum's collections include paintings, sculpture, furniture, costumes, bronzes, firearms, and—yikes!—mummies. Items date from prehistory to the present. For kids, the staff has prepared specials tours on cassette tapes, designed to make art more accessible. The tapes combine fun (treasure-hunt-type questions and clues about the works) and facts (design concepts, how art is made). Wearing the headphones makes kids feel involved, not merely dragged along. Adults can plug in, too. On your way out, don't miss Alexander Calder's huge stegosaurus exhibit.

● New England Air Museum

Bradley International Airport, 10 miles north of Hartford on Rte. 75, off I-91, Windsor Locks; (860) 623-3305. Year-round, daily, 10–5; closed Thanksgiving and Christmas. Adults, $6.50; 6–11, $3. **Ages 3 and up.**

Older kids who think airplanes are neat will enjoy taking a look at the aircraft exhibited here. More than 80 examples are on display, including bombers, fighters, helicopters, and a modern commercial jet. All have been meticulously restored. Children (and adults) will get a kick out of playing with the flight simulator; a museum staffer will supervise you. Aviation-related films are shown several times a day.

● Connecticut Trolley Museum

58 North Rd., Rte. 140, exit 45 off I-91, East Windsor; (860) 627-6540.
Daily, Memorial Day–Labor Day, 11–5; Sat., 10–6; Sun., 12–6. Labor
Day–Thanksgiving (closed Thanksgiving Day), Sat. and Sun., 12–5.
Special events for Halloween and Christmas season. Adults, $6.50; 5–12,
$3; under 5, free. **All ages.**

Take a three-mile ride through scenic New England countryside
on an antique trolley car à la Mister Rogers's Neighborhood. The Halloween special, "Rails to the Dark Side," is a howlin' hoot, but too scary for
small fry.

● Connecticut Fire Museum

58 North Rd., Rte. 140, exit 45 off I-91, East Windsor; (860) 623-4732.
July and Aug., Mon.–Fri., 10–4; Sat. and Sun., 12–5. May–June, Sept.
and Oct., Sat. and Sun., 12–5. Adults, $2; 5–12, $1. **Ages 3 and up.**

It's 100 years of choo-choo history, with old-time fire trucks and
models dating from 1850 to 1950.

● Allen's Cider Mill

Mountain and N. Granby Rds., Rte. 189, Granby; (860) 653-6438. Mid-
Sept.–Dec., Sat. and Sun., 9–5. Call to confirm they're pressing cider before
you visit. **All ages.**

Watch cider being pressed and, even better, sample the results at this
1919 mill.

● Massacoh Plantation

800 Hopmeadow St., Rte. 10, Simsbury; (860) 658-2500. May–Oct.,
Sun.–Fri., 1–4 P.M. ; guided tours 1–3. Phelps House open Mon.–Fri., 1–4
P.M., all year. Adults, $5; 5–18, $2.50. **Ages 5 and up.**

This complex represents three centuries of local history. Older
children will enjoy the Phelps House (1771, formerly a hotel and tavern),
the one-room schoolhouse (1741), and the stocks and pillory. Also on the
grounds are an herb garden, a 1683 meeting house, and a Victorian
carriage house. Guided tours, from 1 to 3 P.M., are lively and geared
toward children.

● Talcott Mountain State Park and Heublein Tower

Rte. 185 at Bloomfield-Simsbury town line; (860) 242-1158. Grounds
open year-round; tower open Memorial Day–Labor Day, Thurs.–Sun., 10–5;
Labor Day–Columbus Day, daily, 10–5. **Ages 3 and up.**

For the best view in the state, take a one-and-a-half mile hike to Heublein Tower in Talcott Mountain State Park. Once the summer home of the Heublein family, the tower offers panoramic views of four states and the Farmington River.

● Stratton Brook State Park

Rte. 305, Simsbury. 8–sunset.

Have bikes, will travel? This small park is best known for its extensive bike trail, winding through white pines and over brooks. Hiking, swimming, fishing, and, come winter, cross-country skiing and ice skating are other possibilities here. There are boathouses and a concession stand, too.

● Old Newgate Prison and Copper Mine

115 Newgate Rd., exit 40 off I-91, East Granby; (860) 566-3005 or (860) 653-3563. Mid-May–Oct., Wed.–Sun., 10–4:30. Adults, $3; 6–17, $1.50. **Ages 6 and up.**

This colonial copper mine served as a Revolutionary War prison—the nation's first state prison—housing British sympathizers. This site served as Connecticut's state prison until 1827. Prowl the dungeonlike chambers to see where the prisoners ate and slept, and hear of their attempted escapes. You can take a tunnel stairway down to the celebrated Simsbury copper mine and walk the narrow mine paths. The mine was worked from 1707 to 1773. Later the Newgate prisoners were kept in the mine at night. It's an unusual glimpse of American history. Today the crumbling jail walls set against a backdrop of foothills and valley forests appear picturesque. The picnic area on the grounds is a pleasant setting. If you have time, take the Newgate Wildlife Trail from the parking lot. The six-mile self-guided nature trail winds around Newgate Pond.

● Lutz Children's Museum

247 South Main St., Manchester; (860) 643-0949. Tues. and Wed., 2–5; Thurs., 2–8; Fri., 9:30–5; Sat., 12–5. Adults, $3; children, $2.50. Free admission Thurs. nights. **Ages 1–12.**

Don't look, just touch . . . what is it? Yes, deer antlers. The "feel boxes" are just one of many exhibits children can get their hands on here. This little charmer is chock-full of fun possibilities: children can put on life jackets and steer a boat through a storm, climb aboard the Alphabet Express, or put on their own puppet show. The museum also has a live animal exhibit. Many of the animals are part of a rehabilitation and release program, making this an ever-changing exhibit. Nearby, the museum's

Oak Grove Nature Center offers self-guided trails through woods, swamps, a hemlock grove and over a covered bridge. Little ones will want to run—not walk—to the outdoor playscape.

● Wickham Park

1329 W. Middle Tpke., exit 92 off I-384, Manchester; (860) 528-0856. April–Oct., daily, 9:30–dusk. **All ages.**

An aviary, a small zoo, and a 1927 log cabin are the featured attractions at this unusual park. The 215-acre site has beautifully manicured grounds with oriental and lotus gardens, toddler play areas, and picnicking facilities. Cross-country skiing in winter.

● Old Tolland Jail Museum

Town Green, exit 68 off I-84, Tolland; (860) 875-3544. Jail museum: May–mid–Oct., Sun., 1–4. Hicks-Stearns Museum: mid-May–mid-Oct., Wed. and Sun., 1–4. Donation of $1 per adult suggested. **Ages 3 and up.**

This site on Tolland Green housed prisoners until the 1960s; now visitors can go into the jail's cells (built in 1856) and tour the country house connected to it where the warden and his family lived. Refurbished in 1990, the warden's home contains farm tools and home furnishings. Across the street, the Hicks-Stearns Museum is worth a visit. This colonial-tavern-turned-Victorian-summer-cottage houses family heirlooms (including toys) and souvenirs of European travel. A Victorian Christmas open house and a summer lawn concert series are local traditions.

● Daniel Benton Homestead

Metcalf Rd., exit 68 off I-84, Tolland; (860) 875-7559. May-mid–Oct., Sun., 1–4. Donations accepted. **Ages 5 and up.**

This center chimney Colonial house, the oldest house in Tolland (constructed in 1720) housed Hessian prisoners during the Revolutionary War. Perhaps the best feature of this historic house is its romantic-yet-spooky ghost story. The guide tells it well, and locals swear it's true. Visit and decide for yourself whether or not the Benton house is haunted.

● Dinosaur State Park

West St., exit 23 off I-91, Rocky Hill; (860) 529-8423. Park: year-round, daily, 9–4:30. Free. Exhibit Center: year-round, Tues.–Sun., 9–4:30. Adults, $2; 6–17, $.50. Track casting permitted May–Oct., daily, 9–3:30. **All ages.**

Imagine finding real, 185-million-year-old (Jurassic Period) dinosaur tracks! That's what happened here in 1966 during excavation for a new state building. The fossil tracks, three-toed impressions ranging from 10 to 16 inches in length, are now protected in a large geodesic dome. What type of dinosaur made these tracks? Nobody knows for sure, but you'll see a full-size replica of the scientists' best guess, a dilophosaurus, on display here. Bring 10 pounds of plaster of Paris and one-quarter cup of vegetable oil, and make your own cast of a dinosaur footprint. The park also has two miles of nature trails (pick up a trail map at the office—no pets or bikes, please) and a gift shop.

● Connecticut Audubon Center at Glastonbury

1361 Main St., exit 7 off Rte. 2, Glastonbury; (860) 633-8402. Tues.–Fri., 1–5; Sat., 10–5; Sun., 1–4. Free. Discovery Room: $1 per person for nonmembers. **Ages 3 and up.**

"Green" tots (and aren't they all, these days?) will love connecting with nature here. The center has a small exhibit area and walking trails through a wooded park, adjacent to the Connecticut River. Best for kids up to the third grade or so, the hands-on Discovery Room offers do-it-yourself craft projects (make footprints with inkpads, for example), a skull collection, a puppet theater, and live animals. Other exhibits feature native flora and fauna and the Connecticut River ecosystem. Wear walking shoes and plan to hike the nature trails in Earle Park; maps are available at the center.

● Mill Pond Falls

Garfield St., Newington; (860) 666-4661. Year-round. **All ages.**

Once surrounded by Indian wigwams, this area is now a lovely town park with its own natural waterfall. Enjoy a picnic here, as ducks paddle across the pond.

● New Britain Youth Museum

30 High St., New Britain; (860) 225-3020. July–Aug., Mon.–Fri., 1–5. Sept.–June, Tues.–Fri., 1–5; Sat., 10–4. Donations requested. **Ages 2–10.**

A doll collection, a miniature circus display, multicultural exhibits, and a small petting zoo are featured here, along with changing exhibits.

● New Britain Youth Museum at Hungerford Park (formerly, Hungerford Outdoor Center)

191 Farmington Ave., exit 35 off I-84, Kensington; (860) 827-9064. Tues.–Fri., 1–5: Sat., 10–5. Summer hours: Tues.–Fri., 11–5, Sat., 10–5. Closed holidays. Animal demonstrations in summer: Weekdays, 2 P.M., and Sat., 11, 1, and 3. Adults, $2; 2–17, $1. **All ages.**

Take a walk on Connecticut's wild side here, where there's plenty to see and do at a family-friendly price. Meet the hedgehogs, ferrets, reptiles, and other curious creatures at the indoor exhibits, then visit the barnyard beasts at the outdoor petting area. Hike the nature trails, view a pond from an observation station, and check out exhibits that explore Connecticut's geology and natural history. Live animal demonstrations add to the fun.

● New Britain Museum of American Art

56 Lexington St., New Britain; (860) 229-0257. Tues.–Fri., 1–5; Sat., 10–5; Sun., 12–5. Closed holidays. Adults, $3; students, $2; under 12, free. **Ages 5 and up.**

American art from 1740 to the present is the focus here, with artists such as Sargent, Benton, Whistler, and Wyeth represented among the 5,000 works. Just for families: During the "Second Saturday Family Fun" program, special tours run the second Saturday of each month (except August) at 10:30 A.M. Special themes are presented each week, such as "Mobiles"; after looking at the featured works, families can create their own examples. (A small materials fee—$1 or so—is charged.) In July and August, a program called "Art Explorers" is offered on Wednesdays. Call the museum for details.

● Hardware City Rock Cats Minor League Baseball

Willowbrook Park Complex, off Rte. 9, New Britain; (860) 224-8383. Season runs April–Sept. Tickets, $2–$7. **All ages.**

With a name like the Rock Cats, how could they not be totally cool? Da Cats are the AA Eastern affiliate of the Minnesota Twins. About 71 home games are scheduled in the team's new $9.25 million stadium.

● Tomasso Nature Park

Granger Ln., Rte. 72, Plainville; (860) 747-6022. Mid-March–mid-Nov., daily, dawn to dusk. Free. **All ages.**

This four-acre wetland area is home to a bounty of plant and animal life, including nearly 600 painted turtles. Nature trails, bridges, and observation areas offer opportunities to view them.

● Hot Air Ballooning

Ever wonder what it would be like to hover over rivers and valleys in a hot air balloon? Central Connecticut is home to several balloon companies, which specialize in sunrise or sunset flights (always followed by a champagne toast). This is a truly unbeatable way to view fall foliage. Most companies are happy to bring along children, even infants, with adult passengers, but it is quite a splurge—often, more than $100 per person. Talk with your balloon pilot about group discounts. Some companies to try: **Emerald City Balloon Co.,** Manchester; (860) 647-8581; **Kat Balloons,** Farmington; (860) 678-7921; and **Berkshire Balloons,** in Southington; (203) 250-8441.

● Fruit Picking

There's plenty of picking outside the city of Hartford, especially to the south of town. Here are some possibilities: **Bell Town Hill Orchards,** 475 Matson Hill Rd., S. Glastonbury, (860) 633-2789 (apples and blueberries); **Riverview Farm,** 593 Tryon St., S. Glastonbury, (860) 633-0200 (apples and strawberries); and **Rose's Berry Farm,** Matson Hill Rd., S. Glastonbury, (860) 633-7467 (strawberries, blueberries, and raspberries). For a complete directory, contact the Connecticut Department of Agriculture, Marketing Division, at (860) 566-3671.

RESTAURANTS

● The Pavilion

State House Square (next to Old State House), Hartford; (860) 247-0845. Garage parking on Market St. Daily, 7–midnight.

For variety and ease, you can't beat the Pavilion Court on the second floor of the Pavilion. The building is smack in the middle of all the action at State House Square and is an architecturally interesting bit of art deco, featuring lots of plants, glass, and lights. Ride the glass elevator to the second floor and take your pick of fare: deli sandwiches, tacos and enchiladas, salads, pizza, and more.

● MEGAbytes Cafe at Scooters

Rte. 6, Bristol; (860) 583-1818.Tues.–Thurs., 11–8; Fri., 11–11; Sat., 10–10; Sun., 10–9. Closed Mon. during school year.

"Most people don't come here for the food," one of the staffers here told us, quite frankly. Still, if you don't mind dining on pizza, popcorn, and cappuccinos, you can get a bite at this entertainment complex and play on an inflatable pirate ship, act out your *Star Wars* fantasies in the lazertron gallery, play Ping-Pong, even surf the 'Net (the tab is $1.50 for 15 minutes).

● Nulli's Restaurant

706 Hartford Rd., Manchester; (860) 647-1500. Tues.–Sat., 11–10. Closed Sun. and Mon.

"The closest you can get to Mama's," is how the folks in Nulli's kitchen describe the Italian food here. Unless Mama opened a can of Beefaroni, how can you go wrong? Everything's tasty, the luncheon specials are bountiful and cheap, there's even a bocce court. Ask to be seated near it, so the kids can have a go at Italy's answer to bowling.

Essex and the Connecticut River Valley

A visit to charming, postcard-pretty Essex is like a trip to the past. Stroll down tree-lined Main Street, and you'll see gracious old colonial homes where sea captains and shipbuilders once lived with their families. Once an important shipbuilding town, Essex is where America's first warship, the *Oliver Cromwell,* was built. Recently, Essex was named the number one small town in the U.S., according to *The 100 Best Small Towns in America.*

Stand at the lower reaches of the Connecticut River and you can almost picture an old side-wheeler riverboat churning up the river on its voyage from New York to Hartford. Although schooners have been replaced by pleasure craft and riverboats have given way to automobiles, it's possible for visitors to get a taste of the river's glory days. You can even take a ride on an authentic riverboat. Combine your cruise with a steam-train ride, and you'll get a delightful tour of the Connecticut River Valley, albeit the 20th-century version. For more river lore, visit the River Museum. Or for something completely different, tour the fantasy castle-turned-state-park or bob along the Farmington River in a giant rubber doughnut.

● Steam Train and Riverboat
Valley Railroad Co., exit 3 off Rte. 9, Essex; (860) 767-0103. May–Dec. Schedules change depending on season; check locally for exact departure times. Every train connects with the riverboat except the last train of the day. No boat service with Christmas train rides. Adults, $14 (train only, $10); 2–11, $7 (train only, $5). **Ages 3 and up.**

There's an old-fashioned magic about a steam train ride. Kids find it exciting—the smoke billowing and whistles blasting—while adults find it relaxing. This attraction combines a Valley Railroad steam-train ride from Essex to Chester with an hour-long riverboat cruise; the whole trip lasts about two and a half hours. The scenery is beautiful and includes rolling hills, flowering meadows, the Connecticut River shoreline, and local attractions such as Gillette Castle and the Goodspeed Opera House. Passengers transfer from steam train to riverboat at Deep River Landing,

boarding the *Becky Thatcher* or *Silver Star* vessels. Bring a picnic to enjoy
on the riverboat, if you wish. Off season, visit in fall for an unforgettable
view of autumn foliage. Or come at Christmastime, when you'll share the
train with Santa, Mrs. Claus, and their elves.

● Connecticut River Museum

*67 Main St., Essex; (860) 767-8269. Year-round, Tues.–Sun., 10–5.
Adults, $4; 6–12, $2.* **Ages 3 and up.**

At the foot of Main Street in Essex, where the old steamboat dock
has been restored, you'll find a full-size replica of America's first submarine. Constructed in 1775, *American Turtle* was clumsy and ineffective
against the British; still, it's interesting to look at. The River Museum
also houses ship models, navigational instruments, shipbuilding displays,
and special exhibits.

● Gillette Castle State Park

*River Rd., off Rte. 82, Hadlyme; (860) 526-2336. Castle: Memorial Day–
Columbus Day, daily, 10–5. Columbus Day–Sun. before Christmas, weekends, 10–4. Park: year-round, 8–7. Castle: adults, $4; 6–11, $2. Park
only: free.* **All ages.**

Your kids may not know who actor William Gillette is—for that
matter, you might not remember him, either. But visiting his 24-room
fantasy castle is a fun way to get acquainted. Best known for his role as
Sherlock Holmes, Gillette was a rather eccentric character himself, and
the house is full of creative mechanical touches. It's also full of feline-
themed artifacts; Gillette shared the castle with 15 cats during his
residence from 1919 to 1937. After his death, the estate was designated
a state park. Now, you can picnic here, take a hike, go fishing, or, for a
real adventure, rent a canoe here and camp at Selden State Park, a 528-
acre island near Gillette Castle that's accessible only by water.

● Goodspeed Opera House

*Rte. 82, East Haddam; (860) 873-8668. Tours offered on Mon., 1–3 P.M.,
July–Oct. (with some exceptions; call to verify). Performances: Wed.–Fri.,
8 P.M., Sat. at 4 and 9 P.M., Sun. at 2 and 6:30 P.M.; Wed. matinee at 2:30.
Season: April–Dec. Tour only: Adults, $2; under 12, $1.* **Ages 6 and up.**

This wonderful Victorian "gingerbread" structure was a popular
riverside theater from the late 1800s to the 1920s. Nearly demolished in
the 1950s, this unique landmark was rescued, restored, and now features
musical theater productions. Take a behind-the-scenes tour of the opera
house or take in a show. Older children who enjoy the performing arts

will find a visit to the Goodspeed a real treat. Three musicals are performed here each season.

● Devil's Hopyard State Park
Three miles north of junction of Rte. 82 and 156, East Haddam; (860) 873-8566. Open mid-April–Sept. **All ages.**

This scenic area offers 15 miles of hiking trails—one steep side, one gentler side. Hike along the stream to Chapman Falls, a 60-foot cascade. Fish in the trout-stocked stream, enjoy a picnic, or bring camping gear and spend the night. Beware: legend has it that the devil lived here. That should inspire some interesting ghost stories around the campfire . . .

● Haddam Meadows State Park
Rte. 154, Haddam; (860) 566-2304. Daily, 8–sunset. **All ages.**

Fly a kite, toss a Frisbee, or just stretch your legs; this 175-acre meadowland (the river floodplain) offers lots of room to roam from sunup to sundown, along with fishing, picnicking, boating, and, in winter, cross-country skiing.

● Mary's Doll House
56 Neptune Ave., Moodus; (860) 873-8301. Sat. and Sun. For hours, and weekday schedule, please call. Free. **Ages 5 and up.**

If someone in your group is a doll fanatic, stop by this family-run doll and miniature museum.

Special Note: While in Moodus, listen for the Moodus Noises. These strange, subterranean rumblings have been variously explained as the threats of evil spirits (according to Indian legend), witches in the mountain (according to early white settlers), and emanations from pearls (according to a British scientist, who disappeared while researching the subject). Modern scientists believe the sounds are caused by movement along intersecting fractures in the earth's crust.

● Canoeing/Tubing
Exploring the serpentine Farmington River is a splendid way to spend a day. Canoeing and tubing are great ways to go with kids. **Farmington River Tubing,** (860) 693-6465 or (860) 739-0791 offers tube rentals, PFDs (personal flotation devices), and a ride back to your starting point. Season runs from Memorial Day to Labor Day. Kids must be age 10 or over, 4 feet 5 inches tall or more, and weigh at least 50 pounds. **Huck Finn Adventures** offers rental canoes (with extra seats for families) for paddling down a tranquil, wooded stretch of the Farmington.

Some kids like to bring fishing gear to troll along while they ride. Shuttle service is available, too. Call (860) 693-0385 for information.

● Fruit Picking

One of the busiest spots in the area is **Lyman Orchards,** Routes 147 and 157 in Middlefield, (860) 349-1566; they offer pick-your-own sweet corn, raspberries, tomatoes, squash, pumpkins, apples, peaches, and strawberries in season. The farm store sells produce and baked goods and hosts special events in summer and fall. For a complete directory of pick-your-own farms, roadside stands, and cider mills, call the Connecticut Department of Agriculture, Marketing Division, at (860) 566-3671.

● Chatfield Hollow State Park

Exit 63 off I-95, .5 mi. west of Killingworth Center on Rte. 80, Killingworth; (860) 566-2304. Daily, 8–sunset. **All ages.**

An old waterwheel, a covered bridge, a pond, a brook, and red pine groves make this a truly exceptional park. Swim in Schreeder Pond, walk the nature trail along the brook, or hike the well-marked trails (a four-and-a-half-mile loop passes points of interest). The pond is stocked with trout. The park is part of Cockaponset State Forest, where you'll find additional hiking trails, cross-country skiing, and snowmobiling in winter.

● Wadsworth Falls State Park

Rte. 157, Middlefield; (860) 566-2304. Daily, 8–sunset. **All ages.**

A beautiful waterfall with a scenic overlook is the most outstanding feature here. Also enjoy fishing, hiking, swimming, picnicking, and, in springtime, colorful laurel. Go ice-skating and cross-country skiing here in winter.

● Hurd State Park

Rte. 151, East Hampton; (860) 566-2304. Daily, 8–sunset. **All ages.**

Located on the east bank of the Connecticut River, this park features several hiking trails—some through the woods, some along the river, and some to high points with scenic views. Pack your gear and fish in the Connecticut River. Go cross-country skiing here in winter.

● Hammonasset Beach State Park

Exit 62 South off I-95, Madison; (203) 245-2785. Year-round, 8–sunset. Parking fees daily, Memorial Day–Labor Day; fee weekends only, mid-April–Memorial Day and Labor Day–Oct.; off-season, free. **All ages.**

A two-mile stretch of sandy beach is the main attraction at this popular recreation area, Connecticut's largest shoreline park. Swim in Long Island Sound, fish, or hike along marked trails through a salt marsh. There's also a nature center with interpretive programs, camping and boating, and concessions.

● Boat Cruises

In addition to the riverboat ride previously described, several other cruise options are available. A pleasant day trip, if your kids can handle a leisurely boat ride: cruise from Haddam to the ports of Sag Harbor and Greenport, New York, along the Connecticut River and across Long Island Sound aboard the *Camelot.* Explore for three hours, then return to Haddam. The trip lasts all day, and is offered from June through Labor Day. Contact **Camelot Cruises,** One Marine Park, Haddam; (860) 345-8591. Or, make believe Mom and Dad are Bogey and Bacall on the original steamboat ***African Queen,*** made famous by the movie of the same name. Departing out of Saybrook, the 45-minute ride is offered July through Oct. Call (860) 388-2007 for details. For an expanded list of tour boat operators, call (800) CT BOUND and ask for the Connecticut Vacation Guide.

RESTAURANTS

Many of the restaurants in this area of Connecticut are found in fine country inns—lovely, but not the best of choices if you're dining with small fry. Your best bet is to head to Old Saybrook, where you'll find fast-food franchises and some casual family restaurants. Here are some restaurants—low-key and not touristy—favored by local parents.

● Pat's Kountry Kitchen

Mill Rd. and Rte. 154, Old Saybrook; (860) 388-4784. Mon.–Sat., 7–9. Sun., 7– 12:30 and 2–9. Fri. and Sat. 'til 10 in summer.

There's a little bit of everything on the menu here: steaks, Italian specialties, seafood, soups, sandwiches. It's a quick breakfast stop, and great for early birds since it opens at seven. Children's lunch and dinner menus offer the usual burgers, dogs, and grilled cheese. The setting is casual; the daily specials are good and cheap. "Nothing changes much here," one of the waitpeople told us, and that's just the way the regulars like it.

● Hale-n-Hearty

38 Town St., East Haddam; (860) 873-2640. Tues.–Thurs., 11:30–9; Fri. and Sat., 11:30–10.

This old-fashioned, country-style restaurant offers steak, seafood, and pasta dishes, but what comes flying out of the kitchen most frequently? Retro classics like pot pies and meatloaf dinners, and, from the kiddie side of the menu, boomlet faves like chicken tenders and pasta.

● Oliver's Taverne

Oliver's Corner Shopping Center, Plains Rd., Essex; (860) 767-2633. Mon.–Thurs., 11:30–10:30; Fri. and Sat., 11:30–11; Sun. brunch, 11:30–4.

A bit fancier than the other two recommendations, this "eating and drinking emporium" (the tavern's words) is a big, multilevel barn-wood affair with lots of wood, brass, and cozy fireplaces. Blackboard specials include everything from fried clams to pot roast to baked stuffed lobster; prices are moderate.

Greater New Haven

The next time you lick a lollipop, munch a burger, fish with a steel fishhook, or pop open a bottle with a corkscrew, thank the folks of New Haven. Those items were invented here, along with the first steamboat and rubber footwear. As if that's not enough "firsts," rumor has it that the first American pizza pie was tossed here, at Frank Pepe Pizzeria Napoleteana. They still make a great pizza. The city also takes credit for creating the sports of football (dreamed up by a Yale rugby coach) and Frisbee throwing (inspired by Yalies tossing Mrs. Frisbee's pie plates into the air). Of course, New Haven residents have a couple of other reasons to boast. The most obvious is Yale University, one of the country's oldest and most respected colleges. Yale's outstanding museums are not to be missed, especially the Peabody Museum of Natural History.

New Haven is also a center for regional theater; the most famous is the Yale Repertory Theater, where many top-flight actors have honed their skills, and the Long Wharf Theater, birthplace of several Broadway plays over the years. Whether you're in town for museum hopping, theater going, or attending the Harvard-Yale game, you'll realize that New Haven is a college town—and more.

Don't forget your lollipop.

● Peabody Museum of Natural History

Yale University, 170 Whitney Ave., exit 3 off I-91, New Haven; (203) 432-5050. Mon.–Sat., 10–5; Sun. and holidays, 12–5. Adults, $5; 3–15, $3. Free hours Mon.–Fri., 3–5 P.M. **Ages 3 and up.**

You don't have to know a pterodactyl from a triceratops to be impressed by this museum, one of the largest and oldest natural history museums in the United States. A massive mural provides a dramatic backdrop for life-size prehistoric creatures in the Hall of Dinosaurs. Youngsters will be amazed, and delighted, by the sight of the 65-foot brontosaurus skeleton, the first brontosaurus skeleton found in North America. Another amazing specimen here is a 75-million-year-old turtle. Elsewhere the natural history of our planet is traced through mineralogy, meteorites, and zoology. The Peabody is one of the best museums of its kind in the country. Don't miss it.

● The Only Game in Town

275 Valley Service Rd., exit 11N/12S off I-91, North Haven; (203) 239-GOLF. Mid-March–Oct., daily, weather permitting. Please call for current hours. Free admission; activities charges. **Ages 5 and up.**

Need to get physical after being on your best behavior in New Haven's museums and theaters? This is the place—it's one of those mega (20 acres!) sports complexes that attract older kids and sports-happy moms and dads. Miniature golf, a driving range, indoor batting cages—it's all here, waiting for you to test your prowess.

● New Haven Colony Historical Society

114 Whitney Ave., New Haven; (203) 562-4183. Tues.–Fri., 10–5; Sat. and Sun., 2–5. Adults, $2; 6–16, $1. Free on Tues. **Ages 6 and up.**

Local antiques are the focus here, including beloved playthings of New Haven children who lived 300 years ago. In addition to the antique dolls and toys, older children may enjoy seeing the photographs of old New Haven and comparing them to the city of today. Other noteworthy items are Eli Whitney's cotton gin and the sign from Benedict Arnold's drugstore on Chapel Street.

● Shore Line Trolley Museum

17 River Rd., exit 51E off I-91, East Haven; (203) 467-6927. Memorial Day–Labor Day, daily, 11–5. May, Sept., Oct., and late-Nov.–late-Dec., Sat. and Sun., 11–5. Rest of Nov. and April, Sun. only. Adults, $5; 2–11, $2. **All ages.**

Kid-appeal is guaranteed here, where the highlight is a three-mile ride on a vintage 1911 trolley car. Adults will get a chuckle out of the old advertising slicks posted in the cars. More than 100 trolley cars are on view, many antique, from the United States and Canada. If you dare, sign up for a special Terrifying Trolley Trip at Halloween. Wear a suitably bewitching costume. Santa rides the trolley during the holiday season.

● Connecticut Children's Museum

22 Wall St. (corner of Wall and Orange), exit 3 off I-91, New Haven;
(203) 562-KIDS. Summer, Tues.–Thurs., 10–2; Sat. and Sun., 10–4.
Fall, winter, and spring, Sat. and Sun., 10–4. Per person, $3. **Ages 1–7.**

This delightful museum is set up like a little village where kids
can indulge in imaginative role playing. There's a hospital, a grocery
store, a school, a restaurant, and more, each equipped with plenty of
props and dress-up clothing. Parents won't feel silly joining in—in fact,
the museum staff encourages it. Young visitors will learn by doing, and
have lots of fun in the process. The recommended age range is toddler to
seven years.

● Shubert Performing Arts Center

247 College St., New Haven; (203) 562-5666 or (800) 228-6622.
Season: Sept.–June. Ticket prices vary. **Ages 5 and up.**

They call this 1914-era theater "the birthplace of the nation's greatest
hits," since *Oklahoma!, South Pacific,* and *The Sound of Music* all premiered
here. Take a backstage tour and see the famous graffiti wall, covered with
autographs of the stars. Current productions include Broadway favorites,
dance, music, and family entertainment.

● New Haven Ravens Minor League Baseball

Yale Field, Derby Ave. (Rte. 34), West Haven; (800) RAVENS-1. Season:
April–Sept. Tickets: $2–$15. **All ages.**

Come to the "Ravens Nest" at beautifully refurbished Yale Field
(built in 1927) to see New Haven's boys of summer pick apart their
opponents. The Ravens, a AA affiliate of the Colorado Rockies, play 70
or so home games a season.

● Yale University Student Guided Tours

149 Elm St., New Haven; (203) 432-2300. Guided tours daily, Mon.–Fri.
at 10:30 and 2; Sat. and Sun. at 1:30. Free. **Ages 3 and up.**

Start at the Yale Visitor Information Center (the oldest surviving
residence in New Haven, they tell us) and begin your hour-long guided
tour of campus. See where former Yalies Eli Whitney, Nathan Hale,
Noah Webster, and George Bush—not to mention President Clinton
and Hillary Rodham Clinton—studied, hung out, and brown-nosed their
professors.

● Audubon Coastal Center at Milford Point

1 Milford Pt. Rd., Milford; (203) 878-7440. Tues.–Sat., 10–4; Sun.,
12–4; gate closes at dusk. Adults, $2; 7–12, $1. **All ages.**

From this dazzling locale, add new species to your lifetime list of birds—it's one of the best birding sites in the state and a mecca for nature lovers in general. Within the building are touch tanks, a huge watershed puzzle, displays, and hands-on exhibits. Craft workshops meet Tuesday afternoons from 1 to 5 P.M.; other programs (usually free) include bird walks, storytelling, and sea creature demonstrations. Outdoors, a 70-foot observation tower offers panoramic views of Long Island Sound, the Housatonic River, and an 840-acre salt marsh.

● New Haven Crypt

311 Temple St., New Haven; (203) 787-0121. Open for tours Tues.–Fri., 10:30–2:30. **Ages 3 and up.**

We don't suppose you're dying to get in here . . . the good news is, you don't have to. This unique, historic crypt is located under the First Church of Christ on the New Haven Green, and bears tombstones that date back to 1687.

● Grove Street Cemetery

227 Grove St., between Prospect and Ashmun streets, New Haven. Gates close at 4. **Ages 3 and up.**

Visit the gravesites of Eli Whitney, Charles Goodyear, Noah Webster, and other famous figures here. Established in 1796, this cemetery is a good place to try your hand at grave rubbing.

● East Rock Park

East Rock Rd., Willow St. exit 6 off I-91, New Haven; (203) 946-6086. Park: daily, sunrise–sunset. Summit: daily, April–Nov., 8 A.M.–sunset; closed to vehicles Nov. 1–April 1, weekdays; open weekends, weather permitting. **All ages.**

The best feature of this 420-acre city park is its summit. Drive up to the top of the Rock and you'll get an aerial view of the city, the harbor, and Long Island Sound. Also on the grounds are a bird sanctuary, playgrounds, nature trails, and picnic facilities. Ranger-lead programs include early-morning warbler walks and a kids' fishing derby.

● West Rock Ridge State Park and West Rock Nature Center

Wintergreen Ave., New Haven; (203) 946-8016. West Rock Park: daily, 9–sunset. Free. Nature Center: Mon.–Fri., 10–4. Free. **All ages.**

Rock on, New Haven. West Rock Park surrounds West Rock, which is 428 feet high. Near the summit is Judges' Cave, a historic landmark. Reach the summit by hiking, biking, or by car. Along the ridge you'll

enjoy excellent views of New Haven harbor and Long Island Sound.
West Rock Nature Center has displays of native birds, insects, butterflies,
reptiles, and mammals. The center is surrounded by 40 acres of woodland
with nature trails, ponds, and meadows.

● Lighthouse Point Park and Carousel

*Two Lighthouse Rd., exit 50 off I-95, New Haven; (203) 946-8005.
Memorial Day–Labor Day, 6–sunset. Carousel: Operates Tues.–Sun. Parking
fee.* **All ages.**

This 82-acre waterfront park and beach, set on Long Island Sound,
has several delightful features, including an antique carousel set in a turn-
of-the-century beach pavilion. There's also a marine touch tank and bird
sanctuary, with bird-watching programs in March and April, and hawk-
watching in September. You'll also find nature trails, playgrounds, picnic
groves, and, when it's steamy outside, lots of happy kids playing on the
beach and splashing in the ocean.

● Fort Nathan Hale and Black Rock Fort

*Woodward Ave., exit 50 off I-95 North, New Haven; (203) 946-8790.
Daily, Memorial Day–Labor Day. Free.* **All ages.**

These reconstructed Revolutionary War and Civil War forts give kids
a chance to play soldier with reasonable authenticity. Located on the
eastern shore of New Haven harbor, the forts have bunkers, gun emplace-
ments, breastworks, and there's even a Civil War–era drawbridge that
really works.

● Sleeping Giant State Park

*200 Mt. Carmel Ave., Hamden; (203) 789-7489 or (203) 272-2841
(hiking information). Daily, 8–sunset. Parking fee, April–Nov., weekends
and holidays.* **All ages.**

Two miles of mountaintop form the outline of a "sleeping giant"
along the skyline. This 1,500-acre park is a popular hiking area, with a
33-mile network of nature trails, and ranger-led hikes throughout the
season. Call first; some hikes are designated for experienced hikers only,
covering rough terrain. Hikes depart from the bulletin board at the park
entrance. A one-and-a-half mile trail leads to a stone lookout tower on the
peak of Mount Carmel, offering great views of Long Island Sound.

● Eli Whitney Museum

*915 Whitney Ave., Hamden; (203) 777-1833. Wed.–Fri. and Sun., 12–5;
Sat., 10–3. Closed Thanksgiving, Christmas, and New Year's Day. Adults,
$3; children, $2.* **Ages 3 and up.**

"Exploring the passion for making things" is the theme here, where features include a water learning lab and a covered bridge. After a visit here, kids will tackle those Lego creations with renewed vigor. The 1816-era barn is a venue for country dances, folk music, and summer theater; call for a schedule.

● General David Humphrey's House

37 Elm St., Ansonia; (203) 735-1908. Year-round, Mon.–Fri., 1–4:30. Free. **Ages 3 and up.**

Humphreys, a Revolutionary War hero and aide to General Washington, built this house in 1698. Now, it's a living history museum, recreating daily life in 1762 with demonstrations of open-hearth cooking and woolspinning. Worth a pass-through if you're in the area.

● Wharton Brook State Park

Rte. 5, North Haven–Wallingford line; (203) 269-5308. **All ages.**

Quiet and peaceful, this park is a pleasant out-of-the-city escape. Fish, swim, or enjoy a picnic here in relative solitude. Ice skating in winter.

● Ansonia Nature & Recreation Center

10 Deerfield Ln., Rte. 243 or Rte. 115, Ansonia; (203) 736-9360. Park: daily, sunrise–sunset. Center: daily, 9–5; closed major holidays. Free. **All ages.**

This lovely, 104-acre park boasts an interpretive center, two miles of nature trails, a fishing pond, picnic pavilions, and beautiful fern and wildflower gardens. Cross-country skiing in winter.

● Milford Amusement Center

1607 Boston Post Rd., exit 39B off I-95, Milford; (203) 877-3229. Daily: Sun.–Thurs., 10 A.M.–1 A.M.; Fri. and Sat., 10 A.M.–2 A.M. Kiddie Land open Sun.–Thurs., 10–9 or –10; Fri. and Sat., 10 A.M.–midnight. **Ages 3 and up.**

When they've had enough wholesome outdoor activity and need a little high-tech fun, this is the place. You'll find amusements ranging from video and pinball games (300 or so) to a giant laser-tag arena. Kiddie Land has coin-operated games and rides and miniskeeball; other options include miniature golf, bumper boats, and batting cages. (Some of these are outdoors, so kids will get a little fresh air in spite of themselves.)

● Boat Cruises

If you want to see the area by sea, you have several options. Great for kids: **Schooner, Inc.** offers narrated tours on the colorful history of New

Haven and its harbor, aboard the *Quinipack,* a 91-foot, gaff-rigged wooden schooner. The boat sails from May through mid-Oct. from Long Wharf Pier; call (203) 865-1737 for information and reservations. Tours of New Haven harbor and Long Island Sound are offered on the *Liberty Belle,* from April through Oct. Visit **Liberty Belle Cruises** on Long Wharf (exit 46 off I-95) or call (800) 745-BOAT.

Several cruise companies offer 40-minute, narrated tours of the 27 tiny Thimble Islands in Long Island Sound. Boats depart from Stony Creek Dock in Branford; most run May through October. Aboard the **Volsunga IV,** the captain tells lively tales of local history and pirate legends as he cruises the Thimble Islands. Call (203) 488-9978 for details. Other boats offering island cruises include **Sea Mist II,** (203) 488-8905; and **The Islander** (Connecticut Sea Ventures), (203) 397-3921.

● Hayrides and Sleigh Rides

Who can resist the lure of a bumpity hayride in autumn? Here are some options: **Field View Farm,** 707 Derby Avenue (Route 34) in Derby, hosts hayrides by appointment, weather permitting. Rides run from 6:30 to 9:30 P.M. "Haunted Hayrides" happen at Halloween. Call (203) 795-5415 for a schedule and rates.

The oldest operating farm in Connecticut, **Field View,** offers hayrides and homemade ice cream. **Rose Orchard,** 33 Branford Rd. (Rte. 139), North Branford, has farm animals, a picnic area, pick-your-own pumpkins and other produce in season, and hayrides. Call (203) 488-7996 or (800) 4-HAYRIDE. **Maple View Farm,** 603 Orange Center Road, Orange, offers hayrides and pony rides by appointment. Call (203) 799-6495. **Jones Family Farm,** Rte.110 and Israel Hill Rd., Shelton, has it all: pick-your-own produce in summer, pick-a-pumpkin (and hayrides) in October, and garland wreaths and Santa in December. Call (203) 929-8425.

RESTAURANTS

● Louis' Lunch

263 Crown St., New Haven; (203) 562-5507. Sept.–July, Mon.–Wed., 11–4; Thurs.–Sat., 11–2 A.M. Closed Aug.

Do your kids consider burgers one of the four major food groups? Take them to the place where America's first hamburger patty was slapped on a bun in 1898 (the original broilers are still in use). There's a children's menu, too. Located downtown, in the theater district.

● Frank Pepe Pizzeria Napoleteana
157 Wooster St., New Haven; (203) 865-5762. Mon., Wed., and Thurs.,
4–10:30; Fri. and Sat., 11:30–midnight; Sun., 2:30–10:30. Closed Tues.

They've been making "tomato pies" here since 1925, so you can bet they're good at it. A must stop—said to be where the original American pizza was born. Try the white cheese pizza with fresh clams or the classic tomato-Parmesan pie.

● Glenwood Drive Inn
2538 Whitney Ave. (at the base of Sleeping Giant State Park), Hamden;
(203) 281-0604. April–Dec., daily, 11–10; Jan.–March, 'til 8.

This is a good, old-fashioned family restaurant, offering grilled hot dogs (with buttery, crunchy grilled buns!) and hamburgers and tasty seafood plates. For dessert, pop in next door at Kelly's Kone Konnection, for freshly made ice cream. Kelly's is a cute, retro parlor, with an outdoor gazebo.

● Libby's Italian Pastry Shop
139 Wooster St., New Haven; (203) 772-0380. Call for hours.

You'll swoon at the sight, and taste, of Libby's homemade Italian pastries. They also offer Italian ices, cappuccino, and espresso.

Southwest Connecticut

The southwest corner of Connecticut offers attractions aplenty for visiting families. State-of-the-art interactive museums and old-fashioned amusement parks wait to be explored; enticing natural attractions include beaches, woodland trails, and wildlife sanctuaries. You could bypass this area on the way to the Big Apple, but look what you'd miss: touring an 1868 lighthouse; taking a sleigh ride on a working farm; playing astronaut at the Challenger Learning Center; admiring the Siberian tigers at the Beardsley Zoo; and petting a shark(!) at Norwalk's Maritime Aquarium. Intrigued? Here are the details, and lots more to tempt you to meander a bit.

● Beardsley Zoological Gardens
Noble Ave., exit 27A off I-95, Bridgeport; (203) 576-8082. Daily, 9–4. Closed Thanksgiving, Christmas, and New Year's Day. Adults, $4; 3–12, $2; under 3, free. Carousel rides, $1. Parking fee. **All ages.**

There are 300 reasons to like the Beardsley Zoo, Connecticut's largest—the 300 species that call this zoo home. Among the residents: toucans, ocelots, and timberwolves. Set on 36 acres, the zoo celebrates the wildlife of North and South America. Not all of the animals are real—a replica turn-of-the-century carousel features fanciful hand-carved creatures. If you're in the area, don't miss it.

● The Discovery Museum

4450 Park Ave., Rte. 15, exit 47, Bridgeport; (203) 372-3521. Tues.– Sat., 10–5; Sun., 12–5. Closed Mon. and major holidays. Adults, $6; 3– 18, $4. **Ages 3 and up.**

Wow. This interactive art-and-science museum features 115 hands-on art and science exhibits, not to mention a planetarium, art galleries, and more. A major attraction is the Challenger Learning Center, where kids aged 10 and up can play astronaut with computer-simulated space missions.

● Captain's Cove Seaport

1 Bostwick Ave., exit 26 off I-95, Bridgeport; (203) 335-1433. March 1– Nov. 1. **All ages.**

This lively Victorian-style boardwalk on Black Rock Harbor is a fun place to stroll. From Memorial Day–Labor Day, you can take a harbor cruise ($3 adults, $2 kids), and tour the historic HMS *Rose*, a Revolutionary War–era 24-gun frigate (when it's in port). You might also want to check out Dundon House, a restored 1893 Victorian mansion with a maritime exhibit ($2 adults, $1 kids) and take a peek inside craft shops, eateries, and a fish market. On Sundays, from June through September, boardwalk band concerts provide a festive touch.

● The Barnum Museum

820 Main St., exit 27 off I-95, Bridgeport; (203) 331-1104. Tues.–Sat., 10–4:30; Sun., 12–4:30; also open Mon., July–Aug., 11–4:30. Adults, $5; 4–18, $3. **Ages 4 and up.**

Your kids may never have heard of tiny Tom Thumb, but they'll probably get a kick out of this circus history "lesson," dedicated to P.T. Barnum and "the Greatest Show on Earth." This century-old landmark building also houses exhibits on Bridgeport's industrial history and 19th-century Americana. The most child-pleasing space here is the third floor, with Tom Thumb's tiny carriage and furniture and a 20-by-40-foot, hand-carved miniature circus. The Clown Corner has clown props and costumes; put your nose to the clown's make-up mirror and see yourself in clown-face.

● Audubon Center of Greenwich

613 Riversville Rd., Greenwich; (203) 869-5272. Year-round, Tues.–Sun., 9–5. Adults, $3; children, $1.50. **All ages.**

Families flock to the bird observation window here (sorry), and you're sure to find some new additions for your lifetime list—this 485-acre sanctuary offers an abundant variety of birds. Guided walks for families are offered on weekends, along sections of the Center's 15 miles of hiking trails; also check out the honeybee exhibit, visitor's center, and gift shop.

● Quassy Amusement Park

Rte. 64, exit 16E/17W off I-84, Middlebury; (203) 758-2913 or (800) FOR-PARK. April–May and Sept.–Oct., Sat. and Sun., 11–9; Memorial Day–Labor Day, daily, 11–9. Free; fee charged for rides and games. Parking fee. **All ages.**

Hot dogs, sno-cones, cotton candy, stomach-churning rides—what more could any kid (or young-at-heart mommy or daddy) ask for? Well, how about swimming and boating in Lake Quassapaug, a video arcade, a petting zoo, and miniature golf? It's an old-fashioned, all-American good time, complete with wandering minstrels, magic acts, and, on Friday nights, live music (heavy on the oldies acts and country western).

● Stamford Museum & Nature Center

39 Scofieldtown Rd., Rte. 15, exit 35, Stamford; (203) 322-1646. Mon.– Sat. and holidays, 9–5; Sun., 1–5. Planetarium shows: Sun., 3 P.M. Closed Thanksgiving, Christmas, and New Year's Day. Adults, $5; 5–13, $4. Planetarium shows: Adults, $3; children, $2. **All ages.**

The showpiece of this 118-acre complex is a 19th-century working farm. You'll enjoy poking around the country store and seven galleries (including one highlighting Native American customs) and meandering the woodland trails. Kids love the "natural playground," too. Be sure to visit the zoo, and catch a show at the planetarium. Seasonal activities, like maple syrup–making demonstrations, are a special delight here. If you're in town, don't miss it.

● Boat Cruises—*Soundwaters* Schooner

4 Yacht Haven West Marina, exit 7 off I-95, Stamford; (203) 323-1978. Weekends, mid-April–mid-Nov. Call for schedule and reservations. Adults, $25; 12 and under, $10. **Ages 5 and up.**

Stowaway on this 80-foot, three-masted sharpie schooner. *Soundwaters* is a replica of a 19th-century vessel, offering a delightful, interactive cruise that's great for families. On a three-hour ecology cruise, you'll help hoist the sails of this tall ship, haul in a trawl net filled with lobster and other creatures of the deep, and learn about Connecticut marine life, firsthand. Five onboard educators will answer your questions about Long Island Sound sea life, and staff the plankton station, the salt marsh station, and the tank station, where daring kids can handle some of the marine animals that are hauled in from the deep.

● Downtown Cabaret Theatre and Children's Theatre

263 Golden Hill St., exit 27A off I-95, Bridgeport; (203) 576-1636. Shows Sat., 12 and 2:30; Sun., 12. Per ticket, $9.50. **Ages 2–12.**

Catch your favorite fairy tales and fables here, updated for contemporary kids and presented with original music. A recent double feature combined *Little Red Riding Hood* and *The Three Little Pigs* with a scene-stealing, hip-hoppin' Big Bad Wolf. Performances are geared toward kids age two to 12. It's a lovely way to spend an afternoon and a splendid rainy day activity. B.Y.O. lunch or treats!

● Seaside Park

Exit 27 off I-95, Bridgeport; (203) 576-7233. **All ages.**

Open year-round, this pretty 370-acre park was donated to the city of Bridgeport by P.T. Barnum. Notable features include a beautiful beach and picnic areas.

● Maritime Aquarium at Norwalk

10 North Water St., exit 14N/15S off I-95, S. Norwalk; (203) 852-0700. July–Labor Day, daily, 10–6; Sept. and June, daily, 10–5. Closed Thanksgiving and Christmas. Adults, $7.50; children, $6.50. IMAX Theater admission: adults, $6.50; children, $5; under 2, free. Discounted combination ticket available. **All ages.**

Sharks, seals, jellyfish, otters, and 125 other marine species are on view here, making the Maritime Aquarium one of the top family destinations in the area. Explore the marine life and maritime culture of Long Island Sound at this waterfront destination, where attractions include an IMAX theater, an aquarium, and a hall dedicated to maritime history with several interactive exhibits. Your kids will love the close-up glimpses of underwater inhabitants (they can even "pet" a shark through the glass); you may be inspired to build your own wooden boat after watching the craftspeople here demonstrate their techniques.

● Sheffield Island Lighthouse

Ferry service from Hope Dock, corner of Washington and North Water streets, Norwalk; (203) 838-9444. Memorial Day–Labor Day; call for daily ferry schedule. Adults, $9; 12 and under, $7. **Ages 3 and up.**

Could you handle living in a lighthouse? You wouldn't need a Stairmaster. Take a scenic ferry boat ride on the *Island Girl* to this three-acre park with an 1868 lighthouse. Explore the lighthouse's four levels and 10 rooms; bring along a picnic. The lighthouse is adjacent to the Stewart B. McKinney U.S. Fish & Wildlife Sanctuary.

● Sherwood Island State Park

Exit 18 off I-95, Westport; (203) 226-6983. Daily, 8–sunset. Parking fee, Memorial Day–Sept.; off-season, free. **All ages.**

When you need a beach break, this one can't miss. It's a mile and a half of beachfront on Long Island Sound, suitable for swimming and saltwater fishing. Large, open fields are a great natural playscape—bring a ball and glove and a picnic. Services include a bathhouse and concessions. Two large picnic groves are situated near the water. Park rangers lead nature walks and interpretive programs; call for a schedule of events.

● Nature Center for Environmental Activities

10 Woodside Ln., exit 17 off I-95, Westport; (203) 227-7253. Year-round, Mon.–Sat., 9–5; Sun., 1–4. Adults, $1; children, $.50. **All ages.**

Find out who's who-o-o in the animal kingdom at this 62-acre wildlife sanctuary. Nature trails, natural science exhibits, a live animal hall, a discovery room, and an aquarium offer plenty to see, do, and explore.

● Concerts on the Green

First Presbyterian Church, 1101 Bedford St., Stamford; (203) 324-9522. Month of July, Thurs., 7 P.M. Free. **All ages.**

If your idea of a classic New England outing includes an outdoor concert on a balmy evening, don't miss the carillon and band concerts here on Thursday nights in July.

● Silverman's Farm

Sport Hill Rd., exit 46I off Rte. 15, Easton; (203) 261-3306. Daily, 9–6. Free. Petting Zoo: adults, $2; children, $1. **All ages.**

This is a combination farmer's market and petting zoo, with pick-your-own produce (in season) and a working cider mill.

● Blue Jay Orchards

125 Plumtrees Rd., Bethel; (203) 748-0119. July–Jan. Free. **All ages.**

Celebrate autumn here, as you stroll the farm market, meet resident barnyard animals at the petting zoo, see the cider mill at work, and pick your own apples and pumpkins (September through October).

● Railroad Museum of New England

176 Chase Rd., exit 36 off Rte. 8, Waterbury; (203) 575-1931. May–Oct., Sat., Sun., and holidays, 9:30–5:30. Adults, $8; children, $6. **All ages.**

Attention, Thomas the Tank Engine fans: take a 10-mile ride on a restored historic railroad. Chug-a-lug your way from brass mills, through a state forest, along the Naugatuck River, and past a dam.

● The Nature Conservancy

33 Pent Rd., Rte. 15, exit 42, Weston; (203) 226-4991. Year-round, dawn–dusk. Free. **All ages.**

They call it Devil's Den, but this nature preserve is heaven to hikers, with more than 20 miles of trails on 1,746 acres. Nearby, the Katharine Ordway Preserve offers three miles of trails and an arboretum on 62 acres. No biking, camping, or dogs allowed. Guided nature walks, such as evening Owl Prowls, and interpretive programs are offered; call for information.

● Sportland America

40 Mill Plain Rd., Danbury; (203) 730-0730. Memorial Day–Labor Day, Mon.–Thurs., 10–10; Fri. and Sat.,10–midnight; Sun., 12–10. Skating day pass: adults, $4; under 6, $2.50. Evening pass: adults, $5; under 6, $2.50. **Ages 3 and up.**

Remember how much fun it was to go to a roller rink? Turn your kids on to the same here, or take advantage of the bumper cars and a miniature golf course.

● Hayrides and Sleigh Rides

Thrill to an old-fashioned, horse-drawn hayride or sleigh ride at **Gems Morgans,** 75 North Poverty Rd., Southbury; (203) 264-6190. Call for rates and reservations.

 RESTAURANTS

● The Restaurant at Captain's Cove

1 Bostwick Ave., exit 26 off I-95, Bridgeport; (203) 335-7104. Memorial Day–Oct., Mon.–Thurs., 11–midnight; Sat., 11–1 A.M.; Sun., 11–11.

Captain's Cove is a great place to knock around, with its boardwalk, charter boats to gawk at, and little Victorian shops. The restaurant fare ranges from a boxed lunch to a lobster bake; kids love the old-fashioned arcade games and rides.

● Sycamore Drive-In

282 Greenwood Ave., Bethel; (203) 748-2716. Year-round, Mon.–Sat., 6:30–9:30.

Picky about your upholstery? Forget this place and skip ahead to the next listing. The Sycamore is one of the last authentic drive-ins on the planet. Yes, they offer car hop service; you flash your lights, they take your order, and eventually the car hop will attach a tray of food to your window. This isn't just a restaurant, it's a cultural experience. And the food's not bad; try the chicken-in-a-basket with a mug of the Sycamore's secret-recipe homemade root beer.

Promise us you'll stop here when you're in the area; we can't let this place go the way of the T'bird.

● Bacco's

1230 Thomaston Ave., Waterbury; (203) 755-0635. Tues.–Thurs., 11:30–10; Fri., 11:30–11; Sat., 4–11; Sun., 12–8:30. Closed Mon.

This is a homey, family-style Italian place, with an absolutely killer pizza. The sublime pie is covered with fresh clams and garlic, and baked to perfection in a brick oven. Not bad for a place that's been around for more than 60 years. Kids won't touch clams or garlic? Order a pizza for the grown-ups, and get the kids a nice order of lasagna. *Mangia!*

Litchfield Hills Area

The village of Litchfield could be a movie set entitled "Quaint New England Town." It has the requisite white clapboard homes, a town green, even pristine 18th-century mansions that could be museums but in fact are private homes. The area is, without question, one of New England's most richly blessed when it comes to natural beauty.

If your children consider the appeal of a picturesque colonial village on par with a trip to a plumbing supply store, not to worry. Litchfield County and the surrounding area offers more than just a pretty face. Northwestern Connecticut is studded with state parks where you can camp, fish, hike, swim, ride, and picnic. Beautiful country walks abound. For hardy hikers, Litchfield County offers a stretch of the Appalachian Trail featuring Connecticut's highest peak, Bear Mountain.

Round out your visit with a museum, take in the action at Lime Rock race track, and stop at a local pick-your-own farm to load up on fresh produce.

● Carousel Museum of New England

95 Riverside Ave., exit 31 off I-84, Bristol; (860) 583-6070. April–Nov., Mon.–Sat., 10–5; Sun., 12–5. Dec.–March, Thurs.–Sat., 10–5; Sun., 12–5. Closed major holidays. Adults, $4; 4–14, $2.50. **Ages 4 and up.**

Remember the thrill of your first carousel ride? Probably not, but you'll have a real appreciation for those painted ponies after a visit here. Housed in a restored, turn-of-the-century factory are wonderful examples of antique carousel art, where painters and carvers work painstakingly to restore old pieces to their past glory. Tours run every half-hour; "Kidstuff" programs offer classes in papier-mache. Call for a schedule.

● Lake Compounce Theme Park & Entertainment Complex

822 Lake Ave., exit 31 off I-84, Bristol; (860) 583-3631. Every day except Tues., 11–10. General admission (no rides), $3.95; all-day ride pass: adults, $18.95; under 48 in. tall, $13.95; 3 and under, free. **All ages.**

Only a true curmudgeon could resist the charms of this attraction. America's oldest continually open amusement park is an appealing blend of Victoriana (old-time shops, a carousel) and contemporary thrills, like the Thunder River whitewater raft ride and the Boomerang roller coaster—fifteen new rides in all. Better eat that corn dog later—the Boomerang turns you upside down six times! Also new at Lake Compounce: a circus-themed Kiddie Land. Stop and catch your breath at one of the live stage shows.

● White Memorial Foundation and Conservation Center

Rte. 202, Litchfield; (860) 567-0857. Conservation Center: Spring–fall, Mon.–Sat., 9–5; Sun., 12–4. Winter hours, Mon.–Sat., 8:30–4:30; Sun., 12–4. Adults, $2; 6–12, $1. Sanctuary open year-round, daily. Free. **All ages.**

This 4,000-acre wildlife sanctuary—including half the shoreline of Bantam Lake and the Bantam River—offers 35 miles of hiking trails. Take a guided tour or set your own pace, with time out for a picnic along the way. Bantam Lake is great for swimming, or rent a rowboat or canoe, or make it a real getaway and camp out at one of the family campgrounds on the property. Be sure to stop by the Conservation Center, near the entrance, for a quick lesson in local flora and fauna. Exhibits include interesting things like a working beehive, an aquarium with turtles, snakes, and fish, and stuffed hawks and owls on display.

● Mt. Tom State Park
Rte. 202, Litchfield; (860) 868-2592. April 1–Nov. 15, daily, sunrise–sunset. Parking fee in season: $4 weekdays, $5 weekends. **All ages.**

Ready for a workout? The summit of this park is 1,325 feet above sea level, crowned by a stone tower. Other features here include a hiking trail, lake swimming, fishing, boating (no motors, please), even scuba diving. Go ice skating here in winter.

● Topsmead State Forest
Buell Rd., Rte. 118, Litchfield; (860) 567-5694. Grounds: Open year-round, 8–sunset. Mansion: June–Oct.; call for hours. Free. **All ages.**

The principal attraction here is an English Tudor-style cottage, the summer home of Edith Morton Chase. Miss Chase donated the 514-acre forest to the state upon her death in 1972. The cottage is open to visitors during the summer; call first to confirm the schedule. The grounds include a 40-acre wildflower preserve and nature trail. Have a picnic at one of the tables, or spread a blanket wherever you choose. Cross-country skiing and snowshoeing in winter.

● Sandy Beach
Bantam Lake, E. Shore Rd. (Rte. 109), Morris; (860) 567-5387. Memorial Day–June, weekends only, 9–7; July–Labor Day, daily, 9–7. $5 fee for vehicles and boats; $1 fee for walkers and bicyclists. **All ages.**

This secluded cove is a welcome find on a balmy day, with lifeguards, bathhouses, a snack bar, picnic area, and canoe launch.

● Horseback Riding
Lee's Riding Stable, in Litchfield, offers guided horseback rides (on easy-going mounts) and pony rides, on beautiful wooded trails. The stables are located at 57 E. Litchfield Rd.; call (860) 567-0785 for information.

H.O.R.S.E. of Connecticut, in Washington, is a non-profit rescue organization, offering daily tours to view and feed the horses. Book in advance for a trail ride. Call (860) 868-1960 for details.

● Bicycle Touring/Mountain Biking
Connecticut's gorgeous countryside, covering nearly 90 percent of the state, is best viewed by bicycle. For a free map of Connecticut's on-road bicycle routes, write to: Connecticut Dept. of Transportation, 2800 Berlin Tpke., P.O. Box 317546, Newington, CT 06131-7546. For mountain

bikers, a best bet is **Woodbury Ski & Raquet Area,** on Rte. 47, in Woodbury. Twenty miles of terrain with 36 trails offers thrills aplenty.

● Canoeing/Kayaking/Tubing

You'll catch glimpses of the Housatonic River as you drive and hike around the Litchfield Hills; if you'd like an on-river experience, a couple of local outfitters will be happy to comply. **Clarke Outdoors,** on Rte. 7 in West Cornwall, (860) 672-6365, offers ten-mile trips on the Housy by canoe, kayak, or raft. Trips run in April through October, daily; call to see which sounds like a good match for your group. Reservations are recommended. **Main Stream Canoe,** based in New Hartford, offers flatwater and whitewater canoe daytrips, moonlight trips (in summer), and kayak "adventures." Trips run daily, Memorial Day through Labor Day, and weekends during spring and fall. Call (860) 693-6791 for details. **Farmington River Tubing** offers thrilling river rapids rides for families with older kids (age 10 and up) who know how to swim. One person rides on each tube, traveling stretches that are alternately calm and peaceful, and wild and woolly. Call (860) 693-6465.

● Meadowbrook Farm

644 Middle Rd. Tpke., Woodbury; (860) 263-3267. April–Oct., Thurs.– Sat., 9–5; Sun., 10–5. Adults, $3.50; children, $2.50. **All ages.**

This farm offers family fun and then some, with farm animals, pony rides, hayrides, nature trails, bird walks, and more.

● American Indian Archaeological Institute

Curtis Rd. off Rte. 199, Washington; (860) 868-0518. Mon.–Sat., 10–5; Sun. 12–5. Adults, $4; 6–16, $2. **Ages 4 and up.**

This museum is more child-pleasing than its name implies. Exhibits highlight the Native American experience in New England, with artifacts spanning 10,000 years. Most kids are intrigued by the re-created Onandaga Indian longhouse filled with household objects and appearing as though the family will return home any minute. Dino-philes will delight in the mastodon skeleton, unearthed in nearby Farmington. Walk along an Indian trail, visit a 17th-century Algonkian Indian village, and view a simulated archaeological dig.

● Gunn Historical Museum

On the Green, cor. of Wykeham Rd. and Rte. 47, Washington; (860) 868- 7756. Thurs.–Sat., 12–4. Free. **Ages 5 and up.**

Of course you'll want to get a peek inside one of the lovely homes here; this 1781 house is furnished with memorabilia from several Washington homes, including exquisite dolls and dollhouses.

● Lime Rock Park

Rte. 112, Lakeville; (860) 435-0896 or 800-RACE-LRP. Racing on most weekends, early April–Nov. Call for schedule. Rates vary with event: $10 and up for adults; 12 and under, free. **Ages 5 and up.**

If your kids love fast cars, lots of noise, and action, head to the track. Pro national and amateur road racing events are held here, with car shows and auto festivals rounding out the calendar. If you're bringing a small child, consider a regional race (not to mention earplugs); they're shorter (30 minutes as opposed to 2.5 hours) and less crowded than other spectator events. Spectators are also welcome at Tuesday practice sessions. Your ticket entitles you to a walk around the paddock area, where drivers and crews are at work on their cars.

● Sharon Audubon Center

Rte. 4, Sharon; (860) 364-0520. Mon.–Sat., 9–5; Sun., 1–5. Closed major holidays. Trails open daily, dawn to dusk. Adults, $3; children, $1.50. (Free to National Audubon Society members.) **All ages.**

This 684-acre sanctuary is a hiker's paradise, with 11 miles of nature trails, and some beautiful wildflower and herb gardens. A stand-out among the trails: the Bog Meadow Trail, a short (1.25 miles), moderately challenging hike through some beautiful territory. Clearly marked, the trail is at its best in autumn, when the maples and aspens are in their fall colors. Walk along the boardwalk and beside a pond that's home to ducks, turtles, minks, and beavers.

● Lake McDonough

Rte. 219 off Rte. 44, Barkhamsted; (860) 379-3036. Boating, mid-April–Labor Day; fishing from shore, Labor Day–Nov.; swimming, Memorial Day–Labor Day. **All ages.**

Rent a rowboat or paddleboat and putter around this pretty, popular lake. You may also B.Y.O.B. (bring your own boat) and pay a small fee to launch it. Or go swimming, fishing, hiking, picnicking—this place has it all.

● Macedonia Brook State Park

Rte. 341, Kent; (860) 566-2304. Daily, 8–sunset. **All ages.**

Beautiful and wild, this park is blessed with forests, mountainous terrain, a deep gorge, upper and lower falls, wildlife, and, of course, a brook. It offers great views of the Catskill and Taconic mountain ranges, too. Hiking trails here are plentiful and color coded, and some extend along the Appalachian Trail. There's fishing, and cross-country skiing in winter.

● Peoples State Forest

East River Rd., Barkhamsted; (860) 379-2469. Grounds: open daily, 8– sunset. Mansion: June–Oct., call for hours. Free. **All ages.**

More great hiking, with trails leading past caves and springs. Look for beavers building dams in the marsh. Stop for a picnic among the 200-year-old white pines in Mathies Grove, and take a peek inside the small nature museum (summer only). Go cross-country skiing and snow-mobiling here in winter.

● Burr Pond State Park

Burr Mountain Rd., Rte. 8, 5 miles north of Torrington; (860) 482-1817. Daily, 8–sunset. Parking fee in season. **All ages.**

Features here include trout-stocked Burr Pond, a sandy beach, streams, rivers, and interesting rock formations. Swimming, boating, and fishing are permitted. It's a great place to paddle a canoe; rent one here from Farmington River Tubing. A scenic path encircles the 88-acre pond. The cross-country skiing is easy, and there's also ice skating in winter.

● Haystack Mountain

Rte. 272, 1 mile north of Norfolk; (860) 566-2304. Daily, 8–sunset. **All ages.**

Drive halfway up the mountain and enjoy the view, especially lovely during fall foliage season. From there, active types can hike the half-mile trail to the top of the mountain. At the summit, you'll see a 34-foot-high stone tower; climb it for dramatic vistas of Long Island Sound and the Berkshires.

● Housatonic Meadows State Park

Rte. 7, 1 mile north of Cornwall Bridge, Sharon; (860) 672-6772. Daily, 8–sunset. Camping: mid-April–Dec. Park: free. Camping: $10 per night. **All ages.**

If your group enjoys fly fishing, the clear, cold Housatonic River is a great place to test your skills on trout and bass. A two-mile stretch of river is limited to fly fishing. Enjoy a picnic under the pines on the riverbank. You can even spend the night, if you wish; call ahead to reserve a space at a riverside campsite. Best hiking is on the Pine Knob Loop trail, which joins the Appalachian Trail.

● Kent Falls

Rte. 7, 3 miles north of Kent; (860) 927-3238. Daily, 8–sunset. Parking fee on weekends and holidays. **All ages.**

This cascading waterfall draws thousands of visitors each year. Climb the pathway adjacent to the falls for great views at all levels. This is a favorite scene for professional and amateur photographers.

● Mohawk Mountain State Park and Forest

Rte. 4, Cornwall; (860) 566-2304. Daily, 8–sunset. **All ages.**

In summer or, even better, during peak fall color, drive to the mountaintop for enchanting views. An abandoned fire tower serves as a lookout. There are plenty of hiking opportunities throughout the forest, with several loop trails and a section of the Appalachian Trail. Don't miss Black Spruce Bog, near forest headquarters, home of a unique community of insect-eating plants. Cross-country ski on forest roads and trails or join the downhill skiers at Mohawk Mountain Ski Area.

● Mohawk Mountain Ski Area

46 Great Hollow Rd., off Rte. 4, Cornwall; (860) 672-6100. Daily, except Christmas, generally Thanksgiving weekend–Easter. Lifts run Mon.–Sat., 8:30–10; Sun., 8:30–4. Full-day lift tickets (anytime): adults, $25; 6–15, $20; under 6, $10. Partial-day passes (morning, 8:30–1; afternoon, 1–6; Sun. only, 1–4; twilight, 4–10): adults, $20; 6–15, $15; under 6, $10. **Ages 3 and up.**

Family skiing is the name of the game at Mohawk Mountain. Run by a mother-daughter team, the resort does not serve alcohol, and it offers a friendly, low-key atmosphere. Noteworthy features include night skiing (except on Sundays), snowmaking over 95 percent of the mountain's skiable terrain, and ski programs for kids as young as age three. Tiny tots can get into the act with Mohawk's "Try-and-see" program; kids from age five to 12 can participate in the SKIwee program, run on weekends and holidays from 10 to 3. Youngsters who can handle the chairlift with ease and make controlled wedge turns can graduate to SKIwee Tigers, a multiday instruction program, while junior speed demons can sign up for Christmas Racing Camp, a five-day course designed to hone racing skills. Group and private lessons are offered daily, and lest you doubt that Mohawk emphasizes learning, group lessons are offered four times a day.

This managable, family-friendly resort is a great place to build your confidence on skis, or to introduce your kids to this exhilarating activity.

● Cross-Country Skiing

Connecticut's numerous state parks and state forests are open to Nordic skiers, as are several nature centers and preserves. There are also a number of cross-country ski centers, offering groomed trails, equipment rentals, and snack bars. Recommended destinations include **Mohawk Mountain** ski resort with more than 40 miles of trails, in Cornwall, (860) 672-6100; the **Blackberry River Inn** in Norfolk, (860) 542-5100, with more than 10 miles of trails, and rentals and lessons; and **White Memorial Foundation** in Litchfield, with 35 miles of trails through varied and beautiful conservation land. Call (860) 567-0857 for information.

 RESTAURANTS

● Deer Island Gate Restaurant

Rte. 209, on Bantam Lake, Morris; (860) 567-4622. Wed.–Sat., 5–10; Sun. buffet, 1–7. Closed for a few weeks each winter; call for reservations.

This is a large, casual restaurant with great views of Bantam Lake. The menu is ambitious, offering daily fish specials, steaks, pork, duck, chicken, lamb, and German dishes. Prices start at around $12.50 and up for entrées; there's no children's menu, but they're happy to offer half-portions of most entrées for half price. Local folks love the Sunday German buffet.

● La Tienda Cafe

Rte. 202, Federal Square shopping center, Litchfield; (860) 567-8778. Tues. and Wed., 4:30–9; Thurs., 11:30–9; Fri. and Sat., 11:30–10; Sun., 12– 9; Mon., 3–9.

Most American kids love Mexican food, as do most grown-ups, so this little place is a happy find. You can tell a lot about a Mexican restaurant by the quality of its tortilla chips; La Tienda's are homemade and just great. Try a Mexican pizza, Arizona-style nachos (topped with ground beef), or a soup-and-appetizer combination. All the Mexican favorites are offered, along with some unique house specialties, all very reasonably priced. There's also a children's menu, but what child doesn't like tacos?

Northeast Connecticut

"Off the beaten track." "Where the crowds aren't." These phrases describe Connecticut's quiet corner. If modern life-with-children has left you worn out, strung out, and in need of escape, this might be the perfect place to reconnect. Besides, how could you miss showing your kids the statue honoring General Israel Putnam, who said, "Don't fire until you see the white of their eyes?" And life is far too short to miss indulging in a homemade ice cream at U-Conn's dairy bar—the perfect reward for hiking local hills and biking country roads.

Rolling countryside, working farms, and historic inns give a pastoral feel to this undiscovered corner of Connecticut; we'll provide suggestions for some pleasant diversions as you roam.

● Connecticut State Museum of Natural History

University of Connecticut, Rte. 195, exit 68 off I-84, Storrs; (860) 486-4460. Videoplace: Mon., Thurs.–Sat., 12–4; Sun., 1–4. (Call ahead to confirm hours.) Museum: Mon., Thurs.–Sat.., 12–4; Sun, 1–4. Closed July 4th, Labor Day weekend, Thanksgiving, Christmas, and New Year's Day. Free. **All ages.**

Great white sharks, a life-size wigwam, mounted birds of prey—these totally cool exhibits will surely capture your child's attention, along with the minerals and fossils on display at the University of Connecticut's natural history museum. And did we mention the 20 life-size interactive video games? Awesome. Special children's workshops and family festivals are held periodically; call for a schedule of events.

● University of Connecticut Dairy Bar and Animal Barns

(See previous listing for address.) Animal barns located at Horsebarn Hill Rd.; dairy bar located at 3636 Horsebarn Rd. Ext. Dairy bar: Year-round, Mon.–Fri., 10–5; Sat. and Sun., 12–5. Animal barns: Year-round, daily, 10–4. Closed July 4th, Easter, Thanksgiving, and Christmas. **All ages.**

The University of Connecticut was founded in 1881 as a land-grant school of agriculture; part of that heritage remains today. Visit the friendly dairy cattle, sheep, horses, and swine housed at U-Conn's barns (time your trip for early spring to see the newborns). Next, head to the dairy bar for the local delicacy—wonderfully sinful homemade ice cream.

● Nathan Hale Homestead

South St., off Rte. 44, Coventry; (860) 742-6917. Mid-May–mid-Oct., daily, 1–5. Adults, $4; children, $1. **Ages 3 and up.**

Explore the life and times of Connecticut hero Nathan Hale at his 1776 family farm. The best feature for kids is a walled-in, grassy field where they can try hoop-rolling and walking on stilts. (Many parents can't resist these stilts, either.) You can picnic on the grounds, keeping an eye out for resident animals. Plan your visit to coincide with one of the special events held here: "Hale to Spring," featuring baby animals; "Muster and Colonial Encampment," with tents and musket shooting, in July; and the "Lantern Tour," a house tour by candlelight, in October. Call for dates.

● Photomobile Model Museum

1728 Rte. 198, Woodstock; (860) 974-3910. Sat., 10–5; Sun., 12–5. Adults, $2; under 16, $1. **Ages 5 and up.**

Now here's something we'll bet you don't see every day—solar-powered model cars, boats, planes, and trains. See 'em demonstrated outdoors (on sunny days) or indoors, under the floodlights.

● River Bend Mining & Gemstone Panning

41 Pond St., Rte. 14A, Sterling; (860) 564-3440. Mid-April–mid-Oct., Tues.–Thurs., 10–5; Fri., 10–8; Sat., 10–7; Sun., 9–5. Mine: adults, $6.50; children, $5.50. Sluice: $3.25. **Ages 5 and up.**

Guided by the lamp on your miner's helmet, enter an authentic mine. Mine for gems, fossils, minerals, and shells, or try panning "sluice" (a gravelly mixture that may contain gemstones) and see what sparkly treasures you uncover. This activity is fairly common in some states, like Montana and Tennessee, but out-of-the-ordinary here in New England. It's semi-educational, and fun. Also see the wildlife exhibit, with 40 animal displays.

● Ballard Institute and Museum of Puppetry

Weaver Rd., off Rte. 44, Mansfield; (860) 486-4605. Mid-April–mid-Nov., Thurs.–Fri., 10–3; Sat.–Sun., 12–5. **Ages 3 and up.**

Beyond Punch & Judy—see more puppets than you've ever imagined here, where changing exhibits highlight puppets from a collection of more than 2,000. Thus inspired, the kids will be ready to put on some whiz-bang puppet productions back home.

● Creamery Brook Bison Farm

19 Purvis Rd., Brooklyn; (860) 779-0837. Year-round, Mon.–Fri., 2–6; Sat., 9–2. Guided tours by reservation. Adults, $6; 3–11, $4.50. **All ages.**

Some people actually do have a home where the buffalo roam. Take a 40-minute ride through this 100-acre dairy farm where the buffalo (more accurately, American bison) roam. A fun way to see it—on a hayride.

● Wright's Mill Farm

63 Creasey Rd., Canterbury; (860) 774-1455. Year-round, daily, 9–5.
All ages.

Hike and picnic amidst the pastoral pleasures of this 250-acre farm complex. Horse-drawn carriage and wagon rides, pumpkin-hunt hayrides, and cut-your-own Christmas trees are offered (in season, of course). Guided tours of the historic mill village are led, by appointment.

● Quinebaug Valley Trout Hatchery

Trout Hatchery Rd., exit 89 off I-395, Central Village; (860) 564-7542. Daily, 10–4. Free. **All ages.**

Fish-o-rama! Nearly 600,000 pounds of brook, brown, and rainbow trout are produced here each year, making this one of the largest hatcheries in the East. Watch them in action through glass viewing walls.

● Roseland Cottage

Rte. 169, exit 72 off I-84, Woodstock; (860) 928-4074. June–mid-Oct., Wed.–Sun., July 4th, and Columbus Day, 11–5. Adults, $4; 5–12, $2; under 5, free. Teas: $12 per person. **Ages 3–14.**

This is one of those local landmarks that just can't be missed. This striking pink Gothic Revival home is now designated a National Historic Landmark. It was built by publisher Henry Bowen as a summer home. Kids will get a kick out of the indoor bowling alley, in the barn. Presidents Grant, Hayes, Harrison, and McKinley visited Roseland (wonder if Bowen made them wear those goofy bowling shoes?). A nice feature for families: special teas are held for children throughout the summer, on various Sundays. Themes (these change from year to year) include a Children's Victorian Tea Party, Miss Tiggy Winkle (from Beatrix Potter stories) Tea, and a Tussy Mussy Tea. Each lasts about two hours. Children age three to 14 take part; parents can join the tea party if they desire. A wonderful event happens here, on the first Saturday in August: an old-fashioned Children's Lawn Party, just as Henry Bowen would've done it, with period games and activities.

● Bigelow Hollow State Park

Rte. 197, Union; (860) 928-9200. Parking fee, weekends and holidays in season. **All ages.**

Explore this scenic woodland area—although, since it's 513 acres, you probably won't see it all—by foot or by boat. Park lands surround Mashapaug Lake. Recreation opportunities include fishing, hiking, boating, and, when the snow piles up, snowmobiling and cross-country skiing.

● Connecticut Audubon/Pomfret Farms

220 Day Rd., off Rte. 169, Pomfret; (860) 928-4041. **All ages.**

Enjoy the pastoral beauty of Connecticut's "Quiet Corner" at this 140-acre property, as you meander the hiking trails that loop around it. Guided bird walks and wildlife workshops are offered on a regular basis.

● Saddletown

281 Newport Rd., Oneco; (860) 564-1171. July–Aug., Sun., 11–6. $5. **Ages 2 and up.**

What's an authentic replica of an old Western town doing in northeast Connecticut? We don't know, either, but if you're curious about their cowboy shows, pony rides, and petting animals, mosey on over.

● Mashamoquet Brook State Park

Rte. 44, Pomfret; (860) 928-6121. Fee, weekends and holidays in season. **All ages.**

This 1,000-acre park is the home of the famous (well, around here, anyway) wolf den, where Reverend Gen. Israel Putnam is said to have slain the last wolf in Connecticut. Follow Wolf Den Trail to the site.

● Horseback Riding

Diamond A Ranch, in Dayville, is home of the "Pizza King ride." No, Pizza King is not a horse; you actually ride to a pizza parlor. Other rides are available, tailored to your interest and ability. Rides are offered year-round, weather permitting. Call the ranch at (860) 779-3000 for details.

RESTAURANTS

● Willington's Pizza

25 River Rd., Rte. 32, Willington; (860) 429-7433. Daily, 11–11.

Not just any pizza—award-winning pizza is served here. So good, *Good Morning America* visited, chowed down, and did a story on them.

● Zip's Diner

Junction, Rtes. 12 and 101, Dayville; (860) 774-6335. Daily, 6–9.

This authentic 1954 diner serves homecooked grub worthy of the "diner" name. Get your meatloaf and mashed or mac-and-cheese here. This is how Mom cooked before she went fat-free.

● We-Li-Kit Ice Cream

728 Hampton Rd., Rte. 97, Pomfret; (860) 974-1095. Summer, daily, 12–9:30.

Lu-Vit, is more like it. This is real ice cream, made from the milk of real Connecticut cows. How do we know for sure? They're right here, on the property, about 150 of 'em. Bet Ben & Jerry can't say that.

● Stoggy Hollow General Store

Rte. 198, Woodstock Valley; (860) 974-3814. Daily, 7–8; Fri. and Sat. 'til 9.

Hard to find but worth it, this general store and eatery is cute as can be. The oversized sandwiches are messy and delicious, and the home-baked sweets are sheer heaven. But wait, there's more. An expanded menu features gourmet pizza, soon-to-be-world-famous hand-cut French fries, and "nostalgia drinks" like root beer floats and egg creams. Sit in the parlor of this 1836 colonial and enjoy the food and atmosphere. Or, sit outside, and watch the world go by. The general store, next door, has fun stuff like penny candies and classic small toys.

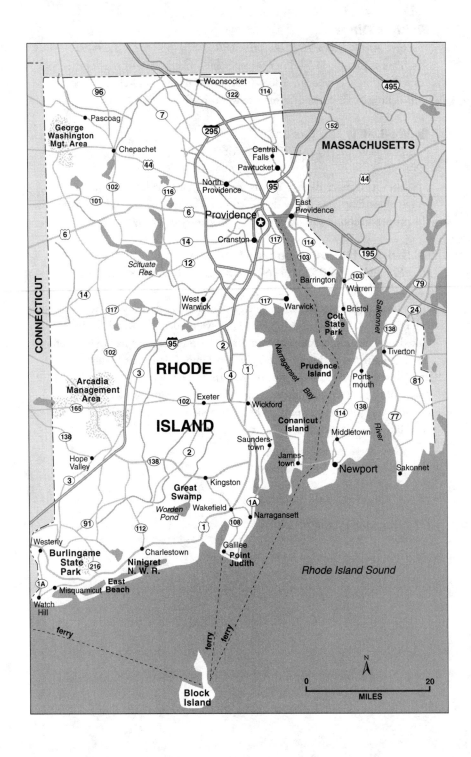

Woonsocket
96
122
114
495
7
Pascoag
George
Washington
Mgt. Area
152
MASSACHUSETTS
295
Chepachet
Central
Falls
44
North
Providence
44
Pawtucket
102
116
95
101
6
Providence
East
Providence
14
6
117
114
Cranston
12
195
103
Scituate
Res.
Barrington
103
Warren
79
14
West
Warwick
117
Warwick
Bristol
24
117
Colt
State
Park
138
102
95
Narragansett Bay
RHODE
2
1
Prudence
Island
Tiverton
3
4
Arcadia
Management
Area
Ports-
mouth
81
165
102
Exeter
Wickford
ISLAND
Conanicut
Island
138
Middletown
114
138
77
Sakonnet River
138
Saunders-
town
2
Hope
Valley
138
James-
town
Newport
Sakonnet
3
Kingston
Great
Swamp
1A
Worden
Pond
Wakefield
91
112
Narragansett
1
108
Westerly
Galilee
Rhode Island Sound
Burlingame
State
Park
216
Charlestown
Point
Judith
Ninigret
N. W. R.
1A
East
Misquamicut Beach
Watch
Hill
ferry
ferry
ferry
N

0   20
MILES

Block
Island

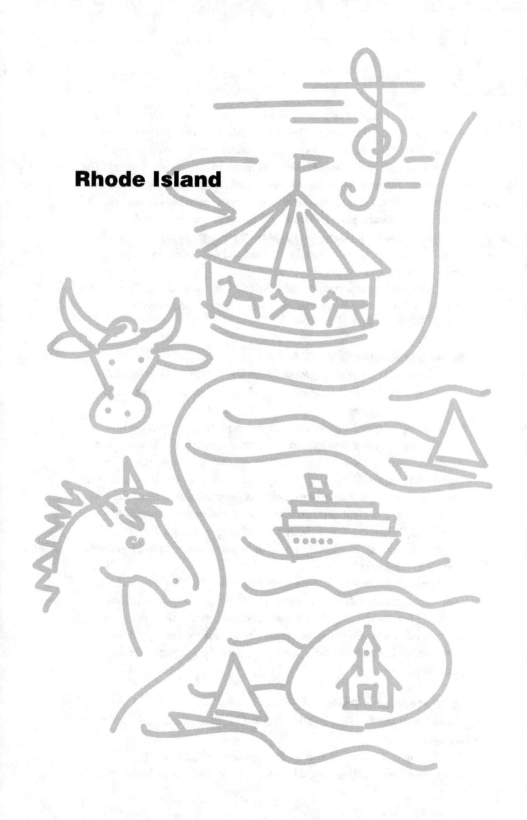

Rhode Island

Providence Area

You might be tempted to pass by the Providence area, in a hurry to get to the Rhode Island resorts of Newport or Block Island, or the beaches of the South County region. Yet this quiet, urban pocket, often named as one of America's most livable cities, has much to offer young visitors. The biggest city in the smallest state boasts a new, four-acre park, smack in the center of town. Landscaped riverwalks and venetian-style footbridges make this a pleasant place to stroll, and perhaps take in an outdoor concert. Window shop along South Main Street, where historic colonial buildings have been authentically restored and now house boutiques, galleries, and restaurants.

Perennial favorites include the exotic animals at Roger Williams Park & Zoo, and, in nearby Pawtucket, a children's museum housed in a unique old mansion.

● Roger Williams Park & Zoo

950 Elmwood Ave. (off I-95), Providence; (401) 785-3510. Park: daily, 7–9. Zoo: Memorial Day–Labor Day, 9–5; rest of year, 9–4. Adults, $5; 3–12, $2.50. **All ages.**

It's easy to spend a pleasant, busy day exploring this wonderland of parks, ponds, lakes, and gardens that cover more than 430 acres. But Roger Williams Park is more than a nature tour; its centerpiece is an award-winning zoo. More than 160 species are housed here in expansive, naturalistic settings. Exhibits are grouped geographically, featuring Plains of Africa (home of elephants, giraffes, zebras, and more), Tropical Rainforest, Madagascar, and the Arctic (where polar bears Norton and Trixie frolic in their pool). One of the oldest zoos in the country, this one keeps getting better.

Don't go home yet—there's more to see and do. Walk the wetlands trail and try to identify native animals and plants. Visit the Museum of Natural History and the planetarium. Don't forget to take a ride on the carousel and the antique railroad train. Or—a must on muggy days— rent a paddleboat at the boathouse and explore the park's connecting waterways.

● Waterplace Park

Memorial Blvd., Providence; (401) 785-9450. Open year-round. Free. **All ages.**

This new, four-acre urban park is a pleasant oasis in the heart of downtown. Surrounding a tidal basin, the park is edged by landscaped riverwalks and venetian-style footbridges. An amphitheater is the site of free concerts throughout the summer.

● Providence Performing Arts Center

220 Weybosset St., Providence; (401) 421-ARTS. Box office hours: Mon.– Fri., 10–6; Sat., noon–5. Ticket prices vary. **Ages 3 and up.**

This historic theater was built in 1928 as a Loew's Movie Palace. Now, live theater offerings include Broadway shows, revivals of classics like *Carousel* and *Grease*, and productions for children such as *Magic School Bus Live!* Free organ concerts here in spring and fall.

● Museum of Art, Rhode Island School of Design

Benefit St., Providence; (401) 454-6500, (401) 454-6331. Open June 30– Labor Day, Thurs.–Sun., noon–5. Rest of year: Tues., Wed., Fri., Sat., 10:30–5; Thurs., noon–8; Sun. and holidays, 2–5. Closed Mon.; also closed Thanksgiving, Christmas, New Year's eve and July 4. Adults, $2; children and students, $.50. Free on Sat. **Ages 5 and up.**

Since RISD is one of the best art and design schools in the country, its art museum is worth a look. Collections include classical art from ancient Greece and Rome, 18th-century European porcelains (you might want to skip this if you've small children in tow), Chinese and Indian pieces, Egyptian objects, and, in Pendleton House, 19th-century American furniture and decorative arts. Perhaps the most interesting space for children is the Daphne Farago Wing, featuring contemporary art in all media.

● Rhode Island State Capitol

82 Smith St., Providence; (401) 277-2357. Mon.–Fri., 8:30–4:30, except holidays. Self-guided tours during business hours; guided tours by appointment. **Ages 3 and up.**

Many believe that this impressive, white-domed Georgian marble structure is the most beautiful capitol building in America. Inside, see the full-length portrait of George Washington painted by Rhode Islander Gilbert Stuart.

● Children's Museum of Rhode Island

Pitcher-Goff Mansion, 58 Walcott St., Pawtucket; (401) 726-2590. Year-round, Tues.–Sat., 9:30–5; Sun.,1–5. Closed mid-June–Oct. Per person, $3.50; under 1, free. **Ages 1–11.**

This warm, lively museum, housed in a 19th-century Victorian mansion, is a place where children aged one to eleven can touch, draw, explore, bounce, read, imagine, and learn. Have a make-believe tea party in Great Grandmother's Kitchen, explore Rhode Island on your hands and knees in the room-size relief map, play hide-and-seek in a climbing maze of tunnels and platforms, and more. The museum hosts traveling exhibits, too.

● Crescent Park Carousel

At end of Bullock's Point Ave., East Providence; (401) 435-7518 or (401) 433-2828. Easter Sunday–Memorial Day, Sat. and Sun., 12–7. After Memorial Day, Fri.–Sun., 12–8. July–Labor Day, Wed.–Sun., 12–8; closed Mon. and Tues., except for summer holidays. Labor Day–Columbus Day, Sat. and Sun., 12–8. $.50 per ride or 5 rides for $2. **All ages.**

What a treasure! More than a century old, this carousel—once part of a large amusement park—is one of the few complete carousels of its type still in operation. Designed in 1895 by Charles I.D. Looff, it features 66 one-of-a-kind figures.

● Slater Memorial Park

U.S. Rte. 1-A, Pawtucket; (401) 728-0500, ext. 252. Park: Memorial Day–Labor Day, 8 A.M.–9 P.M.; Labor Day–Memorial Day, 8–dusk. Carousel: Easter Sunday–June 30, Sat.–Sun., 11–5; July 1–Labor Day, daily, 11–5; Labor Day and Columbus Day weekends, 11–5. **All ages.**

Play some tennis, enjoy a picnic, and take a whirl on the restored 1894 Looff carousel, said to be the fastest Looff carousel ever made.

● Pawtucket Red Sox Baseball

McCoy Stadium, 1 Columbus Ave., Pawtucket; (401) 724-7300. Tickets (general admission): adults, $4; kids, $3. **All ages.**

This is the AAA baseball league farm team of the Boston Red Sox, so you never know if one of the young hotshots on the field will make it to the majors. Cheer 'em on from April through August.

● Slater Mill Historic Site

Roosevelt Ave., Pawtucket; (401) 725-8638. Hours for general public: June–Nov. 1, Sat., 10–5; Sun., 1–5. March–May and Nov.–third Sun. in Dec., Sat. and Sun., 1–5. Closed major holidays. Adults, $6; 6–12, $4, under 6, free. **Ages 5 and up.**

This excursion is for older children who like the sounds of and are intrigued by the mechanisms of machinery. (You know who we're talking about: the kids who can't resist a construction site and adore dismantling small home appliances.) Billed as the birthplace of American industry, the site includes the Sylvanus Brown House (1758), an early skilled-worker's home; the Wilkinson Mill (1810), which houses an authentic 19th-century machine shop; and a working, 16,000-pound waterwheel. The 90-minute tour includes demonstrations of early textile machinery, hand-spinning, and weaving.

● Canoeing and Kayaking

Baer's River Workshop offers guided kayak tours (or canoes, if you prefer) along Rhode Island waterways, featuring close-up looks at the Ocean State's natural side: peaceful woodlands, salt marshes, barrier beaches, and rural landscapes. Wildlife sightings might include king-fishers, muskrat, black ducks, osprey, and great blue herons. No paddling experience is necessary. Full- and half-day tours are offered, departing from (and ending at) Baer's headquarters at 222 South Water St. in Providence. Three-seater canoes are available (great for families); kayaks can take groups of three people. For paddling in individual boats, kids should be 10 or older. Special events, paddling instructions, and kids canoe-kayak camps are available. For information, call (401) 453-1633.

● Fruit Picking

A number of Rhode Island farms offer fruit-picking possibilities—mostly raspberries, strawberries, blueberries, blackberries, and apples in season. Pick-your-own produce farms are located throughout the state, including several in Providence County. For listings, contact the Rhode Island Division of Agriculture, 22 Hayes St., Providence, 02908; (401) 277-2781.

RESTAURANTS

● The Arcade

65 Weybosset St., Providence; (401) 598-1199. Mon.–Fri., 10–6; Sat., 10–5.

Located in the heart of downtown Providence, the Arcade (1828) was the first enclosed shopping center in the United States. Today, you'll find a collection of eateries offering everything from soup to nuts. Whether your bunch likes Greek or Chinese food, pizza or burgers, you'll find it here. Find a table at Center Court and enjoy. Warning: when the business crowd rolls in for lunch on weekdays, the place gets mobbed.

● Angelo's Civita Farnese

141 Atwells Ave., Providence; (401) 621-8171. Mon.–Thurs., 11–8:30; Fri.
and Sat., 11:30–9; also open Sun. 12–6:30, Labor Day–Memorial Day.

This comfortable family restaurant is located in "Little Italy," and it's
a true classic, known for megaportions and miniprices. All your favorite
pasta dishes are on the menu, available in half-size portions for kids. (That
may not be necessary if you have a small child—regular portions are huge
enough to share.) *Mangia, bambini!*

Newport

America's First Resort. Millionaire's Playground. Queen of American
Resorts. Yachting Capital of the World. Visit Newport, and you'll soon
understand why this island seaport has earned such superlative titles. The
city echoes its past, first as a 17th-century colonial town of merchants and
traders, later as the summer resort of America's richest society members.
You'll find the narrow streets surrounding its harbors lined with clapboard houses that were once home to sea captains and traders. You'll also
see magnificent Gilded Age mansions, extravagant summer "cottages" for
the wealthy American aristocracy during the Industrial Age, hugging the
shoreline.

Newport remains a prestigious East Coast resort community;
opulent sailboats and powerboats dot its harbors. The 17th-century
mercantile harbor is now a contemporary center of fine restaurants, shops,
and outdoor cafes. The beauty of the island, with its dramatic views of
Narragansett Bay and the Atlantic Ocean, remains.

The summer season is crowded and congested, so you'll want to
find time to venture out beyond Thames Street (the main drag) and the
wharves. Tour a mansion or two, by all means, but take a drive to Fort
Adams Park for a picnic. Take a harbor cruise, or walk the dunes at
Second Beach for a pretty (and unhurried) view of this elegant coastal
community. Your first stop might be the Gateway Visitor Information
Center. You can park there, or at one of the other public garages, and plan
to tour Newport on foot as much as possible. While it's possible to rent
bicycles to cruise around town, we'd never recommend it with kids in
tow—you'd be a nervous wreck in downtown traffic. Trust us—you'll be
happiest if you travel by foot or by boat as much as possible.

● Newport Mansions

Plan on seeing only one or two mansions during your Newport visit,
especially if your kids are very young. Children quickly tire of the hour-

long tours and the inevitable summer crowds that flock to see how the Vanderbilts, Belmonts, and Berwinds lived. You'll enjoy the tours most with older kids (eight years and up), but if you're taking an infant or toddler, be prepared to carry them—most mansions are not stroller-accessible. Also, note that combination tickets are availble for properties that are part of the Preservation Society of Newport County. These include The Breakers and Green Animals Topiary Gardens. Here are three mansions that families will enjoy the most:

● The Breakers

Ochre Point Ave.; (401) 847-1000. May–Oct., daily, 10–5. Adults, $10; 6–11, $3.50. **Ages 3 and up.**

The Breakers, built for Cornelius Vanderbilt, is the most palatial of Newport's mansions. You'll marvel at this 70-room castle of marble, mosaic, alabaster, and mahogany, resembling a 16th-century Northern Italian palace. View the music room, library, bathrooms that deliver both salt and freshwater, a magnificent double loggia with commanding ocean views, and an opulent dining room. The "cottage" served as a children's playhouse.

● The Beechwood

580 Bellevue Ave.; (401) 846-3772. Mid-May–Oct., daily, 10–5. Nov. 1–Dec. 19, daily, 10–4. Weekends, Feb.–mid-May, 10–4. Adults, $8.50; 13 and under, $6.50; 5 and under free. **Ages 8 and up.**

Kids enjoy The Beechwood; it's a living history tour. Instead of roped-off displays and dry narration, you'll encounter the Astors' staff of servants, who will show you around the house. You are the Astors' guests—and members of high society, no less—for their anniversary ball. The Beechwood Theater Company reenacts life as it would have been at The Beechwood in the summer of 1891. The annual Children's Day features games, story telling, and special activities.

● Hammersmith Farm

Ocean Dr. (adjacent to Fort Adams State Park); (401) 846-7346. Guided tours, April–mid-Nov., daily, 10–5. June–Labor Day, daily, 10–6. Call to confirm closing time. Adults, $8; 6–12, $3. **Ages 8 and up.**

Hammersmith Farm, the Auchincloss family's summer cottage, is the only working farm left in Newport. The informal tour provides personal glimpses into the lives of the Kennedy family. When John Kennedy was in office, Hammersmith was known as the "summer White House." Its seaside location and gardens (originally designed by Frederick Law

Olmstead) are gorgeous, and children love visiting the miniature horses and donkey that graze in the fields. You may wish to combine your tour of Hammersmith Farm with a *Viking Queen* cruise. The narrated cruise passes through the harbor and bay to a private dock at Hammersmith. There, you'll disembark and tour the farm. Call (401) 847-6921 for information about the boat trip.

● Cliff Walk

Put the baby in a backpack and grab the little ones' hands for this dramatic walk overlooking the Atlantic Ocean. On this steep, picturesque hike, you'll see the rocky coastline at its best and pass by some of Newport's mansions. The 3.5-mile trail runs from Memorial Boulevard and Eustis Avenue to Bailey's Beach. Walk all of it or just a part.

● Fort Adams State Park

Ocean Dr.; (401) 847-2400. Year-round, sunrise–sunset. **All ages.**

Built in 1824, the fort was designed to accommodate 2,400 soldiers with 468 mounted cannons. It is not open for public viewing, but its park is a great place to picnic. Features include a small beach, fishing pier, boat launching ramps, barbecue grills, picnic tables, and plenty of room for the kids to run and play while you savor the oceanside setting.

● Newport Aquarium

Easton's Beach; (401) 849-8430. Open Memorial Day–Labor Day, daily, 10–5. Adults, $3.50; 2–12, $2.50; under 2, free. **All ages.**

Get up close and personal with the fascinating undersea residents of Narragansett Bay here, at Rhode Island's only aquarium. Pet a real shark, find out if an ocean pout (a species of fish found in these waters) actually pouts, handle marine creatures in the touch tank. All the specimens here have been caught by local fisherfolk; at the end of the season, there's a "Setting Free" party. Kids can show up with a bucket and help set creatures free. Call for details.

● Rhode Island Fisherman and Whale Center

144 Spring St.; (401) 849-1340. Daily, except Wed., 10–5. Adults, $2; 5–13, $1; under 5, free. **All ages.**

Ahoy, mate! Young salts will enjoy this interactive exploration of the sea. See—and touch—Rhode Island marine life (horseshoe crabs, starfish, sea urchins), and take a turn at the wheel of a fishing boat. Listen to recorded "fish stories," go on a (videotaped) whale watch, and try your hand at tying a bowline and other nautical knots. Test your skill as a quahogger. (Don't know what a quahog is? You'll find out.) You can even eavesdrop on real fishermen chatting over the marine radio.

● International Tennis Hall of Fame

194 Bellevue Ave.; (401) 849-3990. Year-round, daily, 9:30–5. Adults, $8; under 7, $4; family rate, $12. **Ages 6 and up.**

Tennis buffs will not want to miss this. Housed in the Newport Casino Building, it's billed as the birthplace of United States tennis tournaments. Some of the game's greatest players have played here, including Rod Laver, Chris Evert, and Martina Navratilova. Old Davis Cup films are shown in a 450-seat theater. A simulated tennis gallery and interactive videos allow you to test your tennis savvy.

● Green Animals Topiary Gardens

Cory's Lane (off Rte. 114), Portsmouth; (401) 847-1000. Open May–Oct., daily, 10–5. Adults, $6; 6–11, $3. **All ages.**

This maze of charming sculptured geometric figures and animal shapes is sure to delight young children and amaze adults. The gardens contain nearly 80 plant sculptures that have been lovingly pruned and shaped; 21 pieces are animals or birds made of California privet and yew. The main house features Victorian toy collections. Drive to Portsmouth yourself or take the Old Colony and Newport Railway, a 1930s train, from downtown Newport.

● Old Colony and Newport Railway

America's Cup Ave. (across from the Gateway); (401) 849-0546. May–Dec., Sun. and holidays, 12:30 P.M. Adults, $6.50; 14 and under, $3.50; family rate, $16. **Ages 3 and up.**

Board a vintage 1930s railway car for this eight-mile scenic trip to Portsmouth. The three-hour round trip includes a stopover at Green Animals Topiary Gardens. This trip runs on Sundays only. On Tuesday, Wednesday, Thursday, and Saturday, the railway runs one-hour scenic trips along the west shore of Aquidneck Island. No Green Animals on that one, but it might be better for kids who'd get antsy on an 18-mile train trip.

● Sailing

Fort Adams State Park, Ocean Dr.; (401) 849-8385.

Visit the Yachting Capital of the World without getting out on the water? Unthinkable! Plus, you'd miss seeing Newport from the water side. If you're adept at handling a small sailboat, rent one from **Sail**

Newport Sailing Center; they offer six- to 24-foot vessels by the hour or half-day, and (if you need a refresher course) private and group instruction for kids and adults. (A word of advice: This isn't for Nervous Nellies; Newport Harbor is incredibly busy. Keep an eye out for those party boats!) Call ahead to reserve on busy summer weekends. Rate information is available by phone.

● *Viking Queen*

Goat Island Dock; (401) 847-6921. Mid-May–mid-Oct., daily. Reduced schedule spring and fall; call ahead for cruise schedule. Rates (one-hour cruise): Adults, $7; 4–11, $3. Hammersmith Farm cruise: Adults, $14; 4–11, $6. **All ages.**

If a ferry boat cruise is more your style, relax aboard the *Viking Queen*'s bay and harbor cruises. Or tie in your cruise with a visit to Hammersmith Farm. (See Hammersmith Farm, above.)

● **Butterfly Zoo at Newport Butterfly Farm**

594 Aquidneck Ave., Middletown; (401) 849-9519. Open mid-May–Sept., Tues.–Sun. 11–4. Weekend rates: adults, $5; under 12, $3; weekday rates: $4/$3. Under 3, free. **All ages.**

This 20-by-80-foot greenhouse structure is home to butterflies from all over the world. Mingle with these gorgeous insects (hint: they're most active on sunny days) and take pictures if you wish.

● **Newport on Foot**

Tours leave from Gateway Visitor Information Center; (401) 846-5391. March–Oct. One-hour tours; schedule varies. Kids, $5 (must be accompanied by an adult; no charge for adult). **Ages 5 and up.**

What's the story behind those splendid storefronts and stately homes? Who's buried in Newport's ancient graveyards? Find out on a guided, narrated walking tour designed for kids, departing from the Gateway Visitor Information Center. Themed tours include the intriguingly named "Ghosts and Graveyards" (you make grave rubbings) and "Skeletons and Angels." At tour's end, guests enjoy lemonade and cookies.

● **Beavertail State Park and Lighthouse**

Rte. 138, Beavertail Point, Jamestown; (401) 423-3270. Memorial Day– June, weekends only. June–Aug.; tours daily, Wed.–Sun., 10–4. **All ages.**

The centerpiece of this park is the lighthouse at Beavertail Point. Park naturalists give tours three times daily; you'll also enjoy panoramic views of the Atlantic coastline.

● Norman Bird Sanctuary and Museum

583 Third Beach Rd., Middletown; (401) 846-2577. Memorial Day–
Labor Day, daily, 9–5; Labor Day–Memorial Day, Tues.–Sun., 9–5. Trail
use: adults, $4; under 12, $1. Museum is free. Free Sun. morning bird walks
in spring and fall, 8 A.M. **All ages.**

This 450-acre refuge is a wonderful outdoors getaway for families,
with seven miles of walking trails. Don't miss Hanging Rock Trail—this
gently sloping hike (one mile each way) will take you to a dramatic rock
formation overlooking the ocean. Before leaving the sanctuary, stop in at
the trailside museum, housed on the second floor of the large barn. You'll
see specimens of local birds and animals mounted on the walls, with
explanations of their habitats and habits. Kids can crawl into the authentically reconstructed bark wigwam.

● Beaches

Kids might find that the best thing to do in Newport is to head
for one of its beaches. Besides swimming at the small beach area at **Fort
Adams State Park,** you can ride the waves (or just dunk your toes) at
First Beach (Memorial Boulevard, running from Cliff Walk to Middle-
town); the three-mile-long, sandy **Second Beach** (Sachuest Point area
in Middletown); and **Third Beach** (Sachuest Point area on the Sakonnet
River). **Easton's Beach** now has a wonderful feature for kids, the
Newport Aquarium. (See listing.)

 RESTAURANTS

● Inn at Castle Hill

Ocean Dr.; (401) 849-3800. Barbecue, Memorial Day–Labor Day, Sun.,
2:30–6, weather permitting.

If it's a sunny Sunday afternoon, don't miss the barbecue at this
ocean bluff restaurant—part of a recently restored inn. It has the best
view in town—a panorama of Narragansett Bay, Newport Harbor, and
the Atlantic Ocean. Sit on the grassy hill overlooking the water while
listening to live jazz and awaiting barbecued chicken, burgers, and other
favorites. Of, if your kids are older, mom and dad can dine on fresh fish in
one of the inn's dining rooms or outside on the terrace while the youngsters feast on picnic food on the lawn.

● The Market

43 Memorial Blvd.; (401) 848-2600. Open Memorial Day–Labor Day,
daily, 8–8; off-season, open Mon.–Sat., 8–7; Sun., 8–6.

Open for breakfast, lunch, and dinner, this deli/bakery offers carry-out cuisine—perfect for those times when the kids can't handle a sitdown restaurant, but you'd like a tasty bite (hold the fast food, please). This is also a good bet for do-it-yourself grocery items for boating or beach feasts.

● The Best Dressed Bagel

198 Thames St.; (401) 848-BAGL. (Across from Dansk store.) Memorial Day–Labor Day, daily, 8:30–6; rest of year, 8:30–2:30.

Traveling en famille, you may not make it to the fancy Black Pearl restaurant, but you'll be grateful for quickie, fill-up places like the Best Dressed Bagel. Why "best dressed?" You can fix up a hot, New York–style bagel, 51 ways—enough choices to satisfy the most persnickety of youngsters. Bagel dogs (hotdogs wrapped in bagels shaped like a hotdog bun) and pizza bagels are top picks for kids. Gourmet muffins, strudels, specialty coffees, too.

● Bannister's Wharf

In the heart of downtown Newport, you'll find lively Bannister's Wharf. Sit outside under a Cinzano umbrella and order oysters on the half-shell, lobster rolls, or a bowl of chowder. Order sandwiches, salads, sweets, little nibbles—virtually anything—from outdoor cafes while you watch the harbor activity.

South County

Tiny Rhode Island offers an astonishing 400 miles of scenic coastline. Nowhere is this more evident than the South County region. From Narragansett Pier to Watch Hill, the southwestern edge of the state is nearly one continuous stretch of sand, offering beaches for every taste.

Perhaps the best family beach is in **Narragansett—Sand Hill Cove.** This one is inside the breakwall, so the surf is calm. This beach also has a brand-new pavilion and amenities such as lifeguards, bathhouses, and snack bars. **Narragansett Town Beach** is a fun scene for older kids who like wild waves and body-surfing. This beach is popular with surfers, especially when storms threaten. (Some surfers do their thing here year-round, believe it or not, wearing heavy wetsuits.) This beach has facilities as well. Arrive early to find a parking space.

Charlestown Beach, at the edge of the Ninigret National Wildlife Refuge, is popular with residents and visitors alike. You'll find it clean and spacious, with changing rooms, showers, and a small store for refreshments. If you'd like to get away from the ocean beach crowd, pack a picnic basket and head for the Ninigret National Wildlife Refuge. You'll find peaceful walking trails to the small pond beach.

You won't be alone at **East Beach,** but the crowd is a mellow one. Located at the eastern edge of the wildlife refuge, East Beach is considered one of the best around. You'll find nearly three miles of white sand and lots of dunes. Kids enjoy the walk to Ninigret Pond, where they can watch windsurfers sail the protected waters. There are no facilities here, and the small parking lot fills up early (before nine) on weekends, so arrive early. Right next to East Beach is **Blue Shutters Beach,** where many East Beach–goers trek for refreshments and restrooms. Blue Shutters has nearly four miles of clean sand, plus amenities, concessions, and kids, kids, kids.

Like to be where the action is? Proceed to busy **Misquamicut Beach,** where the air is filled with the smell of suntan lotion and the sound of boom boxes, and the sand is a mosaic of colorful beach towels. Of course, kids love all this, especially the snack bars and beachside activities— including minigolf, kiddie rides, and a Ferris wheel. The total opposite experience is at **Watch Hill,** a quiet Victorian town on the western border of the state. Watch Hill Beach is small and rarely crowded, with showers, changing rooms, and a cluster of restaurants and shops nearby. Generations of kids have enjoyed the beach's Flying Horse Carousel.

Beyond the beaches, here's a look at some other favorite South County attractions.

● The Enchanted Forest

Rte. 3, exit 2 off I-95, Hope Valley; (401) 539-7711. May–mid-June, Wed.–Fri., 10–2; Sat. and Sun., 10–5. Mid-June–Labor Day, daily, 10–5; month of Sept., Sat. and Sun., 10–5. Per person, $9.95; under 2, free. Extra charge for go-carts. **All ages.**

Too, too cute, this fairyland-themed amusement park will tickle the small fry in your bunch. Fun features include storybook exhibits, a jump castle, a carousel, tame roller coasters, two Ferris wheels, favorite carnival rides such as "Paratrooper" and "Scrambler," a petting zoo, miniature golf, go-carts, and batting cages. There's a snack bar and picnic area, too.

● Adventureland

Point Judith Rd., Narragansett; (401) 7789-0030. Weekends, mid-April–mid-June and Labor Day–mid-Oct., 11–6. Daily, mid-June–Labor Day, 10–10. Prices, $1.50–$20; discount tickets available. **Ages 7 and up.**

Junior sports fiends will be in heaven here. If yours are into minigolf, they'll find the course here a hoot, with waterfalls, caves, streams, and an island. Bumper boats, batting cages, and a go-cart track round out the offerings. This attraction is recommended for ages seven and up; go-carts require a height of 56 inches.

● Canonchet Farm and South County Museum

Off Boston Neck Rd., Scenic 1-A, Narragansett; (401) 789-1044 or (401) 789-1044. Farm: open daily. Museum: May–Oct., Wed.–Sun., 11–4. Farm only, no charge. Museum: adults, $3.50; 6–16, $1.75; family maximum, $10. **Ages 5 and up.**

Spread over this 174-acre park is a 19th-century working farm, a cemetery with graves dating to 1700, nature trails, picnic areas, and the South County Museum. The museum features articles of early Rhode Island life, including antique toys and dolls and a collection of carriages. Special events and demonstrations are held frequently; call for a schedule.

● Water Wizz

330 Atlantic Ave., across from Misquamicut Beach, Westerly; (401) 596-0110. Memorial Day–mid-June, Sat. and Sun., 11–4. Mid-June–Labor Day, daily, 10–6:30. 40-min. pass, $7 per person; all day pass, $16. **Ages 5 and up.**

If the kids are feeling hot, sticky, and crabby after a couple of hours at the beach, this will cool them down—and give grown-ups a chance to sip an iced tea in peace. Watch them squeal and splash down six giant waterslides, four twisty serpentine slides (including a kiddie version), and two 50-foot-high speed slides. It's best for bigger kids, but little ones can ride with an adult.

● Flying Horse Carousel

Bay St., Watch Hill. Mid-June–Labor Day, daily, 1–9. Children only. $.75 per ride. **Ages 2–12.**

This 1867 merry-go-round is believed to be the oldest in America and is designated as a National Historic Landmark. Each hand-carved horse has a real tail and mane; horses are suspended from a center frame, swinging out or "flying" when in motion. Grab the brass ring and win a free ride.

 RESTAURANTS

● Olympia Tea Room

Bay St., Watch Hill; (401) 348-8211. May–Oct, daily, 8–10.

Had enough of picnics and beach food? Ready for something civilized? You'll find it at this charming classic, part bistro and part soda fountain. Sit at a wooden booth and enjoy the timeless quality of the place, with its black-and-white floor and waitresses garbed in tea room attire (black uniforms, white lace collars). Or, sit outside at a cafe table and enjoy the added bonus of a view of the bay. A children's menu is offered, along with enticing soda fountain creations and the Olympia Tea Room's trademark dessert, the Avondale Swan (a hot fudge sundae in a swan-shaped puff pastry).

● George's of Galilee

250 Sand Hill Cove Rd., Port of Galilee; (401) 783-2306. Mid-Feb.–Memorial Day, 11:30–9; Memorial Day–mid-Oct., 11:30–10; mid-Oct.–mid-Feb., Thurs.–Sun., 11:30–9.

This is one of those big, bustling, shore dinner-with-view outposts. Ferries headed for Block Island depart here, so it gets busy; rather than wait in lines, we advise you to head upstairs to the deck for an inexpensive menu and great views of Long Island Sound. The menu leans toward local fresh fish, including fish and chips, seafood salads, fried clams, and, for those who prefer turf to surf, chicken and beef. They offer a kid's menu, and kids who finish their dinners can pick out a toy (to keep) from the toy chest. Now, there's an inducement to join the Clean Plate Club!

Other Rhode Island Highlights

These family-friendly attractions don't fit neatly into any of our geographic categories, but they merit inclusion anyway. And in Rhode Island, you're never too far from anyplace else!

● Coggeshall Farm Museum

Colt State Park, Rte. 114, Bristol; (401) 253-9062. March–Sept., 10–6; Oct.–Feb., 10–5. Adults, $1; children, $.25. Rates vary for special events.
All ages.

What was it like to live and work on a New England farm in the 18th century? Find out here, at this working coastal farm located near a salt marsh on Narragansett Bay. These days, rare breeds of livestock are raised here, including oxen, pigs, chicken, and sheep, who roam the property freely. Depending on the season, visiting kids can help shear a sheep, see maple sugaring demonstrated, watch a team of oxen till the soil, and see craftspeople at work. The best time to visit with kids is during the Days of Merriment, held in June. Activities include 18th-century children's games. Call for information.

● East Bay Bicycle Path

This paved path is open only to walkers and bicyclists, following 14.5 scenic miles between Providence and Bristol, through parks that line Narragansett Bay. Attractions along the way include a Looff carousel, several state parks, and Brickyard Pond. There are several places to stop for refreshment along the way, too. Restrooms are available at Colt State Park and Haines State Park. Need to rent a bike? Try **Bay Path Cycles,** 13 State Street, in Bristol.

● Casey Farm

Rte. 1-A, Saunderstown; (401) 295-1030. Open June–mid-Oct., Tues., Thurs., Sat., 1–5. **Ages 3 and up.**

This 300-acre working farm is a rare example of the original plantation farms of the Colonial era. The 1750 farm house, overlooking Narragansett Bay, was a site of Revolutionary War activity. Today, the farm is community-supported, and grows Rhode Island–certified organic produce. Tour the house museum and family cemetery, stroll the hiking trails, and perhaps take home some organic seedlings and produce.

● Ruecker Wildlife Refuge

Seapowet Ave., Tiverton; (401) 949-5454. Open daily, dawn–dusk. **All ages.**

Managed by the Audubon Society of Rhode Island, this 48-acre wildlife sanctuary offers 1.5 miles of hiking trails, winding through woodland, meadow, and salt marsh. Look for feeding herons, egrets, and osprey as you wander.

Block Island

"This place is like Martha's Vineyard was, twenty years ago," some say, and they mean it in the best possible way. If your description of the perfect getaway features words like "serene" and "relaxing," and if your vision of the perfect place includes windswept dunes and pastoral vistas, consider Block Island.

There's plenty to do on Block Island, it's just that, once you arrive here, you won't feel compelled to rush around and do them. The pace is slow and the pleasures are simple, building sandcastles on the beach, bicycling around the seven-mile island, kite-flying, kayaking, and fishing along the beach are popular pursuits.

The ferry ride to the island will put you in the mood, as you watch Block Island slowly appear on the horizon. Look closely to see if you can spot the buoys marking the harbor entrance as you get closer to port. Ferries depart to Block Island from Point Judith, Rhode Island, year-round, and from Newport and Providence, Rhode Island, and New London, Connecticut, and Montauk, New York, during the summer season. Even if your ferry accepts cars, don't bother to bring one. The only proper way to do Block Island is on a bicycle. (In bad weather, it's okay to take a taxi.)

Block Island is less pretentious than other New England resorts, and somewhat less expensive as well. It's "less" of a lot of things, which makes it more attractive to families who want a relaxing getaway.

Getting There: For ferry information, call Interstate Navigation Co./ Nelseco Navigation Co. at (401) 783-4613 (reservations) or (860) 442-7881. For Montauk ferry information, call (516) 668-2214.

● Mohegan Bluffs

These rugged clay cliffs may be found at the southernmost tip of the island. Follow Spring Street to Mohegan Trail. Climb up a path to the 200-foot elevation and gaze out over the Atlantic. You'll also see Southeast Light, a beacon to seafarers since 1874. The lighthouse was moved back from the crumbling cliff face, amid much fanfare, in 1993 to ensure it wouldn't tumble into the sea. Wooden stairs will take you back down to Mohegan Bluffs beach, which is secluded but pebbly.

● Block Island Beaches

This island is practically surrounded by beaches. It's hard to tell where one beach ends and the next one begins! There's two-mile **Crescent Beach,** on the starboard side as you arrive by ferry; **Frederick J. Benson Beach** (closest to town) has amenities and rentals. To the north is **Scotch Beach** and, farther north, **Mansion Beach,** where only the stone walls of a vanished mansion remain. South of the ferry landing is **Ballard's Beach.** The best way to discover your favorite: kick off your shoes, slather on the sunscreen, and start walking. You're sure to find an enticing little cove of sand and surf.

● Bicycling

Pedal around this 7-mile-long, 3.5-mile-wide island for views of rolling hills festooned with wildflowers, windswept dunes, and the Victorian architecture of Old Harbor. You may also see Great Salt Pond and the pleasure-boat basin, New Harbor. Old Harbor is the commercial wharf where the ferries dock. At the northern tip of the island, you'll see Settler's Rock and the North Light Lighthouse (open for tours) at Sandy

Point. (Please don't swim at Sandy Point, due to dangerous currents.) You'll also see numerous freshwater ponds and wildlife refuge areas. Bicycles may be rented at several shops, including **Esta's** on Water St. at Old Harbor, (401) 466-2652. They offer child seats and Tag-alongs, those small-sized add-ons that allow small fry to pedal along, much like a bicycle built for two. These are really great because, frankly, Block Island's hilly terrain can be challenging for little legs, and the curvy roadways make it difficult to keep everyone in sight as you roll along. Once you get the hang of pedalling in tandem, a Tag-along bike is a dandy way to tour Block Island.

● Fishing

Block Island is famous for fishing. Besides the deep-sea charter boat trips, you can surfcast for blues, striped bass, or flounder, or get a license and try your luck with the freshwater ponds for bass, perch, and pickerel. To rent a fly rod or surf rod, try **Oceans & Ponds** on Ocean Ave.; they also offer guided fishing trips. Bait and tackle are available at **Twin Maples** at 22 Beach Avenue; (401) 466-5547.

● Rustic Rides Farm

West Side Rd.; (401) 466-5060. Summer and fall; $25 per person. **Ages 3 and up.**

A sunset horseback ride, on the beach, no less, may well be your most special Block Island memory. Try to overlook the rather chaotic appearance of the property (animals and equipment scattered about); soon, you'll be astride a gentle horse—perhaps Cocoa or Mercury—and be heading down the rugosa rose–lined pathway to the beach. The farm is owned by a family with young children, so their guides are good with kids. Rides last about an hour.

● Hotel Manisses Animal Farm

One Spring Rd.; (800) MANISSE; (401) 466-2421. **All ages.**

The Hotel Manisses is certainly lovely, but you don't have to stay there to enjoy its most child-friendly feature: a pasture full of animals, including exotics like llamas, a Scottish Highland steer, and fainting goats. Stroll around—nobody will mind—and take a peek. The hotel is a short walk from Old Harbor.

● Hiking—Clayhead Nature Trails and the Greenway

Entrance to Clayhead Nature Trails and parking off Corn Neck Rd. Guided walks, daily, mid-June–Labor Day. Suggested donation: $2 per person. Schedule printed in Block Island Times *newspaper, or call (401) 466-2129* *for details. Greenway trails have several access points; pick up trail map at Nature Conservancy office, near Deadeye Dick's.* **All ages.**

Hiking families love Block Island, where a quarter of the land is protected from development. Hiking trails offer plenty of variety. Don't miss the Greenway, a network of trails that wind through park, conservancy, and private lands from the center of the island to the southern shore, and Clayhead Nature Trails, on the north side of the island. The Nature Conservancy offers naturalist-led nature walks; guides point out Island birds and plant life, with (depending on your guide) a smattering of natural history and coastal ecology. Or, go it alone, armed with a trail map. Pick up a map, with all Block Island trails diagramed, at the Nature Conservancy office. Clayhead Trails are hilly, but not too steep (stay on the trails to avoid poison ivy); follow side trails to the beach. On the way back, stop by Littlefield Bee Farm, across the street. See how honey is produced, and pick up a jar of Block Island honey at their farm stand for a sweet souvenir. The Greenway trails have serveral access points. Inspired by the Greenway system of trails in England, these consist of more than 12 miles of clear paths, winding through the southern half of Block Island. A highlight is the Enchanted Forest, a cool oasis of tall red pines, spruce, and maples.

● Kayaking/Canoeing

Block Island's Great Salt Pond is a haven for paddlers. The folks at **Oceans & Ponds** on Ocean Street will direct you to the best places to go, based on your abilities. Most paddlers put in at Great Salt Pond for a leisurely paddle in protected water. After a short briefing from the folks at Oceans & Ponds, even neophytes can handle this serene inner pond or the inland tributaries of Trims and Harbor ponds. Or perhaps Sachem Pond, to the north, great for swimming, picnicking, and birdwatching. Don't want "serene?" Rent an ocean kayak, and get a rousing workout, versus the ocean waves and currents. If you're looking for a real adrenalin rush, surf-ride the ocean waves in a sit-upon Kahuna, also available from this Orvis retailer. They also rent canoes. Call (800) ORVIS or (401) 466-5131.

● Shellfishing

A license is required for shellfishing. Obtain one at the Block Island Police Station on the corner of Beach and Ocean avenues.

● Block Island Farmer's Market

In season, Wed., 9–11 A.M., near Rebecca's; and Sat., 9–11, at Negus Park on Ocean Ave. **All ages.**

Block Island's bounty is on display at the farmer's market, where island farmers and artisans offer locally-grown produce, baked goods, and homemade crafts. You'll find much more interesting souvenirs than the same old T-shirts, along with great goodies to pack for a picnic at the beach.

 RESTAURANTS

● Ernie's

Water St., Old Harbor; (401) 466-2473. Open daily, 6:30–noon, May– mid-Oct.

Every island has its breakfast hang-out, where the gossip and hot coffee flows. Here, Ernie's is it. Since 1961 (practically forever, as restaurants go), they've been offering all the standards, served in the casual dining room or out on the deck. Grab a copy of the *Block Island Times* and have at it.

● Finn's

Water St., Old Harbor; (401) 466-2473. End of April–Columbus Day, 11:30–9 or 10.

Eat indoors or outdoors at Finn's and watch the ferries docking at Old Harbor. They have their own fish market next door, so you know the catch is fresh. You can get an inexpensive sandwich or a lobster dinner or anything in between all day, so the kids can choose fun food while adults enjoy a leisurely meal. The number-one kid's choice here is the fish sandwich; adults rave about Finn's baked stuffed shrimp.

● Rebecca's

Water St., Old Harbor; (401) 466-5411. Memorial Day–Labor Day, 7–9.

Want to take a picnic to the bluffs or the beach? Sure you do. Many delis and restaurants on the island offer food to go. We like Rebecca's, where you can get child-pleasing dogs and super sandwiches (try the marinated-chicken speidi), packed to go.

Annual Events

MASSACHUSETTS

January
Butternut Basin Kids' Festival, Great Barrington; (413) 528-2000

February
Washington's Birthday Celebration, Old Sturbridge Village, Sturbridge;
  (508) 347-3362
Winter Week, Hancock Shaker Village, Pittsfield; (413) 443-0188

March
Otis Ridge Ski Area Fun Days, Otis; (413) 269-4444
Saint Patrick's Day Parade, South Boston; (617) 268-8525

April
Boston Marathon, Boston; (508) 435-6905
Reenactment of the Battle of Lexington and Concord, Lexington Green;
  (781) 861-0928
Daffodil Festival, Nantucket Island; (508) 228-1700

May
Museum-Goers' Month, Greater Boston; (800) 888-5515
Seaport Festival, Salem; (978) 262-1414
Art Newbury Street, Boston; (617) 267-7961
Sheep-Shearing Day, Gore Place, Waltham; (781) 894-2798
Sheep-Shearing Festival, Museum of American Textile History, North
  Andover; (978) 686-0191

June

Art in the Park Festival, DeCordova Museum, Lincoln; (781) 259-8355
St. Peter's Fiesta, St. Peter's Square, Gloucester; (978) 283-1601
Hyannis Harbor Festival, Bismore Park, Hyannis; (508) 775-2201
Blessing of the Fleet, MacMillan Wharf, Provincetown; (508) 487-3424
St. Anthony's Festival, North End, Boston; (617) 536-410.

July

Boston Harborfest, Boston; (617) 227-152.
Boston Pops Fourth of July Concert, Charles River Esplanade, Boston;
    (617) 266-1492
Yankee Homecoming Days, Newburyport; (978) 462-6680
Lowell Folk Festival, Market St., Lowell; (978) 459-1000
Feast of the Blessed Sacrament (largest Portuguese feast in America),
    Maderia Field, New Bedford; (508) 992-6911
Barnstable County Fair, East Falmouth; (508) 563-3200
Independence Day Celebration and Parade (historical parade), Old
    Sturbridge Village, Sturbridge; (508) 347-3362
Turn-of-the-Century Ice Cream Social, Old Deerfield; (413) 774-7476
Your Hometown America Parade (one of the largest Fourth of July
    parades in America), Pittsfield; (413) 499-3861

August

Gloucester Waterfront Festival, Gloucester; (978) 283-1601
Fall River Waterfront Festival, Fall River; (508) 676-8226
Plymouth Lobster Festival, Plymouth; (508) 746-8500
Sand Castle and Sculpture Day, Jetties Beach, Nantucket; (508) 228-1700
Celebrate Holyoke (food and music festival), Holyoke; (413) 536-4611
Teddy Bear Rally, Amherst Town Common, Amherst; (413) 256-8983

September

Cambridge River Festival, Memorial Dr., Cambridge; (617) 349-4380
Newburyport Waterfront Festival, Plum Island Fairgrounds,
    Newburyport; (978) 262-1414
Essex Clamfest, Memorial Park, Essex; (978) 283-1601
Bourne Scallop Fest, Buzzards Bay Park, Bourne; (508) 759-3122
Tivoli Day and Annual Pro/Am Bicycle Races (bike races for kids and
    adults), Oak Bluffs, Martha's Vineyard; (508) 693-5511
The Big E (state fair), Eastern States Exposition fairgrounds, West
    Springfield; (413) 737-2443
Franklin County Fair, Wisdom Way, Greenfield; (413) 774-4282

October

Head of the Charles Regatta (rowing event), Charles River, Cambridge/
   Boston; (617) 864-8415
Haunted Happenings, Salem; (978) 744-0004
Westport Harvest Festival, Main Rd., Westport; (508) 636-6504
Cranberry Harvest Festival, South Carver; (508) 747-2350
Topsfield Fair, Topsfield Fair Grounds, Topsfield; (978) 887-2212

November

Plimoth Plantation Thanksgiving Celebration, Plymouth; (508)
   746-1622
Old Sturbridge Village Thanksgiving Day Celebration, Sturbridge; (508)
   853-6015

December

Christmas Tree Lighting and Carol Sing, Prudential Center, Boston; (617)
   236-3744
Boston Common Tree Lighting, Boston Common; (617) 635-4505
Chain of Lights (holiday festival), Worcester County, (508) 753-2920
Nantucket Noel and Christmas Stroll, Nantucket Island; (508) 228-1700
First Night Boston (New Year's Eve celebration), Boston; (617) 542-1399

NEW HAMPSHIRE

January

Cross Country Apres Ski Socials, Jackson Touring Center; (603) 383-9355
Winter Workshops, Appalachian Mountain Club, Gorham; (603)
   466-2727
Family Discovery Weekends, Appalachian Mountain Club, Gorham;
   (603) 466-2727

February

Family Frolics Weeks, Cranmore Ski Resort, North Conway; (800) SUN-
   N-SKI
Winter Workshops, Appalachian Mountain Club, Gorham; (603) 466-2727
Winter Carnival, King Pine, East Madison; (603) 367-8896 or (800)
   FREE-SKI

March

Spring Carnival, Cranmore, North Conway; (603) 356-5544 or (800)
   SUN-N-SKI

Annual Coca-Cola Rites of Spring, Black Mountain, Jackson; (603) 383-4490

March Madness, King Pine, East Madison; (603) 367-8896 or (800) FREE-SKI

Telemark Skiing Camp, Appalachian Mountain Club, Gorham; (603) 466-2727

April

Annual Spring Fest Weekend, Waterville Valley; (603) 236-8311

Annual Beach Party, Bretton Woods; (800) 232-2972

Festival of Flowers, Sunapee; (603) 763-4914

May

Wood Day, Canterbury; (603) 783-9511

Sheep and Wool Festival, New Boston; (603) 352-4550

Lilac Family Fun Festival, Rochester; (603) 332-8863

Wakefield Pride Day, Wakefield; (603) 522-6106

New Hampshire's Annual Lilac Time Festival, Lisbon; (603) 838-6336

Annual Chowder Festival, Portsmouth; (603) 436-2848

June

Fields of Lupine Festival, Sugar Hill; (603) 823-5661

AMA Cycle Week, Loudon; (603) 783-4931

Market Square Day, Portsmouth; (603) 431-5388

Victorian Games Day, Nestlenook Farm, Jackson; (603) 383-9443

Annual Open Water-ski Tournament, Wolfeboro; (603) 569-3132

Colonial Follies, Keene; (603) 352-2033

Trout Tournament, Littleton; (603) 444-6561

International Children's Festival, Somersworth; (603) 692-5869

Mt. Washington Road Race, Pinkham Notch; (603) 466-3988

Strawberry Moon Festival, Warner; (603) 456-2600

Seacoast Jazz Festival, Portsmouth; (603) 436-2848

Mt. Washington Auto Road Hill Climb, Gorham; (603) 466-3988

Strawberry Festival, Laconia; (603) 524-8813

Annual Fiddler's Contest, Lincoln; (603) 745-3563

July

Fourth of July Celebration, Gorham; (603) 466-5538

Independence Day Gala Celebration, Bretton Woods; (603) 278-1000

Fourth of July Celebration, Littleton; (603) 444-6561

Parade and Celebration, Lebanon; (603) 448-5121

Annual Gunstock Crafts Festival, Gilford; (603) 293-4341

Fourth of July Celebration, Jackson; (603) 383-9356

Old Home Days, Warren; (603) 764-9901

Hanover Street Fest, Hanover; (603) 643-3115

Annual Birthday Celebration, Portsmouth; (603) 436-3853

Annual Native American Cultural Weekend, Twin Mountain; (603) 846-5058

Hillsborough Balloon Fest and Fair, Hillsborough; (603) 464-5858

Revolutionary War Festival, Exeter; (603) 772-2622

Annual Crafts Fair at the Bay, Alton; (603) 755-2166

Annual Northeast Antique and Classic Boat Show, Weirs Beach; (603) 524-0348

Canterbury Fair, Canterbury; (603) 783-4349

Annual Daylily Festival, Bethlehem; (603) 869-3131

Annual Lakes Region Open Water-ski Tournament, Wolfeboro; (603) 569-3132

August

Annual Huggins Hospital Street Fair, Wolfeboro; (603) 569-2200

Attitash Bear Peak Blueberry Festival, Bartlett; (603) 374-2368

Annual League of New Hampshire Craftmen's Fair, Newbury; (603) 224-3375

Annual New Hampshire Antiques Show, Manchester; (603) 239-4188

Old Time Farm Day, Milton; (603) 652-7840

Children's Festival, Hampton Beach; (603) 926-8718

Candlelight Tour of Historic Houses, Portsmouth; (603) 436-1118

Annual Children's Fair, New Ipswich; (603) 878-1327

Attitash Bear Peak Equine Festival, Bartlett; (603) 374-2368

Annual Fine Arts and Crafts Festival, Meredith; (603) 279-6121

Annual Professional Lumberjack Festival, Lincoln; (603) 745-8111

September

World Championship Mud Bowl, North Conway; (603) 356-3171

Annual Riverfest Celebration, Manchester; (603) 623-2623

Annual Seafood Festival, Hampton Beach; (603) 926-8717

Annual Hew Hampshire Highland Games; (800) 358-SCOT

Harvest Weekend, Milton; (603) 652-7840

Deerfield Fair, Deerfield; (603) 463-7421

Grand Old Portsmouth Brewer's Festival, Portsmouth; (603) 433-1100

October

Annual Bavarian Fall Foliage Festival, Lincoln; (603) 745-8111

Annual Wool Arts Tour, Henniker; (603) 588-6637

Annual Gunstock Oktoberfest, Gilford; (603) 293-4311
Halloween Haunted Hike, Bristol; (603) 744-2713
Halloween Hauntings, Holderness; (603) 968-7194
Guinness Book of Records Pumpkin Festival, Keene; (603) 358-5344

November
Turkey Trotter at Conway Scenic Railroad; (603) 356-5251 or (800) 232-5251

December
Santa Claus Express, Conway Scenic Railroad; (603) 356-5251 or (800) 232-5251
First Night, Portsmouth; (603) 436-2848
Festival of Lights, Enfield; (603) 632-7087

MAINE

January
Ski Fest, Sunday River Cross Country Ski Center; (207) 824-2410
Children's Festival Week, Sugarloaf USA; (207) 237-2000
Snowmobile Snodeo, Rangeley; (207) 864-3368
White White World Week, Sugarloaf USA; (207) 237-2000

February
Annual U.S. National Toboggan Championships, Camden Snow Bowl; (207) 236-3438
Family Fling Week, Sugarloaf USA; (207) 237-2000
International Snowmobilers Festival, various towns; (207) 728-7000
Mushers Bowl, West Bridgton; (207) 539-4324

March
Rangeley Lakes Sled Dog Races, Rangeley; (207) 864-5364
Northern Maine Trade Fair, Fort Fairfield; (207) 472-3802
Maine Maple Sunday, sugar houses around the state; (207) 287-3491
Norlands Maple Days, Norlands Historical Living Center; (207) 897-4366

April
Aucocisco, Maine's Bay Region; (207) 772-6828

May
St. John Valley Antique Car Show, Madawaska; (207) 543-6150
Bar Harbor Lobster Race, Bar Harbor; (207) 288-3511

June
Old Port Festival, Portland; (207) 772-6828
Dixfield Summerfest, Dixfield; (207) 562-8151
Boothbay Harbor Windjammer Days, Boothbay Harbor; (207) 633-2353
Acadian Festival, Madawaska; (207) 728-7000
Norlands Annual Heritage Days, Norlands Historical Living Museum;
  (207) 897-4366
Whatever Family Festival, Kennebec Valley; (207) 623-4559
Castine's Annual Summer Festival, Castine; (207) 326-4884
Ogunquit Strawberry Festival, Ogunquit; (207) 363-2749

July
Houlton Agricultural State Fair, Houlton; (207) 532-3250
Boothbay Harbor Old-Fashioned Celebration, Boothbay Harbor; (207)
  633-6201
Schooner Days, Rockland; (207) 596-0376
Kittery Seaside Festival, Kittery; (207) 439-3800
Annual Maine Potato Blossom Festival, Fort Fairfield; (207) 472-3802
Native American Festival, Bar Harbor; (207) 288-3519
Annual Yarmouth Clam Festival, Yarmouth; (207) 846-3984
Annual Camden Arts and Crafts Show, Camden; (207) 236-4404
Annual Central Maine Egg Festival, Pittsfield; (207) 487-5282
Friendship Sloop Days Annual Homecoming, Rockland; (207) 272-9658
Logging Museum Festival Days, Rangeley; (207) 864-5364
Annual Country Fair, Jefferson; (207) 549-5224
Annual East Benton Fiddler's Contest, East Benton; (207) 2017
Annual Lobster Festival, Rockland; (207) 596-0376
Annual Maine Festival, Brunswick; (207) 772-9012

August
York Days, York; (207) 363-1040
Skowhegan State Fair, Skowhegan; (207) 474-2947
Annual Maine Antiques Festival, Union; (207) 563-1013
Wilton Blueberry Festival, Wilton; (207) 645-2214
Annual Machias Wild Blueberry Festival, Machias Bay; (207) 255-4402
Rangeley Lakes Blueberry Festival, Rangeley; (207) 864-5364
Houlton Potato Feast Days, Houlton; (207) 532-4216
Camden Windjammer Days, Camden; (207) 236-4404

September
Wooden Boat Sail-In, Brooklin; (800) 807-WIND
Oxford County Fair, Oxford; (207) 743-6723

Franklin County Fair, Farmington; (207) 778-4215
Common Ground County Fair, Windsor; (207) 623-5115
Fryeburg Fair, Fryeburg; (207) 935-3268

October
Apple Festival, Rangeley; (207) 864-5595
Annual Fall Festival, Camden; (207) 236-4404
St. Johns Valley Fall Fest, Madawaska; (207) 728-7000
Annual Fall Foliage Fair, Boothbay; (207) 633-4924
Harvestfest Celebration, York Village; (207) 363-4422

November
Lighting of Nubble Lighthouse, York; (207) 363-4422
Santa Claus Parade, Houlton; (207) 532-4216
Victorian Holiday Horse and Carriage Parade, Portland; (207) 772-6828

December
York Village Festival of Lights, York Village; (207) 363-4422
Christmas-at-Norlands, Norlands Historical Living Museum; (207)
   897-4366
Harbor Lights Festival, Boothbay Harbor; (207) 633-2353

VERMONT

January
Dairy Farmer's Appreciation Day, Jay Peak Ski Resort; (802) 988-2611 or
   (800) 451-4449
Stowe Winter Carnival, Stowe; (802) 253-2329
Dog Sled Saturday, Montshire Museum; (802) 649-2200
Sleigh Ride Weekends, Billings Farm and Museum; (802) 457-2355
Boy Scout Championships, Bromley Mtn. Resort; (802) 824-5522

February
Tubbs Family Snowshoe Fest, Stratton; (802) 297-2200
Sugar on Snow Celebration, Okemo Mtn. Resort; (802) 228-4041
Snowflake Festival, Lyndon and East Burke; (802) 626-5475
Igloo Build, Montshire Museum; (802) 649-2200
Winter Carnival, Brattleboro; (802) 254-4565

March

Ontario Week Celebration, Jay Peak Ski Resort; (802) 988-2611 or (800) 451-4449

Vermont Maple Syrup Experience, Arlington, Dorset, and Manchester; (802) 375-2269

April

Bear Mountain Mogul Challenge, Killington Ski Resort, Killington; (802) 422-6252

May

Annual Spring Farm Festival, Billings Farm and Museum, Billings; (802) 457-2355

Burlington Annual Kids Day, Burlington; (802) 864-0123

June

Lake Champlain Balloon and Craft Festival, Champlain Valley Expo; (802) 899-2993

Annual Ben & Jerry's One World One Heart Festival, Sugarbush Resort, Warren; (800) BJ-FESTS or (800) 53-SUGAR

Annual Caledonia Classic Auto Club Car Show, Lyndonville Fairgrounds; (802) 748-3678

Stowe Flower Festival, Stowe; (802) 253-7321

Quechee Hot Air Balloon Festival and Crafts Fair, Quechee; (802) 295-7900 or (800) 295-5451

Rutland Region Ethnic Festival, Rutland; (802) 747-3950

Ethan Allen Days Festival, Arlington; (802) 375-9491 or (800) 375-2800

July

Grafton Annual Fair Day, Grafton; (802) 843-2230

Victorian Ice Cream Social and Croquet, Montpelier State House; (802) 295-5200

Cracker Barrel Bazaar, Newbury Common; (802) 866-5518

Summerfest, Newport; (802) 334-6345

Swanton Summer Festival, Swanton Village Green; (802) 868-7200

August

French Heritage Gathering, Hardwick; (802) 434-3190

Castleton Colonial Day, Castleton; (802) 273-2122

Rutland Air Show, N. Clarendon; (802) 273-2747

Dummerston Annual Fair, Dummerston; (802) 254-2249

September

Bennington Fair, Bennington; (802) 442-2911

Sugarbush Brewers Festival, Mad River Valley; (802) 583-2381

Woodstock Wool Day, Billings Farm and Museum, Billings; (802) 457-2355

Annual Harvest Festival, Shelburne Farms; (802) 985-8686

Festival of Traditional Crafts, Fairbanks Museum and Planetarium, (802) 748-2372

October

Townshend Pumpkin Festival, Townshend; (802) 365-7793

Northeast Kingdom Annual Fall Foliage Festival, various towns; (802) 748-3678

Burlington Autumn Fair, Burlington; (802) 865-4556

Fall Foliage Fair, Chester on the Green; (802) 875-3267

Annual Vermont Apple Festival and Craft Show, Springfield; (802) 885-2779

Annual Foliage Craft Fair, Brattleboro; (802) 257-7145

November

Annual Holiday Craft Show, Burlington; (802) 223-2636

Festival of Lights, Essex Junction; (802) 878-5545

Festival of Trees, Bennington; (802) 447-3311

December

The Nights Before Christmas, Mount Snow Resort; (802) 464-8092

Prelude to Christmas, Manchester and the Mountains Region; (802) 362-2100

Holly Days Festival, Brattleboro; (802) 254-4565

Annual Blessing of the Sleds, Wilmington; (802) 464-8092

Christmas at Billings Farm, Billings Farm and Museum; (802) 457-2355

Christmas Market, St. Johnsbury; (802) 626-5836

CONNECTICUT

January

Warm Up to Winter celebration, Farmington Valley Area; (800) 4-WELCOME

May

Lobsterfest, Mystic Seaport, Mystic; (860) 572-5315

Lime Rock Grand Prix (largest race in North America), Lakeville; (800) RACE-LRP

June
Yale-Harvard Regatta on the Thames River, New London; (203) 432-4747
Taste of Hartford, downtown, Hartford; (860) 728-3089

July
Fourth of July Town Celebration, Enfield; (860) 749-1820
Riverfest, Hartford and East Hartford locales; (860) 293-0131
Guilford Handcrafts Exposition, Town Green, Guilford; (203) 453-5947

August
Connecticut Summer Dance Festival, various locales, Watertown; (860) 274-0004
SONO Arts Celebration, Washington and S. Main Sts., South Norwalk; (203) 866-7916
Mark Twain Days, citywide, Hartford; (860) 247-0998
Brooklyn Fair, fairgrounds, Brooklyn; (860) 774-7568
Woodstock Fair, South Woodstock; (860) 928-3246

September
Norwalk Oyster Festival, Veteran's Memorial Park, East Norwalk; (203) 838-9444
Durham Fair (Connecticut's largest agricultural fair), Durham; (860) 349-9495
Bethlehem Fair, fairgrounds, Bethlehem; (203) 266-5350

October
Chowderfest, Mystic Seaport, Mystic; (860) 572-5315
Apple Harvest Festival, Town Green, Southington; (860) 628-8036

November
Live Turkey "Inn-vitational," (turkey contests) Inn on Lake Waramaug; (860) 868-0563
Victorian Holiday Celebration, Gillette Castle State Park, East Haddam; (860) 526-2326

December
Christmas at Mystic Seaport (holiday lantern light tours), Mystic; (860) 572-5315

Torchlight Parade & Carol Sing, Main St. to Town Green, Old Saybrook;
(860) 395-3123

First Night Hartford (New Year's Eve celebration), Hartford; (860)
728-3089

RHODE ISLAND

January

Polar Bear and Penguin Plunges (ocean swims to benefit charities),
Wickford Town Beach, North Kingstown; Newport Beach, Newport;
Mackeral Cove, Jamestown

February

Newport Winter Festival (New England's largest winter festival),
Newport; (401) 849-8048

Mid-Winter Eastern Surfing Championships, Narragansett Town Beach,
Narragansett; (401) 789-1954

March

Irish Heritage Month, citywide, Newport; (401) 849-8098

May

Gaspee Days, various locations in Cranston and Warwick; (401) 781-1772

June

Great Chowder Cook Off, Newport; (401) 846-1600

Newport Outdoor Art Festival, Newport; (401) 431-2913

Big Easy Bash, Stepping Stone Ranch, West Greenwich; (401) 351-6312

Rhode Island National Guard Open House & Air Show, Quonset State
Airport, North Kingstown; (401) 886-1423

July

Bristol 4th of July Parade (the nation's oldest), Bristol; (401) 253-7215

Ancient & Horribles Parade, Chepachet; (401) 568-4412

Black Ships Festival (Japanese cultural events/kite competition), Newport;
(401) 846-2720

South County Hot Air Balloon Festival, Kingston; (401) 783-2801

August

Narragansett Heritage Days, Narragansett; (401) 783-7121

Charlestown Chamber Seafood Festival, Ninigret Park, Charlestown;
(401) 364-4031

Fools' Rules Regatta ("anything that floats" contest), Town Beach, Jamestown; (401) 423-1492

International Quahog Festival, Wickford; (800) 854-3584

September

Providence Waterfront Festival, Providence; (401) 785-9450

Heritage Festival, State House Lawn, Providence; (401) 277-2669

Taste of Rhode Island, Newport Yachting Center, Newport; (401) 846-1600

October

Newport Harvest-by-the-Sea Festival, citywide, Newport; (401) 849-8048

Octoberfest, Pawtucket; (401) 738-2000

Autumnfest, Woonsocket; (401) 762-9072

November

Montgolfier Day Balloon Regatta, State House lawn, Providence; (401) 253-0111

December

Christmas in Newport, citywide, Newport; (401) 849-6454

Festival of Lights, Wickford Village, North Kingstown; (401) 295-5566

First Night Providence (New Year's Eve celebration), Providence; (401) 521-1166

Tourist Information

Massachusetts
Massachusetts Office of Tourism, 100 Cambridge St., 13th Floor, Boston, MA 02202; (617) 727-3201; fax, (617) 727-6525; (800) 227-MASS offers Great Dates in the Bay State; (800) 447-MASS offers Massachusetts Getaway Guide

New Hampshire
New Hampshire Office of Travel and Tourism Development, PO Box 1856, Concord, NH 03302-1856; (603) 271-2343; fax (603) 271-2629 or 6784

Maine
Maine Office of Tourism, 33 Stone St., Augusta, ME 04333; (207) 287-5710; out-of-state, (800) 533-9595; fax, (207) 287-8070

Vermont
Vermont Department of Tourism and Marketing, 134 State St., Montpelier, VT 05602; (802) 828-3236; fax, (802) 828-3233; (800) 833-9756 (automated fax service)

Connecticut
Connecticut Department of Economic and Community Development, 865 Brook Street, Rocky Hill, CT 06067; (860) 258-4355; (800) CT-BOUND; fax, (860) 258-4275

Rhode Island
Rhode Island Tourism Division, 1 West Exchange St., Providence, RI 02903; (401) 277-2601; (800) 845-2000; fax, (401) 277-2102

Index by Age Group

Alphabetical Index